new inspiration

Judy Garton-Sprenger and Philip Prowse
with Amanda Bailey, Tim Bowen
and Susannah McKee

Teacher's Book 3

MACMILLAN

Macmillan Education
4 Crinan Street
London N1 9XW
A division of Macmillan Publishers Limited
Companies and representatives throughout the world

ISBN 978-0-230-41020-6

This edition published 2012
First edition published 2006

Original design by Giles Davies Design Limited and eMC Design Limited
Page make-up by Expo Holdings, D&J Hunter Design
Illustrated by Kathy Baxendale, p178; Mark Davis, pp164, 176, 179 and 180; Gillian Martin, pp174 and 182; Julian Mosedale, p173; Julia Pearson, p165; Simon Smith (Beehive Illustration), p171; and Harry Venning, pp167, 169, 170, 177 and 181.
Cover design by Designers Collective

The authors and publishers are grateful for permission to reprint the following copyright material:
Page 186: *You've Got A Friend* Words and Music by Carole King copyright © Screen Gems-EMI Music Inc, USA 1971, reprinted by permission of EMI Music Publishing Ltd, London, WD2H 0QY and International Music Publications Ltd. All Rights Reserved;
Page 187: *Celebrate the Future Hand in Hand* Words by Cheryl Berman Music by Ira Antelis copyright © Wonderland Music Company Incorporated 2003, administered and reprinted by permission of Warner/Chappell Music Ltd, London, W6 8BS. All Rights Reserved;
Page 188: *Brown-eyed Girl* Words and Music by Van Morrison copyright © Web IV Music Incorporated, USA/Universal Music Publishing Limited 1967, reprinted by permission of Music Sales Limited & Hal Leonard Corporation. All Rights Reserved. International Copyright Secured;
Page 189: *I Will Survive* Words and Music by Dino Fekaris & Freddie Perren copyright © Perren-Vibes Music Company/PolyGram International Publishing Incorporated, USA/Universal Music Publishing Limited 1978, reprinted by permission of Music Sales Limited & Hal Leonard Corporation. All Rights Reserved. International Copyright Secured.

For full photographic acknowledgements please refer to the Student's Book.

Printed and bound in Thailand

2018 2017 2016
11 10 9 8 7 6

Contents

NEW INSPIRATION

New Inspiration is a four-level course designed to take teenagers from beginner to intermediate level (CEF A1–B1+). The course aims to appeal to the modern teenager through imaginative and exciting topics, introduces up-to-date language and expressions, increases confidence through learner independence activities, provides regular opportunities for revision and self assessment, and caters for different learning styles. For the teacher it offers everything needed for successful lessons with full support at every stage.

KEY IDEAS

A fundamental concept in the organisation of *New Inspiration* is that of *difference*.

Different ages

Teenagers are passing through a challenging period of their lives with great physical, social and psychological changes. A 16-year-old lives in a different world from a 13-year-old. In designing *New Inspiration* our aim has been to create a course which grows with its students.

Different abilities

Every class is a mixed-ability class. We see mixed ability not as a problem, but as a fact of life to which we need to respond in our teaching. Our response in creating *New Inspiration* has been to develop *flexible* materials which offer a variety of learning paths to success.

Different interests

One of the most striking findings of the research phase in preparing this course was the wide variety of different interests among students. We have therefore provided a broad range of materials to engage students in challenging but achievable tasks. The topic syllabus gives the opportunity for cross-curricular and cross-cultural work so that students learn about life and the world at the same time as learning English. Language learning also needs to be fun to be effective, so we have included lots of games, poems and puzzles, as well as a story in the Workbook and songs in the Teacher's Book.

Different backgrounds

Teenagers come to the language classroom with a wide range of backgrounds – not only in social and educational terms, but also because of different learning histories. Students in the same class may have had positive, negative or no language learning experiences at primary level; they may have started learning another language, or had private lessons or extra classes in English. Students who started learning English at primary level may have been exposed to predominantly oral activities, games and songs, and be surprised at the different demands of the class they are now in.

New Inspiration aims to provide a safe transition to the new level, and to revise and recycle language in fresh contexts.

Different learning styles

We believe that it is important for students to 'learn how to learn'. We have provided opportunities for students to experiment with different learning styles and develop language learning strategies which suit them. We have tried to make students aware that, while they may have a preferred learning style, they could benefit from experimenting with others.

Different aspirations

Within each teenager there is a young adult in the making, and all have differing goals and aspirations for the future. We have aimed to provide students with practical language skills and a positive attitude to learning. This will lead them to success in examinations and prepare them for using English in the real world.

Different class sizes and numbers of hours a week

The Teacher's Book provides lesson plans full of extra optional activities which can be given to less confident learners or to fast-finishers, and the Workbook exercises can all be used for self-study. Teachers with more hours at their disposal will find that they have material for considerably more than the 90–120 hours of the core course if they use the optional activities.

KEY FEATURES OF *NEW INSPIRATION*

Multi-syllabus

The course has a topic-led syllabus which integrates separate communicative, lexical, grammatical, pronunciation skills and learner independence syllabi. This provides a principled approach to vocabulary acquisition and to the development of the four skills. The Contents pages of the Student's Book list the topics, lesson titles, communicative aims, language areas, pronunciation points, skills and learner independence training.

Reading and Listening

At Level 3, students encounter new language in the first three lessons of each unit through a variety of reading and listening texts which focus on topics of interest and relevance to the students' lives and studies. These texts are preceded by tasks to give students a purpose for reading/listening and to develop predictive skills.

Vocabulary and Grammar

The topic-led syllabus provides a firm basis for systematic coverage and development of vocabulary. Lessons contain Word Banks and activities to revise and extend lexical fields, and students are encouraged to maintain their own vocabulary notebooks. At the back of the Student's Book there is a unit-by-unit Word List with phonemic transcriptions.

There is a clearly structured approach to grammar, leading to fluency activities where students apply the target language in communicative situations. Language Workout boxes at the end of each lesson are cross-referenced to a comprehensive Language File at the back of the Student's Book, which provides detailed explanations of grammatical points with controlled practice exercises.

Pronunciation

The first three lessons of each unit provide explicit work on pronunciation, stress and intonation arising from the lesson language. Phonemic symbols are given as support where relevant; these are intended for recognition only. There is a Pronunciation Guide at the back of the Student's Book.

Skills development

Careful attention is paid to the development of the four language skills in each unit, both in the first three lessons and in the fourth Integrated Skills lesson. Guided writing, a carefully staged programme of tasks, helps the growth of students' writing skills. There is further work on reading and writing skills in the Workbook, together with suggestions for extensive reading.

Learner independence

The Integrated Skills lessons in each unit offer work on the development of learner independence, and this is supported by parallel sections in the Workbook and advice in the Teacher's Book lesson notes.

Cognitive development, and language awareness and enjoyment

New Inspiration contains a range of activities, such as quizzes and questionnaires, which encourage students to think in English. 'Your response' activities after reading and listening also encourage the development of critical thinking and personal responses to texts.

Inspiration EXTRA! sections at the end of each Student's Book unit contain either a full project, or a Language Links activity focusing on plurilingualism and a sketch for students to act out. There are also games, puzzles and limericks. Games can also be found in the Student's Book lessons, and the Workbook contains more puzzles, crosswords and brainteasers.

Mixed ability

The first three lessons of each unit contain Extension activities for fast-finishers. Inspiration EXTRA! also includes both a Revision and an Extension section which caters for two different ability levels – revising and extending language from the preceding four lessons – and a Your Choice! section where students can choose between activities reflecting different learning styles. There are further Revision and Extension sections in the Workbook.

Recycling and reviewing

The syllabus regularly recycles new language. In addition to the Revision and Extension sections, there are four Review sections at each level, providing further revision and learner independence self assessment sections. There are further Review sections in the Workbook.

Culture and CLIL

Each level also features four Culture sections which build cross-cultural awareness, encourage discussion, develop vocabulary, and lead up to Mini-projects. The Workbook contains further Culture sections with reading, writing and vocabulary exercises. There is a wealth of CLIL material appropriate to the students' age and level throughout the course, including a dedicated section in each Workbook.

COURSE COMPONENTS

Student's Book

The Student's Book provides 90–120 hours of teaching material within eight units. Each unit has four lessons – each on two pages for ease of use – and an Inspiration EXTRA! section. The first three lessons in each unit present and practise new language, and the fourth is an Integrated Skills lesson. Each pair of units is preceded by a Preview, which gives the learner a taste of what is to come, and followed by a Review. At the back of the book there is a Language File, a Word List, a Pronunciation Guide and a List of Irregular Verbs.

Workbook

The Workbook offers exercises which can be done in class or as self-study. It mirrors the Student's Book in its organisation, providing a wealth of extra language practice material, integrated skills and learner independence work, mixed-ability Revision and Extension exercises, Culture pages and Review sections. It includes pronunciation exercises, brainteasers, crosswords and suggestions for follow-up work on the Internet. The Workbook also contains CLIL materials linked to other subjects studied at this level, and a unit-by-unit story for extensive reading with associated language practice activities.

Teacher's Book

The Teacher's Book features a practical approach to methodology with step-by-step lesson notes. There are stimulating ideas for warmers to start each lesson as well as optional activities throughout the lesson notes. There are follow-up activities at the end of each lesson and suggestions for homework. Useful cultural information is provided to help answer student queries, and photocopiable songs with activities are also included. Full audioscripts are integrated within the notes, as are answers to all the Student's Book exercises. There is also a complete Workbook Answer Key.

Tests CD

The editable Tests are designed to cater for mixed-ability classes by providing Basic, Standard and Higher Tests for each Student's Book unit. Teachers can use the test that best suits their students and adapt it as necessary. The CD also provides a placement test, three end-of-term tests and an end-of-course test. Tests include grammar, vocabulary, reading, listening and writing.

Class Audio CD

All the Student's Book texts, dialogues and pronunciation exercises are recorded, as well as the songs in the Teacher's Book. Recorded items are indicated by the symbol ⊙ in the Student's Book and Teacher's Book.

New Inspiration Digital

Interactive Whiteboard Software is available for the course. Macmillan Practice Online – New Inspiration provides self-marking support materials which mirror the structure of the course. The *New Inspiration* Resource Site provides the teacher with extra language practice materials, CLIL cross-curricular or culture lessons and a social networking section.

www.macmillanpracticeonline.com
www.macmillanenglish.com/inspiration

New Inspiration and the Common European Framework

The Common European Framework (CEF) is a widely used standard created by the Council of Europe. In the classroom, familiarity with the CEF can be of great help to any teacher in identifying students' actual progress and helping them to set their learning priorities.

New Inspiration offers a wide range of teaching materials in various components which give teachers the opportunity to develop all aspects of their students' language ability. The CEF can be used to follow their progress.

Below are the B1–B2 descriptors (description of competencies) covered in *New Inspiration* 3 which students are aiming to reach. A1–A2 descriptors are available in the *New Inspiration* 1 and 2 Teacher's Books and also on the *New Inspiration* teacher's website. A high level of confidence with the A1–A2 descriptors is expected along with a basic level of confidence of the B1 descriptors as students start using *New Inspiration* 3. By the end of the course students should be able to accomplish all the B1 level and some of the B2 level descriptors. Many of the B1 descriptors talk of greater confidence with the same kinds of ability already described at A2: others only emerge for the first time at B1.

On the teacher's website you will also find a list of unit by unit descriptors with suggested targets which you can print out and copy for your students to assess themselves. Students can use these at any point to get a detailed picture of their own individual progress.

What is a CEF Portfolio?

If you are using portfolios as a way of evaluating your students' coursework over the year, you will find a wide variety of opportunities within each *New Inspiration* unit to provide material for the dossier.

A portfolio is a means to document a person's achievements. Artists, architects or designers collect samples of their work in portfolios. The basic idea is that students collect samples of their work in their portfolio. Most of the time, these samples will be texts created by the students, but they could also include photos of classroom scenes, wall displays, audio recordings and DVDs. All these documents provide evidence of a student's performance, e.g. during a discussion, an oral presentation or a role play.

The portfolio consists of three parts: the Language Passport with information about a student's proficiency in one or more languages i.e. qualifications, the Language Biography where students reflect their learning process and progress and say what they can do in their foreign language(s) and the Dossier, a collection of materials and data put together by students to document and illustrate their learning experiences.

Although it may be a demanding task to set up in the beginning, the overall aim is for students to be involved in planning, collecting and evaluating their own work – taking responsibility for their own learning. This in turn may lead to increased participation and autonomy on the learner's part.

	New Inspiration 3 TB descriptors	Unit 1	Unit 2	Unit 3	Unit 4	Unit 5	Unit 6	Unit 7	Unit 8
Listening B1	I can follow clearly articulated speech directed at me in everyday conversation, though I sometimes have to ask for repetition of particular words and phrases.								
	I can generally follow the main points of extended discussion around me, provided speech is clearly articulated in standard dialect.	10	23, 24, 29	38, 47	53, 55	62, 70		91	102, 103
	I can listen to a short narrative and form hypotheses about what will happen next.				51				
	I can understand the main points of radio news bulletins and simpler recorded material on topics of personal interest delivered relatively slowly and clearly.	14, 15, 17	23, 27, 29, 30	38, 40, 43, 47	55	62, 69, 73	79, 81	89, 91, 95	102, 103, 106, 107
	I can catch the main points in TV programmes on familiar topics when the delivery is relatively slow and clear.								
	I can understand simple technical information, such as operating instructions for everyday equipment.								

Listening B2	I can understand in detail what is said to me in standard spoken language even in a noisy environment.	13	24, 27			69			104, 105
	I can follow a lecture or talk within my own field, provided the subject matter is familiar and the presentation straightforward and clearly structured.		30	43					
	I can understand most radio documentaries delivered in standard language and can identify the speaker's mood, tone etc. by using contextual clues.	15						95	
	I can understand TV documentaries, live interviews, talk shows, plays and the majority of films in standard dialect.							93	
	I can understand the main ideas of complex speech on both concrete and abstract topics delivered in a standard dialect, including technical discussions in my field of specialisation.								
	I can use a variety of strategies to achieve comprehension, including listening for main points; checking comprehension.	10, 11, 13	23	40, 43, 47	53, 55	69, 73	79, 81	89, 93	102, 103, 104, 105, 107
Reading B1	I can understand the main points in short newspaper articles about current and familiar topics.	14, 18		36, 39, 42		63	80		
	I can read columns or interviews in newspapers and magazines in which someone takes a stand on a current topic or event and understand the overall meaning of the text.			40, 42	48, 52	64, 70	76	99	100
	I can guess the meaning of single unknown words from the context thus deducing the meaning of expressions if the topic is familiar.	16	28			68, 69	79	94	
	I can skim short texts (for example news summaries) and find relevant facts and information (for example who has done what and where).	10, 12, 16	22, 26, 28	36, 42	48, 52	63, 64, 66, 70	78, 80	88, 90, 92, 94	100, 101
	I can understand the most important information in short simple everyday information brochures.	14, 20, 21	26			72		96	106
	I can understand simple messages and standard letters (for example from businesses, clubs or authorities).								
	In private letters I can understand those parts dealing with events, feelings and wishes well enough to correspond regularly with a pen friend.								
	I can understand the plot of a clearly structured story and recognise what the most important episodes and events are and what is significant about them.	16		46, 47	48, 54			92	

Reading B2	I can rapidly grasp the content and the significance of news, articles and reports on topics connected with my interests or my job, and decide if a closer reading is worthwhile.					64		92	
	I can read and understand articles and reports on current problems in which the writers express specific attitudes and points of view.			42		66, 72	74, 76	88, 98	100
	I can understand in detail texts within my field of interest or the area of my academic or professional speciality.		26			68, 70, 72	74	90, 98, 99	
	I can understand specialised articles outside my own field if I can occasionally check with a dictionary.		28			66, 68, 69			
	I can read reviews dealing with the content and criticism of cultural topics (films, theatre, books, concerts) and summarise the main points.								
	I can read letters on topics within my areas of academic or professional speciality or interest and grasp the most important points.								
	I can quickly look through a manual (for example for a computer program) and find and understand the relevant explanations and help for a specific problem.								
	I can understand in a narrative or play the motives for the characters' actions and their consequences for the development of the plot.				54				
Spoken Interaction B1	I can start, maintain and close simple face-to-face conversations on topics that are familiar or of personal interest.	11, 13	29	38, 47				93	103
	I can maintain a conversation or discussion that may sometimes be difficult to follow when trying to say exactly what I would like to.	13, 15	25	43, 47	51			93	
	I can deal with most situations likely to arise when making travel arrangements through an agent or when actually travelling.					69			
	I can ask for and follow detailed directions.								
	I can express and respond to feelings such as surprise, happiness, sadness, interest and indifference.								
	I can give or seek personal views and opinions in an informal discussion with friends.	17	25, 27, 29	36, 37, 38, 41, 47	50	62, 64, 65, 73		95	102, 103, 107
	I can agree and disagree politely.				50				

Spoken Interaction B2	I can initiate, maintain and end discourse naturally with effective turn-taking.	13		41		67		95	
	I can exchange considerable quantities of detailed factual information on matters within my fields of interest.			38	55	73	75		108
	I can convey degrees of emotion and highlight the personal significance of events and experiences.								101, 102
	I can engage in extended conversation in a clearly participatory fashion on most general topics.	13				65, 69			102, 103, 108
	I can account for and sustain my opinions in discussion by providing relevant explanations, arguments and comments.			41		65, 73			102, 103
	I can help a discussion along on familiar ground confirming comprehension, inviting others in, etc.								
	I can carry out a prepared interview, checking and confirming information, following up interesting replies.	11, 15, 17	25, 27	38, 47		62, 65, 67	75, 79	96	102, 105, 107
Spoken Production B1	I can narrate a story.				54				
	I can give detailed accounts of experiences, describing feelings and reactions.								
	I can describe dreams, hopes and ambitions.								
	I can explain and give reasons for my plans, intentions and actions.					63			
	I can relate the plot of a book or film and describe my reactions.			46, 47					
	I can paraphrase short written passages orally in a simple fashion, using the original text wording and ordering.			41, 47	52, 54	67			101
Spoken Production B2	I can give clear, detailed descriptions on a wide range of subjects related to my fields of interest.		30		48, 49, 56		81	91	101
	I can understand and summarise orally short extracts from news items, interviews or documentaries containing opinions, argument and discussion.					69			
	I can understand and summarise orally the plot and sequence of events in an extract from a film or play.		30						
	I can construct a chain of reasoned argument, linking my ideas logically.		24	41	52	67	76, 81		
	I can explain a viewpoint on a topical issue giving the advantages and disadvantages of various options.				52			89, 91	
	I can speculate about causes, consequences, hypothetical situations.			41	48, 51, 53, 54			92	101, 102
Strategies B1	I can repeat back part of what someone has said to confirm that we understand each other.								

	I can ask someone to clarify or elaborate what they have just said.								
	When I can't think of the word I want, I can use a simple word meaning something similar and invite 'correction'.		29	43					
Strategies B2	I can use standard phrases like 'That's a difficult question to answer' to gain time and keep the turn while formulating what to say.								
	I can make a note of 'favourite mistakes' and consciously monitor speech for them.								
	I can generally correct slips and errors if I become aware of them or if they have led to misunderstandings.								
Language Quality B1	I can keep a conversation going comprehensibly, but have to pause to plan and correct what I am saying – especially when I talk freely for longer periods.	13	29	38, 43	54		81		107
	I can convey simple information of immediate relevance, getting across which point I feel is most important.		23, 27, 29, 30	41	48	67, 70	75	89, 95, 97	101
	I have a sufficient vocabulary to express myself with some circumlocutions on most topics pertinent to my everyday life such as family, hobbies and interests, work, travel, and current events.	13, 14, 17, 18, 19	22, 23, 26, 29	36, 38, 41, 43	48, 51, 56	63, 65, 67, 69, 73	77, 79, 81, 82	89, 91, 92, 95, 96	101, 102, 103, 106, 107, 109
	I can express myself reasonably accurately in familiar, predictable situations.	13, 16, 19	23, 25, 27, 29, 31	36, 37, 39, 41	49, 51, 53, 55, 56	63, 65, 67, 69, 71, 72	75, 77, 79, 81, 82	89, 91, 93, 95, 97	101, 103, 105, 107, 109
Language Quality B2	I can produce stretches of language with a fairly even tempo; although I can be hesitant as I search for expressions, there are few noticeably long pauses.		30		49	69			
	I can pass on detailed information reliably.						77		
	I have sufficient vocabulary to express myself on matters connected to my field and on most general topics.			41		69		95	
	I can communicate with reasonable accuracy and can correct mistakes if they have led to misunderstandings.								
Writing B1	I can write simple connected texts on a range of topics within my field of interest and can express personal views and opinions.	13, 19, 21	25, 29	37, 39, 43	49, 53, 56	62, 63, 65, 71, 73	75, 77	89, 93	101, 103, 109
	I can write simple texts about experiences or events, for example about a trip, for a school newspaper or a club newsletter.	13, 15, 17, 19	23			69	75		

	I can write personal letters to friends or acquaintances asking for or giving them news and narrating events.	17		41					
	I can describe in a personal letter the plot of a film or a book or give an account of a concert.								
	In a letter I can express feelings such as grief, happiness, interest, regret and sympathy.								
	I can reply in written form to advertisements and ask for more complete or more specific information about products (for example a car or an academic course).								
	I can convey – via fax, e-mail or a circular – short simple factual information to friends or colleagues or ask for information in such a way.							91, 93	
	I can write my CV in summary form.								
Writing B2	I can write clear and detailed texts (compositions, reports or texts of presentations) on various topics related to my field of interest.	21	30		55, 56	65, 73	81	91, 95	101, 105, 107, 109
	I can write summaries of articles on topics of general interest.								
	I can summarise information from different sources and media.	15	30		56		79, 82	99	108
	I can discuss a topic in a composition or 'letter to the editor', giving reasons for or against a specific point of view.								
	I can develop an argument systematically in a composition or report, emphasising decisive points and including supporting details.			43			79, 81		
	I can write about events and real or fictional experiences in a detailed and easily readable way.	19				69	77	95	105
	I can write a short review of a film or a book.		23, 27						
	I can express in a personal letter different feelings and attitudes and can report the news of the day making clear what – in my opinion – are the important aspects of an event.				51				103

Using *New Inspiration*

There are four **Preview** sections at each level of *New Inspiration* giving students a brief introduction to the communicative aims and topic/vocabulary areas they will cover in the following two units.

Communicative Aims

Students match pictures with captions or speech bubbles to the correct communicative aims from the box. This activity helps prepare students for the context in which they will learn each communicative aim.

Topics and Vocabulary

Categorisation activities introduce students to some of the key vocabulary of the following two units, and they are also encouraged through brainstorming to identify other words that they already know for some of the topics.

PREVIEW

UNITS 5–6

COMMUNICATIVE AIMS
LEARNING HOW TO ...

1 Talk about what has and hasn't happened
2 Talk about experiences
3 Talk about achievements and important events
4 Describe a sequence of past events
5 Talk about past habits and states
6 Talk about inventions

TOPICS AND VOCABULARY

Countries
Phrases with *go, learn* and *ride*
Sport
Geographical features
Disability
Recycling
Household items
Materials
Inventions
Phrases with *do* and *make*

A They didn't use to have electric light.

B They haven't reached the USA yet.

1 Match four of the communicative aims (1–6) with the pictures (A–D).

2 Complete the words and put them into categories.

Sport | Materials | Household items

car_et co_ton c_cling
cu_board cu_tains gla_s
ic_ho_key m_tal mirr_r
plas_ic p_per r_nning sai_ing
sa_cepan s_iing su_fing
va_uum cle_ner wo_l

3 2.15 Listen to extracts 1–3 from Units 5 and 6. Match them with A–C below.

A An extract from an autobiography
B A description of an invention
C Information about a new sport

60

Listening Preview

Students listen to short extracts from the following units and identify what kind of passage the extracts are taken from or what topic they discuss.

The car, which was sketched by da Vinci in 1478, runs by clockwork.

h had planned to go to university, but instead
e left school and started her own business.

PREVIEW

4 Play *What kind of person?*

Work in pairs and make notes describing four other students under these headings.

What kind of person?

Colour ....

Day of the week ....

Month of the year ....

Place ....

Clothes ....

Household item ....

Food ....

Animal ....

Take turns to read out your descriptions to another group. Can they guess who the people are?

This person is red. She is Monday. June. And a beach. She is a pair of blue jeans. A phone. Pizza. And a cat.

Believe it or not!

Who is the world's greatest inventor? Many people think that Thomas Edison registered the most inventions – he had over 1,000 patents, including the light bulb. But Dr Yoshiro Nakamatsu from Tokyo has 3,200 patents, including the floppy disk! Although he's 78, he's still going strong, so that number will probably increase.

61

Speaking activity

Students carry out an interactive speaking activity related to the next two units. This may be a game, as here, a questionnaire or a survey. The Teacher's Book provides suggestions for students to use the results of the game to complete a project.

Believe it or not!

Interesting facts related to one of the topics of the following units.

The first three lessons in each unit present **new language**. While these lessons follow a similar pattern up to the After Reading/Listening exercise, the subsequent practice activities vary from lesson to lesson but always include pronunciation and end with writing and Language Workout. Lessons may also include Word Banks and vocabulary exercises, games and role plays, as appropriate for the lesson aims. There are always one or two Extension activities for fast-finishers. In every case there is a progression from controlled presentation and practice of new language to freer, more communicative activities.

Lesson heading
The heading shows the unit topic – in this case Challenges – and the communicative aim(s) and target language of the lesson.

Warmers
The Teacher's Book suggests at least two warmers for each lesson. These may revise previously learnt language or prepare students for the lesson topic.

1 Opener
The aim of the Opener is to set the scene for the reading text or listening passage or to pre-teach vocabulary, or both.

2 Reading/Listening
The new language is presented in a text or listening passage which is preceded by pre-reading/listening tasks or prediction activities. Students then read the text or listen to the passage. Teachers may then wish to play the recording, pausing to answer queries about language or content, or to ask students to close their books and listen without reading.

5 CHALLENGES
3 We've been friends ever since we me

Talking about achievements and important events
Present perfect with *for* and *since*

1 OPENER
Look at the photo of Usain Bolt. How is he feeling? What has he done?

2 READING
2.21 Read the text and match six of these headings with quotations 1–6.

Something I'd like to change
What I do at a race
Drugs
The future
Someone I rely on
Winning
Charity work

Usain Bolt: 9.58

Usain Bolt was born in Trelawney, Jamaica in August 1986. At the 2008 Olympics® in Beijing he won three gold medals (100 metres, 200 metres and 4x100 metres relay). He set a new world record in each event. In 2009 at the World Championships in Berlin he set new world records in both the 100 metres (9.58 seconds) and 200 metres (19.19 seconds). In his autobiography, *Usain Bolt: 9.58*, he talks about his life.

1 ____
'I've won hundreds of medals since I was at school. It's special when you win your first one, but after a while the novelty wears off. It's not the piece of metal that matters, it's the achievement itself. I don't need to see the medals to know I won, and I don't have to show them to anyone to prove it. Everybody knows.'

2 ____
'My best friend in the world is still NJ, or Nugent Walker Junior. We've been friends ever since we met on the first day at primary school and I can't remember ever falling out with him. We hit it off straight away and now he's my personal assistant, someone I can turn to at any time of day or night, who is always, always there for me.'

3 ____
'I don't worry about who I'm racing against or what's going to happen. I just go out there, entertain the crowd and win.'

4 ____
'I'd like to cut out the habit of looking around me as I run, because I know it would improve my times. It's a bad habit I've had since high school.'

5 ____
'My fame gives me an opportunity to help those who are less fortunate and assist other charitable agencies. I've been involved in a number of projects including work in the health, education, community development and sports sectors.'

6 ____
'My attitude to drugs has always been to stay away from them. I tried a cigarette when I was 13 years old, but I've never touched one since. I've had to do drug tests for years – I had my first drug test in Miami just before I was 17. I'm tested after every race, and every day I have to tell the authorities where I'm going to be in case they want to do a test.'

66

Weblink
The Teacher's Book provides at least one URL relevant to each lesson. Teachers are advised to check these links before sharing them with the students as web addresses frequently change.

4 Vocabulary
Lessons may also offer explicit lexical development through Word Banks of lexical sets and vocabulary exercises.

3 After Reading/Listening

These exercises use a variety of different formats including true/false, open questions, matching questions and answers, and completion. The aim is intensive reading/listening. After Reading/Listening ends with Your response: an activity which invites the student to respond personally to the text or dialogue.

Follow-up activities and homework

The Teacher's Book offers optional follow-up activities, usually including a game, to help with mixed-ability teaching and to cope with variable aptitude and amounts of time available. Homework suggestions (usually writing) are also provided for each lesson.

UNIT 5

AFTER READING

Match the questions with the answers. There are two wrong answers.

1 How many medals did Usain Bolt win at the 2008 Olympics®?
2 How many medals has he won since he was at school?
3 How long has he known his personal assistant?
4 Why would he like to get rid of a bad habit?
5 What does being famous give him a chance to do?
6 What happens to him after every race?

a For three years.
b So he could run faster.
c He's tested for drugs.
d More than a hundred.
e Since they were at primary school.
f Help people who are less lucky than him.
g Travel around the world.
h Three.

Your response What do you admire about Usain Bolt? What does it take to be a successful athlete? What problems can fame and success cause?

VOCABULARY

Complete with the correct preposition: *about, at, in, to, with.*

1 be ___ the Olympic® Games
2 show something ___ someone
3 worry ___ something
4 fall out ___ someone
5 be involved ___ something
6 be ___ a class
7 be ___ school
8 live ___ a house

PRONUNCIATION

Mark the stressed syllable.

achievement attitude
authorities community
development entertain
fortunate novelty
opportunity primary

2.22 Now listen and check. Repeat the words.

6 SPEAKING

Make questions and interview another student. Note down the answers.

How long/you/be/at this school?
A How long have you been at this school?
B For three years./Since September 2010.

When/you/get/to school today?
A When did you get to school today?
B At eight o'clock.

1 How long/we/have/this coursebook?
2 When/you/start/learning English?
3 Who/you/know/the longest in this class? When/you/first/meet/them?
4 Which friend/you/have/the longest? How long/you/be/friends?
5 What's your favourite band? When/you/first/hear/them?
6 What's your favourite sport? How long/you/play/it?
7 How long/you/live/in this town?
8 How long/you/live/in the same house or flat?
9 What colour are your favourite shoes? When/you/get/them?
10 Has your family got any pets? How long/you/have/them?

Now tell another student about the most interesting answers.

Extension Ask another student to interview you. Give some true and some false answers to the questions. Your partner has to guess which answers are false.

7 WRITING

Look at questions 3–10 in exercise 6 again. Write a paragraph about yourself answering some of the questions.

LANGUAGE WORKOUT

Complete.

Present perfect with *for* and *since*
I've won hundreds of medals ___ I was at school.
I've had to do drug tests ___ years.

We can use the present perfect with *for* and *since* to talk about the unfinished past.
We use ___ to say *how long* something has lasted.
We use ___ to say *when* something started.

▶**Answers and Practice**
Language File pages 117–118

67

6 Speaking

In the Speaking activity, students *use* the target language to communicate, in this case interviewing each other about how long they've done things for, and when they did things. This activity often also *personalises* the target language and students use it to talk about their own lives and opinions.

Extension

Lessons have one or more Extension activities offering more challenging practice for fast-finishers.

7 Writing

Each of the first three lessons in each unit ends with a writing activity. These typically have the dual function of writing skills development and reinforcement of the target language. In this lesson students write a paragraph about how long they've done things for, and when they did things.

Language Workout

The Language Workout boxes highlight the target language with sentences from the lesson or paradigms for the students to complete. The bottom of the box refers students to the Language File at the back of the book where they can check their answers, find a fuller treatment of the grammatical point and do a practice exercise focusing on the form of the target language. The Teacher's Book provides suggestions for further practice activities and additional information about the target language.

Teachers may decide when to draw students' attention to the Language Workout, and the Teacher's Book gives suggestions for when it can be used. For example, it may be appropriate to refer to it before learners are expected to produce the target language, and/or for consolidation at the end of the lesson.

5 Pronunciation

Each of the first three lessons in every unit contains a pronunciation exercise focusing on particular sounds or stress and intonation. The Teacher's Book provides more information about the phonological area being taught and suggests further activities.

The fourth lesson in each unit is an **Integrated Skills** lesson. In these lessons the four skills support each other, usually moving from a reading text to a listening activity, then to a speaking activity based on the listening or reading and concluding with a writing activity for which the reading, listening and speaking have prepared the students. The lesson ends with a Learner Independence section.

Lesson heading
The lesson heading identifies the text type, in this lesson, Describing personal experiences.

1 Opener
The aim of the Opener is to introduce the topic or to revise and pre-teach vocabulary, or both.

Warmers
The Teacher's Book suggests two or three warmers. These may revise vocabulary or prepare students for the lesson topic.

2 Reading
There are usually one or two reading activities encouraging detailed reading. Detailed comprehension questions have the dual function of encouraging intensive reading and highlighting the structure of the text in preparation for the subsequent skills activities.

5 CHALLENGES

4 Integrated Skills

Describing personal experiences

1 OPENER

How much do you know about Peru? Do the quiz: choose A or B.

1 Peru is on the … coast of South America.
A Atlantic B Pacific

2 Its capital is …
A Lima B Santiago

3 It shares a border with …
A Bolivia B Paraguay

4 The Andes … runs through Peru.
A river B mountain range

5 The … built Machu Picchu.
A Aztecs B Incas

READING

2 Students Julie and Simon are backpacking round South America. Read and complete Julie's blog with phrases a–f.

a and rises to over 4,000 metres in some places
b which tastes a bit like beef
c it was the capital of the Inca empire
d it's 3,809 metres above sea level
e for a hot shower and a rest before dinner
f on the edge of the mountain

2.21 Now listen and check. Which words in the phrases helped you to complete the text?

We've been busy since we arrived in Peru from Ecuador a week ago! It's our fourth country so far. First we took a bus from Lima, the capital, to Cuzco (24 hours!). Somewhere on the journey I lost my watch, but it wasn't **valuable**, so it didn't really matter. Cuzco is a beautiful old town surrounded by the Andes mountains – __1__. We spent a night in a **hostel**, and the next morning we started to walk the Inca trail to the city of Machu Picchu. The trail is often very **steep** __2__, so lots of people suffer from **altitude** sickness. I've bee[n] lucky because I haven't felt ill, but Simon has had a bad headache for a couple of days.

The trek along the Inca **trail** took four days and it was **exhausting**. But it was well worth it. On the last day, we got up at 4am to reach Machu Picchu in time for sunrise. When we got there, the city was **invisible** because it was covered in cloud. But suddenly the cloud lifted, and there was Machu Picchu __3__. It was magic!

We spent several hours **wandering** round the site – what an incredible place! Then back to Cuzco by bus and train __4__. We've had some interesting food in Peru. I've already tried llama, __5__. A local speciality in Cuzco is roast guinea pig, but I couldn't face it!

Tomorrow we're going to Lake Titicaca, on the border between Peru and Bolivia. It's the largest freshwater lake in South America and one of the highest in the world – __6__. The weather has been great – let's hope it stays that way.

68

Weblink
The Teacher's Book provides at least one URL relevant to each lesson (in this case a website with information about travel in Peru). Teachers are advised to check these links before sharing them with the students as web addresses frequently change.

5 Listening

These activities develop intensive listening skills. Here students listen for the order in which two people are visiting certain countries.

Learner Independence

Learner Independence sections typically include three activities, focusing on learning to learn, word creation, and idiomatic expressions.

UNIT 5

Find the highlighted words in the text which mean:

1 cheap hotel *n*
2 height *n*
3 walking in a relaxed way *v*
4 path through the countryside *n*
5 rising quickly *adj*
6 very tiring *adj*
7 worth a lot of money *adj*
8 something you can't see *adj*

Linking words: *so* and *because*.

Find examples of *so* and *because* in the text. Then complete these rules.

We use ____ to talk about reason or cause.
We use ____ to talk about consequence or result.

Now complete these sentences with *so* or *because*.

1 They were tired ____ the bus journey took 24 hours.
2 Cuzco is surrounded by mountains, ____ it gets very cold at night.
3 We got up early ____ we wanted to see the sunrise.
4 Lots of people visit Machu Picchu ____ it's very beautiful.
5 I haven't got much money, ____ I can't go on holiday this year.

LISTENING

2.24 Listen to Julie and Simon talking to Rod, an American backpacker in Cuzco. Follow their route on the map and number the countries in the order they're visiting them.

SPEAKING

Look at your answers to exercise 5. Use the map and tell each other which countries Julie and Simon have already visited, and which countries they haven't visited yet.

Plan a backpacking trip with another student. Choose a country or group of countries, and decide which places you want to visit. Plan your itinerary.

GUIDED WRITING

Imagine you are on the road! Write a blog about the backpacking trip you planned in exercise 7. Use the text in exercise 2 to help you and include this information.

- Where are you now?
- Where is it exactly, and what's it like?
- How did you get there?
- Where have you already been?
- What have you done?
- Where are you going next?

LEARNER INDEPENDENCE

9 Self assessment: Look back over this unit, think about what you've learnt and make a list.

Information I've found out more about South America.
Grammar I've learnt how to use 'already' and 'yet' with the present perfect.
Vocabulary I've learnt new words for sports.

If there are any areas where you have problems, look back at the lesson again and refer to the Language File.

10 Word creation: Make nouns ending in *-ity* from these adjectives and complete the sentences.

active electric national popular possible real responsible special

1 Seafood is a ____ in this restaurant.
2 Reading is my favourite leisure ____.
3 There's a ____ of rainstorms later today.
4 The ____ of backpacking holidays has grown recently.
5 Where are you from? What's your ____?
6 Parents have a ____ to look after their children.
7 If we turn off the lights, we'll save ____.
8 Snowboarding looks difficult, but in ____ it's quite easy.

11 2.25 **Phrasebook**: Find these useful expressions in Unit 5. Then listen and repeat.

I didn't have a clue.
Have you ever wondered what it's like?
I've never had so much fun.
I've never done anything like it before.
It didn't really matter.
It was well worth it.
It was magic!
What an incredible place!
I couldn't face it.
Let's hope it stays that way.

Now write a five-line dialogue using three or more of the expressions.

69

9

In this lesson students look back at what they have learnt and think about any problem areas. Discussion may take place in English or the mother tongue, as appropriate to the learner's level. The emphasis here is on learning *how* to learn. The Teacher's Book offers optional activities to further explore this area.

10

The aim here is to increase students' vocabulary by noticing how to make nouns from adjectives.

11 Phrasebook

This section occurs in every unit and helps students learn idiomatic expressions in context. Students find the expressions from within the unit, practise pronunciation and then complete a small follow-up activity, in this case writing a dialogue with some of the expressions they have learnt.

Follow-up activities and homework

The Teacher's Book offers optional follow-up activities, usually including a game, to help with mixed-ability teaching and to cope with variable aptitude and amounts of time available. Homework suggestions (usually writing) are also provided for each lesson.

8 Guided Writing

Here students can write a blog about the trip they planned. The Teacher's Book suggests that students use a range of adjectives to describe their journey, and also provides further optional activities.

6 & 7 Speaking

Students now use their answers to the Listening activity to plan their own backpacking trip. The Teacher's Book offers further optional activities.

Inspiration EXTRA! follows the Integrated Skills lesson in each unit. The left-hand page includes either Language Links and a Sketch, or a Project. There is always a Game/Puzzle, and sometimes a Limerick.

On the right-hand page there are mixed-ability activities giving opportunities for both revision and extension, and Your Choice!, which allows students to choose from four different activities.

Language Links

The aim of the Language Links section is to raise plurilingual awareness. Here, students are encouraged to see how knowing one or two languages can often help them to identify words in other languages.

Project

The projects in Units 2, 4, 6 and 8 provide a valuable resource for student creativity, self-expression and language consolidation. They also allow students of varying abilities to contribute. Students are encouraged to save their projects to add to their portfolios. While intended for use with the whole class, the projects could also be used for homework or as supplementary material with more confident students in mixed-ability classes. The group size for projects will vary from class to class, but teachers may prefer to have groups of three to six members.

1 Projects require students to go back through part of the unit which models the writing they will do. Then students brainstorm ideas, choosing a few to write about.
2 There is then a research phase using reference books, libraries or the Internet to gather information for the project. This could involve interviewing people, for example, family members.
3 Finally the group work together to produce their project, reading each other's work, editing and illustrating it. The Teacher's Book offers suggestions for organisation.

Game/Puzzle

Here, students play a miming game. There is often a puzzle on this page, and there are also games throughout the book in the lessons and in the Teacher's Book optional activities.

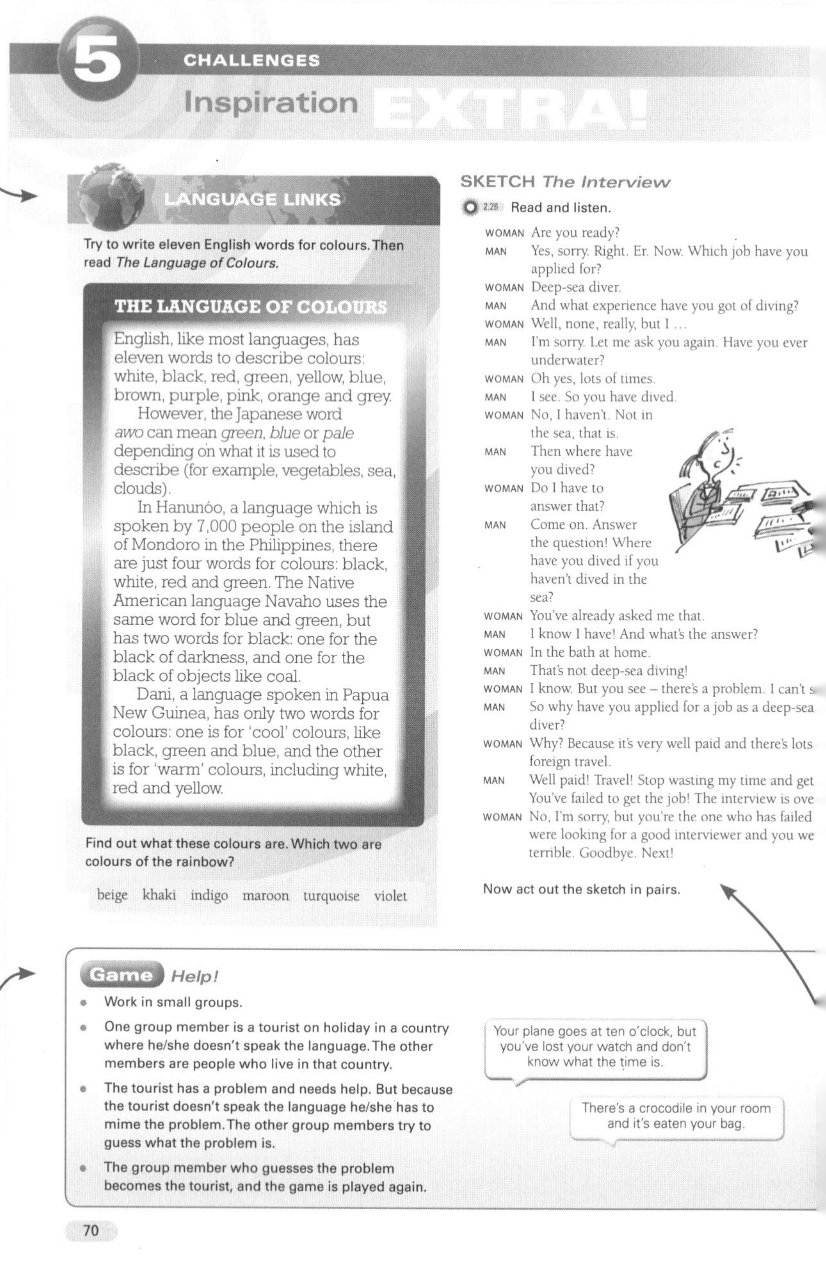

5 CHALLENGES

Inspiration EXTRA!

LANGUAGE LINKS

Try to write eleven English words for colours. Then read *The Language of Colours.*

THE LANGUAGE OF COLOURS

English, like most languages, has eleven words to describe colours: white, black, red, green, yellow, blue, brown, purple, pink, orange and grey.

However, the Japanese word *awo* can mean *green, blue* or *pale* depending on what it is used to describe (for example, vegetables, sea, clouds).

In Hanunóo, a language which is spoken by 7,000 people on the island of Mondoro in the Philippines, there are just four words for colours: black, white, red and green. The Native American language Navaho uses the same word for blue and green, but has two words for black: one for the black of darkness, and one for the black of objects like coal.

Dani, a language spoken in Papua New Guinea, has only two words for colours: one is for 'cool' colours, like black, green and blue, and the other is for 'warm' colours, including white, red and yellow.

Find out what these colours are. Which two are colours of the rainbow?

beige khaki indigo maroon turquoise violet

SKETCH *The Interview*

2.26 Read and listen.

WOMAN Are you ready?
MAN Yes, sorry. Right. Er. Now. Which job have you applied for?
WOMAN Deep-sea diver.
MAN And what experience have you got of diving?
WOMAN Well, none, really, but I …
MAN I'm sorry. Let me ask you again. Have you ever underwater?
WOMAN Oh yes, lots of times.
MAN I see. So you have dived.
WOMAN No, I haven't. Not in the sea, that is.
MAN Then where have you dived?
WOMAN Do I have to answer that?
MAN Come on. Answer the question! Where have you dived if you haven't dived in the sea?
WOMAN You've already asked me that.
MAN I know I have! And what's the answer?
WOMAN In the bath at home.
MAN That's not deep-sea diving!
WOMAN I know. But you see – there's a problem. I can't s
MAN So why have you applied for a job as a deep-sea diver?
WOMAN Why? Because it's very well paid and there's lots foreign travel.
MAN Well paid! Travel! Stop wasting my time and get You've failed to get the job! The interview is ove
WOMAN No, I'm sorry, but you're the one who has failed were looking for a good interviewer and you we terrible. Goodbye. Next!

Now act out the sketch in pairs.

Game *Help!*

- Work in small groups.
- One group member is a tourist on holiday in a country where he/she doesn't speak the language. The other members are people who live in that country.
- The tourist has a problem and needs help. But because the tourist doesn't speak the language he/she has to mime the problem. The other group members try to guess what the problem is.
- The group member who guesses the problem becomes the tourist, and the game is played again.

Your plane goes at ten o'clock, but you've lost your watch and don't know what the time is.

There's a crocodile in your room and it's eaten your bag.

70

Sketch

The aim of the sketches is for students to enjoy using English while also getting valuable stress and intonation practice. The Teacher's Book has suggestions for using the recording and for acting out the sketches.

Revision

The Revision exercises provide further writing practice for less confident students in mixed-ability classes. In this unit, students write sentences about what two people have or haven't done, information based on an interview and sentences using time phrases. They are always given sections of the unit to refer back to.

UNIT 5

EVISION

ESSON 1 Look at *10 things to do before you're 20* on page 62. Use your answers to exercise 2 to write eight sentences about Lisa and Steve.

Lisa's already been to lots of gigs. She hasn't learnt first aid yet.

ESSON 2 Look at exercise 8 on page 65. Write six sentences about the student you interviewed.

Helena has never wanted to change her name because she likes it.

ESSON 3 Write five sentences using these phrases.

last four days last Wednesday I got up a couple of minutes summer

She's only been here for a couple of minutes.
I haven't felt well since I got up.

EXTENSION

LESSON 1 Look at exercise 5 on page 63. Imagine it is 17 July. Write eight questions about McGregor and Boorman's trip using verbs from the text in the present perfect and *yet*. Answer the questions using *just, yet*, or *already*.

Have they been to the Czech Republic yet?
Yes, they've already been there.

LESSON 2 Look at the chart you completed in exercise 5 on page 65 and write a paragraph about the students you interviewed.

Kris and Stephanie haven't been water-skiing, but Nadia has. She went water-skiing when she was on holiday in Spain last summer.

LESSON 3 Look at exercise 2 on page 66. Imagine you are interviewing Usain Bolt. Choose some of the questions 4–10 in exercise 4 and write his answers.

YOUR CHOICE!

CONSTRUCTION Present perfect or past simple?

Complete with the present perfect or past simple of the verbs.

Zorbing is quite a new sport and many people __1__ (not try) it yet. Dwane van der Sluis and Andrew Akers __2__ (invent) zorbing in New Zealand in the 1990s. The inventors __3__ (want) to design a ball so that people could 'walk' on water, but it __4__ (not work) very well. Then they __5__ (try) rolling it down a hill with great success. Now zorbing centres __6__ (open) around the world and soon everyone will know someone who __7__ (try) the sport. 'Once you __8__ (have) a go, you want to do it again and again,' a teenage zorber said.

REFLECTION Present perfect

Choose the correct rule.

- We use *for* to refer to
  A a period of time. B a point in time.
- We use *since* to refer to
  A a period of time. B a point in time.
- We use the present perfect with just to talk about things that
  A happened a long time ago. B happened very recently.
- We use the present perfect with *already* to talk about things that
  A have happened. B haven't happened.
- We use the present perfect with *yet* to talk about things that
  A we expect to happen. B have happened recently.
- We usually use *ever* in
  A questions. B negative statements.
- We use *never* in
  A affirmative statements. B negative statements.

ACTION Make yourself look good!

- Work in groups of four. Use these verbs: go, kiss, meet, see, talk, win.
- Student A makes a sentence using one of the verbs in the present perfect.
  I've been to India.
- Student B repeats the sentence and adds to it.
  I've been to India and China.
- Student C repeats Student B's sentence and adds to it.
  I've been to India, China and Egypt.
- Student D repeats Student C's sentence and adds to it.
  I've been to India, China, Egypt and Antarctica.

INTERACTION The present I've always wanted

- Work in a small group.
- We are given presents on our birthdays and at other times of the year. Imagine it's one of those days and you can choose the present.
- What present have you always wanted but never got? It could be a thing, or an event, or a skill you'd like to have, or something you'd like for someone else.
- Take turns to tell each other about the present you've always wanted and why it has been such an important wish.

71

Extension

The Extension exercises provide challenging writing activities for more confident students in mixed-ability classes. In this unit, students write questions and answers in the present perfect, summarize information in a chart and imagine they are interviewing Usain Bolt and write his answers to their questions.

The Revision and Extension exercises are a flexible resource and may be done at the end of the unit or after the relevant lesson. Alternatively the students can do them as homework. Where possible, the Teacher's Book provides answers.

Your Choice!

The aim here is for students to choose and do the activity they like best. The activities reflect different learning styles and the aim is to encourage awareness of learning styles and to foster learner independence. Your Choice! activities may involve individual, pair or group work.

Culture

There are four Culture sections at each level of *New Inspiration* providing both factual information and the opportunity for cross-cultural comparisons. The section illustrated here deals with the topic of tourism.

1 Reading

Here, students three texts which discuss the impact of tourism and identify the text which performs each of the functions listed.

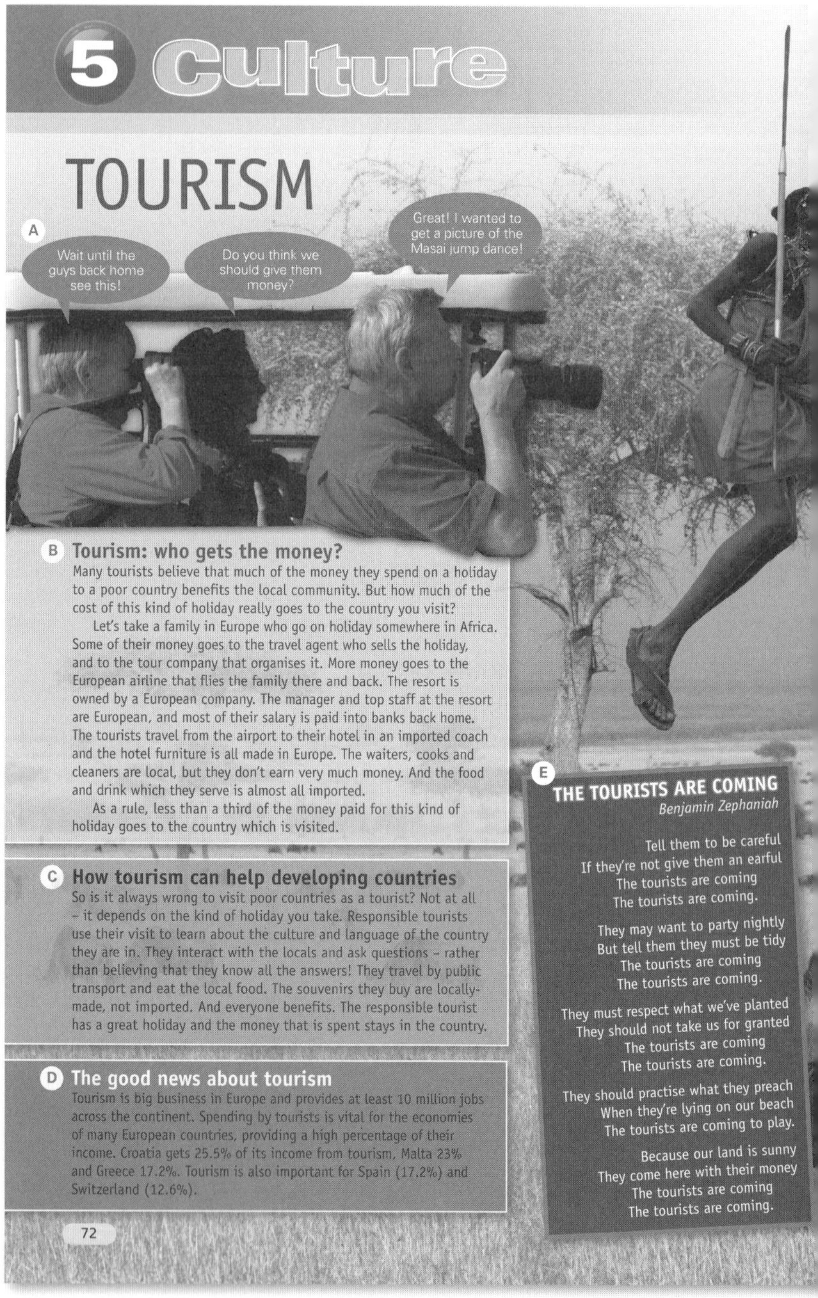

5 Culture

TOURISM

A

Wait until the guys back home see this!

Do you think we should give them money?

Great! I wanted to get a picture of the Masai jump dance!

B **Tourism: who gets the money?**

Many tourists believe that much of the money they spend on a holiday to a poor country benefits the local community. But how much of the cost of this kind of holiday really goes to the country you visit?

Let's take a family in Europe who go on holiday somewhere in Africa. Some of their money goes to the travel agent who sells the holiday, and to the tour company that organises it. More money goes to the European airline that flies the family there and back. The resort is owned by a European company. The manager and top staff at the resort are European, and most of their salary is paid into banks back home. The tourists travel from the airport to their hotel in an imported coach and the hotel furniture is all made in Europe. The waiters, cooks and cleaners are local, but they don't earn very much money. And the food and drink which they serve is almost all imported.

As a rule, less than a third of the money paid for this kind of holiday goes to the country which is visited.

C **How tourism can help developing countries**

So is it always wrong to visit poor countries as a tourist? Not at all – it depends on the kind of holiday you take. Responsible tourists use their visit to learn about the culture and language of the country they are in. They interact with the locals and ask questions – rather than believing that they know all the answers! They travel by public transport and eat the local food. The souvenirs they buy are locally-made, not imported. And everyone benefits. The responsible tourist has a great holiday and the money that is spent stays in the country.

D **The good news about tourism**

Tourism is big business in Europe and provides at least 10 million jobs across the continent. Spending by tourists is vital for the economies of many European countries, providing a high percentage of their income. Croatia gets 25.5% of its income from tourism, Malta 23% and Greece 17.2%. Tourism is also important for Spain (17.2%) and Switzerland (12.6%).

E **THE TOURISTS ARE COMING**

Benjamin Zephaniah

Tell them to be careful
If they're not give them an earful
The tourists are coming
The tourists are coming.

They may want to party nightly
But tell them they must be tidy
The tourists are coming
The tourists are coming.

They must respect what we've planted
They should not take us for granted
The tourists are coming
The tourists are coming.

They should practise what they preach
When they're lying on our beach
The tourists are coming to play.

Because our land is sunny
They come here with their money
The tourists are coming
The tourists are coming.

72

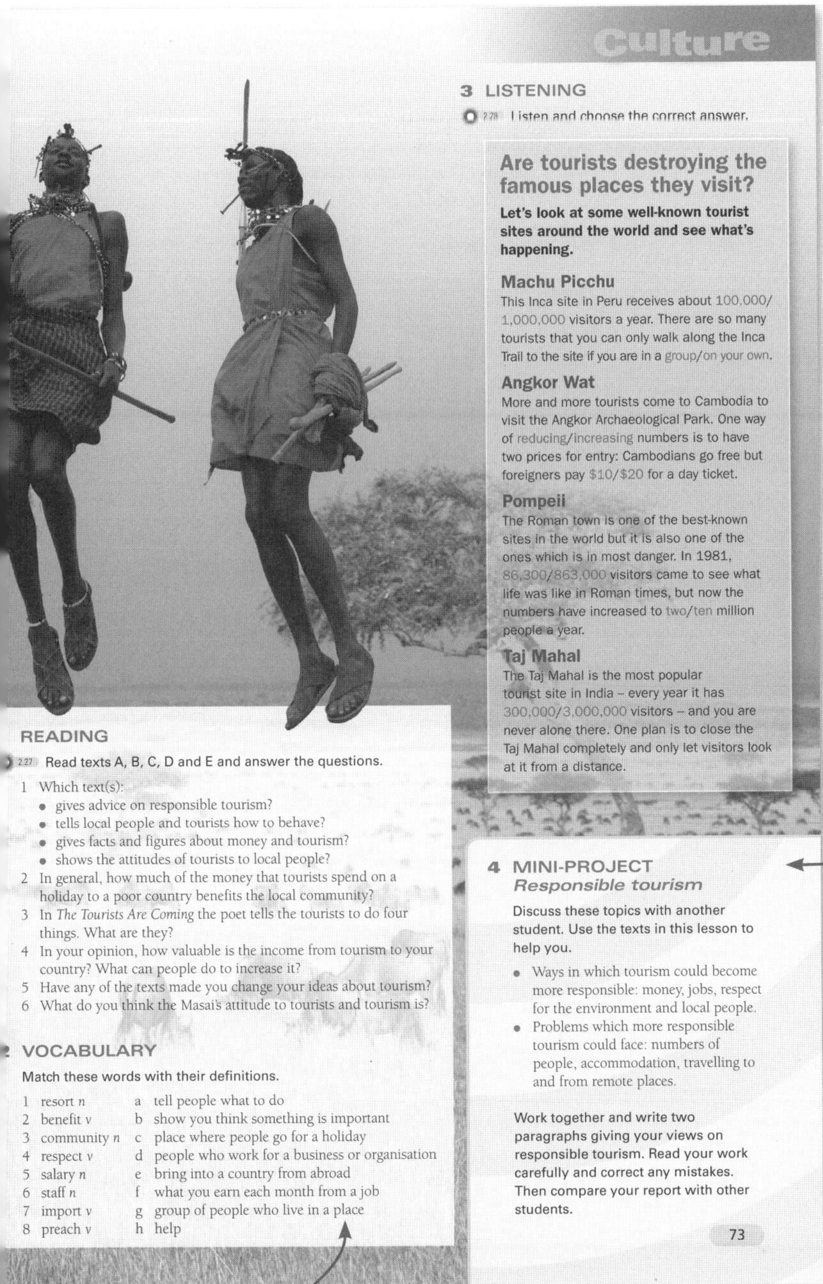

Culture

3 LISTENING

2.28 Listen and choose the correct answer.

Are tourists destroying the famous places they visit?

Let's look at some well-known tourist sites around the world and see what's happening.

Machu Picchu
This Inca site in Peru receives about 100,000/1,000,000 visitors a year. There are so many tourists that you can only walk along the Inca Trail to the site if you are in a group/on your own.

Angkor Wat
More and more tourists come to Cambodia to visit the Angkor Archaeological Park. One way of reducing/increasing numbers is to have two prices for entry: Cambodians go free but foreigners pay $10/$20 for a day ticket.

Pompeii
The Roman town is one of the best-known sites in the world but it is also one of the ones which is in most danger. In 1981, 86,300/863,000 visitors came to see what life was like in Roman times, but now the numbers have increased to two/ten million people a year.

Taj Mahal
The Taj Mahal is the most popular tourist site in India – every year it has 300,000/3,000,000 visitors – and you are never alone there. One plan is to close the Taj Mahal completely and only let visitors look at it from a distance.

READING

2.27 Read texts A, B, C, D and E and answer the questions.

1 Which text(s):
- gives advice on responsible tourism?
- tells local people and tourists how to behave?
- gives facts and figures about money and tourism?
- shows the attitudes of tourists to local people?

2 In general, how much of the money that tourists spend on a holiday to a poor country benefits the local community?
3 In *The Tourists Are Coming* the poet tells the tourists to do four things. What are they?
4 In your opinion, how valuable is the income from tourism to your country? What can people do to increase it?
5 Have any of the texts made you change your ideas about tourism?
6 What do you think the Masai's attitude to tourists and tourism is?

VOCABULARY

Match these words with their definitions.

1	resort *n*	a	tell people what to do
2	benefit *v*	b	show you think something is important
3	community *n*	c	place where people go for a holiday
4	respect *v*	d	people who work for a business or organisation
5	salary *n*	e	bring into a country from abroad
6	staff *n*	f	what you earn each month from a job
7	import *v*	g	group of people who live in a place
8	preach *v*	h	help

4 MINI-PROJECT
Responsible tourism

Discuss these topics with another student. Use the texts in this lesson to help you.

- Ways in which tourism could become more responsible: money, jobs, respect for the environment and local people.
- Problems which more responsible tourism could face: numbers of people, accommodation, travelling to and from remote places.

Work together and write two paragraphs giving your views on responsible tourism. Read your work carefully and correct any mistakes. Then compare your report with other students.

73

4 Mini-Project
The Mini-Projects in the Culture sections typically use the text as a model and invite the students to work in pairs and write about aspects of their own culture.

Vocabulary
The Culture section texts provide a rich source of useful new vocabulary, and there are a variety of activity types here to give practice.

Weblink
The Teacher's Book provides at least one relevant URL (in this case a website with information about responsible tourism). Teachers are advised to check these links before sharing them with the students as web addresses frequently change.

There are four **Reviews** at each level of *New Inspiration*. Each Review covers the new language of the preceding two units. The Teacher's Book contains the answers to all the exercises.

Review exercises are contextualised, often using information from the relevant lesson, so that students are creating meaningful sentences.

Language points reviewed include not only main verb tenses but problem areas such as *already/yet* and *for/since*.

The Workbook offers a parallel Review with text and multiple-choice questions, examination-type exercises, and a self assessment Progress Check consisting of 'I can do …' statements.

Exercise 1

Each review begins with a text covering the new language of both units with KET/PET examination-type objective test questions, usually multiple-choice cloze.

Weblink

The Teacher's Book provides at least one relevant URL (in this lesson a website giving tips on how to sleep well). Teachers are advised to check these links before sharing them with the students as web addresses frequently change.

REVIEW

UNITS 5–6

1 Read and complete. For each number 1–12, choose word or phrase A, B or C.

Teen sleepwalks to top of crane

A teenage sleepwalker __1__ after she __2__ asleep on the arm of a 40-metre-high crane, police have __3__ reported.

Police and firefighters __4__ to a building site in south-east London after a passer-by __5__ the girl on the crane. A firefighter __6__ up and discovered the 15-year-old girl was fast asleep. He didn't want to wake her in case she panicked and fell off the crane. Luckily he __7__ the girl's mobile phone and called her parents. They then phoned their daughter to wake her up, and she __8__ safely down to the ground. The rescue operation lasted __9__ two hours.

Apparently the unnamed girl __10__ her home in the middle of the night and climbed the crane while she was asleep. An expert at the London Sleep Centre said, 'I've treated people who __11__ cars and ridden horses while asleep. One patient has even tried to fly a helicopter. But I've __12__ heard of a more unusual case than this.'

	A	B	C
1	A rescued	B is rescued	C was rescued
2	A found	B was found	C were found
3	A ever	B just	C yet
4	A called	B was called	C were called
5	A had noticed	B has noticed	C did notice
6	A has climbed	B climbed	C was climbed
7	A found	B was found	C has found
8	A brought	B had brought	C was brought
9	A for	B since	C during
10	A leaves	B has left	C had left
11	A drive	B has driven	C have driven
12	A ever	B never	C yet

2 Rewrite the sentences using the present perfect with *just*.

The match began a minute ago.
The match has just begun.

1 The plane landed five minutes ago.
2 We saw the film last night.
3 It started raining a few seconds ago.
4 The students left school last month.
5 I bought some new trainers yesterday.
6 We heard the news half an hour ago.

3 Two students are going backpacking in Asia. Write sentences using the present perfect with *yet* and *already*.

buy the plane tickets
They've already bought the plane tickets.

read all the guidebooks
They haven't read all the guidebooks yet.

1 book somewhere to stay the first night ✗
2 apply for visas ✓
3 plan their route ✓
4 buy a phrasebook ✗
5 have the necessary vaccinations ✓
6 save up enough money ✓
7 pack their rucksacks ✗
8 organise travel insurance ✗

4 Ask and answer questions using the present perfect with *ever*.

Rob/try snowboarding ✗
A Has Rob ever tried snowboarding?
B No, he hasn't.

1 Sophie/go on a roller coaster ✓
2 Steve/eat sushi ✗
3 Lisa/try bungee jumping ✓
4 Julie and Simon/visit Mexico ✗
5 Lisa/win a race ✓
6 Julie and Simon/be on TV ✗

Now write sentences.

Rob has never tried snowboarding.

5 Complete with the present perfect or past simple.

A __1__ you ever __2__ (make) a parachute jump?
B No, I __3__ never __4__ (want) to. What about you?
A I __5__ (do) it last year.
B Really? __6__ you __7__ (enjoy) it?
A I __8__ (be) terrified before I __9__ (jump). But when my parachute __10__ (open) I __11__ (feel) great.
B Parachute jumping isn't for me – I __12__ (be) afraid of heights all my life!

6 Write sentences using the present perfect with *for* and *since*.

they/live in this town/1980
They've lived in this town since 1980.

1 he/have guitar lessons/six months
2 she/not/contact us/last Friday
3 I/be awake/6am
4 you/know each other/two weeks
5 my parents/be married/25 years
6 we/live here/I was born
7 you/not/go on holiday/ages
8 I/have a headache/yesterday

84

Complete with the past perfect where possible. Otherwise use the past simple.

Chris Haas, 15, __1__ (invent) the Hands-On Basketball as a school project when he __2__ (be) nine. 'The idea __3__ (be) to make an invention to help people do something better,' he remembers. Chris's father __4__ (be) a basketball coach for many years before he __5__ (retire). 'I __6__ (know) how to shoot properly because my father __7__ (teach) me,' Chris says, 'so I __8__ (paint) hands on a basketball to show the other players how to hold it.' No one __9__ (think) of this before, and Chris __10__ (sell) his idea to a big company. He __11__ (not expect) to make a lot of money, but last year he __12__ (earn) $50,000 from his invention.

Think about life 300 years ago. Write sentences about what people used to do and didn't use to do.

travel by plane
They didn't use to travel by plane.

1 drive cars
2 travel by boat
3 cook food over a fire
4 buy frozen food
5 send emails
6 listen to the radio
7 read by candlelight
8 wash clothes by hand

Write sentences using the past simple passive.

the vacuum cleaner/invent/Herbert Booth/1901
The vacuum cleaner was invented by Herbert Booth in 1901.

1 radium/discover/Marie and Pierre Curie/1898
2 the first printed books/produce/China
3 the electric light bulb/invent/Swan and Edison/1879
4 Mount Everest/first climb/Tenzing and Hillary/1953
5 mobile phones/first use/1978
6 the London underground/open/1863
7 the first colour photos/take/James Maxwell/1861
8 potatoes/bring/to Europe/the 16th century

VOCABULARY

0 Complete with ten of these words.

accident award brick carpet cans
float habit headache inspiration
kite medal metal mend tyre

1 You can't fly a ____ if there's no wind.
2 A carpenter managed to ____ the broken chair.
3 A beautiful Indian ____ covered the floor.
4 Could I have two ____ of cola, please?
5 Smoking is a very dangerous ____.
6 It's easier to ____ in the sea than in a freshwater pool.
7 He had a motorbike ____ but luckily he wasn't hurt.
8 It must be wonderful to win an Olympic® gold ____.
9 They say genius is one per cent ____, and 99 per cent hard work.
10 She was delighted to win an ____ for her first novel.

11 Match these words with their definitions.

blind combine deaf entertain foreigner
recycle reduce simplify sphere vehicle

1 give a performance that people enjoy
2 bring or put together
3 something round, like a ball
4 unable to see
5 unable to hear
6 process waste so it can be used again
7 machine that travels on roads
8 opposite of *increase*
9 person from another country
10 make easier or less complicated

12 Match the words in list A with the words and phrases in list B.

	A	B
1	become	a candle
2	do	by 50%
3	earn	damage
4	light	of an idea
5	perform	a language
6	reduce	money
7	think	in a play
8	translate	underwater
9	swim	well known

REVIEW

LEARNER INDEPENDENCE SELF ASSESSMENT

Look back at Lessons 1–3 in Units 5 and 6.

How good are you at ...?	✓ Fine	? Not sure
1 Talking about what has and hasn't happened Workbook pp50–51 exercises 1–4	☐	☐
2 Talking about experiences Workbook pp52–53 exercises 2–4	☐	☐
3 Talking about achievements and important events Workbook pp54–55 exercises 1–5	☐	☐
4 Describing a sequence of past events Workbook pp62–63 exercises 2 and 3	☐	☐
5 Talking about past states and habits Workbook pp64–65 exercises 2 and 3	☐	☐
6 Talking about inventions Workbook pp66–67 exercises 1–3	☐	☐

Not sure? Have a look at Language File pages 117–119 and do the Workbook exercise(s) again.

Now write an example for 1–6.

1 Lisa has already been to lots of gigs but she hasn't learnt first aid yet.

85

Collocation
All the Review sections include an exercise to raise awareness of the importance of collocation.

Learner Independence Self Assessment
This self assessment section for each two units lists the communicative aims and invites students to rate their confidence in each one. Students who are not sure about their ability in a particular area are referred to the Language File and the relevant Workbook exercises. The Teacher's Book offers guidance on handling this.

Follow-up activities and homework
The Teacher's Book offers optional follow-up activities, usually games. Homework suggestions (usually writing) are also provided.

Vocabulary
Vocabulary exercises include completion, matching words with their definitions, and collocation (in this case matching verbs and phrases).

Welcome!

WHAT KIND OF LANGUAGE LEARNER ARE YOU?

- The aim is to help students gain awareness of their language learning style(s) in order to help them learn more effectively and enable them to choose the most appropriate activities from Your Choice! in the Revision and Extension sections.
- Before reading the questions, set the context by putting a few questions on the board for students to discuss in pairs: *Why are you learning English? What do you like doing in language lessons? How can you get better at English?* Elicit one or two example responses as a class.
- Ask students to read the profiles of Carla and Carlos and decide who they are more like. Be prepared to explain *learn by heart*, *rules* and *look up* (a word).
- Check that students have made a decision by asking those that have chosen Carla to raise their hand. Ask these students to decide if they are more like Silvio or Silvia. Those who have chosen Carlos should decide if they are more similar to Leonie or Leo. Encourage students to deduce the meaning of vocabulary from context or ask *What does … mean?*
- Ask students to sit in four groups according to who they are most like: Silvia, Silvio, Leonie or Leo. Students then read about their learning style and discuss with a partner from their group if they agree with the results and why they have these preferences.
- Ask students to read about the other learning styles and decide if they are sometimes like them. They could discuss this with a partner either from their own group or a different group. Encourage students to identify at least one or two statements from other learning styles which are true for them, to remind them to try different ways of learning.
- Show students Your Choice! on page 19 of the Student's Book and tell them that they should remember their learning style so that they will be able to choose the best activities for themselves in future lessons.

Optional activities

- With their books closed, students try to remember as much as possible about their learning style, writing three sentences in their notebooks about how they learn best.
- Students work with a partner who has a different learning style. They try to find three differences and one similarity between themselves. Put some prompts on the board to help them: *pair work*, *group work*, *homework*, *grammar exercises*, *speaking*, *tests*, *games* and remind them to use the question *Do you like …?*
- Students look quickly through the first unit of the book and identify an exercise or activity which they think will particularly suit their learning style.

Units 1–2

Activities		Project	Vocabulary	Optional Aids
Identifying communicative aims Categorising vocabulary	Contextualising listening extracts	Yesterday questionnaire	Music and dance Films Feelings	Warmers 1 and 2: a soft ball Follow-up activity: slips of paper

WARMER 1

Play a name game. Students stand in a large circle at the front of the class. Throw the ball to a student so he or she can catch it. That student says his name and then follows it with a food or drink that begins with the same letter, e.g. *I'm Paul and I like pasta.* He then throws the ball to another student and she says her name, e.g. *I'm Suzanne and I like strawberries.* Continue until everyone has said their name and the food they like.

WARMER 2

Students stand in a large circle again. This time they throw the ball to another student and say that student's name and what he or she likes, e.g. *You're Paul and you like pasta, You're Suzanne and you like strawberries.*

WARMER 3

Students stand in a line at the front of the class with their backs to the wall. Explain that the furthest position on the left represents January 1st and the furthest position on the right represents December 31st. Students should ask questions to find out each other's birthday and re-order the line so they are in the correct order from January 1st to December 31st. Check the order is correct by asking them to say their birthday. Make sure they say it in the correct way, e.g. either *June the second* or *the second of June.*

1
- The aim is to introduce the students to the main areas of communicative language they will cover in Units 1 and 2, and to encourage them to think about the function of the language.
- Explain the task to the class. Students look at the photos and match them with the communicative aims, using the captions to help them. Point out that there are six pictures and eight communicative aims so two of them are not used.
- Ask students to do the task individually and then compare their answers in pairs. Check the answers with the whole class.

Answers

A 5 B 1 C 7 D 8 E 4 F 2

Optional activity

Use picture F to revise weather vocabulary. Write *It's raining again* on the board. Ask students to work in pairs and make a list of other types of weather, e.g. *It's snowing again. It's windy.* Listen to their ideas as a class and make a list on the board.

2
- Check that students understand the words in the three boxes. Point out that *cartoon* is another word for *animation* and that *happy* is another word for *cheerful.*
- Ask the students to work in pairs and add four more words to each category. Check the answers with the whole class. Write the three categories on the board and invite students to come to the board and write their words in the correct category.

Optional activity

With a less confident class, write some of the possible answers below on the board in random order and ask students to sort them into the correct categories.

Suggested answers

Music and dance – indie, hip-hop, blues, rap, classical, rock, heavy metal, country; salsa, tango, waltz, disco, flamenco, lambada, samba, river-dance
Films – science fiction, fantasy, horror, thriller, crime, romantic, action, musical, war, western
Feelings – sad, embarrassed, confident, bored, excited, tired, nervous, scared

Optional activity

When students have written their extra words on the board, focus on the word stress in some of these words, e.g. *breakdancing, comedy, cheerful.* Invite students to come to the board and mark the stress on other multi-syllable words.

3
- The aim of the activity is for students to contextualise a short listening extract by working out what kind of passage it is extracted from.
- Explain to students that they should listen for the main gist of each passage and that it does not matter if they do not understand every word.

- Play the recording. Students match each extract 1–3 with the summaries A–C.

1.01 Recording

(From Unit 1 Lesson 2, Exercise 4)

1

JONI *Hello?*

MOTHER *Hi Joni. Mum here. I'm sorry about phoning you.*

JONI *No, it's really nice to hear you.*

MOTHER *I just wanted to check that you're all right.*

JONI *Oh – yes, I'm OK.*

2

(From Unit 2 Lesson 4, Exercise 2)

It shows a group of friends who are enjoying lunch together. They're in a restaurant with a river in the background. Some of the people are sitting at tables, eating and drinking, while others are standing chatting behind them. In the foreground, a woman is holding a dog and there are two boatmen in white vests and straw hats.

3

(From Unit 1 Lesson 1, Exercise 2)

INTERVIEWER *Sophie, what do you usually do at weekends?*

SOPHIE *I work in a shoe shop every Saturday and I often go to clubs with my friends on Saturday night. Or we listen to music and play video games.*

INTERVIEWER *How often do you go to the cinema?*

SOPHIE *Once or twice a month.*

Answers

1B 2C 3A

Optional activity

Write these questions on the board: *What is the girl's name in the first extract? Where are the friends in the second extract? How often does Sophie go to the cinema?* Play the recording again and ask students to write down the answers. Check the answers with the whole class. (Joni; in a restaurant; once or twice a month)

4
- The aim of this activity is to encourage students to talk about things that happened in the past.
- Ask students to look at the picture and describe the people. Are they happy, angry, excited? Ask why and where they are and what they are doing.
- Ask students to read the four questions. Check that they understand the task and all the vocabulary, especially the word *event* – something that happened. Give them two or three minutes to think about four different events and to make a few notes.
- Divide the class into groups of four. Ask them to ask and answer the questions and make notes about their group's answers, especially any that are interesting or surprising.
- Ask each group to tell another group about what they learnt from the members of their group, e.g. *It was Sonia's birthday yesterday and all her friends came to her party.* An alternative is to give each group member a letter (A, B, C, D) and ask all the As to form one group, all the Bs another and so on. Then they should tell their new group what they learnt in their first group.

Last Year Questionnaire Project

- Students use the Yesterday Questionnaire to formulate a new questionnaire called the Last Year Questionnaire. For example, the first item in the Yesterday Questionnaire becomes *Think of an international event that happened last year.* Ask them to write four new questions on a sheet of paper with space for answers.
- Have students stand up, walk around the class and interview as many students as possible in 10 minutes, noting down their answers.
- Students write a short report about their findings, e.g. *Both Carla and Martin mentioned the tsunami in Japan. They were very sad about it.*

- Books closed. Write the word *the* on the board. Tell the students that this word is special because it is the most common word in English. Then write *Go.* on the board. Remember to write a full-stop after it. Tell the students there is something special about this word too as it holds another record in the English language. Elicit suggestions from the class.
- If they cannot work out the answer, ask them to open their books and read the explanation in the Believe it or not! box.

Follow-up activities

- ♦ Students write four important dates on a piece of paper, e.g. *9th July 2009*. They then work in pairs, exchange papers and guess what happened on each other's dates. The person answering may only say *Yes* or *No*. For example: *Was it a personal event? Yes. Was it your birthday? Yes!*
- ♦ Remind students of the three categories in the vocabulary exercise on page 8: music and dance, films and feelings. Ask students to work in groups of four with their books closed. Give each group small slips of paper to write on. Tell them they have five minutes to write as many words as possible related to the three categories (these can be words they remember from the exercise or other related words). They should write one word on each slip of paper. At the time limit, collect the slips from each group and give them to another group. Ask them to sort the words into the correct categories.

HOMEWORK

Ask students to use the Yesterday Questionnaire to interview a family member or a friend who is not in the same class at school and write down their answers.

1 TURNING POINTS

1 How are you feeling?

Communicative Aims	**Language**	**Pronunciation**	**Vocabulary**	**Optional Aids**
Talking about states and regular activities Talking about what's happening now Talking about future arrangements	Present tense review Adverbial phrases of frequency	/ɒ/ job /ʌ/ club	Leisure activities School subjects Clothes	Warmer 2: sticky notes with UK cities Follow-up activities: large pieces of paper; a box and blank cards

WARMER 1

Ask students to write their first name vertically on a piece of paper. They should then use three of the letters in their name to begin or be included in three words about themselves, e.g. their hobbies, names of family members, etc.
Students then circulate around the room, showing their papers and asking questions to other students based on the information in their name.

WARMER 2

Tell students that in the first unit they will meet young people from different parts of Britain. Ask students if any of them have visited Britain or other English speaking countries or know the names of any towns/cities. Put the names of famous cities, including Manchester, London, Liverpool and Brighton, on sticky notes. Draw a rough map of Britain on the board and invite students to come and stick the names in the correct place on the map. Encourage other students to help them, e.g. *No, it's in the north* and elicit any information students may know about the places, e.g. *It's a big city, it's by the sea*, etc.

LANGUAGE WORKOUT OPTION

If you want to focus on the language students will be using in these activities, you may like to go to the Language Workout box now.

1 OPENER

- The aim is to get students to think about their answers to the everyday questions in the questionnaire.
- Ask students to read the questions carefully and make notes for their answers. Then ask them to compare their answers in pairs.

2 READING

- Before you ask the students to read the answers, ask them to look at the picture of Sophie and tell you what she's wearing, what she's doing and how she's feeling. Then ask them to read the answers and match them with the questions in the questionnaire. Play the recording. Students read, listen and check their answers. Encourage them to guess unfamiliar words from context. Be prepared to explain *environment* and *fed up* (bored). Explain that *scary* is another word for *frightening* and that *half term* is usually a short holiday in the middle of each of the school terms.

Answers

1 j 2 h 3 i 4 a 5 c 6 k 7 d 8 e 9 b 10 g 11 l 12 f

1.02 Recording

INTERVIEWER *Sophie, what do you usually do at weekends?*
SOPHIE *I work in a shoe shop every Saturday and I often go to clubs with my friends on Saturday night. Or we listen to music and play video games.*
INTERVIEWER *How often do you go to the cinema?*
SOPHIE *Once or twice a month.*
INTERVIEWER *What are you reading at the moment?*
SOPHIE *A science fiction novel by Stephenie Meyer called* The Host. *It's brilliant.*
INTERVIEWER *What are your favourite school subjects?*
SOPHIE *Biology and Spanish.*
INTERVIEWER *What do you and your friends talk about?*
SOPHIE *School, TV, boys!*
INTERVIEWER *Do you have a boyfriend?*
SOPHIE *Yes, he's 17, and he's a student at sixth form college.*
INTERVIEWER *What are you wearing today?*
SOPHIE *A hoodie, a denim skirt and boots.*
INTERVIEWER *How are you feeling?*
SOPHIE *I'm fed up with the weather – it's raining again.*
INTERVIEWER *What are you looking forward to?*
SOPHIE *Half term – I'm spending a week in Spain on a school trip. I can't wait!*
INTERVIEWER *And what do you care about?*
SOPHIE *I care about the environment and I work as a volunteer at our local park.*
INTERVIEWER *What do you worry about?*
SOPHIE *There's a lot of street crime round here. It's quite scary.*
INTERVIEWER *What's your ambition?*
SOPHIE *I want to be a doctor. And I'd like to travel round Latin America.*

3 AFTER READING AND LISTENING

- Students read and listen to the dialogue again and decide if sentences 1–8 are true or false. Ask them to underline the words in the dialogue that helped them decide on their answers.
- Check the answers before students write corrections for the false sentences. Monitor and help where necessary.

Answers

1 True
2 False. She goes once or twice a month.
3 False. It's brilliant.
4 True
5 False. She's feeling fed up.
6 True
7 False. She cares about the environment.
8 True

Your response

Give the students a couple of minutes to think about similarities and differences. Then ask them to work in pairs and discuss the questions. Ask them to say why they would like to meet Sophie or why not.

Optional activities

- Students read and act out the interview in pairs.
- In pairs, student A covers the text and tells Student B everything he/she remembers about Sophie. Student B listens and checks in the book.

4 LISTENING

- The aim is to predict before listening.
- Ask the students to read the text and guess what the eight mistakes are, eliciting *every Sunday night* as a possible example if necessary.
- Play the recording. Students listen and underline the eight differences.
- Use the example in the book to elicit the first correction from the students.
- Ask students to work in A/B pairs to correct the other seven mistakes in the same way.
- Encourage students to add extra stress to the word they are correcting to make the correction clearer.

1.03 Recording and answers

INTERVIEWER *Rob, what do you usually do at weekends?*
ROB *I play the **guitar** in a band on Saturdays. And I go swimming every Sunday **morning**.*
INTERVIEWER *How often do you go to the cinema?*
ROB *Not very often. About once a **month**.*
INTERVIEWER *What are you reading at the moment?*
ROB *I'm not reading anything.*
INTERVIEWER *What are your favourite school subjects?*
ROB ***History** and art.*
INTERVIEWER *What do you and your friends talk about?*
ROB *Music and **football**.*
INTERVIEWER *Do you have a girlfriend?*
ROB *No – anyway, I'm not looking for a girlfriend.*
INTERVIEWER *What are you wearing today?*
ROB *A **red** top, jeans and trainers.*
INTERVIEWER *How are you feeling?*
ROB ***Excited**, because it's my birthday tomorrow!*
INTERVIEWER *What are you looking forward to?*
ROB *The holidays.*
INTERVIEWER *What do you care about?*
ROB *People who aren't as lucky as I am. I help at a club for disabled people.*
INTERVIEWER *What do you worry about?*
ROB *I worry about exams. I get really nervous.*
INTERVIEWER *What's your ambition?*
ROB *I want to **pass** all my exams and go to university.*

Optional activity

Remind students of Sophie Miller from exercise 1. Read some information about her which includes mistakes, e.g. *Sophie wants to be a teacher.* When they hear a mistake, students shout *Stop!* and correct it.

5 PRONUNCIATION

- Ask students to look at the words in the box. Play the first part of the recording, pausing after each word for students to repeat. Demonstrate the difference in mouth position for the two sounds, highlighting the rounder lip shape and stronger lip tension for /ɒ/.

1.04 Recording

college does London month novel often once want what worry

- Ask the students to copy the chart into their notebooks.
- Play the recording again. Students write the words from the box in the correct column. Pause after each word to give students time to write.

1.04 Recording and answers

/ɒ/ *job college novel often want what*
/ʌ/ *club does London month once worry*

6 SPEAKING

- Tell students they are going to interview a partner using the questions in Teenage Life on page 10. Remind students to note down the answers and to ask about boyfriend/girlfriend as appropriate.
- Before they start the interview, check that students can answer *How often* questions covered in the adverbial phrases of frequency box in the Language Workout. Ask students to recall how often Rob goes to the cinema (once a week). Check students' understanding of *once* by asking *How many times?* (one) and try to elicit other possible responses (twice a week, every day), referring students to the Language Workout box as necessary.

Extension Explain to students that they need to write three questions they would use to find out about another person's character and lifestyle. Tell them they can use or adapt the questions in the questionnaire on page 10 or think of their own. When they have written their questions, ask them to work in groups of four and ask and answer each other's questions. Ask each group to report back to the whole class.

7 WRITING

- The aim is to write a personal profile using a model for guidance.
- Ask students to look again at the profile of Rob and identify which questions are answered in which paragraph without looking back at the questionnaire on page 10. Check the answers with the class.

Answers

Paragraph 1: What do you usually do at weekends?
How often do you go to the cinema?
What are you reading at the moment?
What are your favourite school subjects?
What do you and your friends talk about?
Do you have a girlfriend?
Paragraph 2: What are you wearing today?
How are you feeling?
What are you looking forward to?
Paragraph 3: What do you care about?
What do you worry about?
What's your ambition?

- Students write a similar three-paragraph profile based on the notes from their interview. Remind students to take care when choosing the present simple or continuous. Give students a few minutes to check their paragraph for grammar, spelling and capital letters. They then give it to another student to check.

LANGUAGE WORKOUT

- Ask students to complete the Language box, using contractions where possible. Confident students can complete first and then check, while others can look back at exercises 2 and 3 and then complete.
- Students turn to page 112 of the Language File to check their answers.

Answers

work lives go does(n't) do
's is(n't) are I'm
simple continuous

- Highlight that:
  - we use the present simple to talk about things we do every day, week, month and when using state verbs, e.g. *like, believe.*
  - we add *-s* for *he/she/it* in the affirmative form.
  - we form the question with *do/does* + verb and the negative with *don't/doesn't* + verb.
  - we use the present continuous to talk about temporary events and what is happening now. We can also use it to talk about future arrangements.
  - we form the present continuous with *am/is/are* + verb + *-ing*
- Drill the examples in chorus for pronunciation and stress. Encourage students to use contractions like *we're* in the continuous form.

PRACTICE

- Students do Practice exercise 1 on page 112 of the Language File.
- Ask students to compare their answers in pairs.

Answers

1 What does Rob usually do after school?
2 He goes to the park with his friends and they play football.
3 What is Sophie doing at the moment?
4 She is listening to music.
5 Does she work every Saturday?
6 Where is she spending half term?
7 Do you worry about street crime?
8 I think some city streets are getting quite dangerous.

Follow-up activities

- ♦ Students make personal posters, with their name in the centre, surrounded by key words about them and illustrations/photos. Students circulate, presenting themselves via their posters and asking each other follow-up questions.
- ♦ Students start a Vocabulary box. They look back through the unit for new words and expressions and write them on cards with an explanation, translation or illustration on the other side.

HOMEWORK

Students write a personal profile about themselves (based on the Rob model) to include on a class webpage. If computers/digital camera are available, these could be put on the computer at a later date.

WEBLINK

Students may like to visit www.bbc.co.uk/videonation/feature/teenagers for articles of interest to teenagers.

Revision and Extension p19

Language File p112

Workbook Unit 1 Lesson 1 pp2–3

Photocopiable worksheet p162, notes p154

2 Why didn't I enjoy it more?

Communicative Aims
Describing past events

Language
Past simple review

Pronunciation
/θ/ both
/ð/ together

Vocabulary
Adjectives for feelings

WARMER 1

In pairs, ask students to write a list of things to take on a beach holiday, e.g. *suncream*. The first pair to think of ten things should shout *Stop!* Check their list as a class.

WARMER 2

Ask students if they have been on holiday with friends rather than parents. Brainstorm possible advantages (freedom, meeting new people, holiday romance) and disadvantages (homesickness, paying for yourself).

1 OPENER

- The aim is to introduce the context for the reading.
- Students discuss the title and question in pairs. The emphasis here is on generating ideas and students may not arrive at the answers given below but that is OK.

Answers

She's feeling homesick/miserable because the holiday hasn't gone as planned.

2 READING

- Play the recording. Students read, listen and check their predictions from exercise 1. Encourage them to guess unfamiliar words from context and ask *What does … mean?* Check that students understand *accent* by asking *What's the word for the way Joni speaks?* and ask for synonyms for *miserable* (unhappy, sad, depressed). Note that *Newquay* is pronounced /'nju:ki:/.

1.05 Recording

See text on page 12 of the Student's Book.

3 AFTER READING

- Students read and listen to the dialogue again and answer questions 1–8.
- Check the answers by asking different students to ask and answer the questions.

Answers

1 *Because it was their first holiday without parents.*
2 *No, they made different friends.*
3 *She didn't like them.*
4 *They thought she wasn't good enough for them.*
5 *No*
6 *Because she missed Sara.*
7 *Because she didn't want her Mum to know she was miserable.*
8 *Sara*

Your response

Give the students a couple of minutes to think about a situation when this happened to them. Then ask them to work in pairs and tell their partner about it. Ask them to report what their partner said to the whole class.

Optional activity

In pairs, ask students to write two lists of what was good and bad about the holiday, e.g. *good: Newquay was a great place; bad: Joni felt sad and lonely*.

LANGUAGE WORKOUT OPTION

If you want to pre-teach the language students will be using in the following activities, you may like to go to the Language Workout box now.

4 LISTENING

- Tell the students they are going to listen to the phone conversation between Joni and her mother. Check students understand *fortune teller* (someone who predicts your future, for example by reading your palm).
- Ask students to read the list of activities and predict which Joni did in the morning, afternoon or night.
- Play the recording. Students compare their predictions with the recording.
- Check the answers as a class. Highlight the use of prepositions: *in the morning/afternoon, at night*. With a confident class, ask students to give their answers in the past simple form, e.g. *In the morning, she walked around the harbour.* With a less confident class, check the time of day first and then elicit the whole sentence in the past simple.

1.06 Recording

JONI *Hello?*
MOTHER *Hi, Joni. Mum here. I'm sorry about phoning you.*
JONI *No, it's really nice to hear you.*
MOTHER *I just wanted to check that you're all right.*
JONI *Oh – yes, I'm OK. Newquay is cool.*
MOTHER *Are you sure you're OK? You don't sound very happy.*
JONI *No, I'm fine, really. I'm just a bit tired after yesterday.*

MOTHER	*So what happened yesterday?*
JONI	*Um, in the morning it was cloudy, so I walked round the harbour. And I visited a fortune teller!*
MOTHER	*Really?*
JONI	*Uhuh. And in the afternoon the sun came out, so I went for a swim in the sea. Then I had a picnic with some friends. After that, I fell asleep on the beach.*
MOTHER	*And did you go out last night?*
JONI	*Yes, I met my friends in a club, and then we went to a party, and I danced for five hours.*
MOTHER	*No wonder you feel tired!*
JONI	*Mm. Um, how's everyone at home?*
MOTHER	*Oh, we're all fine. Well, I just wanted to say hello, and enjoy the rest of the holiday.*
JONI	*Thanks for calling, Mum. See you at the weekend. Bye.*

Answers

Morning: walk round the harbour, visit a fortune teller
Afternoon: go for a swim in the sea, have a picnic, fall asleep on the beach
Night: meet her friends in a club, go to a party, dance for five hours

5 SPEAKING

- The aim is for students to describe past events using the context of Joni's day.
- Read the question in the example out loud. Elicit possible responses, checking correct use of past simple.
- In pairs, students follow the example, asking and answering questions about the rest of her day.

6 ROLE PLAY

- Explain that students are going to roleplay a similar phone conversation between Sara and her father. Divide the class into pairs, with one student as Sara and the other, her father.
- From the prompts, elicit what Sara and her father will say first, checking correct question formation and use of past simple. With a less confident class, the dialogue could be put on the board and later gradually removed as students do the role play.
- In pairs, students do the role play, if possible sitting back to back and holding their mobile phones. Encourage 'Sara' to give as much detail as possible about what she did yesterday.

Optional activity

Elicit and write on the board different past time expressions e.g. *yesterday morning, last night*. In pairs, students ask each other what they did at these times.

7 PRONUNCIATION

- Demonstrate the two sounds, reading the examples *both* /bəʊθ/and *together* /tə'geðə/ and asking students to repeat. Highlight that the mouth position is the same, with the tongue at the base of the front teeth. Get students to feel the vibration of /ð/ by placing their hand at the front of their throat. Ask students to copy the chart into their notebooks and write the words in the correct column.
- Play the recording, pausing for students to repeat after each word.

1.07 Recording and answers

/θ/ *both anything maths month thought*
/ð/ *together mother other weather without*

Optional activity

In pairs, students try to make one sentence using as many of the words from the pronunciation box as possible, e.g. *Last month I thought that maths was better than anything*. The pair that include the greatest number of these words are the winners.

8 VOCABULARY

- Books closed, students brainstorm adjectives for positive and negative feelings. Put their ideas on the board in two columns.
- Ask students to look at exercise 8 to see if their adjectives are in the box. In pairs, students then write them in the correct column.
- Check the answers as a class. Drill examples in chorus for pronunciation. Then have students look for these adjectives in Joni's blog.

Answers

☺ *cheerful excited happy pleased*
☹ *angry bored depressed embarrassed lonely miserable nervous sad scared tired worried*
Adjectives in Joni's blog: excited, depressed, bored, sad, lonely, cheerful, miserable, happy

Optional activity

Ask students to count the number of syllables in each adjective and mark the stressed syllable.

- Read the examples out loud and ask students if they have had these experiences.
- In pairs, students tell each other when they had happy/ unhappy feelings.

Extension Students describe an experience, and have their partner guess how they felt.

9 WRITING

- The aim is to write a diary entry, practising the past simple and feelings vocabulary, using Joni's blog as a model.
- Ask students to re-read Joni's blog entry and find the answers to the five questions.

Answers

Where did you go? Newquay (paragraph 2)
Who were you with? My best friend, Sara (paragraph 1)
Who did you meet? New friends (paragraph 3)
What did you do? Spent time with new friends (paragraph 4), went surfing and went to parties (paragraph 2)
How did you feel? Bored and depressed (paragraph 2), excited (paragraph 1), sad and lonely (paragraph 4), miserable (paragraph 5).

- Ask students to make notes to answer the same questions about their imaginary holiday.
- Students then write their diary entry from these notes, based on the model. Remind them to use 'I', and to check they have included the past simple and a range of feelings adjectives.

Optional activity

Students read their partner's diary entry and write three more questions in the past simple. Students ask and answer the questions in pairs.

LANGUAGE WORKOUT

- Ask students to complete the Language box. Confident students can complete first and then check, while others can look back at exercises 2 and 3 and then complete.
- Students turn to page 112 of the Language File to check their answers.

Answers

were was(n't) Was -ed -d -ied
did(n't) did(n't) did(n't) Did
negative questions

- Highlight that:
  - the verb *be* is different from other verbs. The negative form is *wasn't/weren't* and the question form is *was/were* + subject …?
  - regular verbs form the past simple by adding *-ed* or just adding *-d* if the verb already ends in *e*. For verbs ending in consonant + *y*, change *y* to *i* and add *-ed*. Verbs ending in vowel + *y* do not drop the *-y*.
  - both regular and irregular verbs form the negative with *didn't* + verb and the question with *did* + subject + verb …?
- Drill examples in chorus for pronunciation and stress. Highlight weak forms of *was* /wəz/ and *were* /wə/.

Optional activity

Game *Left or Right?* Read out verbs in the infinitive form. Students raise their right hand if the verb is regular in the past simple or their left if it is irregular. Choose a student with the correct hand raised to say the verb in the past simple.

PRACTICE

- Students do exercise 2 on page 112 of the Language File. Students complete the answers on their own.
- Ask students to compare their answers in pairs.
- Check the answers by asking individual students to read out what they have written.

Answers

1 Where did Sara and Joni go for their holiday?
2 Were Sara and Joni on holiday with their parents?
3 How long did the parties last?
4 Was Joni good enough for Sara's friends?
5 Did Joni like Sara's friends?
6 How did Joni feel when her mum phoned?
7 When did Joni nearly cry?
8 Why did Joni turn round?

- Ask students to look at Joni's blog on page 12 again and answer the eight questions.

Answers

1 Newquay 2 No 3 All night 4 No 5 No
6 Pleased 7 When she heard her Mum's voice.
8 Because she felt someone's eyes on her.

Follow-up activity

Game *Memory chain* Write *Last year on holiday, I …* on the board. The first student finishes the sentence, e.g. *I went to the beach.* A second student repeats the first example and adds an activity, e.g. *I went to the beach and I met new friends.* Continue around the class or in small groups.

HOMEWORK

Ask students to find photographs of their past holidays (or excursions/visits if they haven't been on holiday) and prepare some sentences in the past simple to explain where they visited, when they went and what they saw and felt. They bring these to the next lesson.

WEBLINK

Students may like to visit www.visitnewquay.org/ for more information about Newquay.

Revision and Extension p19

Language File p112

Workbook Unit 1 Lesson 2 pp4–5

Photocopiable worksheet p163, notes p154

3 She was surfing

Communicative Aims	Language	Pronunciation	Vocabulary	Optional Aids
Describing what happened and what was happening	Past simple and past continuous	/ʃ/ splash /ʧ/beach	Water Parts of the body Phrasal verbs with *get*	Warmer 1: students' own holiday photos

WARMER 1

If you set the homework from the last lesson, put students in groups to show each other their photos, share their sentences and ask each other questions.

WARMER 2

Game *Shark* On the board, draw a staircase with eight steps and a person on the top step. At the bottom, draw the sea and an open-mouthed shark. Think of a word connected with water, e.g. *rain, wave, swimming* and indicate the number of letters in the word with dashes. Students say letters of the alphabet to try to guess the word. Correct guesses should be added to the word in the correct place, while incorrect guesses mean the person moves one step nearer to the shark. The aim is for students to guess the word before reaching the shark.

1 OPENER

- The aim is to introduce the context for the article in exercise 2 and predict the content of the article.
- Students answer the questions orally as a class. Prompt students to predict what happened to her, if possible eliciting *shark*. The emphasis here is on generating ideas and students may not arrive at the answers below at this point.

Answers

She's surfing. She's only got one arm. A shark attacked her.

2 LISTENING

- Students read the short text about *Soul Surfer* and predict what words could go in the gaps, e.g. 2 could be days, weeks, months or years. Play the recording. Students read, listen and check their predictions.

1.08 Recording

Soul Surfer is a film about the life of one-armed surfer Bethany Hamilton. Bethany was 13 when a four-and-a-half-metre tiger shark bit off her left arm. The film tells how Bethany started surfing again less than four weeks after the accident and now competes successfully in international surfing championships. Although Anna Sophia Robb plays Bethany, it is Bethany herself who does most of the surfing in the movie. An interesting fact is that the children of two famous film stars are in the movie – Jack Nicholson's daughter, Lorraine, plays Bethany's friend Alana, and Pierce Brosnan's son, Sean, plays Bethany's brother, Noah.

Answers

1 13 2 weeks 3 international 4 daughter 5 son

3 READING

- Students read and listen to the text and answer the question. Encourage students to guess unfamiliar words from context. Be prepared to explain *jaws, paddle* and *recover*.

1.09 Recording

See text on page 14 of the Student's Book.

4 AFTER READING

- Students read and listen to the article again and answer questions 1–6.
- Check the answers as a class.

Answers

1 They often took part in surf competitions.
2 She hoped to be a professional surfer.
3 She was thinking 'I hope the surf gets better soon …'
4 It turned bright red.
5 'Get to the beach.'
6 When can I surf again?

Your response

Give the students a couple of minutes to think about their answer to the question. Then ask them to compare their ideas in pairs or small groups. Listen to their ideas as a class.

Optional activities

- Give students five minutes to study the text and remember as much as possible. They then close their books. Ask students quiz questions about the story, e.g. *Where was Bethany surfing?*
- As a class, brainstorm other water sports, e.g. *sailing, windsurfing, white-water rafting*. In pairs, students discuss which they like or want to try and which they think are difficult or dangerous.
- If appropriate to your class, ask them which of these is the worst to lose in an accident: an arm, a leg, your sight or your hearing. Have them give reasons for their choice.

LANGUAGE WORKOUT OPTION

If you want to pre-teach the language students will be using in the following activities, you may like to go to the Language Workout box now.

5 LISTENING

- Before students read the headline, brainstorm other animals, apart from sharks, which can attack/hurt people, e.g. *snake, lion, tiger, bear, polar bear, wolf*. Try to elicit *crocodile* if students don't produce it.
- Focus students on the headline and check that students understand *punch*, asking for a synonym or translation. Try to elicit ideas from the students about what the article will be about.
- Ask students to read sentences 1–10. Be prepared to explain *splash*.
- Play the recording. Students check if the sentences are true or false.
- Check the answers as a class, encouraging students to correct the false sentences.

1.10 Recording

An Australian teenager survived a dramatic crocodile attack last week.

16-year-old Shane Peters was helping his father, Clive, in the garden at their home near Darwin. It was really hot. 'Dad, I'm going down to the river for a swim,' Shane told his father. Shane got to the river, took off his clothes and jumped in.

The river wasn't very deep by the side so Shane started to swim out to the middle. While he was swimming, he heard a splash behind him. He looked around but didn't see anything. The river water was cold and Shane felt great. In the middle he turned around and started to swim back. Then he had a shock. A large crocodile was swimming towards him.

Shane thought quickly and then shouted 'Help! Dad! Crocodile!' Clive heard his son but thought he was joking. 'Come back here and do some more work!' he shouted back. 'But Dad …' Shane began, but before he said anything more the crocodile took his arm and pulled him under the water.

Shane kicked the crocodile hard and to his surprise the animal opened its jaws and let him go. Shane started to swim to the side as fast as he could. But the crocodile was faster and came after him. The water wasn't very deep now and Shane stopped swimming and stood up. He turned and there was the crocodile right in front of him. They were face to face. Before the crocodile opened its huge mouth again, Shane punched it hard on the nose. The crocodile didn't move and Shane punched it hard again on the nose. To Shane's great surprise the crocodile slowly turned and swam away.

Shane got out of the water as fast as he could, got his clothes and ran back to the garden. His father was waiting for him and looked at Shane's arm. 'So it was a crocodile! Quick! Let's get you to hospital.' At the hospital they cleaned the bites on Shane's arm and he returned home. The next day at school everyone wanted to hear the story of the teenager who punched a crocodile!

Answers

1 *True*
2 *False. He decided to swim in the river.*
3 *True*
4 *False. He saw a large crocodile.*
5 *True*
6 *False. The crocodile took his arm and pulled him under.*
7 *False. When he kicked the crocodile, it opened its jaws.*
8 *False. When he stood up, he saw the crocodile right in front of him.*
9 *False. He punched it on the nose.*
10 *True*

Optional activity

1.10 Students listen to the recording again and write down two examples of verbs in the past continuous and two in the past simple. After listening, more confident students can try to remember the whole sentences which the verbs were used in.

6 SPEAKING

- Put students into A/B pairs. Student B closes their book, while student A asks them questions 1–5. Encourage student A to prompt their partner if they cannot remember the answer.
- Students reverse roles with student B asking student A questions 6–10.
- Monitor and note examples of good language and errors. Put these on the board and ask students to identify and correct the errors.

Answers

1 *He was helping his father.*
2 *He went for a swim in the river.*
3 *He heard a splash behind him.*
4 *He saw a large crocodile swimming towards him.*
5 *He thought he was joking.*
6 *It pulled him under the water.*
7 *The crocodile opened its jaws and let him go.*
8 *He saw the crocodile right in front of him.*
9 *He punched it hard on the nose.*
10 *He got out of the water as quickly as he could.*

Optional activity

Fast finishers can make up another question about the text for their partner.

Extension Ask students to work with the same partner as in exercise 6. Have them decide who will play the role of Shane and who will be Clive. Give an example of the kind of question Clive could ask, e.g. *What happened? What did you do next?* When students have finished the role play, ask two or three more confident pairs to act out their role plays for the whole class.

7 PRONUNCIATION

- Demonstrate the two sounds, reading the examples *splash* /splæʃ/and *beach* /biːtʃ/, asking students to repeat. Highlight that the /ʃ/ sound is often used to ask people to be quiet (demonstrate Ssh!), while the other sound is similar, but starts with the tongue in the same position as for /t/ with the tip of the tongue touching the ridge behind the upper teeth. Point out that /tʃ/ is almost always represented by *ch* in spelling.
- Ask students to copy the table into their notebooks, read the words in the box quietly to themselves and write them in the correct column.
- Play the recording, pausing for students to repeat after each word.

1.11 Recording

championship change competition international ocean professional punch shark shout watch

Answers

/ʃ/ *competition, international, ocean, professional, shark, shout*
/tʃ/ *championship, change, punch, watch*

Optional activity

Dictate some extra words containing one of the above sounds for students to copy down into the correct column, e.g. *each, she, shop, cheque/check, child, shy, cheer, shock.*

8 VOCABULARY

- Explain that the recording and article contained different phrasal verbs using *get*. Ask students to match the phrasal verb with the meaning. Encourage students to look back at the recording/articles to deduce meaning from context and/or underline where each phrasal verb was used.

Answers

1 get on (ex 3 reading text)
2 get over (ex 2 reading text)
3 get away (ex 3 reading text)
4 get back (ex 3 reading text)
5 get out of (ex 5 listening)

Extension Have students write five new sentences using the phrasal verbs from the word bank.

Optional activity

Students find examples of other phrasal verbs being used in this unit, e.g. *stand up, take off, look around.* They then write them on cards, putting a definition or illustration on the back, to add to the Vocabulary box.

9 WRITING

- Tell students that they are going to write a short newspaper article about what happened to Shane and ask them in pairs to brainstorm key points which they remember from the story. They can refer to exercise 5 to help them.
- Play the recording again, asking students to note down any extra information which they could include in their article.
- Remind students to include a headline such as *Teenager punches crocodile*. Students then write their article.
- Give students a few minutes to check their paragraph for grammar, spelling and capital letters. They then give it to another student to check.

Optional activity

With a less confident class, dictate the first three lines of the recording for students to write down. Then as a class, brainstorm key points to include in the rest of the article and put these on the board for students to follow.

LANGUAGE WORKOUT

- Ask students to complete the Language box with verbs in the past simple or past continuous. Confident students can complete first and then check, while others can look back at exercises 2 and 3 and then complete.
- Students turn to page 113 of the Language File to check their answers.

Answers

was waiting saw asked was recovering
simple continuous

- Check that students have completed the tense descriptions accurately and ask students *Which verb describes longer activities?* (was recovering) *Which describes background to events?* (was waiting).
- Highlight spelling rules:
  - most verbs ending in *e* drop the *e* before adding *-ing*, e.g. *taking*
  - but verbs ending *ee* don't drop the final *e*, e.g. *seeing*
  - most one syllable verbs ending vowel + single consonant double the final consonant before adding *-ing* (except if the final consonant is *w*, *x* or *y*).
- Drill examples in chorus for pronunciation and stress. Highlight the weak pronunciation of *was* /wəz/ and *were* /wə/, encouraging students to put greater stress on the main verb rather than these auxiliaries.

Optional activities

♦ Put short sentences from the article on the board including verbs in both past simple and past continuous. For example, *Bethany was surfing, she won her first national championship*. In pairs students put the sentences in chronological order, reconstructing the story. Encourage students to link phrases with *when*, *while*, *suddenly*, etc.

♦ Give students a spelling test on *-ing* forms. Dictate verbs such as *seeing*, *swimming*, *taking*, *being*, for students to write down.

PRACTICE

- Students do exercise 3 on page 113 of the Language File. Students complete the answers on their own.
- Ask students to compare their answers in pairs.
- Check the answers by asking individual students to read out what they have written.

Answers

1 escaped 2 went 3 didn't see 4 was pulling
5 came 6 were laughing 7 changed 8 noticed
9 were swimming 10 got 11 went
12 was moving 13 was looking 14 appeared
15 was swimming 16 crashed 17 looked
18 were screaming 19 crying 20 disappeared

Follow-up activities

♦ Tell the students that some of them will be journalists interviewing Shane and Bethany. Brainstorm possible questions that the journalists could ask each person, e.g. *How did you learn to surf again so quickly?* Divide students into groups of three, one to be a journalist and the other two to be Shane and Bethany. Journalists choose which two/three questions they are going to ask each person. Other students re-read their story and plan what they are going to tell the journalist. Journalists then interview the other two. If there is time, journalists could report back to the whole class.

♦ Students make a wordmap for *water*. Write *water* in a circle in the centre of the board and lines coming from it to categories such as *water sports, wet weather, things that live in water*. Students then add words to each category, e.g. *scuba diving, umbrella, octopus*, looking back through the unit to help them.

HOMEWORK

Students invent their own *Lucky escape in the water* story. Give students the questions *Where were you? What were you doing? What happened? How did you escape? How did you feel?* and ask them to include their answers to all these questions in their own story.

WEBLINK

Students may like to visit Bethany's own website for news about her progress and to add a message to her message board. www.bethanyhamilton.com

Revision and Extension p19

Language File p113

Workbook Unit 1 Lesson 3 pp6–7

Photocopiable worksheet p164, notes p154

4

Integrated Skills
Describing a significant event

Skills			Learner Independence	Vocabulary
Reading Connecting ideas: *It all started on a bus* article	*Listening* Identifying speakers and noting details: personal anecdotes	*Speaking* Interviewing *Writing* Describing a significant event	Learning Diary Word creation: prefixes *dis-* and *un-*	Feelings Useful expressions

WARMER 1

If you set the homework from the last lesson, ask students to read each other's Lucky escape stories in groups of four students. Each student should think of one question about the story to ask the writer, who should answer. As a group they could vote on the best story.

WARMER 2

Lead in to the theme of the unit by putting names, places or dates associated with some important events on the board, e.g. *Neil Armstrong, Nelson Mandela, July 4th, 1776.* Elicit what happened in each case, e.g. *the moon landing, the first black president of South Africa, American independence.* Ask if the students know any other important events like these.

1 OPENER

- The aim is to set the context for the reading.
- Ask students to work individually and choose three important international, national or local events that happened during the last five years. Ask them to work in pairs and compare their ideas.
- Ask each pair to give key information such as names, dates or places to the whole class and the other students guess what the important events were.

2 READING

- Books closed. On the board write the headline *It all started on a bus.* Explain that this is the headline to a story about a very important event. Elicit suggestions from the class. Then ask them to read the text quickly and check their predictions.
- Ask students to read the seven questions carefully and then to read the text and find the answers.
- Encourage them to guess unfamiliar words from context, but not worry about the highlighted words at this stage.
- Students listen to the recording to check their answers.

1.12 Recording

See text on page 16 of the Student's Book.

Answers

1 To go home
2 Trains and buses
3 To the window seat in the same row
4 Because she was tired of giving in.
5 He called the police.
6 The US Supreme Court decided it was illegal to separate whites and blacks on buses.
7 The civil rights movement

Optional activity

Fast finishers can review tenses by finding three examples of regular past simple, irregular past simple and past continuous in the text.

3

- The aim is to encourage the students to deduce meaning from context.
- Ask the students to match highlighted words in the text with definitions 1–10.

Answers

1 separate 2 row 3 boycott 4 fare 5 arrested
6 minister 7 civil rights 8 department store
9 giving in 10 fine

Optional activity

Fast finishers can put this vocabulary on cards to add to the Vocabulary box.

4 LISTENING

- Ask students to look at the photos. The aim is to set the context for and predict the content of the listening.
- Use the photos to elicit the following vocabulary from the students: *ice-hockey, skates, wolf, wild animal, moon, polar bear, iceberg.*
- Students listen to the recording and match each one with a photo. More confident students can note down any vocabulary which helped them reach a decision. Less confident students can read the texts as they listen.

1.13 Recording and answers

1

I'll never forget the first time I was close to a wild animal. It happened when I was [1] ***16****. I was on a camping holiday with my* [2] ***parents*** *on Vancouver Island in Canada. It was a fine night and we were sleeping in the open around the fire. Suddenly I woke up in the middle of the night. The stars were really beautiful and I felt so* [3] ***happy****. But what woke me? Then I realised something was sitting by the fire, only a metre away from us. It was a wolf! I was really* [4] ***frightened*** *– in fact I was terrified. Then the wolf stood up and slowly walked away. I couldn't believe it! And I couldn't go back to sleep. In the morning I was very* [5] ***tired****. But when I told my parents about the wolf, they didn't believe me!*

2

I'll always remember when I first played for the school ice hockey team. It was November 23rd – I can't forget the [6] ***date!*** *I was 15 and I was wearing a new pair of skates I got for my* [7] ***birthday****. It was a home game and lots of people were watching. I felt quite* [8] ***nervous*** *at the start, but I soon relaxed. The crowd were cheering and screaming. And when we scored a goal the noise got even louder. It was an* [9] ***amazing*** *experience. I didn't score a goal, but that didn't matter. I was part of the hockey team now – that was the* [10] ***important*** *thing.*

Answers

1 C 2 B

- Ask students to read the two texts and try to predict/ remember the words that go in the gaps.
- Students listen again and complete the gaps. Ask them to compare their answers with a partner and then check the answers as a class.

Optional activities

- ♦ If the students found the exercise difficult, play the recording again, pausing after each gap to check each answer, replaying as necessary.
- ♦ Dictate five or six sentences from the recordings for students to write down. Try to choose those with a clear link to each speaker/story, e.g. *The crowd were cheering and screaming. I woke up in the middle of the night. I couldn't go back to sleep. I was wearing a new pair of skates.* Students then try to remember which of the two recordings each sentence came from. They look back at the text to check their answers, also checking their spelling.

5 SPEAKING

- Tell the students they are going to interview another student about a significant event in their life. If necessary, brainstorm possible topics and write them on the board, e.g. *a new sport/hobby, travel/transport, technology, music, people and relationships*.
- Give students a few minutes to plan their own answers to the questions in exercise 5.
- Students interview each other in pairs, taking notes of their partner's answers.
- Ask students to tell a new partner about their previous partner, using their notes.

Optional activity

Students could use their notes to report back the story to their partner, but including two or three mistakes. Their partner must stop them to correct the wrong information. For example: *You were 14 when you first tried skiing – No, I wasn't 14. I was 13.*

6 GUIDED WRITING

- Ask the students to write a paragraph about a significant event. More confident students could think of another event, while other students could use the same example from exercise 5. Encourage all students to refer to the models and the questions in exercise 5 and check they have included all the points covered in exercise 5.
- Students exchange writing, read for interest and to correct each other's work for spelling, grammar and punctuation.

7 LEARNER INDEPENDENCE

- The aim is to encourage students to reflect on what they have learnt and how to consolidate their learning for the future.
- Ask students to copy the headings into the back of their notebooks and write a first Learning Diary entry.
- Remind students that they can add new entries to their Learning Diary as often as they like.

Optional activity

Students could share their ideas with a partner for the *My plan and What I did outside class* sections. Then each pair suggests their best idea(s) to the rest of the class, who write them down for future reference, and choose their favourite idea to add to their current diary entry.

8 WORD CREATION

- The aim is for students to recognise the meaning of the two prefixes and extend their vocabulary.
- Write the sentence from exercise 1 on the board with a gap: *Joni didn't enjoy her holiday – she was* ________. Ask students to remember the missing word *unhappy*.
- Before looking at exercise 8, put the prefixes *un-* and *dis-* on the board and ask students if they know any words starting with these prefixes.
- Ask students to choose the correct prefix for the words in the box. Students can check back in the book or in dictionaries, before checking as a class.

Answers

disagree disappear uncomfortable unfriendly
unhappy unlucky unpopular unusual

- Students use the words to complete the sentences, reminding them they may have to change the tense.
- Check the answers as a class. Drill examples in chorus for pronunciation and stress.

Answers

2 unusual 3 disagreed 4 unlucky 5 unpopular 6 uncomfortable 7 disappeared 8 unfriendly

Optional activities

- Fast finishers can write their own sentences using words from the exercise.
- Ask the students to use dictionaries to find three more words which begin with the prefixes *dis-* or *un-*.
- **Game** *Left or right?* Follow the instructions in Unit 1, Lesson 2, p32. In this game you will read out words without a prefix. Students decide if the prefix is *dis-* or *un-*.With a confident class, the game could be continued with words not on the list, e.g. *untidy, unfashionable, disadvantage, dishonest.*

9 PHRASEBOOK

- Play the recording for the students to listen and repeat the idiomatic expressions.
- Ask students to find the expressions in Unit 1.
- Students find which expressions have the meanings 1–4.

1.14 Recording and answers

I can't wait! (Sophie, L1, ex2)
I'm fed up with … (Sophie, L1, ex2)
once or twice a month (Sophie, L1, ex2)
Everything went wrong. (Joni, L2, ex2)
I didn't care. (Joni, L2, ex2)
I'll never forget the first time I … (Speaker 1, L4, ex4)
I couldn't believe it! (Speaker 1, L4, ex4)
I'll always remember when … (Speaker 2, L4, ex4)

1 I didn't care.
2 I couldn't believe it!
3 I can't wait!
4 I'm fed up with

Optional activity

Students begin a Personal Phrasebook, copying the phrases from this exercise, together with any other new phrases learnt. Be ready to help with explanations as necessary.

Follow-up activities

- Give students the question stem *Can you remember the first time you …?* and a list of verbs in the infinitive form, e.g. *eat, see, hear*. Students choose five verbs to put into past simple and make questions of their choice, e.g. *Can you remember the first time you went to a football match?* Students then circulate, asking students their questions and trying to find five different people who answer *yes* to their questions. Confident students should ask further questions about their experiences.
- **Game** *Vocabulary race* Divide the class into groups of four or five students. Give each group three words from the Vocabulary box. The group must work together to write three sentences including each of the three words, without turning them over to look at the definition or translation. The first group to write three correct sentences wins the game.

HOMEWORK

Students find the lyrics to a favourite song on the Internet and use dictionaries to look up five unknown words. They should copy these words and definitions/examples into their vocabulary notebooks.
Students put into action the *My Plan* section of their Learning Diary.

WEBLINK

Students may like to visit www.famoushistoricalevents.net to find out more significant events in world history.

Revision and Extension p19

Workbook Unit 1 Lesson 4 pp8–9

Inspiration EXTRA!

LANGUAGE LINKS

- Books closed. Write *hello* on the board. Ask students if they know how to say this in other languages – apart from their own language of course! Elicit some examples and write them on the board. Then write the word *polyglot* on the board. Elicit that a polyglot is a person who can speak several languages.
- Ask students how many languages there are in the world. Elicit different suggestions from the class. Then ask how many languages they think one person can speak. Again, elicit different suggestions but do not give any answers at this point.
- Students open their books and look at the eleven ways of saying hello. Ask if they recognise any of these languages (Portuguese, Spanish, Italian, French, German, Turkish, English, Czech, Swedish, Polish and Swahili). Explain the task. Students should read the text and find examples of people who speak or spoke many languages and how many languages they can or could speak.
- Check answers with the whole class. Point out that *claim* means to say something is true but without proof or evidence.
- Ask students to read the two questions at the bottom of the text. Give them a couple of minutes to think about their answers and make notes. Ask them to compare their answers in pairs. Then ask each pair to report to the whole class, e.g. *Peter's father speaks French and German. His grandparents can speak Italian.*

Answers

Ziad Youssef Fazah can speak 59 languages.
Professor Alexander Arguelles knows more than 34 languages.
Sir John Bowring spoke 100 languages.

GAME WORD MAZE

- Ask the students *What's the opposite of beautiful?* (to elicit ugly), and show them that they can find *ugly* in the first line of the maze.
- Tell students to work in pairs to move from line to line of the maze by finding pairs of opposites, until they reach *calm*. To win, they need to do this as quickly as possible.
- Remind students to note down all the pairs of opposites in their notebooks.

Answers

beautiful – ugly – happy – sad – boring – interesting – better – worse – right – left – easy – difficult – fast – slow – same – different – nervous – calm

Optional activities

- ♦ In pairs, one student closes their book and their partner tests them on the pairs of opposites, by saying only one of each pair. Their partner must say the opposite.
- ♦ **Game** *Stress patterns* Draw a stress pattern on the board, making sure that the students understand the shapes represent syllables, with the larger shape being the stressed syllable, e.g. *o O o important, unusual; O o boring, trendy.* In pairs students find as many examples as possible of words from the maze which follow the given pattern. The pair with the most wins.

SKETCH THE MIRROR

- The aim is for students to enjoy using their English while also getting valuable stress and intonation practice. Ask the students to look at the cartoon and establish that the sketch is about a man looking at a man in a mirror.
- With a more confident class, play the recording with books closed. Then play it again with books open. With a less confident class, play the recording once while the students follow in their books, and then once again with books closed.

1.15 Recording

See text on page 18 of the Student's Book.

- Divide the class into two equal groups and play the recording again, with one group repeating in chorus as Man 1 and the other group as Man 2. Encourage students to exaggerate stress and intonation.
- Ask the students to close their books and play the recording again. Then ask the students to work in pairs and read the sketch aloud. Choose several pairs to act out the sketch in front of the class.

Optional activity

Make an audio or video recording of students performing the sketch.

REVISION

Lesson 1

- If necessary, point out that Rob's profile is made up of three paragraphs and ask students to identify which questions from the Teenage Life questionnaire are answered in each paragraph.

Lesson 2

- If necessary, point out the different formation of subject questions (Who hated every minute of her holiday?) and object questions (Who did Joni miss?)

Suggested questions and answers

Who was Joni on holiday with? Her best friend, Sara.
Who phoned Joni? Her mum.
Who did Joni miss? Sara.
Who did Sara and Joni meet on the first day? New friends
Who didn't Joni like? Sara's new friends
Who did Joni like? Her new friends.
Who felt sad and lonely? Joni (and possibly Sara too)
Who did Joni see when she was on the phone to her mum? Sara, also on the phone.

Lesson 3

- Refer students to the first half of the article on page 14. Encourage students to re-read, taking notes on what Alana saw and how she probably felt. Also refer students to Feelings vocabulary on page 13.

EXTENSION

Lesson 1
Students' own answers

Lesson 2

- Refer students to the blog on page 12. If necessary, give students a first line to start the dialogue, for example *Hello, Joni. It's Mum. How are you enjoying your holiday?*

Lesson 3

- Refer students to the stories in Lesson 3. Encourage students to make notes first about where they were, what happened and how they escaped. Remind students to take care when choosing between the past simple and continuous.

YOUR CHOICE!

- Ask students to look back at the learning styles table on page 7 and remember which learning style they were. Divide the class into groups according to their learning style to do the relevant activity: Construction, Reflection, Action or Interaction.
- Monitor and help groups. Check answers if necessary, or provide written answers for groups to check their own work against.
- Encourage students to experiment with other learning styles and try one of the other activities of their choice.

Language File pp112–113

CONSTRUCTION

- Students complete the gaps with the verbs in past simple or continuous.

Answers

1 rode 2 was staying 3 was cleaning 4 asked 5 said 6 was going 7 heard 8 was shouting 9 put 10 fell

REFLECTION

- Students complete the gaps.

Answers

Past simple
-ed (students' own example, such as walked)
-d (students' own example, such as lived)
i (students' own example, such as carry)
(students' own example, such as play)
Past continuous
was/were (students' own example)
(students' own example, such as take -taking)
-ing (students' own example, such as seeing)
Doubling consonants
(students' own examples, such as stop)
-ing or -ed (students' own examples)

ACTION

- Divide the class into groups of four. With an uneven number, have a group of three with one student taking the role of students A and D.
- Elicit an example with one verb. Students then follow the instructions in their groups.

INTERACTION

- Ask two confident students to read the example out loud.
- Ask students to work in small groups and ask each other similar questions following the model. Remind students to use the past continuous for the longer/background activity they were doing at that time, and to use a range of feelings adjectives.

Workbook Unit 1 Inspiration EXTRA! pp10–11

Women in the world

Useful information

Valentina Tereshkova was born in Russia in 1937. She spent nearly three days in space in her spacecraft, Vostok 6.
Aung San Suu Kyi was imprisoned under house arrest by the Burmese military government for 15 years before her release in November 2010.
Junko Tabei was the first woman to climb Mount Everest, but since then more than 75 women have reached the summit of the world's highest mountain.
Jennifer Murray's solo flight took a total of 99 days and covered a distance of nearly 60,000 kilometres.
Sirimavo Banadaranaike served three terms as Prime Minister of Sri Lanka, from 1960 to 1965, 1970 to 1977 and 1994 to 2000.
Indira Gandhi was prime minister of India from 1966 to 1977 and again from 1980 to 1984. She was assassinated in 1984.
Margaret Thatcher was born in 1925 and studied chemistry at university. She was prime minister for 11 years from 1979 to 1990.
Benazir Bhutto was prime minister of Pakistan twice – from 1988 to 1990 and 1993 to 1996. She was leader of an opposition party that was favourite to win the next election when she was assassinated in 2007.

1 READING

- Ask students to look at the picture. Ask where these women are and what they are doing. (In Jodhpur, India – they're breaking up bricks.)
- Students do the True or False quiz individually. Ask them to compare their answers in pairs. Point out that all the statements are, in fact, true. Check students understand *illiterate* (unable to read or write).
- Ask students to read the information in the three texts and note down the most surprising facts. Ask them to compare their answers in pairs or small groups. Elicit from the class which facts are the most surprising.
- You could ask students to listen to the recording and follow in their books.

1.16 Recording
See text on page 20–21 of the Student's Book.

2

- Ask students to read the questions first. Then students read the texts again to find the answers.
- Check the answers with the whole class by asking individual students to read out their answers.

Answers
1 Russia 2 Finland 3 Sri Lanka 4 Saudi Arabia 5 Liechtenstein 6 Aung San Suu Kyi 7 Men 8 Junko Tabei 9 Benazir Bhutto 10 Native Americans

3 VOCABULARY

- Students work individually to match the words with the definitions and then compare their answers in pairs.

Answers
1c 2i 3b 4f 5a 6e 7h 8d 9g

Optional activity

In pairs, students discuss which of the achievements in the three texts was the most impressive and why. When they have discussed this question, ask each pair to tell the class their answer and their reasons. Alternatively, take a class vote.

4 MINI-PROJECT WOMEN IN MY COUNTRY

- Put the students into pairs.
- Ask students to answer as many of the questions as they can. If they are unsure of any of the answers, they should check their facts using the Internet or the library.
- Students then write a short paragraph about the position of women in their country, using the answers to the six questions to help them.
- Give students a few minutes to check their paragraph for grammar, spelling and capital letters. They then give it to another student to check.

WEBLINK

For more information on women in the world, students may like to visit www.womeninworldhistory.com

Workbook Culture pp12–13

2 ARTS

1 You can't help laughing

Communicative Aims	Language	Pronunciation	Vocabulary	Optional Aids
Talking about likes and dislikes Agreeing and disagreeing	Verb/Preposition + gerund *So/Nor* + auxiliary verbs	Syllable stress	Films Adjectives for opinions	Exercise 8 Optional activity: an example film review

WARMER 1

Game *Password* Organise students into teams of at least three. One student from each team sits with their back to the board. Write on the board the name of an actor/actress that your students will know. The teams describe the actor/actress to the team member who can't see it. They must not say the name. The first student to guess correctly wins a point for their team. Students move so a different student has their back to the board and then continue. It would help students recognise the names of the actors/actresses in exercise 7 if you include these here: Johnny Depp, Zac Efron, Kristen Stewart, Robert Pattison, Zoe Saldana, Ben Stiller.

WARMER 2

Tell students the topic of the lesson is films. Write jumbled questions related to the topic on the board e.g. *do cinema often you how to go the? film is what favourite your?* Students re-order questions and then ask and answer the questions in pairs. Nominate one or two students to report back on their partner's answers.

1 OPENER

- The aim is to introduce vocabulary for film types and prepare students for the reading.
- Write the film types on the board and ask students to suggest the names of films in each category. You could have a class vote to see which type of film is the most popular. Ask students to look at the DVD covers on pages 22 and 23 and match these to categories.

Answers

A musical B action film C comedy
D horror film/romantic film
E animation/science fiction film

2 READING

- In pairs, students tell their partner what, if anything, they know about the five films. Do one with the whole class as an example. If students know the film but lack some vocabulary, particularly key words in the text, e.g. *pirate, kidnap, curse, vampire,* provide this vocabulary and write it on the board.
- Explain that they will read and listen to five descriptions and they need to match them to the five films.
- Play the recording, pausing after each description for students to compare their ideas with a partner. Play the recording again while students read the descriptions in their books.

1.17 Recording

See text on page 22 of the Student's Book.

Answers

1 D Twilight 2 C Night at the Museum 3 E Avatar
4 B Pirates of the Caribbean 5 A High School Musical

3 AFTER READING

- Students read and listen to the dialogue again and decide if sentences 1–10 are true, false or there is no information about this in the descriptions. Check the answers before students write corrections for the false sentences. Monitor and help where necessary.

Answers

1 *True*
2 *False. Edward is afraid of losing Bella.*
3 *True*
4 *False. He's fed up with looking for work.*
5 *True*
6 *True*
7 *No information.*
8 *True*
9 *False. They are good at singing.*
10 *No information*

Your response

Put students into pairs. They ask each other if they have seen any of the five films. If so did they enjoy them or did they find them boring? Ask them to give reasons and say what kind of films they enjoy watching. If necessary, refer them to the list of film types in the Opener on page 22.

Optional activities

- Fast finishers find all the gerunds in the text in preparation for the Language Workout.
- **Game** *Spelling race* Books closed, do a spelling test of 10 words in the text, e.g. *incredibly, divorced, museum, audition, guard.* This could be done as a team competition. The team with the most correct answers is the winner. With a confident class, give a definition of the word rather than the word itself.

4 VOCABULARY

- Tell students to copy the chart into their notebooks. In pairs, students categorise the words as good or bad. Do one as an example with students. Do not check the answers yet.

5 PRONUNCIATION

- Play the recording. Students listen for the first time to check their answers. With a less confident group, check understanding by asking further questions, e.g. *Which word is the same as exciting? Which word means frightening?*
- Ask students to predict/remember where the stress is on each word. Do one as an example with students. Play the recording again. Pause after each word to check the answers. Have students repeat each word.

1.18 Recording and answers

☺ *amazing brilliant excellent exciting funny interesting thrilling*

☹ *awful boring disappointing scary silly terrible*

Optional activity

In pairs, students name films they think are awful, brilliant, etc. Ask them to use at least five of the adjectives.

6 LISTENING

- Ask students to predict which adjectives the speakers will use for each film. Play the recording. Pause after each extract for students to note and compare answers. Play the recording again if necessary.
- Check the answers with the whole class. If any students have seen the films, ask them if they agree with the opinions.

1.19 Recording

1

Twilight *isn't really a horror film. There are some scary moments, and you jump out of your seat sometimes, but often it's quite silly.*

2

Night at the Museum *is a great movie – it's exciting and extremely funny. I laughed until I cried. And the animation and effects are excellent.*

3

I really enjoyed watching Avatar. *The story isn't original at all, but that doesn't really matter – the film is still interesting. And the special effects are amazing.*

4

The best thing in Pirates of the Caribbean *is Johnny Depp – he's brilliant as the pirate Jack Sparrow. But I think Keira Knightley is awful – she plays Elizabeth.*

5

I was looking forward to seeing High School Musical *because my friends said good things about it. But it's a disappointing film – sometimes it's quite boring.*

Answers

1 Twilight – *scary, silly*
2 Night at the Museum – *exciting, funny, excellent*
3 Avatar – *interesting, amazing*
4 Pirates of the Caribbean – *brilliant (Johnny Depp), awful (Keira Knightley)*
5 High School Musical – *disappointing, boring*

LANGUAGE WORKOUT OPTION

If you want to pre-teach the language students will be using in the following activities, you may like to go to the Language Workout box now.

7 SPEAKING

- Give students two minutes to think about how they could complete the sentences so that they are true for themselves.
- Ask students to look at the example dialogues.
- Highlight that:
  - *so* and *nor* are used if you agree with the first person's statement.
  - *so* is used in response to a positive statement.
  - *nor* is used in response to a negative statement.
  - the response is formed using *so/nor* + auxiliary from first statement or *do/does/did* if there is no auxiliary in the first statement + *I*.
  - if you disagree with the first statement, the response is usually *I* + auxiliary in opposite form from first sentence, e.g. *I love …, I don't; I'm scared of …, I'm not*.
- With a less confident group, check the necessary auxiliary for each of the sentence heads they are going to use.
- Nominate a student to say one of their sentences and respond appropriately using *So …* or *Nor …* Nominate two confident students to demonstrate with a different sentence for the whole class.
- Students continue in pairs. Monitor and help where necessary.
- Nominate some students to tell the class one thing they have learnt about their partner.

Optional activity

Encourage confident students to give more information, e.g. why they are not keen on something or how often they do what they love.

Extension Have the class do a class survey to find out what the three most popular kinds of film are. Then have a class vote on what is the most popular film at the moment.

8 WRITING

- Students work in pairs or individually. Ask students to think about a film they have seen recently. Students look at the questions and note answers. Encourage students to use vocabulary from exercises 1 and 4. Students then use these notes to write a short review. Encourage confident students and fast finishers to provide more details.

- Monitor and note examples of good language and errors. Put these on the board and ask students to identify and correct the errors.

Extension Ask one student to read their review. Tell them not to say the name of the film. The other students guess the name of the film. Continue in open class or in smaller groups depending on the size of your class. You could organise this as a team competition with the first student to guess winning a point for their team.

Optional activity

With less confident students, write a model review for the students. Students read the review and guess the name of the film. They can then use the structure and language in this review to write their own.

LANGUAGE WORKOUT

- Ask students to complete the Language box. Confident students can complete first and then check, while others can look back at the film descriptions on page 22 and then complete.
- Students turn to page 113 of the Language File to check their answers.

Answers
seeing going fighting losing
with looking in rescuing at singing

- Drill the examples in chorus and individually for pronunciation. Pay particular attention to the linking between the verbs and prepositions and the weak forms of *of*, *for* and *at*:
afraid of /əfreɪdəv/, *good at* /'gʊdət/ and *look for* /lʊk fə/.

PRACTICE

- Students do Practice exercise 4 on page 113 of the Language File on their own.

- Ask students to compare their answers in pairs.
- Check the answers by asking individual students to read out what they have written.

Answers
1 buying 2 shopping 3 seeing 4 watching 5 getting 6 being 7 talking 8 making 9 meeting

Optional activity

Students make two lists in their notebook:
1 Verb + gerund, e.g. *risk, like, keep, can't help*.
2 Word + preposition, e.g. *interested in, fed up, good at*.
Make sure that they leave lots of space to add to both these lists in later lessons.

Follow-up activities

♦ Students think of as many examples as possible for these three categories: books, TV programmes, computer games. Write their examples on the board. Drill the question *What do you think of …?* Students ask each other's opinions of the examples in pairs. Encourage students to use the adjectives in exercise 4. Demonstrate with one or two confident students first.

♦ **Game** *Noughts and crosses* Draw this grid on the board:

scary	keen	interested
good	succeed	avoid
fed up	bored	famous

Divide the class into two teams. One team is Noughts (O) and one team is Crosses (X). Team O chooses a square first. They must make an accurate sentence using the word in the square followed directly by a correct preposition. If they answer correctly, write O in the square. If they answer incorrectly, Team X can answer and win the square. The first team to get a line of three in any direction wins the game.

HOMEWORK

Students interview a friend or relative about a film they have seen (in their own language if necessary). They can ask the questions in exercise 8. They then write up the dialogue, translating it into English.

WEBLINKS

Students may like to visit www.imdb.com where can they read about the latest films.

Revision and Extension p31

Language File p113

Workbook Unit 2 Lesson 1 pp14–15

Photocopiable worksheet p165, notes p155

2 Promise to work together

Communicative Aims	Language	Pronunciation	Vocabulary
Talking about skills, abilities and ambitions	Verb (+object) + infinitive	Syllable stress	Music and dance Skills

WARMER 1

Game *What?* Organise students into teams. One student from each team stands at the front of their team. You show them a word and they mime it. The first team to guess the word wins a point. Continue with different students. Revise words from the Vocabulary box/previous lessons, e.g. *skateboard, miserable, scared, scream.*

WARMER 2

Elicit some current TV shows. Write them on the board. Ask students what type of TV show it is, e.g. *soap opera, reality show, chat show*. In pairs, students tell each other what their favourite TV show is and why.

1 OPENER

- Set the scene for the reading/listening by asking students to look at the magazine extract and photos on page 24. Ask *What kind of show is Star School?* Give students one minute to read the introduction to find the answer. Elicit that it is a show where contestants learn to improve their singing and each week perform a song on TV. Each week the public *vote one contestant off the show until there is a final winner. If there is a similar show in your country, ask students for the name and whether they watch/enjoy it.
  *vote off = make someone leave because they don't get enough votes.

2 LISTENING

- If your students are familiar with this type of programme, ask them what the different teachers in a school of this type teach, e.g. dance, voice. Elicit/tell students that this type of teacher is called a *coach*. Write the roles on the board. Include the four roles given here, i.e. director, voice coach, dance coach, songwriting coach.
- Students read the ten sentences and predict which person says each of the sentences. Ask them to compare their ideas in pairs. Listen to their suggestions but do not correct them at this point.
- Play the recording. Students listen and check their predictions.

1.20 Recording

TONY *Hi! I'm Tony, the director of Star School, and I'd like to welcome you. While you're here, we expect you to obey the rules and attend all your classes. Our teachers are great and they can help you to develop your talents. So let's meet the team: this is Jess – she's your voice coach.*

JESS *Hello there! Everyone can sing, but not everyone can sing like a star. I hope to help you to find your special voice. I want you to practise your songs hard and help each other. That's the best way to make the most of your time here, OK? And here's Adam, your dance coach.*

ADAM *Hey, good to see you all. I can teach you to dance in a range of styles including ballet, jazz, breakdancing, ballroom and salsa. But I want to you to promise me something. Promise to work together because you can't learn to dance alone. Try out new dance routines and don't refuse to experiment. And now, Rachel.*

RACHEL *Hi, I'm your songwriting coach. Songwriting is cool, but don't pretend to be a poet when you aren't one! The important thing is that you manage to fit the words to the music. Most contestants learn to do it, and performing your own song is a great feeling. Best of luck!*

Answers

Tony: E, I, C Jess: F, D Adam: A, J, H Rachel: B, G

3 AFTER LISTENING

- Students read the questions. Play the recording again for students to read and listen.
- Students answer the questions using the information in exercise 2 to help them. Make sure they understand that two answers are not needed.
- Students compare answers. Check their answers by asking one student to read a question and then another student to answer it. Note that there are several language changes from the statements in exercise 2, e.g. *We expect you to attend all your classes* becomes *He expects them to attend all their classes.*
- Check students understand key vocabulary – *expect, pretend, manage, promise, refuse.* Ask students to use the context to guess meaning.

Answers

1 *He expects them to obey the rules and attend all their classes.*
2 *He says their teachers are great and they can help them to develop their talents.*
3 *She hopes to help them find their special voice.*
4 *She wants them to practise their songs hard and help each other.*
5 *He can teach them to dance in a range of styles.*
6 *He asks them to promise to work together.*
7 *She tells them not to pretend to be a poet.*
8 *The important thing is that they manage to fit the words to the music.*

Your response

Students work individually, read the questions and make notes. Then ask them to discuss their answers to the questions in pairs. Ask each pair to report back to the whole class.

4 PRONUNCIATION

- Write *hopeful* and *attend* on the board. Elicit the number of syllables and which syllable the main stress falls on.
- Ask students to look at the words in the box and, in pairs, recall/guess which stress pattern they follow.
- Tell them to copy the chart into their notebooks. Play the recording. Students listen and write the words in the correct column.
- Students compare their answers and then listen again to check. Check answers by asking different students to read the words in one column aloud.

1.21 Recording and answers

■▪ *hopeful manage practise promise special talent*

▪■ *attend expect obey perform pretend refuse*

LANGUAGE WORKOUT OPTION

If you want to pre-teach the language students will be using in the following activities, you may like to go to the Language Workout box now.

5 LISTENING

- Students read the truth questionnaire. Check understanding of *a skill* by eliciting examples, e.g. *knowing a language, playing a musical instrument*.
- Students look at photos of the two teenagers and predict some of their answers.
- Play Anna's interview and then pause for students to compare answers. If necessary play Anna's section again. Repeat this procedure with Will's interview.
- Check the answers with the whole class.

1.22 Recording

INTERVIEWER *Now Anna, you're first, here we go with the Truth Questionnaire.*
ANNA *OK.*
INTERVIEWER *Question 1: do you promise to tell the truth?*
ANNA *I don't know what the questions are yet – but yes.*
INTERVIEWER *What new skill do you want to learn?*
ANNA *Um, I want to learn to dance the salsa.*
INTERVIEWER *And what would you like to teach your friends to do?*
ANNA *That's easy – I'd like to teach them to listen to me sometimes.*
INTERVIEWER *Question 4: is there something you pretend to like, but don't really like?*
ANNA *That's difficult … um, I know – salad. I pretend to like it but I don't really!*
INTERVIEWER *Mmm. Next question: is there anything you refuse to eat?*
ANNA *Yes, I really don't like pizza so I refuse to eat it.*
INTERVIEWER *Question 6: what do your parents ask you to do which you don't enjoy?*
ANNA *Oh, lots of things – Um, they ask me to do the washing up, for example.*
INTERVIEWER *What can you just manage to do but would like to do better?*
ANNA *Just manage to do – you mean something I don't do very well? Yeah. Um, we learned to use PowerPoint® at school, but I'm not very good at it.*
INTERVIEWER *And the last question. What do you hope to do when you leave school?*
ANNA *Oh, I want to travel around the world.*
INTERVIEWER *And now your turn, Will. Are you ready?*
WILL *Sure. Are they the same questions?*
INTERVIEWER *Yes, they are. Question 1: do you promise to tell the truth?*
WILL *Of course.*
INTERVIEWER *Right. What new skill do you want to learn?*
WILL *A new skill? Yes, I want to learn to drive a car when I'm older.*
INTERVIEWER *And what would you like to teach your friends to do?*
WILL *My friends? I don't think I can teach them anything!*
INTERVIEWER *Question 4: is there something you pretend to like, but don't really like?*
WILL *Yes, I pretend to like dancing but I don't really enjoy it.*
INTERVIEWER *And is there anything you refuse to eat?*
WILL *Yes, I hate eggs – I can't stand them.*
INTERVIEWER *OK. Question 6: what do your parents ask you to do which you don't enjoy?*
WILL *Oh yes! They always want me to write thank-you letters when I get presents and I can never think of anything to write.*
INTERVIEWER *Next question. What can you just manage to do but would like to do better?*
WILL *That's easy – speak Italian!*
INTERVIEWER *And the last question: what do you hope to do when you leave school?*
WILL *You mean this evening? Play football.*
INTERVIEWER *No, Will – when you finish school and leave.*
WILL *I hope to go to university.*

Answers
Anna
1 True 2 False. To learn to dance the salsa.
3 False. To listen to me sometimes. 4 True
5 False. Pizza. 6 True 7 True
8 False. To travel round the world.
Will
1 True 2 False. To drive a car. 3 True
4 False. I pretend to enjoy dancing.
5 False. Eggs. 6 True 7 False. To speak Italian.
8 False. To go to university.

Extension Nominate a student to read the example comparing Anna and Will's answers. Do the second question with the whole class, showing that you can say *and* or *but* to connect the ideas, e.g. *Anna wants to learn to dance and/but Will wants to learn to drive a car.* Students continue in pairs.

6 SPEAKING

- Write the following chart on the board for the students to copy into their notebooks. Continue the question numbers to 8.

Question	Me	Name:_____	Name:_____
1			
2			

- Tell students that they can answer *yes* or *no* to the first answer. If they answer *no*, they must invent an answer.
- Give students a few minutes to think about their responses to the eight questions in the questionnaire and write them in the *Me* column.
- Students interview two other students and note their answers in the other columns. Make sure students do not show each other their charts. Encourage a confident class/confident students to give more information, e.g. why they want to learn that skill.
- Nominate students to say how they were similar or different from the students they interviewed.

7 WRITING

- Ask students to use their notes in the chart to write a paragraph comparing each other's answers. Ask students to read the example. Set a 10-minute time limit.
- Students exchange writing and correct each other's work for spelling, grammar and punctuation.

Extension Ask students to take a sheet of paper and write the questions *What new skills do you want to learn?* and *What do you want to do when you leave school?* at the top of the page. Then they write the names of their classmates in a list down the left-hand side. Ask them to stand up and walk around the class, interviewing their classmates and noting down their answers. When they have finished, they work in groups and evaluate their results, reporting back to the whole class, e.g. *Five people in the class want to learn to play the guitar.*

LANGUAGE WORKOUT

- Ask students to complete the Language box. Confident students can complete first and then check, while others can look back at exercises 2 and 3 and then complete.
- Students turn to page 114 of the Language File to check their answers.

Answers
to to help to work to experiment
to be to do you to you to you to

- Drill the examples in chorus and individually, paying particular attention to the weak pronunciation of *to* /tə, tʊ/.

PRACTICE

- Students do Practice exercise 5 on page 114 of the Language File.

Answers
1 us to obey 2 her to help 3 you to find
4 to learn 5 us to promise 6 to work
7 to be 8 us to write 9 to do
10 to try

Follow-up activity

Game *Word association* Divide students into groups of three or four. Student A thinks of a word from the unit, e.g. *voice*. Student B has to say a word associated with voice, e.g. *mouth*. Student C has to say a word associated with *mouth*, e.g. *sing*, and so on.

HOMEWORK

Students imagine they are a contestant at Star School. Have them write an email to family or friends, saying what happened on the first day and how they felt.

WEBLINK

Students may like to visit www.lamda.org.uk/drama for information on a music and dance school.

Revision and Extension p31

Language File p114

Workbook Unit 2 Lesson 2 pp16–17

Photocopiable worksheet p166, notes p155

3 Books are left in public places

Communicative Aims	Language	Pronunciation	Vocabulary	Optional Aids
Describing a system	Present simple passive	Linking: consonant sound + vowel	Books Phrasal verbs with *up* World records	Warmer 2: books or book covers Follow-up activity: copies of text, recording track 1.25

WARMER 1

Game *Broken telephone* Organise students into groups of 10. Give one student in each team a sentence. The student memorises the sentence and then whispers it to the next student. The next person whispers the sentence to the next and so on until it gets to the last person in the group. That person then stands up and says the sentence. Use sentences which are relatively long and revise grammar and vocabulary from previous lessons, e.g. *He pretends to be rich but he always avoids paying in expensive restaurants.*

WARMER 2

Tell students the topic of the lesson is *books*. Show the students some book covers. Elicit what type of book they think each one is. In pairs, students say which of the books they would most like to read based on the covers.

1 OPENER

- The aim is to personalise the topic and set the scene for the reading.
- Students discuss the questions in pairs. Make a list on the board of the places students suggest where you can get books, e.g. *bookshop, internet, school library, public library, from a friend*. Ask students which they prefer and why.

2 READING

- Explain that they are going to read about another place where they can get books. Students look at the headline. Ask *How much does the book cost?* (It's free)
- Ask *Why do you think it is free? Where does it come from? Can anyone pick it up?* Play the recording. Students listen and read to see if they were right.

1.23 Recording

See text on page 26 of the Student's Book.

3 AFTER READING

- Students read the text again and answer the questions with short answers.
- Encourage them to guess the meaning of unfamiliar vocabulary from context and ask *What does … mean?*
- They check their answers in pairs. Ask students to read their answers to the class.

Answers

1 *Casino Royale*
2 *To take the book home and read it.*
3 *Ron Hornbaker*
4 *About one million members around the globe*
5 *In public places – on buses, on park benches, in cafés*
6 *To report back to the website when they find a book.*
7 *Register the next book you finish at the website, label it with its ID number and then leave it in public place for someone else to pick up and enjoy.*

Your response

Ask students to make a list of other public places where you could leave a book. In pairs, students race to write five, e.g. *on a train, in a museum*. Students decide which book they would leave in a public place for others to read. In small groups, they say why they would choose this particular book. Each group reports back to the whole class, e.g. *Marcus would leave Jurassic Park because he has already read it.*

Optional activities

- Ask *Have you heard of this before? Have you ever seen a book with the label on it? Is it a good idea?*
- Check some of the new vocabulary in the text by giving students definitions. In pairs, students look at the text and try to find the words.

4 PRONUNCIATION

- Have students look at the sentences in the box and the linking between the words.
- Demonstrate the wrong pronunciation of the first sentence, with each word pronounced separately with a pause between them. Then play the recording of the first sentence for students to hear the difference. Play the sentence again, pause the recording and ask the students to repeat the sentence. Continue, pausing after each sentence for students to repeat.
- Ask students if they can work out when the words link together. Elicit that it happens when the first word ends with a consonant sound (not necessarily a consonant letter) and the second word begins with a vowel sound (not necessarily a vowel letter).

1.24 Recording

See text on page 26 of the Student's Book.

5 VOCABULARY

- Ask students to find examples of phrasal verbs with *up* in the text. There are four (see below). Students can use the context in the text to work out the correct definitions for these.
- In pairs, students match the phrasal verbs and definitions. Check the answers with whole class.

Answers

1 turn up 2 grow up 3 look up 4 pick up
5 stand up 6 give up 7 set up 8 come up with
In Free books!: came up with, set up, pick up, turn up

Extension Students complete the sentences in pairs and check their answers as a group. (1 Pick up 2 give up 3 turn up 4 grows up 5 stand up)

Optional activity

Write *an idea/a plan, smoking, a word/an expression, a pen/a book, a company* in a random order on the board. Students match these to the verbs they go with, e.g. *give up smoking*.

LANGUAGE WORKOUT OPTION

If you want to pre-teach the language students will be using in the following activities, you may like to go to the Language Workout box now.

6 LISTENING

- Ask students to read the list of verbs first and check that they understand them all.
- Explain the task. They will hear a recording and they should write the verbs in the correct spaces.
- Ask them to compare their answers in pairs. Check the answers by asking different students to read out each sentence.

1.25 Recording

*Books are 1 **made** of paper, and most of the world's paper is 2 **produced** from pine trees. These trees are 3 **grown** in countries such as Canada, the USA, Sweden, Finland and Japan.*
*A book is 4 **published** somewhere in the world every 20 seconds – that's over 1.5 million books a year! Many books are 5 **sold** by town bookshops, but now increasing numbers are 6 **bought** online through virtual bookshops like Amazon.*
*In the UK, about 60% of the population is 7 **registered** with a library. About one third of the books which are 8 **taken** out of libraries are 9 **borrowed** by children. More books are 10 **read** by girls than boys, and most reading is 11 **done** in bed. It's 12 **said** that a good book is the best of friends. So find a new friend today!*

Optional activity

1.25 With a more confident class, ask them to complete the text without listening to the recording. They then listen to check their answers.

7 SPEAKING

- The aim is to develop students' fluency and to provide natural spoken practice of the present simple passive.
- Give students five minutes to think about their answers to the questions.
- Tell students to listen to their partner's answers carefully and say whether they have read the book they are talking about and, if so, do they agree? If they haven't read it, are they interested in reading it now?
- Students could work in pairs, in groups or stand up and move around the classroom talking to different students. Set a 10-minute time limit.
- Monitor and note examples of good language and errors. Put these on the board and, at the end of the activity, ask students to identify and correct the errors.
- Ask if anyone has heard about a book that they would now like to read.

8 WRITING

- Tell students to use their answers to exercise 7 to write a book review. Tell students the reviews will be put on the class/library noticeboard if this is possible. Tell students to give their review a title, e.g. *A book you must read.* Elicit the first sentence, e.g. *I strongly recommend …* Set a 10-minute time limit.
- Students read each other's reviews and choose one book they would like to read. Encourage a book exchange if appropriate.

9 SPEAKING

- Write the prompts for the first question on the board and elicit the full question. Ask *What do you think is the answer?* Encourage students to say *I think it's …*
- Students continue asking and answering the questions in pairs. Tell students that they must write the same answer as their partner. They should discuss their ideas if they disagree. They write their answers in their notebooks.
- Do not check the answers as a class. Play the recording for students to listen and check their answers.

1.26 Recording

1 Where are the most newspapers sold? China
2 Where are the most films made? India
3 Where are the most cars sold? China
4 Where is the most coffee produced? Brazil
5 Where is the most coffee drunk? Scandinavia
6 Where is the most tea produced? China
7 Where is the most tea drunk? Turkey
8 Where are the most bananas grown? India
9 Where is the most rice grown? China

Answers
1 A 2 B 3 B 4 A 5 C 6 B 7 C 8 B 9 A

Extension In pairs, students write more quiz questions. Make sure that students realise they must know the answers to the questions. Each pair gives their questions to the teacher. Divide the class into teams of four. Ask the questions and have teams note down the answers. The team with the most correct answers is the winner.

LANGUAGE WORKOUT

- Ask students to complete the Language box. Confident students can complete first and then check, while others can look back at exercise 2 and then complete.
- Students turn to page 114 of the Language File to confirm their answers.

  Answers
  is are is are
  be
- Highlight that:
  - in active sentences the subject is the 'doer' of the verb.
  - in passive sentences the subject is not the 'doer' of the verb. If you mention the 'doer' of the verb you use *by* + the person.
  - the passive is used (a) to focus on the main topic of the sentence, e.g. *The books are found by other people* (the books are the main topic of the text, not the people who find them), (b) because the 'doer' of the verb is unknown, unimportant or obvious, e.g. *You are invited to pick it up* (obviously by the label).
  - the passive is usually used in more formal contexts, e.g. newspaper articles.
- To revise past participle forms, refer students to the list of irregular verbs at the back of their books on page 127.
- Drill the examples chorally and individually for pronunciation. Pay particular attention to the weak form of *are* /ə/.

Optional activity

In pairs, one student has their book closed and the other student looks at the irregular verb list on page 127 and tests their partner.

PRACTICE

- Students do Practice exercise 6 on page 114 of the Language File on their own.
- Ask students to compare their answers in pairs.
- Check the answers by asking individual students to read out what they have written.

Answers
1 Sushi is eaten in Japan.
2 Saris are worn by women in India.
3 Portuguese is spoken in Brazil.
4 Kangaroos are found in Australia.
5 Over 250 kinds of olives are grown in Spain.
6 A lot of cotton is produced in Egypt.
7 Ferrari sports cars are made in Italy.
8 The sitar is played in India.

Follow-up activities

♦ **Game** *Passive tennis* Divide the class into two teams. Students 'serve' a verb in the infinitive to the other team, who must 'return' within one minute with a passive sentence using that verb. Teams change roles after three verbs have been 'served'.

♦ **Game** *Running dictation* Write out the recording text track 1.25. Put copies of the text at the front of the class where students can't read it. In pairs, one student runs up to the text, reads and remembers as much as they can, runs back and dictates it to their partner. Their partner writes the text. The two students can change roles halfway through. The first pair to finish shouts *Stop!* They then exchange their text with another pair and compare them to the original. Each text starts with 50 points but loses a point for each error in spelling, punctuation or missing word.

HOMEWORK

Students write a short story of at least 80 words including as many of the phrasal verbs from exercise 5 as possible. The story should make sense but can be fantasy.

WEBLINK

Students may like to visit www.bookcrossing.com for more information.

Revision and Extension p31

Language File p114

Workbook Unit 2 Lesson 3 pp18–19

Photocopiable worksheet p167, notes p155

4 Integrated Skills
Describing a picture

Skills
Reading Matching texts with pictures: *What's your favourite picture?*
Listening Listening for details in a description
Speaking Interviewing
Writing Describing a picture

Learner Independence
Classroom English
Word creation: adjective suffixes *-ful* and *-less*

Vocabulary
Art styles
Feelings
Useful expressions

Optional Aids
Exercise 7 Optional activity: a range of pictures
Follow-up activities: large pieces of paper or card; pictures

WARMER 1

If students wrote the stories for homework, organise students into groups to read their stories to each other.

WARMER 2

Ask *Who teaches Maths?* Prompt students to answer the question beginning with the word *Maths* … They need to form a present simple passive sentence, e.g. *Maths is taught by Mr Brown.* In pairs/groups, students try to be first to form four more sentences about school using the present simple passive, each one using a different verb.

WARMER 3

Ask students to think about all the pictures they have in their house: photos, paintings, posters. In pairs, students describe these pictures to their partner.

1 OPENER

- The aim of the questions is to engage students' interest in the text. This can be done as a whole class activity with a confident class.
- Ask students to read the words for the five art styles and then decide which style is represented by the three paintings.

Answers
A impressionism B expressionism C pop art

Useful information

Picture A is *Luncheon of the Boating Party*, painted in 1881 by French impressionist Pierre-Auguste Renoir. Picture B is *Weeping Woman* by Pablo Picasso. It was painted in 1937 as a response to the bombing of the town of Guernica in the Spanish Civil War.
Picture C is by Roy Liechtenstein who, along with Andy Warhol, is probably the best-known American pop-artist.

2 READING

- The aim is for students to read and listen for general understanding before focusing on the language in the text.
- Set a two-minute time limit for students to match the texts with the pictures.
- Play the recording. Students listen and read. Students compare their answers in pairs and then as a class.
- Elicit the key words that helped students to make their decisions. Ask students if they agree with the opinions of the three speakers.

1.27 Recording
See text on page 28 of the Student's Book.

Answers
1 B 2 C 3 A

3

- The aim is to encourage students to deduce the meaning from context.
- Students find the highlighted words and match them with the definitions. They then compare answers in pairs.

Answers
1 attractive 2 realistic 3 wonder 4 war 5 background 6 expression 7 a great deal 8 foreground

4

- The aim is to raise students' awareness of the use and form of pronouns in making texts more readable and cohesive.
- Write on the board *I like the fact that the picture suggests a story and the picture looks like an image from a comic book.* Ask students to find the same sentence in the text and write it on the board and highlight the difference. Ask why the second sentence is better: because it doesn't repeat the word *picture* and uses a pronoun instead.
- Students find the other sentences in the text and identify which word is replaced by the word in italics.

Answers
1 this painting 2 favourite picture 3 a group of friends 4 the painting

5 LINKING WORDS

- Ask students to find three examples of sentences with *which* and three with *who* in the text. Ask which word is used for things (*which*) and which word is used for people (*who*).
- Students identify what or who is referred to in each of the six sentences. Do the first one with the whole class as an example.

Answers

There's a painting which means a great deal to me. (Text 1) which = painting
She has an expression on her face which shows that something is very wrong. (Text 2) which = expression
It's an impressionist painting which shows beautiful treatment of light and colour. (Text 3) which = painting
It's a picture of a woman who's crying. (Text 1) who = woman
It shows an attractive girl and a dark-haired man who's turned away from her. (Text 2) who = man
It shows a group of friends who are enjoying lunch together. (Text 3) who = a group of friends

6 LISTENING

- The aim is for students to listen for specific information.
- Tell students they are going to listen to the description of another picture. Give students one minute to read the interview.
- Play the recording. Students listen and choose the correct answers. Play the recording again, pausing to check the answers to each question. Ask students *Do you think you would like this picture? Why/why not?*

1.28 Recording and answers

SPEAKER 1 *Do you have a favourite picture, or one which means a lot to you?*
SPEAKER 2 *Yes, there are several pictures which I like a lot, but there's one in particular.*
SPEAKER 1 *What kind of picture is it?*
SPEAKER 2 *It's a* ***painting*** *on my* ***bedroom*** *wall.*
SPEAKER 1 *Can you describe it?*
SPEAKER 2 *It's a picture of a sunset in the Greek islands. There aren't any people or* ***boats*** *in it, just the sea, the sky and the islands. I don't know who painted it but there's a date on it –* ***75****. So I think it's from* ***1975****.*
SPEAKER 1 *Why is it important to you?*
SPEAKER 2 *It reminds me of holidays in Greece. I love travelling around the islands.*
SPEAKER 1 *How does it make you feel?*
SPEAKER 2 *Happy and relaxed. The colours are fantastic – the sea is* ***black*** *and grey, some of the islands are green and blue, but the mountains in the background are* ***pink****. And the sky is yellow and blue.*

Optional activity

1.28 Shadow reading: In pairs, one student is the interviewer and the other responds. They practise the conversation in the book. Explain that you are going to play the recording again and they should try to say the words at the same time as the recording. Allow them to mouth the words the first time. Typically students find this very difficult the first time the recording is played, but easier with each try. Repeat a maximum of three times.

7 SPEAKING

- Students use the questions in exercise 6 to interview each other about their favourite pictures. Give students time to think about their answers to the questions and ask for necessary vocabulary.
- Demonstrate the interview, with students asking you the questions.
- Monitor and provide help. Make a note of examples of good language and errors. Put these on the board and ask students to identify and correct the errors.

Optional activities

- If you think your students need ideas, provide a range of pictures for students to choose from, e.g. postcards or pictures downloaded from the Internet.
- Students repeat the activity with different students. This enables them to correct the mistakes they made in the first interview and be less dependent on any notes they have prepared.

8 GUIDED WRITING

- The aim is for students to write a short description of a picture using the texts in exercises 2 and 6 as models.
- Students exchange texts and read them, first for interest, and then again to check spelling and punctuation.

9 LEARNER INDEPENDENCE

- The aim is to provide students with useful language for the classroom. This should encourage students to ask these questions when they need to, and also help promote more English in the classroom.
- Students match the questions and the answers. Check answers by asking one student to ask and another to answer each question.

Answers

1 f 2 d 3 b 4 c 5 a 6 e

Optional activity

Use the opportunity to look at the pronunciation guide on page 127 with the students.

10 WORD CREATION

- The aim is for students to learn the meaning of the two suffixes and extend their vocabulary.
- Write *careful* and *careless* on the board and elicit the difference: *-ful* means with and *-less* means without. Write *stressful* on the board. Elicit/give the opposite: *stress-free*. Use this to illustrate that you cannot always use both suffixes.
- Students complete the sentences individually and then compare in pairs. Check answers as a whole class.

Answers

1 careless 2 painful 3 truthful 4 colourful 5 hopeful 6 careful 7 painless 8 hopeless 9 colourless 10 successful

Optional activity

In pairs, students note other things which can be described using the adjectives, e.g. *painful – breaking your leg, colourless – air*. Students then change partners. They read their list and their new partner says the appropriate adjective.

11 PHRASEBOOK

- Ask students to look through the unit to find the expressions, and look at how they are used.
- Play the recording, pausing after each expression for students to repeat.
- Ask students to work in pairs and write a five-line dialogue using three of these expressions.
- Students read their dialogues to the whole class.

1.29 Recording and answers

You can't help laughing. (L1, Ex 2.1)
Best of luck! (Rachel L2, Ex 2)
The important thing is … (Rachel L2, Ex 2)
Do you promise to tell the truth? (Interviewer L2, Ex5)
Why not try it? (L3, Ex2)
Who knows? (L3, Ex2)
It depends. (L4, Ex2.2)
I wonder what's happened. (L4, Ex2.2)
I like the fact that … (L4, Ex2.2)
It reminds me of … (Female L4, Ex6)

- Students can add expressions they like to their Personal Phrasebooks. Help with translation where necessary.
- Ask students to work in pairs to make up the five-line dialogue. Invite some pairs to act out their dialogues in front of the class.

Follow-up activities

- ♦ Draw a word map on the board. Write *ARTS* in the centre. Elicit different categories and write them on the word map, e.g. *film, books, pictures, theatre*. Divide students into small groups to draw their own word map on a large piece of paper or card. Encourage them to think of their own categories, and add as many words as they can. Set a time limit and give out bi-lingual dictionaries if available. The word maps can be displayed in the classroom.
- ♦ Organise students into teams. Tell students they are going to redecorate the school with some (new) pictures. Give students a selection of pictures to choose from. Give teams ten minutes to choose some pictures and prepare to present their ideas to the rest of the class. The class hears each presentation and then votes on the best suggestions.

HOMEWORK

Students find one picture that they can bring to class and prepare to say what they like or dislike about it in the next lesson. The picture should not be the same as their favourite picture. They could use personal photos, travel photos, album covers, postcards, birthday cards.
Students review vocabulary from the four lessons in this unit.

WEBLINK

Students may like to visit www.tate.org.uk for the Tate Galleries in London where they can look at pieces of art by subject or artist.

Revision and Extension p31

Workbook Unit 2 Lesson 4 pp20–21

Inspiration EXTRA!

PROJECT TWO-MINUTE TALKS

1
- Explain to students that the aim of the project is to give a talk about films or novels.
- Divide the students into groups and appoint a 'secretary' for each group. The 'secretary' is responsible for taking notes for the group.
- Give students three minutes to make a list of all the books and films they have read or seen recently. Each group then chooses one of each to prepare a short talk about.

2
- Students look at the headings and the questions and make notes. Every student in the group needs to write these notes in their notebook. Encourage students to write notes rather than complete sentences. This should improve their fluency and presentation skills when they give the talk. They may need to research their information on the Internet or at home. Students may also like to collect some visual material, e.g. book covers or pictures from the film, to support their talks.

3
- Tell students they will hear an example of a two-minute talk about a film.
- Play the recording and ask the students if they know the title of the film (*ET*).

1.30 **Recording**

I'm going to talk about one of my favourite films. Steven Spielberg directed the film and it won three Oscars. The film is about a little alien who comes to Earth in a spaceship. The story takes place in a suburb of Los Angeles in the USA at the end of the twentieth century. The main characters are the alien and a young boy called Elliott.

At the beginning of the film the little alien is alone on Earth because the spaceship leaves without it. The young boy Elliott finds the alien, takes it into his house and makes friends with it. Elliott lets his brother and sister meet the alien, but he hides it from his mother and other adults because he knows the adults will take the alien away and do experiments on it. Soon the alien learns some English and says it wants to phone home. It manages to send a message into space. But then the alien gets very ill. Scientists and doctors arrive at the house, and they think the alien is dead. But it isn't! Elliott and his brother escape with the alien and they drive off in a van. Then they ride on bicycles to the forest, but police cars chase them. So the alien and the children take off on their bicycles and fly up in the sky over the treetops. That's the part I like best!

At the end of the film, the spaceship comes back for the alien. The children are very sad when they say goodbye to it. Then the little alien returns to the spaceship, and it takes off. The alien finally goes home!

It's an old movie but it's one of the most popular science-fiction films of all time, and I think it's absolutely brilliant!

Optional activity

1.30 Write *Who directed the film? How many Oscars did it win? Where did the story take place? What happens at the end?* on the board. Play the recording again. Students write the answers in their notebooks. Check the answers with the class. (Steven Spielberg, Three, (In a suburb of) Los Angeles, The alien goes home)

4
- Students organise their notes following the structure given.
- Every student in the group chooses one of the two prepared talks and practises it with the group. The group listens and times the talk. They then make suggestions for improvements, e.g. how to make it last the two minutes, how to shorten it so it fits into two minutes, words which are mispronounced, using pauses and intonation for dramatic effect, using the visuals effectively. Monitor and help where necessary.

5
- Each group chooses two students to give the two talks. These two students do a final practice with their group before giving the talk to the whole class. Remind students not to say the title. Ask the rest of the class to listen and, at the end, say what the title is.

Optional activities

- ♦ With a less confident class, students give their talks to small groups within the class.
- ♦ Tell listeners that they have to ask the speaker at least one question about their topic at the end.

POEMS

- The aim is to enable students to be creative with their English while also focusing on the form of the language they are using.
- Ask students to close their books. Tell students you are going to read a poem and they must try to guess the title. Read the first poem and elicit the title *Peace*. Students read the poem in their books.
- In pairs, students make up another verse using the same pattern. First they need to choose a theme, e.g. *English, their country, being a teenager, family*. Set a five-minute time limit. Monitor and help as necessary.
- Ask students to read the second poem. Read it aloud to them. Ask students to suggest other topics they could write about, e.g. *winter, a different country, the sea*. In pairs, students make up another verse. Again, set a five-minute time limit and monitor and help.
- Collect the poems and read some of the best ones aloud. Students listen and guess who wrote them.

REVISION

Lesson 1
Students' own answers

Lesson 2

Suggested answers
The contestants learn to sing, dance and write songs.
The contestants hope to win the competition.
The contestants promise to work together.
Jess asked them not to pretend to be a poet.
Rachel wants them to practise their songs.
Adam can teach them to dance.
The coaches can help them to develop their talents.

Lesson 3

Answers
2 The most films are made in India.
3 The most cars are sold in China.
4 The most coffee is produced in Brazil.
5 The most coffee is drunk in Scandinavia.
6 The most tea is produced in China.
7 The most tea is drunk in Turkey.
8 The most bananas are grown in India.
9 The most rice is grown in China.

EXTENSION

Lessons 1–2
Students' own answers

Lesson 3

Answers
1 made 2 are cut 3(are) sent 4 is chopped
5 are mixed 6 is removed 7 is dried 8 is turned

YOUR CHOICE!

- Organise students into groups depending on their learning style. Each group does the activity which relates to their own learning style.
- Monitor and help groups. You could provide written answers for groups to check their own work.
- Encourage students to experiment with other learning styles and try one of the other activities of their choice.
- Some activities may take less time than others, particularly the structure section. Ask students to write more examples for the rules.

CONSTRUCTION

Answers
1 buy 2 is designed 3 is built 4 come 5 build
6 are made 7 are produced 8 come 9 is flown
10 is put 11 is made 12 is sold

REFLECTION

Answers
infinitive: to phone
gerund: phoning
infinitive, gerund: raining

ACTION

- Organise the students into two teams. Students follow the instructions in the box. Point out that the questions all use the passive.
- The teams ask and answer questions. Point out that if they answer a question correctly, they ask the next question. If they answer incorrectly, they need to answer another one.

INTERACTION

- Divide students into small groups. Suggest students take a few minutes to make their lists. They then take turns to ask and talk about the topics.
  You may now like students to do the song *You've Got A Friend*. See p161 for the notes and p186 for the worksheet.

Language File pp113–114

Workbook Unit 2 Inspiration EXTRA! pp22–23

Song – photocopiable worksheet p186, notes p161

Units 1–2

Optional Aids

Follow-up activity: pieces of blank paper

1 Ask students to look at the photo and the title and find out how much they know about money in their country. For example, *how much does it cost to buy a house?* Give students two minutes to read the text and find out if British teenagers could answer the same question correctly. Students read the text again and choose the appropriate word for each space. Do the first one together as an example. This can be done in pairs or individually as a short test.

Answers

1 B 2 A 3 A 4 B 5 A 6 A 7 C 8 A 9 C 10 A

Optional activity

Confident students can first attempt the task without looking at the word options.

2 Students complete the sentences with the appropriate form of the verb in brackets. Do the first one together as an example.

Answers

1 do … do, go 2 are … feeling 3 does … learn, learns, is learning 4 do … care, do … care 5 do … go, am going 6 is wearing 7 is looking, gets 8 does … have, is … looking

3 In pairs, students tell each other what they can remember about Joni and her holiday in Newquay. Students complete the sentences with the appropriate form of the verbs in the box.

Answers

1 went 2 did … want 3 made 4 did ... like 5 did … spend 6 missed 7 cried ... heard 8 tried

4 In pairs, students tell each other what they can remember about Bethany and the shark attack. Ask students to look at the example. Students complete the sentences with the appropriate form of the verb in brackets.

Answers

1 were waiting, attacked
2 was thinking, saw
3 didn't scream, feel
4 did she ask, was recovering
5 felt, surfed

5 Students complete the sentences with the gerund of the verbs. Do the first one together as an example.

Answers

1 laughing 2 making 3 listening 4 going 5 borrowing, watching 6 having

6 In pairs, students tell each other what they can remember about Star School. Students complete the sentences with the infinitive of the verbs.

Answers

1 to sing 2 to go 3 to become 4 to practise 5 to help 6 to dance

7 Students match the beginnings and endings.

Answers

1 c 2 f 3 a 4 b 5 e 6 d

Optional activity

Students cover the endings. In pairs, students read the beginnings and say how the sentence ends.

8 Students complete the paragraph with the appropriate form of the verb. Do the first two together as examples.

Answers

1 are sold 2 buy 3 are sent 4 are recorded 5 listen 6 are downloaded 7 are read 8 (are) listened

Optional activity

Students discuss *Do you think there will be books in the future?*

VOCABULARY

9 Students complete the sentences with the words in the box.

Answers

1 denim 2 upset 3 warning 4 scream 5 calm 6 handkerchief 7 documentary 8 avoid 9 library 10 bench

Optional activity

Fast finishers mark the stress on the words in the list of more than one syllable

■▪ denim, warning, library
▪■ avoid, upset
■▪▪ handkerchief
▪▪■▪ documentary

10 Confident students can first cover the list of words and try to work out what the definitions refer to.

Answers
1 illegal 2 terrified 3 genius 4 recover 5 obey 6 ambition 7 paperback 8 enthusiastic

Optional activity

Students write definitions for other words. They exchange definitions and guess each other's words.

11 Remind students that it is useful to learn verbs in phrases like these.

Answers
1 fail examinations 2 fall in love 3 go wrong 4 obey rules 5 perform a song 6 tell the truth 7 visit a website 8 wear boots

12 Students choose one word in each group which is different in some way. Ask students to explain their choices. Do the first one together as an example.

Answers
1 brilliant (all the others are negative adjectives)
2 bored (all the others are positive adjectives)
3 hopeful (all the others are negative adjectives)
4 intelligent (all the others describe appearance)
5 routine (all the others are forms of dance)
6 break (all the others are positive/creative)

LEARNER INDEPENDENCE SELF ASSESSMENT

- Explain to students that the aim of the self assessment is to help them check their own progress and take any action necessary to improve. Point out that the list 1–9 covers language from Units 1 and 2.
- Have students look at the table and tick the Fine box for language they feel confident using or put a question mark in the Not sure box if they feel they still have some difficulties.
- Encourage students to look at the Language File and re-do exercises from the lessons, the Revision and Extension section and the Workbook in areas where they have problems.
- Students write an example sentence for each language area in the list. You may like to elicit the language students need for each example before students write sentences, e.g. *Talking about states and regular activities: present simple*. Students can refer back to the lessons and the Language Workout box and Language File.

Follow-up activities

♦ **Game** *Connect Four* Draw this grid on the board:

keep	hope	start	expect
manage	avoid	risk	pretend
feel like	dream	refuse	promise
teach	help	succeed	give up

Divide the class into two teams and give each team a symbol. Team 1 chooses a square and makes a sentence using that verb plus a second verb. If their answer is grammatically correct and makes sense, write their symbol in the appropriate square. If it's incorrect, Team 2 can correct the sentence and win the square. Teams continue taking turns. The first team to connect four squares wins.

♦ **Game** *Taboo* Organise students into teams. Each team has ten blank pieces of paper. At the top of each paper they write a word from Unit 1 or 2. They underline this word and then write three words underneath to describe it, e.g. *Pizza: Italy, cheese, round.* Each team passes its cards to another team. The cards are placed face down on the table. The first student turns over a card and defines the word at the top to his/her team. They cannot use the three words under the line. If the team cannot guess the word, they leave it. The next student then takes a card and so on. The team that successfully defines the most words in three minutes wins.

HOMEWORK

Students prepare a questionnaire on money to ask each other in the next lesson. Elicit possible questions for the questionnaire, e.g. *How much does a kilo of potatoes cost? Do you think money is important in life?*

WEBLINK

Students may like to visit www.bbc.co.uk/arts where they can read more about books and art.

Language File pp112–114

Workbook Review Units 1–2 pp24–25

Units 3–4

Activities		Project	Vocabulary	Optional Aids
Identifying communicative aims Categorising vocabulary	Contextualising listening extracts	Stories from my week	Space Rules and regulations Sounds	Follow-up activity: slips of paper

WARMER 1

If students have prepared their questionnaires on money from the previous lesson, ask them to work in groups of four and ask and answer each other's questions. Each group then reports back to the class with any interesting or surprising facts they learnt.

WARMER 2

Write the phrase *solar system* on the board. Students work in groups of four and make as many words as possible using only the letters in *solar system*, e.g. *least, try, most, early*. They score a point for each correct word they make and the team with the longest word scores an extra five points. The team with the most correct words wins.

WARMER 3

Revise some of the vocabulary from Unit 2 by writing words for adjectives to describe films on the board with the letters in the wrong order, e.g. *CITEINGX* (exciting), *FLAUW* (awful) and *LILIRGTHN* (thrilling). Students work in pairs to unscramble the letters and spell the adjectives correctly. The first pair to spell all the words correctly is the winner.

1
- The aim is to introduce the students to the main areas of communicative language they will cover in Units 3 and 4, and to encourage them to think about the function of the language.
- Explain the task to the class. Students should look at the photos and match them with the communicative aims, using the captions to help them. Point out that there are five pictures and seven communicative aims so two of them are not used.
- Ask students to do the task individually and then compare their answers in pairs. Check the answers with the whole class.

Answers

A 6 B 2 C 4 D 1 E 3

Optional activity

Ask students to work in pairs and think of other things people must or mustn't do when they drive a car. Ask each pair to report their ideas back to the whole class. Examples might include *You must pay attention to other drivers, You must stop when traffic lights are red* and *You mustn't send text messages.*

2
- Explain that the words in the box are related to three different categories. Point out that if students do not know the meaning of one or more words in the box, they should guess what category they go into. Tell students you will explain the meaning of any words they are not sure about when you check the answers.
- This exercise could be done in pairs. Check the answers with the whole class. Write the three categories on the board and invite students to come to the board without their books and write any words they can remember in the correct category.

Answers

space – astronomer, moon, planet, star, universe, world
rules and regulations – allowed, arrested, forbidden, illegal, law, police
sounds – cheer, clap, whistle, laugh, shout, scream

Optional activity

Ask students if they can add one or more words to each of the groups. Possible words include *rocket, sky, galaxy; jail, court, judge; cry, whisper, sing.*

3
- The aim of the activity is for students to contextualise a short listening extract by working out what kind of passage it is extracted from. Explain to students that they should listen for the main gist of each passage and that it does not matter if they do not understand every word.
- Play the recording. Students match each extract 1–3 with the summaries A–C.

1.31 Recording

1

(Extract from Unit 3 Lesson 2, Exercise 3)

GIRL *Right – what do you know about laws in the UK? How old do you have to be to drive a car?*

BOY *Oh, I know that one – you have to be 17.*

GIRL *Yes, that's right – that's when I learnt to drive. What about getting married – when can you get married?*

BOY *Erm, I think people can get married when they're 16.*

2

(Extract from Unit 3 Lesson 4, Exercise 2)

A quarter of the world's population live without electricity, including over 500 million people in Africa alone. However, there's lots of sun in Africa and it's free, so people ought to use its energy. The developing world should use more solar power.

3

(Extract from Unit 4 Lesson 2, Exercise 4)

A doctor is driving home along a quiet country road. It's late at night and it's raining hard. Suddenly he sees a girl walking along the road. She looks like a student.

Answers

1 C 2 A 3 B

Optional activity

1.31 Write *How old do you have to be to get married in the UK? How many people in Africa live without electricity? What was the weather like when the doctor was driving home?* on the board. Play the recording again and ask students to write down the answers. Check the answers with the whole class. (16, 500 million, It was raining hard)

4
- The aim of this activity is to encourage students to use past tense forms to talk about things that happened to them last week, both positive and negative experiences. You could introduce this activity by giving a brief example yourself – for example, something that made you angry (There was a traffic jam when you were driving to school and you were late. This made you very angry).
- Ask students to read the two lists. Check that they understand the task and all the vocabulary. Give them two or three minutes to think about what happened to them and to make a few notes.
- Divide the class into groups of four. Ask each student to tell the other members of their group about two things that happened to them.
- Ask each group to tell another group about anything interesting or surprising they learnt from the members of their group. An alternative is to give each group member a letter (A, B, C, D) and ask all the As to form one group, all the Bs another and so on. Then they should tell their new group what they learnt in their first group.

Stories of My Week Project

- Students use the ten items in the Stories of My Week as the basis of a questionnaire. For example, the first item in the first group is transformed into the question *What made you happy last week?* the first item in the second group to *What kind of surprise did you have last week?*
- Monitor while they are writing and make sure their questions are accurately formed.
- Ask them to interview two members of the class that they didn't work with in the previous activity. Alternatively, this activity could be done as a timed mingling exercise where students stand up, walk around the class and interview as many students as possible in a set time (for example, 10 minutes), noting down their answers.
- Ask them to take notes about their partners' answers and then report back to the rest of the class.

- Books closed. Write the sentence *The quick brown fox jumps over the lazy dog* on the board. Tell the students there is something special about this sentence that is connected with the letters of the alphabet. Elicit suggestions from the class.
- If they cannot work out the answer, ask them to open their books and read the explanation in the Believe it or not! box.

Optional activity

Ask students if they know a sentence in their language that includes every letter of the alphabet.

Follow-up activities

- Students think of three more questions to add to their Stories of My Week project. They then work in pairs and ask and answer the questions.
- Do the activity in Preview 1–2 Follow-up activities on p26 but using the three categories in the vocabulary exercise on page 34 of the Student's Book: space, rules and regulations and sounds.

HOMEWORK

Ask students to use the Stories of My Week questionnaire to interview someone in their family or a friend from another school and to write a short paragraph about their answers.

3.1 OPINIONS

There could be tens of billions of planets

Communicative Aims	Language	Pronunciation	Vocabulary	Optional Aids
Making logical deductions and discussing possibility	*must* and *can't* *could, may* and *might*	Silent letters	Space The solar system	Follow-up activity: a non-transparent bag, small objects

WARMER

Game *Word association* See Unit 2, Lesson 2, p48 for instructions. Start with the word *sky*.

LANGUAGE WORKOUT OPTION

If you want to pre-teach the language students will be using in the following activities, you may like to go to the Language Workout box now.

1 OPENER

- The aim is to introduce the context and some vocabulary for the reading in exercise 2.
- Ask students to look at the photo and elicit that it shows a sun and a planet. Students do the exercise individually and then compare their answers in pairs. Elicit the names of the planets: *Mercury, Venus, Earth, Mars, Jupiter, Saturn, Uranus, Neptune.*

Answers

from biggest to smallest: galaxy, solar system, star, planet

2 READING

- Read the headline and have students predict what the text is about. Elicit suggestions such as *life in other solar systems, aliens, space travel*. Check that students understand the task. Ask them to read the text and write down the fact they find the most surprising. They compare their ideas in pairs and then report back to the class. Students could listen to the text and follow in their books.

1.32 Recording

See text on page 36 of the Student's Book.

3 AFTER READING

- Ask students to read the questions carefully. Be prepared to explain items of vocabulary, especially *up to* (as many as) and *Earth-like* (similar to Earth).
- Ask students to do the exercise individually and then to compare their answers in pairs.

Answers

1 True 2 True 3 True
4 False. They are in our galaxy.
5 No Information
6 False. It's three to four times the size of Earth.
7 True
8 False. It's 20 light years away from Earth.

Your response

Students read the questions, think about their answers and make notes. They discuss the questions in small groups or use the questions for a whole class discussion.

4 SPEAKING

- The aim is to get students to make logical deductions and discuss possibility using *can't be/must be*.
- Write *can't be* and *must be* on the board and encourage students to use these when discussing the questions.
- Look at the table as a class. Ask students to say what the table shows. Note the pronunciation of *Jupiter* /ˈdʒuːpɪtə/ and *Uranus* /ˈjʊərənəs/. Put the students into groups and use the information in the table to answer the questions.

Answers

1 Mars 2 Saturn 3 Venus 4 Uranus 5 Venus

Extension Explain that students should write true or false statements about the solar system using *near* and *far*. Do one example with the class and write it on the board, e.g. *Jupiter is nearer to Mars than to Saturn*. Ask students to work in pairs and read out their sentences in turn. Their partner should say whether the sentences are true or false by checking the information in the table.

5 VOCABULARY

- Students look at definitions 1–6 and match them with a word or phrase from the box.
- Choose students to read definitions out loud and different students to give the word/phrase they describe.
- Drill the vocabulary in chorus for pronunciation.

Answers

1 solar system 2 gravity 3 atmosphere 4 universe
5 galaxy 6 orbit

6 SPEAKING

- Have students work in pairs and discuss what the photos show. Encourage them to use the phrases *It could/may/might be* ... or *It must/can't be ... because ...*

Answers

1 a rocket 2 the moon 3 the sea 4 a space helmet
5 a telescope 6 a light

7 PRONUNCIATION

- Tell students that the words in the box contain silent letters. Give an example of a word containing a silent letter, e.g. *know, knee*. Ask students to work in pairs to identify the silent letters. Tell them to shout *Stop!* when they have found all of them.
- Play the recording, pausing after each word for students to repeat and check which the silent letters are.

1.33 Recording and answers

biscuit could light might scientist white whole

Optional activity

Game *Noughts and crosses* For instructions, see Unit 2, lesson 1, p45 of this book. Test the correct spelling of words from the pronunciation exercise.

8 LISTENING

- Explain the task. Students will hear eight definitions and they should discuss what it could be, using *could be, might be, must be, can't be*. If necessary give an example first, e.g. *It's a machine with four wheels that four or five people travel in. It can't be a bicycle. It must be a car.* Point out that all the items were in exercise 6.
- Play the recording, pausing after each item. Give students time to make notes. When they have heard all the definitions, ask them to work in pairs and discuss what the items are.
- Check the answers by playing the recording again, pausing after each definition and inviting suggestions from the class. Point out that *UFO* is pronounced by saying the individual letters (U – F – O).

1.34 Recording

1 It's a special kind of glass and you can see yourself in it.
2 It's a hard hat that you wear to protect your head.
3 It's a long thin tube and it travels in space.
4 It's a long thin tube, and it makes distant objects look closer and larger.
5 It's a strange object in the sky that no one can identify.
6 It's a flying machine with wings.
7 It looks like sugar but it's cold and falls from the sky.
8 It's a machine that can do work by itself, and sometimes looks like a human.

Answers

1 a mirror 2 a (space) helmet 3 a rocket 4 a telescope 5 a UFO 6 a plane 7 snow 8 a robot

9 WRITING

- In pairs, ask students to think of five other objects and write definitions for them. Tell them they can look at the words in the box in exercise 6 for ideas.
- Students give their definitions to another pair, who guess the words. Encourage them to use *It could/may/might/must/can't be* when discussing possible answers.

LANGUAGE WORKOUT

- Ask students to complete the Language box using either *must* or *can't*.
- Students turn to page 114 of the Language File to check their answers.

Answers

can't must must can't

- Highlight that:
  - *must, can't, could, may* and *might* are all followed by the verb in the infinitive form.
  - when making deductions, *must* shows we feel sure something is true and is the opposite of *can't*, which shows we feel sure something is untrue. We don't use *mustn't* or *can* in this context.
  - *could, may* and *might* all have the same use, to show we think something is possibly true. *Could* does not refer to the past in this context.
- Drill the examples in chorus for pronunciation.

PRACTICE

- Students do Practice exercise 7 on page 114 of the Language File.

Answers

1 must 2 can't 3 can't 4 must 5 can't; must 6 can't; must

Follow-up activity

Game *What's in the bag?* Put random objects like a ruler, a key or an orange into a non-transparent bag. Students put their hand into the bag and guess what the object(s) are, without seeing them.

HOMEWORK

Ask students to think of five to eight words related to *space* and write them in a crossword. They then create a blank crossword grid and write definitions (crossword clues) for their words.

WEBLINK

Students can visit kids.yahoo.com/reference/encyclopedia/entry?id=EurpnSpac to read about space travel.

Revision and Extension p45

Language File p114

Workbook Unit 3 Lesson 1 pp26–27

Photocopiable worksheet p168, notes p155

2 When can you drive a car?

Communicative Aims	Language	Pronunciation	Vocabulary	Optional Aids
Expressing obligation and prohibition	*must* and *mustn't/can't have/has to* and *don't/ doesn't have to* Reflexive pronouns	Syllable stress	Rules and regulations Laws and age limits	Follow-up activity: signs or pictures of signs

WARMER 1

If students did the homework from the previous lesson, they can exchange crosswords with their partner, who tries to complete it correctly according to the definitions.

WARMER 2

Have students imagine they are going on a trip around America. They can choose three different cities/places to visit. They compare their plan with a partner and discuss reasons for their choices and say what they might see and do on the way.

1 OPENER

- The aim is to introduce the context of laws.
- Check first that students understand *break the law* by giving an example of a law in your country and asking *What's the expression for 'doing something illegal/not following the law'?* Ask students to look at the photos and discuss in pairs which laws are being broken. Ask one or two pairs to report back to the rest of the class. The emphasis here is on generating ideas and students may not arrive at the exact answers below at this point, especially as there may be some unknown vocabulary, e.g. *litter, graffiti.*

Answers

You mustn't use a mobile phone while driving.
You mustn't draw graffiti.
You mustn't drop litter.
You mustn't cycle/ride a bike on the pavement.

2 SPEAKING

- The aim is to get the students to discuss laws in their country and the UK, using *can*.
- Tell students they are going to discuss laws in their country. Do the first one as an example as a class, asking students to complete the three sentences about driving a car.
- In pairs, students discuss each law and complete the *Age in my country* column. Ask them to leave the *Age in the UK* column blank for the time being.
- Encourage students to discuss if they feel any of the age limits in their country should be different.

LANGUAGE WORKOUT OPTION

If you want to pre-teach the language students will be using in the following activities, you may like to go to the Language Workout box now.

3 LISTENING

- Ask students if they know any ages for the laws in the UK.
- Play the recording and ask students to complete the *Age in UK* column.

1.35 Recording

GIRL *Right – what do you know about laws in the UK? How old do you have to be to drive a car?*
BOY *Oh, I know that one – you have to be 17.*
GIRL *Yes, that's right – that's when I learnt to drive. What about getting married – when can you get married?*
BOY *Erm, I think people can get married when they are 16.*
GIRL *Yes, but they must have their parents' permission. Otherwise they have to be 18. OK. And how old do you have to be to join the army?*
BOY *Well again, people can join the army at 16, but they must have their parents' permission.*
GIRL *Yes, otherwise they can't join the army until they're 17.*
BOY *17 – it's still very young to be a soldier.*
GIRL *Yes, it is. What about voting? How old do you have to be to vote in an election?*
BOY *You know, I'm not sure … is it 17?*
GIRL *No, you can't vote until you're 18.*
BOY *So you can fight for your country at 17, but you can't vote?*
GIRL *That's right.*
BOY *That's terrible!*
GIRL *How old do you have to be to live by yourself?*
BOY *Erm – I think that's 16, lots of people leave home at 16.*
GIRL *Yes, you're right. And how old do you have to be before you can buy a pet?*
BOY *No idea!*
GIRL *You can't buy a pet until you're 12.*
BOY *That sounds sensible.*
GIRL *And when can you leave school?*
BOY *The school-leaving age is 16, you can't leave until you're 16.*
GIRL *Correct. How old do you have to be to buy a lottery ticket?*

BOY *Erm, is it 18?*
GIRL *No, it's 16, actually.*
BOY *Really?*
GIRL *Yup. What about flying a plane?*
BOY *Flying a plane? Well, is it the same as driving a car?*
GIRL *Yes – it is. You can fly a plane when you're 17. And last question – how old do you have to be to get a part-time job?*
BOY *Oh, I don't know.*
GIRL *You have to be 13 – but you can't work more than two hours a day.*
BOY *That's fine, I don't want to work more than two hours a day!*

Answers

	Age in UK
You can drive a car.	*17*
You can get married.	*16/18*
You can join the army.	*16/17*
You can vote in an election.	*18*
You can live by yourself.	*16*
You can buy a pet.	*12*
You can leave school.	*16*
You can buy a lottery ticket.	*16*
You can fly a plane.	*17*
You can get a part-time job.	*13*

Extension In pairs, students discuss the differences in laws between the UK and their country.

Optional activity

Game *Memory game* In pairs, one student is not allowed to look at the completed table. Their partner tests them by saying an age and a country (UK or their own) and they say something that you *can/can't/have to do* at this age.

Useful information

In the USA, different states have different laws but you can get a driving licence at the age of 16 and you can drive a car at the age of 15 if there is an adult in the car with you. You can't get married until you are 18 and you have to be 18 to vote in a presidential election.

4 SPEAKING

- Ask students to read the questions. Check that they understand all the vocabulary, e.g. *full-time job* and *seat belt*.
- Put students into groups of 3–4 and ask them to discuss the questions. Ask them to report their group's answers to the whole class.

Useful information

Before doing exercise 5, it may be helpful to give students some background information to American law. Although Americans are all governed by US Federal Law, each state has its own constitution and laws, which have a greater influence on daily life. Laws can vary greatly from state to state, in areas such as crime and punishment, health, drugs and education, e.g. serious crimes are punishable with the death penalty in some, but not all, states.

5 READING

- Ask students to look at the photo. Ask them to read the text and find what law the person in the photo is breaking.

1.36 Recording

See text on page 39 of the Student's Book.

Answer

You mustn't cross the road on your hands.

6 AFTER READING

- Ask students to match the questions with the answers, reading the article again to help them.
- Check the answers by asking different students to ask and answer the questions.

Answers

1c 2f 3h 4g 5e 6a

Your response

In pairs, students discuss what they think of the students' holiday plans and any silly laws in their country. Ask them to share their ideas with the whole class.

Optional activities

- ♦ Fast finishers can cover the questions and try to remember them, looking only at the answers.
- ♦ On the board, put key words from the laws in the article e.g. *cheese, golf, lion, fishing*. Books closed, students try to remember the laws from the words.

7 PRONUNCIATION

- On the board, put the example words *factory* and *allowed*. Ask students *How many syllables? Where is the stress?* for each word.
- Ask students to copy the chart into their notebooks. Students say the words in the box quietly to themselves and write them in the correct column according to stress pattern.
- Play the recording, pausing after each word for students to repeat and check their answers.

1.37 Recording and answers

■▪ *factory journey limit ocean partner purpose ticket*
▪■ *allowed arrest asleep avoid himself include intend*

Optional activity

Students add two words to each list, checking in a dictionary if they are unsure of the stress pattern.

8 WRITING

- Ask students to write ten more laws for their country. Encourage them to use their imagination and invent two silly or strange laws. Make sure they use *must/have to*, *mustn't/can't* and *don't have to*.
- Monitor and help with any vocabulary students need.
- Ask students to compare their list with a partner and try to agree on the best and silliest law from their combined lists.

LANGUAGE WORKOUT

- Ask students to complete the Language box using *must* or *mustn't/can't* for the first section and *have to* or *don't have to* for the second. Confident students can complete first and then check, while others can look back at exercises 2 and 3 and then complete.
- Students turn to page 115 of the Language File to check their answers.

Answers

must mustn't/can't mustn't/can't
have to don't have to
have to can't have to
had to

- Highlight that:
  - *must, can* and *can't, have to* and *don't have to* are all followed by the verb in the infinitive form. *Must, can* and *can't* are never followed by *to*.
  - *don't have to* is not the same as *mustn't*. It expresses lack of obligation rather than prohibition.
  - in this context, *mustn't* can be used as the opposite of *must*, unlike when using *must* for deduction in the previous unit.
- Drill the examples in chorus for pronunciation and stress. Encourage students to use the weak form of *to* /tə/.Remind them that the first *t* in *mustn't* is always silent and that the final *t* in can't and *mustn't* is not always fully pronounced. Point out that *have* is usually pronounced with a /f/ sound and not a /v/ sound at the end when followed by *to*.

PRACTICE

- Students do Practice exercise 8 on page 115 of the Language File, writing the sentences on their own. Check the answers by asking individual students to read out what they have written.
- Ask them to work in pairs and discuss which of the laws they think is the strangest and why.
- Students report their ideas back to the whole class.

Answers

1 can't whistle 2 mustn't sing 3 You can't keep
4 have to wear 5 You can't eat 6 have to wear
7 you can't lie down 8 mustn't walk 9 must wear

- Students do Practice exercise 9 on page 115 of the Language File. Students complete the answers on their own and then compare their answers in pairs.
- Check the answers by asking individual students to read out what they have written.

Answers

1 ourselves 2 herself 3 himself 4 yourselves
5 myself 6 yourself

Follow-up activities

- ♦ **Game** *Signs competition* On the board, draw or stick pictures of signs, e.g. road signs, no smoking signs. Write a number next to each one. Divide students into four teams. Teams take turns to choose a number and make a sentence to explain the rule. They get a point for a correct sentence. Remove signs that have been correctly described until all signs have been used.
- ♦ With a confident and mature class, write some more controversial laws on the board e.g. *You can carry a knife. You can't smoke in public places. Shops can open on Sundays.* Put students into groups according to whether or not they agree, so they can prepare a list of their reasons for agreeing/ disagreeing. Students then present their arguments to the other group and debate each issue as a class.

HOMEWORK

Ask students to write a list of what they consider to be 10 important rules for teenagers of their age and their parents. They can be real rules which they have or rules which they would like to have.

WEBLINK

Students may like to visit translationbooth.com/Unusual-Laws/_/page.html for more examples of unusual or funny laws around the world.

Revision and Extension p45

Language File p115

Workbook Unit 3 Lesson 2 pp28–29

Photocopiable worksheet p169, notes p156

3 You should calm down!

Communicative Aims	Language	Pronunciation	Vocabulary	Optional Aids
Giving advice	*Should/ought to* and *shouldn't* *had better (not)* Adjective + infinitive	/æ/ s**a**d /e/ s**ai**d	School life Teenage problems Adjectives for opinions Phrasal verbs with *down*	Warmer 2: a teen magazine Follow-up activity: large pieces of paper, pairs of scissors

WARMER 1

Game *Adjectives alphabet* Divide the class into four teams and have each group write the letters of the alphabet on a piece of paper vertically. Teams have five minutes to think of one adjective beginning with each letter of the alphabet and write it next to the letter on their page.

WARMER 2

Bring a teenage magazine into class, either in English or your own language, and elicit from the students what they expect to find inside, e.g. *celebrity interviews, horoscopes, song lyrics, problem page*. Put students into pairs to discuss if they read these magazines, which ones and which sections they like/dislike.

1 OPENER

- The aim is to pre-teach and recycle vocabulary for the reading in exercise 2 and help students to predict the content of the text.
- Check that students are familiar with teenage problem pages by asking *Who can teenagers turn to for help with their problems? Have you seen these online?* Ask students to work in pairs to guess which of the words in the box will be in the problem page. Be prepared to explain *bullying, cheating, concentrate* and *marks*.

Answers

bullying, cheating, concentrate, diet, embarrassed, mood, panic

2 READING

- Ask students to read the messages and match the problems with the advice, looking out for any of the words that were in exercise 1 as they read.
- Encourage students to guess the meaning of unfamiliar vocabulary from context and ask *What does … mean?*
- Play the recording to check the answers, and also ask students if they found any words from exercise 1.

1.38 Recording

Lara
It's about my best friend. Her mood changes so quickly. One minute she's happy and cheerful, and the next she's really sad and depressed. It's hard for her to concentrate for long – she often lies down on her bed and falls asleep. I don't want to panic, but I'm really worried about her. What should I do?
D
I think you should calm down! It's quite normal for teenagers' moods to change rapidly. It doesn't always mean that something is wrong. It's helpful to talk about things, so why don't you sit down with her and have a chat? If she doesn't want to talk, perhaps you ought to have a word with her parents.
Sam
I get good marks at school, so my friends all want to copy my homework. But I spend a lot of time working while they're having fun. It's not fair, and I'm getting fed up with it. But how do I tell them they can't copy my work? I don't want to lose my friends – help!
B
Your friends ought to know that they shouldn't copy your work. It's cheating and they'd better not do it any more. The next time they ask, say 'No' nicely but firmly. Explain that they have to do the work themselves or they won't learn anything. If they don't understand, they aren't real friends.
Joe
Two older boys at my school are bullying me. Every time I see them they say something rude. They tell other people lies about me and they send me horrible text messages – the last one said: 'Everyone hates you'. I don't want to go to school because I can't take it any more. What should I do?
A
You'd better tell a teacher or your parents about the text messages at once – cyber bullying is very serious. But try not to show the bullies that you are upset or angry – I know it's difficult, but you should try to ignore them.
Abbie
I know lots of people would like to have my 'problem', but I'm so upset and miserable. I'm really thin and I can't put on weight. It doesn't matter how much I eat, I still stay the same. I'm too embarrassed to talk to my friends about it – they'll just think it's funny.

C

Take it easy and don't worry so much! It's silly to get stressed about something you can't change. Of course, it's sensible to make sure that you eat a balanced diet. But for some people it's more or less impossible to put on weight.

Answers

Lara – D Sam – B Joe – A Abbie – C

Optional activity

1.38 Play the recording again sentence by sentence for students to repeat for pronunciation practice.

3 AFTER READING AND LISTENING

- Ask the students to work in pairs to identify the correct person for questions 1–8. Make this into a competition by asking students to shout *Stop!* when they have answered all the questions. Check the answers by asking the fastest pair to read them to the class. Encourage students to identify where the answers can be found in the text. Be prepared to explain *ignore* and *cyber bullying*.

Answers

1 Joe (I don't want to go to school any more)
2 Lara (why don't you sit down with her and have a chat?)
3 Sam (say no nicely but firmly)
4 Joe (try to ignore them and walk away)
5 Lara (You ought to have a word with her parents)
6 Abbie (Take it easy and don't worry so much)
7 Sam (I spend a lot of time working)
8 Abbie (They'll just think it's funny)

Your response

Students discuss in pairs which is the most serious problem and whether or not they agree with the advice. If they don't agree with the advice, what alternative advice would they give?

4 PRONUNCIATION

- Highlight the /æ/ sound in *sad* and the /e/ sound in *said*.
- Play the recording and ask students to listen and repeat. Highlight that the mouth shape is more relaxed for /æ/, while the sides of the mouth are pulled outwards for /e/.

1.39 Recording

/æ/ *sad and bad had sand sat*
/e/ *said end bed head send set*

- Ask students to listen and write down the words they hear in their notebooks.
- Ask students to compare what they have written in pairs.
- To check the answers, nominate different students to say each word and spell it. Write their spelling on the board and ask other students if they agree.

1.39 Recording and answers

end bad had send set

5 SPEAKING

- The aim of this activity is for students to give their opinions using phrases like *It's difficult to* …, *It's rude to* … and so on.
- On the board, put an example of the adjective + infinitive pattern from the text, but leave a gap for the adjective and elicit what it was, e.g. *It's* ______ *to have a regular routine* (helpful). Highlight the pattern for the students, drill the example in chorus, encouraging students to produce the weak forms of *to* /tʊ/. Ask students to work in pairs to make similar sentences using the adjectives from the box and the phrases. Remind students that they can express a different opinion from their partner by using another adjective, or agree with them using *So do I*.
- Ask confident students to report back on their opinions to the rest of the class and encourage other students to express their agreement or disagreement.

6 VOCABULARY

- Explain that the problem page messages contained different phrasal verbs, e.g. *calm down, lie down, sit down*. Ask students to complete the sentences using the phrasal verbs in the box. Encourage students to look back through the lesson to try to find these phrasal verbs if they are unclear about their meaning. Point out that in sentence 3, the phrasal verb is separated because of the word *it* – we cannot say *turn down it*.

Answers

1 slow down 2 lie down 3 turn it down 4 calm down 5 write down 6 sit down

Extension Have the student work in pairs and see how many other phrasal verbs with *down* they can think of.

LANGUAGE WORKOUT OPTION

If you want to pre-teach the language students will be using in the following activities, you may like to go to the Language Workout box now.

7 SPEAKING

- Ask a student to read number 1 as an example and elicit possible sentences from other students, encouraging use of a range of structures from the Language Workout box to say what should be done.
- In pairs, students make similar sentences for the other situations.

Suggested answers

1 You should tell your friend not to steal again.
2 You should lie and say you like it.
3 You'd better not keep it. You should take it to the police.
4 You ought to/should ask her to change it for another colour.
5 You ought to/should tell Maria.

8 WRITING

- Ask students to write a note describing a problem and asking for advice. Remind them that it does not need to be a real problem they have. Encourage them to look back at those in exercise 2 for ideas, and highlight useful language for asking for advice, e.g. *What should I do? What can I do? Help!*
- Give students a few minutes to check their message for language, spelling and capital letters.
- Students then exchange their message with another student, read the message and write a reply giving helpful advice. Remind students to look back at the advice in exercise 2 and to try to include some of the advice expressions from the Language Workout box, the adjective + infinitive pattern and imperatives, e.g. *explain, try not to …*

LANGUAGE WORKOUT

- Ask students to complete the Language box using *should/ought to/shouldn't* or *had better*. Confident students can complete first and then check, while others can look back at exercises 2 and 3 and then complete.
- Students turn to page 115 of the Language File to check their answers.

Answers

should shouldn't should ought to
better better not

- Highlight that:
  - all the forms give advice/suggestions.
  - *should, ought to* and *had better* are all followed by the verb in the infinitive form. *Should* and *had better* are never followed by *to*.
  - *should* is more frequent than *ought to*, but the meaning is the same.
  - *had better* is used when something is important now. The contraction *'d* is common, representing *had*, not *would*.
  - the negative form of *had better* is *had better not*. We never say *hadn't better*.
- Ask students *Which is stronger: should or must?* to check understanding.
- Drill the examples in chorus for pronunciation and stress.

PRACTICE

- Students do Practice exercise 10 on page 115 of the Language File.

Answers

1 *You should do revision for your exams.*
2 *He was rude to his parents and he ought to say sorry.*
3 *It's nearly midnight – you had better go to bed.*
4 *You shouldn't wear uncomfortable shoes.*
5 *You had better not be late for school tomorrow.*
6 *You ought to listen to your teacher.*

Follow-up activity

Divide the students into groups of five. Give each group a large sheet of paper folded in half and a title, e.g. *school/study problems, problems on holiday*. In groups they brainstorm problems in their category and make a list on one half of the paper. They then give their paper to another group, who think of possible solutions and write them on the other half of the paper. Groups receive their original paper back and read their advice. They then cut up the paper, each piece containing either one problem or one solution. They pass the pieces to a different group, who read and match problems with solutions.

HOMEWORK

Ask students to imagine that they doing an exchange with an English student, who is coming to stay with them for a week. Students write an email to their exchange partner, offering advice about things they should bring, behaviour/local customs etc.

WEBLINK

Students may like to visit teenadvice.about.com/mlibrary.htm for advice on typical problems for teenagers.

Revision and Extension p45

Language File p115

Workbook Unit 3 Lesson 3 pp30–31

Photocopiable worksheet p170, notes p156

4 Integrated Skills
Discussing facts and opinions

Skills
Reading Comparing the language of fact and opinion: *Global Issues*
Listening Noting details about saving energy
Speaking Interview
Writing Expressing opinions about saving energy

Learner Independence
Learning contracts
Word creation: adjective prefixes: *il-*, *im-* and *in-*

Vocabulary
Poverty and aid
Energy-saving
Useful expressions

WARMER 1

Game *Sit down* Ask all the students to stand up. Go round the class, asking each student to say the name of a country. Students who can't think of a country within three seconds or who repeat a country that has already been named, must sit down and are out of the game. Continue round the students as many times as necessary until there is only one student left standing – the winner. With a large class, this could be played in smaller groups.

WARMER 2

Game *Alphabet game* Put the students into groups of four. Ask each group to choose one person who will write. They should write a noun beginning with each letter of the English alphabet. The other students in the group help by suggesting words and how to spell them. The first team to write down 26 correct words is the winner.

1 OPENER

- The aim is to set the context for the reading.
- Ask students to work in pairs and agree on the answers to the questions. Play the recording so the students can check their answers. Find out which pair has the most correct answers. Ask them which fact is the most surprising and which is the most shocking.
- Ask students to look at the photo on page 42 and describe what they can see and where they think these children are.

1.40 Recording

1 The population of the world today is seven billion.
2 The population of the world in 2050 will be nine billion.
3 A billion children in the world live in poverty.
4 150 million 5 to 14-year-olds in the developing world work for a living.
5 100 million children get no primary education.
6 80% of all illness in the world is caused by dirty drinking water.

Answers

1 C 2 C 3 C 4 C 5 C 6 C

2 READING

- Write the words *fact* and *opinion* on the board and ask the students what the difference is. Elicit that a fact is something that is true and an opinion is what someone thinks. Have them read the text and decide which statements are facts and which are opinions.
- Ask one or two confident students to identify facts/opinions and ask how they reached their decision.
- Ask students to make a list of the verbs which indicate opinions rather than facts.
- You could ask students to listen to the text as they follow in their books.

1.41 Recording

See text on page 42 of the Student's Book.

Answers

Income
The first statement is a fact, the second an opinion.
Children
The first statement is an opinion, the second a fact.
Water
The first statement is an opinion, the second a fact.
Energy
The first statement is a fact, the second an opinion.

3

- Ask students to work in pairs and discuss which of the facts in the text are surprising and why. Ask them to share their ideas with the whole class.

4

- Ask students to read the examples of language used in facts and opinions and decide which refer to facts and which to opinions. Explain that opinions are also indicated by: the use of some adjectives, e.g. *successful*, *incredible*, the use of phrases like *a lot of*, *not enough* and other phrases, e.g. *In my opinion*, *I agree*.

Answers

Facts: statistics
Opinions: pronouns like I and we; verbs like should and ought to; words like agree, believe and think

Optional activity

Ask students to close their books. Put some numbers from the text on the board, e.g. *$10 a day, 500 million*. Then read information from the text, e.g. *the number of people in Africa without electricity*, and ask students to guess which number goes with it.

5 LINKING WORDS

- Ask the students to find examples of *however* in the text. (One in *Income*, one in *Water* and one in *Energy*)
- Highlight that:
  - *however* expresses a contrast, like *but*.
  - *however* is more formal than *but* and more common in writing than speaking.
  - *however*, unlike *but*, is often placed at the beginning of a sentence, where it is followed by a comma.
- Students complete the text with *however* and *and*.
- Check the answers as a class.

Answers

1 and 2 However 3 and 4 However 5 and 6 However

6 LISTENING

- Before students read or listen, write on the board *How you can save energy* and elicit any ideas from students about the likely content of the list.
- Ask students to read the text and try to guess any of the words or types of word which may go in the spaces, e.g. *It's a number.*
- Play the recording for students to listen and complete.
- Check the answers together as a class, writing them on the board to check spelling.

1.42 Recording and answers

You can make a difference!

How can you make a difference to the world? You can save energy!

1 *Switch off the lights when you leave a* ***room****.*

2 *When you make hot drinks, just boil the water you need. In a* ***week*** *you can save enough energy to light your house for a* ***day****.*

3 *Run the washing machine at 40°Celsius not 60°Celsius and use a* ***third*** *less energy.*

4 *Turn down the heating in your house by 1°Celsius – it will cost* ***10%*** *less!*

5 *Turn your TV, radio or DVD player off at the wall. When you leave them on standby, it uses 10–****60*** *% more electricity.*

6 *Walk, cycle or, if you must, take the* ***bus*** *to school. Don't let your parents drive you – be impolite and say 'no'!*

7 *Buy local food, not fruit or vegetables from the other side of the* ***world****.*

8 *Think before you fly. A New York-Paris return flight gives out about* ***1.5*** *tonnes of CO_2 (a greenhouse gas) per passenger.*

Optional activity

1.42 With a less confident class, write all the words/numbers for the gaps in a jumbled order on the board before the students listen. Have them guess which word goes in which gap and listen to check.

7 SPEAKING

- Explain the task to students. They should transform the statements into questions. You may need to do one more example to help them, e.g. *2 Do you just boil the water you need when you make hot drinks?*
- Give students time to copy the questions into their notebooks with space to note the replies of two students.
- Put the students into groups of three to ask and answer the questions. Monitor and help where necessary.

8 GUIDED WRITING

- Ask students to read the different ways of expressing opinions. Encourage them to use them when writing their paragraph and to use *however* and *and* to link ideas. Explain that they can also use the information in exercise 6 to help them.
- Monitor and help with any vocabulary students need. If possible, make sure at this stage that their writing is accurate.
- Ask students to work in pairs and read their partner's paragraph.

9 LEARNER INDEPENDENCE

- The aim is to encourage students to acknowledge the rights and responsibilities of teachers and students and use language from lessons 1–3, as well as expressions of opinion.
- Introduce the idea of classroom rights, asking students who has rights in the classroom and eliciting students and teachers.
- Ask a confident student to read out loud the sentence *It is a good idea …* and elicit from students why a class contract could be useful.
- Highlight the example rules given for students and teachers and tell students that they can keep or change these, but should also add more rules for both.
- Give students five minutes to write down their ideas in pairs. Then join pairs together into groups of four to tell each other their ideas and try to come to agreement within their group about what to include in the contract. Repeat this procedure, joining groups of four students into groups of eight to again present their ideas and try to reach agreement within their larger group. Continue to group students into progressively larger groups until the whole class is working together. You could have a class vote on the final points to include in the contract, with rules being accepted if the majority vote for them and the teacher agrees.

Optional activity

Groups of students make posters of their suggested class contract. They then read other groups' suggestions and add their signature at the bottom of the poster if they agree with all the points.

10 WORD CREATION

- Write the following sentence on the board: *I agree that it's an in/il/im/perfect world.* Ask students if they can remember the correct prefix, encouraging them to look back at the *Income* section of the text on p42 to check. Check that they understand *imperfect* is the opposite of *perfect*.
- Students choose the correct prefix, *il-*, *in-*, or *im-* to make the opposites of the words in the box. Be prepared to translate *logical* and *visible* if necessary.
- Students can check back in the book or in dictionaries, before checking as a class.
- Ask students to copy the words into their vocabulary notebooks.

Answers

incorrect incredible illegal illogical imperfect impolite impossible invisible

- Ask students if they can see any repeated patterns in the use of the prefixes. Highlight the use of *il-* with the adjectives beginning with *l* and *im-* for those with *p*.
- Students use the words to complete the sentences.
- Check the answers as a class, drilling examples in chorus for pronunciation and stress.

Answers

1 illegal 2 incredible 3 invisible 4 impossible 5 incorrect 6 illogical 7 impolite 8 imperfect

Optional activity

With a confident class, elicit any other negative prefixes that they know, e.g. *un-, anti-, non-, dis-* (refer students back to Unit 1, Lesson 4 on p17) and ask students to suggest example words for each.

11 PHRASEBOOK

- Play the recording for the students to listen and repeat the expressions.
- Students look through Unit 3 to find the expressions, noting how they are used.
- Students find which expressions go with meanings 1–4. Remind them that there may be more than one expression for each meaning.

1.43 Recording

In other words … (L1, Ex2)
You aren't allowed to … (L2, Ex5)
What should I do? (Lara L3, Ex2)
It's not fair. (Sam L3, Ex2)
I'm getting fed up with it. (Sam L3, Ex2)
I can't take it any more. (Joe L3, Ex2)
Take it easy. (agony aunt L3, Ex2)

Answers

1 Take it easy.
2 What should I do?
3 I'm getting fed up with it/I can't take it any more.
4 You aren't allowed to.

Optional activities

- ♦ Students think of a situation in which they might say each expression, e.g. *Take it easy: to someone who is angry about something.*
- ♦ Students can add expressions which they like to their Personal Phrasebook. Be ready to help with explanation as necessary.

Follow-up activity

Students make an advertising poster for ways of saving energy. They should include some of the facts from Exercise 6 on page 43 and any other ideas they may have. They can illustrate their posters with drawings or photos taken from magazines or the Internet. The class could vote on which is the most effective poster and the best posters could be displayed in the classroom.

HOMEWORK

Ask students to write a short paragraph explaining how they are going to try and save energy at home.

WEBLINK

Students may want to find out more about saving energy at www.loseyourexcuse.gov

Revision and Extension p45

Workbook Unit 3 Lesson 4 pp32–33

Inspiration EXTRA!

LANGUAGE LINKS

- Explain the task. Students should find the names for different sections of a menu in each of the five languages and group them together. For example, *starters* in English goes with *Vorspeisen* in German. To complete this group, students must find the word for starters in French, Italian and Spanish.
- Ask students to work in pairs to complete the exercise.
- Check the answers by asking stronger students to read out the groups to the class. Correct errors of pronunciation in the English words but don't worry if they make mistakes in the pronunciation of the terms in the other languages. Note the pronunciation and word stress of desserts /dɪ'zɜːts/.

Answers

Starters, Hors D'oeuvres, Vorspeisen, Antipasti, Entremeses
Fish, Poissons, Fischgerichte, Pesce, Pescados
Meat, Viandes, Fleischgerichte, Carne, Carnes
Vegetables, Légumes, Gemüse, Contorno, Verduras
Desserts, Desserts, Nachspeisen, Dolci, Postres

- Ask students to categorise the words in the box according to the menu section they belong to. Have them complete this task individually and then compare their answers in pairs.
- To check the answers, write the headings for each language on the board and ask students to come to the board and write words under the correct headings.

Answers

Starters – soup, Fish – trout, Meat – ham, Vegetables – potatoes, Desserts – ice cream
Hors d'oeuvres – soupe, Poisson – truite, Viandes – jambon, Légumes – pommes de terre, Desserts – glace
Vorspeisen – Suppe, Fischgerichte – Forelle, Fleischgerichte – Schinken, Gemüse – Kartoffeln, Nachspeisen – Eis
Antipasti – minestra, Pesce – trota, Carne – prosciutto, Contorno – patate, Dolci – gelato
Entremeses – sopa, Pescados – trucha, Carnes – jamon, Verduras – patatas, Postres – helado

PUZZLE

- Explain that the students are going to solve a puzzle, using clues to work out information about the jobs, pets and favourite activities of five different people.
- Check that the students understand the jobs, pets and activities in the boxes by asking questions like *Which job do you do in a hospital? Which activities can you do in the sea?*
- Ask students to read the clues, discuss them in pairs and complete the chart. Remind them that they can use *must* or *can't* to make guesses when they feel sure and *might, may* or *could* when they don't feel sure, as in the examples. Check that they know that Alice, Claudia and Elena are the women.
- Check the answers as a class, asking students to use *must* or *can't* now that they are sure, and to give a reason from the clues, e.g. *Ben must be a nurse because he works in a hospital.*

Answers

Name	*Job*	*Pet*	*Activity*
Alice	*artist*	*snake*	*riding*
Ben	*nurse*	*dog*	*swimming*
Claudia	*scientist*	*rabbit*	*dancing*
Dave	*reporter*	*cat*	*surfing*
Elena	*politician*	*goldfish*	*skiing*

Optional activity

Game *Guess what?* In pairs, students think of a person, place or thing. They then write eight clues about it, e.g. *It's round, it's made of metal, it has two different sides.* The order of the clues should make it progressively easier to guess what it is. Students then work in small groups. They give the first clue and the other students speculate about what it might be, e.g. *It might be a clock, it could be a ball.* They continue giving clues until one student guesses correctly. This student wins a point.

SKETCH SIGN LANGUAGE

- The aim is for students to enjoy using their English while also getting valuable stress and intonation practice.
- Ask the students to look at the cartoon and establish that the sketch is set in Downing Street, where the British Prime Minister lives, which is guarded by police. Check understanding of *No Entry* by asking *Can you go in?*
- With a more confident class, play the recording with books closed. Then play it again with books open. With a less confident class, play the recording once while the students follow in their books, and then once again with books closed.

1.44 Recording

See text on page 44 of the Student's Book.

- Check that the students understand the joke that *can* is used to express both ability and permission, and that *Police No Entry* could have two possible meanings for who is not allowed to enter.
- Divide the class into two equal groups and play the recording again, with one group repeating in chorus as Man and the other group as Officer. Encourage students to exaggerate stress and intonation.
- Ask the students to close their books and play the recording again. Then ask the students to work in pairs and read the sketch aloud. Choose several pairs to act out the sketch in front of the class.

REVISION

Lesson 1

Answers

2 It must be a dictionary. It can't be a newspaper.
3 It must be an elephant. It can't be a mouse.
4 It must be a motorbike. It can't be a car.
5 It must be a helicopter. It can't be a train.

Lesson 2

Answers

You can't fall asleep in a cheese factory in South Dakota – you have to stay awake.
You can't/mustn't play golf in the streets of Albany, New York.
You mustn't take a lion to the cinema in Baltimore.
You can't/mustn't go fishing in your pyjamas in Chicago.
You can't/mustn't sleep on top of a refrigerator in Pennsylvania.
You can't drive round the town square in Oxford, Mississippi more than 100 times.

Lesson 3

Suggested answers

You ought to calm down. You ought to/should sit down with her and have a chat. You ought to have a word with her parents.
You ought to/should say no nicely but firmly to your friends. You ought to/should explain that they have to do the work themselves.
You ought to/should try to walk away. You should tell your parents or a teacher about it if the bullying continues. You should try to ignore them.
You should take it easy. You shouldn't get stressed about something you can't change. You should eat a balanced diet.

EXTENSION

Lesson 1
Student's own answers

Lesson 2
Student's own answers

Lesson 3

- Refer students to the expressions for giving advice in Unit 3, Lesson 3.

Suggested answers

I think you should join a club to meet other people who have the same interests as you. You ought to try chatting to the person who sits next to you in class.
You should ask your parents to introduce you to their friends' sons and daughters.
You should join an Internet chat room.

YOUR CHOICE!

- Divide the class into groups according to their learning style to do the relevant activity.
- Monitor and help groups. Check answers if necessary.
- Encourage students to experiment with other learning styles and try one of the other activities of their choice.

CONSTRUCTION

- Students complete the gaps with *must, mustn't* or *don't have (to).*

Answers

1 must 2 must 3 don't have 4 must 5 must
6 don't have 7 mustn't 8 don't have 9 must
10 mustn't

REFLECTION

- Students match the examples a–e with the language functions 1–5.

Answers

1 b 2 e 3 a 4 c 5 d

ACTION

- Divide students into three groups.
- Students then follow the instructions in the box, taking it in turns to think of and mime using their object. Remind them that they cannot speak, although they can make noises.
- The other students in their group guess what the object is, making sentences like the examples.

INTERACTION

- Divide students into small groups.
- Check that students understand that *a fortnight* is two weeks. Then ask students to plan their ideal fortnight's holiday, deciding on all the points mentioned in the box. Remind students to use language to express opinions from Unit 3, Lesson 4.
- Students could report back to the rest of the class on their final decisions.

WEBLINK

Students may want to see more examples of funny and interesting signs at www.flickr.com/photos/chris_radley/sets/72157622076190561/

Language File pp114–115

Workbook Unit 3 Inspiration EXTRA! pp34–35

Good reads

Useful information

Gandhi was one of the world's most famous civil rights campaigners. He was born in 1869 in India and was a key figure in the fight for India's independence from Britain.

Live and Let Die is the second novel in the James Bond series of novels, written by Ian Fleming. It was first published in 1954 and was made into a film in 1973, with Roger Moore appearing as James Bond for the first time.

The Sign of Four was written by Sir Arthur Conan Doyle in 1890. It was the second of the numerous stories which he wrote about fictional detective, Sherlock Holmes. It, too, has been made into a film version.

Persuasion is Jane Austen's final novel, written in 1816. It was adapted for the TV by the BBC in 1995 and again in 2007.

1 READING

- Ask students to look at the book covers/titles of the four books on pages 46 and 47 and find out if they know anything about the books and their authors or if they have seen any of the books in film version.
- Ask students to read the profiles of the four teenagers. Explain the task. They should read the short summaries of each book and decide which book is most suitable for each teenager.
- When they have made their decisions, they should compare their answers in pairs, discussing any differences.
- You could have students listen to the recording as they follow the text in their books.

1.45 Recording

See text on pages 46–47 of the Student's Book.

Answers

Alesha B   Maria C   Kazuo A   Paolo D

2 LISTENING

- Tell students that they are going to listen to extracts from three of the books. Their task is to identify which books the extracts are from.
- Ask students to compare their answers with a partner. Then check the answers as a class.

1.46 Recording

1

Captain Wentworth had just returned from sea and was ready to marry. He was rich and was now looking for a wife.

'A little beauty and a few smiles, and I will be a lost man,' he laughed to his sister, when she asked him what kind of wife he wanted. But his sister knew that he was a good man. She knew that other things were more important to him.

'I would like a woman with a strong mind and a gentle character,' he said, more seriously now. 'That is the kind of woman I want.'

2

There were many people outside the theatre. Everyone was meeting friends and going in to see the play. We waited. Suddenly a small dark man appeared.

'Are you Miss Morstan and her friends?' he asked.

'Yes,' she said.

'You must promise me that these men are not policemen,' said the stranger.

'They are not policemen,' replied Miss Morstan.

'Then come with me,' said the man.

We passed through so many streets that I was very soon lost. I had no idea where we were going. I was feeling nervous and Miss Morstan's face looked white. Sherlock Holmes was calm.

At last we stopped. We were outside a house in a dark quiet street. It had only one light in the kitchen window. There were no lights in any of the other houses in the street.

3

Bond saw the head of a huge fish come out of the water. It dived down onto something. There was a long and terrible scream, then two arms suddenly went up into the air and disappeared again.

Two men started to swim towards the reef. One stopped, his hands splashing the water wildly before they disappeared under the waves. He began to scream as he was attacked under the water. The other man was getting nearer to Bond and Solitaire. Bond saw a large head with blood pouring down over its face. It was Mr Big. His eyes were wide open and he was staring madly as he swam towards Bond.

Answers

1 C   2 D   3 B

Optional activities

- Write the names of the four books on the board and ask students if they can remember any characters from each. Write the names they give and add any others they forget. Then dictate examples of direct speech from the novel extracts/recordings for students to write down, e.g. *We shall go tonight to the Lyceum*. Students then compare their sentences in pairs for accuracy and spelling and discuss which novel they came from and which character said each sentence.
- Students work in groups to act out a scene from one of the books. First they should write a script from the information in the extracts, then assign roles and perform their extract for other students.

3 SPEAKING

- In pairs, students tell each other which of the four books they would most like to read. Encourage them to give reasons for their preferences.
- Ask one or two confident students to report their own or their partner's opinion to the rest of the class. You could take a class vote on the most popular book.

Optional activities

- If you have copies of Macmillan Readers *Ghandi, The Sign of Four, Live and Let Die* or *Persuasion*, students could borrow their favourite and read it at home.
- Ask students to write a paragraph about their favourite character from the four books. They should include any information they know about their character from the extracts, adjectives to describe the character and reasons why they found this character interesting.

4 MINI-PROJECT READING SURVEY

- Explain the task to the class and check that students understand all the vocabulary, especially *graphic novels* (novels written in comic book form with pictures).
- Divide the class into groups of four and ask them to record the answers for their group. Ask each group to report their findings to another group. Then ask the groups to report back to the whole class. Record their answers on the board, e.g. *the number of books each student reads each month*. Work out the average number for the class. Find out which of the nine categories of books is the most popular and which is the least popular. Ask students to explain why they like some of the authors they have chosen.

WEBLINK

Students can find resources related to the four books and details of how to buy Macmillan Reader versions at www.macmillanreaders.com

Workbook Culture pp36–37

1 She saw furniture moving

Communicative Aims	Language	Pronunciation	Vocabulary	Optional Aids
Describing what you can see and hear Describing a picture Listening to a story in sounds	Verbs of perception + present participle *can/could* + verbs of perception	/eə/ hair /ɪə/ hear	Sensations and sounds	Warmer 2: slips of paper with names of famous dead people Follow-up activity: DVD clips, DVD player and television

WARMER 1

In groups, students note ten words they have learnt recently. Allow them to look back at previous units and look at their notebooks. Write all their words on the board. In groups, students then make a story using at least five of the words on the board. Set a five-minute time limit. Students tell the class their story. Hold a class vote to decide which story is the best.

WARMER 2

Game *Twenty Questions* Write the names of famous dead people on cards/slips of paper. Choose people who your students will know. Organise students into groups of three or four. Each student in the group has a card with a different name on it. The student must not say the name on their card. The rest of the group asks questions to try to find out who they are. The student can only answer *yes* or *no*. The group are allowed a maximum of twenty questions before guessing who the person is.

1 OPENER

- The aim is to set the context for the reading comprehension.
- Ask students to look at the picture. Ask *What is happening to these objects?* and *What could be the cause?*
- Ask students to read the story headline. Check that they understand the verb *knock*. If necessary, demonstrate by knocking on a desk or on the classroom door.
- Students look at the list of words and predict which ones will be in the text. Listen to their suggestions but do not correct them at this point.

2 READING

- Students read and listen to the article and check their predictions from exercise 1.

2.01 Recording

See text on page 48 of the Student's Book.

Answers

bruise family fright haunted hear investigate move psychic strange video

3 AFTER READING

- Students read and listen to the article again and choose the best answer for the questions. Ask them to note the words in the article that help them decide on their answers. Encourage them to guess the meaning of unfamiliar vocabulary from context.

Answers

1 A 2 A 3 C 4 B 5 B 6 C 7 A 8 C

Optional activities

- Fast finishers write sentences to describe five strange things that happened in the house using a different verb in each sentence, e.g. *A hairbrush flew through the air.*
- Focus on some of the vocabulary in the text, especially *haunted* (a haunted house has a ghost in it), *float, play back, code* and *bruise*.

LANGUAGE WORKOUT OPTION

If you want to pre-teach the language students will be using in the following activities, you may like to go to the Language Workout box now.

Your response

Students discuss the question in pairs. Ask a few students to report back to the class on their discussion. If students say that they do not believe in ghosts, ask them to explain what happened in the house in the story in exercise 2.

4 SPEAKING

- Ask students to look at the picture and say what they can see. Refer them to the examples and the need for a complete sentence beginning with *I can see*, e.g. *I can see a boy juggling.* Students continue in pairs. Monitor and help as necessary.
- The exercise could also be done as a competition with the pair that makes the most sentences being the winners.

Suggested answers

I can see …
a boy skateboarding
a man singing
a group playing instruments
some boys playing football
some children swimming
a girl flying a kite
a man walking a dog

Optional activities

- With a less confident group, allow students time to look up/ask about the vocabulary they will need.
- Fast finishers look out of the window of the classroom (or imagine they are looking out of a window in the school) and say what they can see and hear.
- Students work in pairs. One student closes his/her book and tells the other student as many things as possible that he/she saw in the picture. Then students swap roles and repeat the activity.

5 LISTENING

- Tell students the words in the box are all sounds. Ask students to look at the words and encourage them to ask each other *What does … mean?* if any of the words are unfamiliar. Be prepared to demonstrate/provide a situation for *a door bangs*, *cheer* and *clap*.
- Tell students they are going to hear one of the sounds. Students listen and tell their partner what they can hear. Do the first one together as an example. Play the recording and pause after each sound for students to answer. Monitor and re-play any sounds which the students have difficulty identifying.
- Elicit what is happening in the sequence of sounds. If students have problems guessing the context, tell them it's a wedding (in a church).

2.02 Recording

Man and woman running and getting into car.
Car starting and driving off fast.
Tyres screaming as car stops.
Car doors open and are slammed shut.
Male and female feet running along gravel path and up steps.
Big heavy creaking wooden door opening.
Organ music – 'Here comes the bride'.
Church bells ringing.
People clapping and cheering.
Car driving off amid 'Byes'.

Answers

A I can hear people running.
B I can hear a car starting.
C I can hear a car stopping.
D I can hear a door opening.
E I can hear a door closing.
F I can hear people running again.
G I can hear a door opening.
H I can hear music playing.
I I can hear bells ringing.
J I can hear people clapping and cheering.
K I can hear a car driving off.

Optional activity

With less confident students, students write their answers first.

Extension Students work in pairs and write a paragraph about what happened. Less confident students can write the sequence of sounds, e.g. *First we heard people running. Then we heard a car starting.* More confident students can interpret the whole situation and add reasons, e.g. *First we heard people running because they were late for a wedding.*

6 PRONUNCIATION

- Write the words *hair* and *hear* on the board. Elicit the pronunciation of the words and then ask students to take off the *h* to pronounce the two sounds. Demonstrate the two sounds, showing students that the mouth is more open and rounded for the /eə/ sound and more stretched for the /ɪə/ sound.
- Ask students to look at the words in the chart. Play the first part of the recording, pausing after each word for students to repeat.

2.03 Recording

/eə/ *hair air chair dare pair wear*
/ɪə/ *hear ear cheer dear pier we're*

- Play the second part of the recording. Students listen and write the words they hear. Ask students to compare answers. If necessary, play the recording again. Ask different students to say and spell the answers.

2.03 Recording and answers

hear air chair dear pair we're

Optional activity

If these are difficult sounds for your students, ask them to write five of the words from the chart in their notebook. They then dictate them to their partner and compare to see if the communication was successful. Monitor and help as necessary.

7 WRITING

- Ask students to close their eyes. Tell them to imagine it's Saturday evening. Tell them to think about what they can see, hear and smell. Give them a minute to create the scene in their head.
- Ask students to open their eyes and write five sentences using *I could hear/smell …* Set a time limit. Students compare their sentences and find out if there are any that are the same.

Optional activity

Give students more options, e.g. *It's Saturday or Monday morning/it's now* or *they are living in the future* or *in the past/they are themselves* or *they are rich and famous*. When students tell each other their sentences, their partner guesses the situation.

LANGUAGE WORKOUT

- Ask students to complete the Language box. Confident students can complete first and then check, while others can look back at exercise 2 and then complete.
- Students turn to page 116 of the Language File to check their answers.

  Answers

  moving flying hear see
- Highlight that:
  - the verb of perception is followed by an object: *see/hear* + someone + *-ing*
  - there are other verbs which can be used in this way, e.g. *watch, notice, listen to, smell, feel.*
- Drill the examples in chorus for pronunciation, paying particular attention to the pronunciation of *can* /kən/ and *could* /kʊd/.

Optional activities

♦ Students make sentences with the other verbs that follow the same pattern, e.g. *I watched him walking down the road.*

♦ With confident students, point out that the infinitive can be used instead of the present participle, e.g. *They heard him sing.* Highlight that the present participle is used when you are interested in the activity that is happening. The infinitive is used when you are interested in the complete, finished event.

PRACTICE

- Ask students to look at exercise 11 of the Language File on page 116 and complete the sentences with the present participle of the verbs. Do the first one together as an example.
- Check the answers by asking different students to say the completed sentences.

Answers

1 singing 2 walking 3 dancing 4 playing 5 cooking 6 leaving 7 touching 8 sitting

Follow-up activities

♦ Play a DVD clip. Allow students to listen to the sound but turn the television off so they cannot see the screen. Students tell each other what they heard. They then predict what is happening. Play the clip again and students watch the scene to check their predictions. Finally they tell their partner what they saw.

♦ **Game** *Am I pretending?* Student 1 thinks of a place. They do not say which place it is. They describe one thing they can hear/see/smell. Student 2 privately guesses the place and adds another thing they can hear/see/smell there. Student 3 continues and so on. A student must stop playing if they cannot continue the chain or they are challenged to name the place where all these things can be seen/heard/smelled and are unable to do so. If they are challenged and they can name a place where all these things are heard/seen/smelled, then the challenger must stop playing.

HOMEWORK

Ask students to imagine that they meet a famous dead person. Students write a description of the meeting using *I heard/saw him/her …*

WEBLINK

Students may like to visit www.the-atlantic-paranormal-society.com.
This is a society that investigates hauntings like the one experienced by the Hodgson family.

Revision and Extension p57

Language File p116

Workbook Unit 4 Lesson 1 pp38–39

Photocopiable worksheet p171, notes p156

2 I'll keep my fingers crossed!

Communicative Aims	Language	Pronunciation	Vocabulary	Optional Aids
Making predictions, promises and offers Talking about plans and intentions	Future review: *will/ won't, shall* and *going to*	/æ/ bad /ʌ/ luck	Superstitions Phrasal verbs with *out*	Exercise 7 optional activity: small cards for Vocabulary box

WARMER 1

If students wrote about meeting famous dead people for homework, ask them to tell each other their stories in groups.

WARMER 2

Re-tell the story of the haunting at the house in north London (page 48) but make some factual mistakes, e.g. *A toothbrush flew through the air hitting Janet's sister on the arm.* Students listen and shout *Stop!* when they hear a mistake. They correct the mistake.

WARMER 3

Students see how many words they can make from *superstition*. Students may not use a letter more than once unless it appears more than once in the word itself. The student with the greatest number of words wins.

1 OPENER

- The aim is to set the scene and pre-teach the vocabulary for the reading.
- Books closed, give one example of a superstition, e.g. *seeing a black cat, the number 13* and ask students if it brings good luck or bad luck.
- Ask students to work in pairs and discuss which of the UK superstitions bring good luck and which bring bad luck. Check their answers as a class.
- Ask *Do we have the same superstitions? Are there any different ones here? Are there any we have which are not here?*

Answers

Good luck: catching a falling leaf in autumn, crossing your fingers, throwing a coin into a fountain
Bad luck: breaking a mirror, opening an umbrella indoors, walking under a ladder

2 READING

- Students look at the pictures with the magazine article. Pre-teach and review vocabulary by asking *Which superstition does the first picture represent? Which superstition does the second picture represent? What time of day is it in the third picture?*
- Students look at the title and sub-title. Ask *What's another word for down-to-earth?* (practical, realistic). Give students five minutes to complete the questionnaire. Be prepared to explain *touch wood* (people say this and often try to touch something made of wood when they hope something good will happen or something bad won't happen) and *lucky charm*.
- You could ask students to listen to the questionnaire and check their answers.

2.04 Recording

See text on page 50 of the Student's Book.

3 AFTER READING

- Students turn to page 121, work out their score and read the paragraph which relates to them.
- Students compare their scores with each other. Find out if they agree with the description of themselves.

Your response

Students work in pairs and discuss the first question. Ask each pair to report back to the whole class. Take a show of hands to find out how many students in the class are superstitious and count the number of boys and the number of girls in the class who say they are superstitious.

Extension Students work individually and make a list of superstitions they have in their country. Then ask them to work in small groups of 3–4 and compare their lists. Ask each group to report back to the whole class and make a list of superstitions in note form on the board, e.g. *broken mirror, black cat, ladder.*

LANGUAGE WORKOUT OPTION

If you want to pre-teach the language students will be using in the following activities, you may like to go to the Language Workout box now.

4 LISTENING

- Students tell their partner what they can see in the picture. Read the first part of the story and the question aloud. Encourage students to say *I think he'll …* Accept all suggestions.
- Play the recording. Pause at the end of the next part of the story. Did anyone guess correctly? Play this part of

the story again, including the question. Students answer the question in pairs. Ask one or two students to tell the class their ideas. Repeat the procedure until the end of the story.

2.05 Recording

A doctor is driving home along a quiet country road. It's late at night and it's raining hard. Suddenly he sees a girl walking along the road. She looks like a student.
What do you think the doctor will do?
The doctor stops the car and asks 'Are you all right? Where are you going?'
The girl replies, 'I'm walking home – I missed the last bus.'
What do you think the doctor will say?
'Shall I give you a lift?' offers the doctor. 'Oh, yes please,' says the girl and she gets into the back of the car. 'I live about five kilometres up the road – it isn't far.' The man starts the car and asks for the girl's address. But at that moment, a lorry comes very fast towards them. 'Look out!' cries the girl.
What do you think will happen next?
The doctor manages to avoid the lorry. 'Phew, that was lucky!' he says. The girl doesn't answer so he turns round. There's no one in the back of the car! But then he sees the girl's bag lying on the seat.
What do you think he will do next?
The doctor stops the car, picks up the bag and opens it. He finds a wallet with the girl's address in it.
What do you think the doctor will do now?
The doctor drives to the girl's house and rings the doorbell. Finally a woman with grey hair opens the door. 'Good evening,' says the doctor. 'I'm sorry to trouble you, but a girl left this bag in my car … '
What do you think the woman will say?
'Thank you,' says the woman. 'The bag is my daughter's. But she died in a car accident exactly a year ago.'

Extension Ask students if they think it is a true story and why/why not.

5 SPEAKING

- In pairs, one student reads the statement and their partner responds. Do one with the whole class.

Answers

1 I won't forget anything.
2 I'll drive carefully.
3 I'll look at the map.
4 I'll phone once a week.
5 I won't be away for long.

- Ask students to look at the Language File on page 116. Highlight the use of *Shall I* + infinitive to make an offer. Highlight that *shall* is only used in questions, not statements. Drill the example sentence.
- In pairs, one student reads the statement and their partner responds. Do one with the whole class.

Answers

6 Shall I turn off the lights?/I'll turn off the lights.
7 Shall I lend you one?/I'll lend you one.
8 Shall I close the window?/I'll close the window.
9 Shall I turn down the heating?/I'll turn down the heating.
10 Shall I carry it for you?/I'll carry it for you.

Optional activity

Less confident students write the responses first.

6 PRONUNCIATION

- Play the recording, pausing after each word for students to repeat. Note that the mouth is more open and the lips more spread for /æ/ and more closed with the lips more rounded for /ʌ/.
- In pairs, students practise saying the words.

2.06 Recording

/æ/ *bad cat cap match ran sang*
/ʌ/ *luck cut cup much run sung*

- Play the second part of the recording. Students listen and write which of the words they hear each time.
- Check by asking individual students to read out the words they have written. Write exactly what you hear on the board. For example, if a student says *cat* when the correct answer is *cut*, write *cat* and ask the student to pronounce *cut* correctly.

2.06 Recording and answers

cut cup match run sang

7 VOCABULARY

- In pairs, students match the phrasal verbs and definitions. Check the answers with the whole class.
- Ask students to find three examples of phrasal verbs with *out* in the questionnaire on page 50. Students can use the context to work out the correct definitions for these.

Answers

1 look out 2 read out 3 find out 4 go out 5 try out 6 take out
In this lesson: find out, read out and *go out.*

Extension Students work individually to complete the sentences with verbs from the word bank. Then have them check their answers in pairs. (*1 go out 2 find out 3 read out 4 try out 5 Look out*)

Optional activity

If you have a Vocabulary box, students copy the phrasal verbs onto cards, putting the definitions and examples on the back and add them to the box.

8 WRITING

- Ask one student to read the instructions aloud. Brainstorm some possible topic areas with the students, e.g. *school, family, friends, free time, weather*. Check which verb form students use to talk about plans and which verb form is used with *think* and *hope*. Set a 10-minute time limit. Monitor and help as necessary.

LANGUAGE WORKOUT

- Ask students to complete the Language box. Confident students can complete first and then check, while others can look back at exercise 2 and then complete.
- Students turn to page 116 of the Language File to check their answers.

Answers

won't 'll 'll 'll I'm going
you going is going

- Highlight that:
  - both *will/won't* and *going to* can be used for predictions: *Will/won't* is usually used when there is no evidence, it is just something you believe; *going to* is used when there is some present evidence. Check students understand 'present evidence' by asking what the present evidence is in the example sentence (footsteps).
  - *will/won't* is used for decisions made at the time of speaking and *going to* is used for plans or intentions.
  - *will* is contracted in spoken English, e.g. *I'll*.
  - the pronunciation of *to* in *going to* is /tə/
- Drill the examples in chorus and individually.

PRACTICE

- Ask students to look at Practice exercise 12 of the Language File on page 116 and complete the conversation with the correct form. Do one with the whole class as an example.
- Check answers and ask students to say why they chose *will/going to*.

Answers

1 *'m going to (prediction from present evidence)*
2 *'m going to (plan/intention)*
3 *'ll (offer)*
4 *'ll (decision made at the time of speaking)*
5 *'s going to (prediction from present evidence)*
6 *won't (prediction)*
7 *'ll (prediction)*
8 *'ll (promise/decision at moment of speaking)*

Follow-up activities

- Students conduct a survey to find out the percentage of students in the class who believe in the superstitions listed in exercise 1 and any other national superstitions. Students prepare a question for each superstition, e.g. *Do you think touching wood is good luck?* They interview everyone in the class, collect the information and then write up their results as percentages, a bar graph or a pie chart.
- Write the following on the board:

Find someone who …	Name
thinks he/she will … tomorrow/ next week/next month/next year	
hopes he/she will … tomorrow/ next week/next month/next year	
is going to … tomorrow/next week/next month/next year	
isn't going to … tomorrow/next week/next month/next year	

Students complete the four sentences with ideas and choose one of the time references. They then move around the classroom, asking the appropriate question until they find someone who says *yes*. They write that student's name next to the sentence.

HOMEWORK

Tell students they can write about themselves or any famous person. Students write a paragraph about their future plans, beliefs and hopes as if they were this person. As in exercise 8, students write about what they know is going to happen and what they think and hope will happen.

WEBLINK

Students may like to visit worldsuperstitions.blogspot.com where they can read about superstitions around the world.

Revision and Extension p57

Language File p116

Workbook Unit 4 Lesson 2 pp40–41

Photocopiable worksheet p172, notes p156

3 If you follow this advice ...

Communicative Aims	Language	Pronunciation	Vocabulary	Optional Aids
Talking about future possibility	First conditional	Syllable stress	Memory School life	Follow-up activity: pictures from magazines

WARMER 1

If students wrote about the future plans of a famous person, ask them to read their paragraph to their partner without saying the name of the famous person. Their partner guesses who the famous person is.

WARMER 2

Students choose a current topic, e.g. a *sports competition, TV show, music awards*, and say if they are going to watch it, where and when they are going to watch it, and what they think/hope will happen. Students tell their partner/ group their ideas and their partner responds.

1 OPENER

- The aim is to set the context for the reading.
- Ask students to work individually and answer the questions, making notes in their notebooks. Then ask them to compare their answers in pairs. Have the whole class suggest answers.
- Ask students if they know any interesting memory techniques that help people remember things. Give an example of a memory trick (mnemonic) – *Richard of York gave battle in vain.* This helps people remember the colour spectrum – red, orange, yellow, green, blue, indigo, violet. Ask students if they know any examples in their language.

2 READING

- The aim is to encourage students to read for gist.
- Ask students to read the five headings first. Then read the article and match the headings and paragraphs.
- Play the recording so that students can check their answers.

2.07 Recording

See text on page 52 of the Student's Book.

Answers

1 Say it aloud 2 Put it in writing 3 Make connections 4 Pay attention 5 Go to bed early

3 AFTER READING AND LISTENING

- Students find the answers in the text individually, and then compare answers in pairs.
- Check the answers orally with the whole class. Check students understand that landmarks are things you notice on a regular journey.

Answers

1 *Because they will stay in your memory longer.*
2 *Things you have to do, things you need to buy and words and phrases you want to learn.*
3 *To remember a person's name, think of someone with a similar name. Associate new facts with landmarks on your way to school. Put new words together in a sentence or a story.*
4 *Because you won't remember if you don't concentrate.*
5 *It will help to process new information and fix it in your memory.*

Your response

Students work individually to answer the questions and make notes. Then ask them to work in pairs and compare their answers to the questions. Ask each pair to report their ideas to the whole class.

Optional activity

Students note all the vocabulary in the text related to memory: *forget, remember, learn, associate, link, consolidation, process, categories*. Encourage students to organise the vocabulary, e.g. *verbs/nouns, opposites*.

4 LISTENING

- If your students are familiar with Murphy's Law, ask them for a definition. If they are not familiar with it, read the definition. Students match the beginnings and endings.
- Check the answers. Check students understand *the computer will crash* (suddenly stop working).

2.08 Recording and answers

1 *If you are early, the school bus will be late.*
2 *If you are late, the school bus will be on time.*
3 *If you want a book from the library, it won't be on the shelves.*
4 *If you do homework on a computer, it will crash before you save your work.*
5 *If you forget your calculator, you will have a maths test.*
6 *If you copy someone else's homework, the teacher will find out.*
7 *If you lend friends your notes, they will lose them.*
8 *If you have to decide between two answers, you will choose the wrong one.*

5 SPEAKING

- Ask students to look at the cartoons and the beginnings of the sentences. Students complete the sentences with an appropriate phrase.

Suggested answers

1 miss the train. 2 have to pay for them.
3 lend me your jacket. 4 tidy your room.
5 don't finish your homework. 6 turn it off.

6 PRONUNCIATION

- Students look at the words in the box and predict the number of syllables and the stress.
- Play the recording. Pause after each word and check the answers. Play the recording again, pausing for students to repeat the words.

2.09 Recording and answers

calendar concentrate connection improve
information memorable memory organise
personalise process remember similar

7 SPEAKING

- Students read the questionnaire. Write the following chart on the board for the students to copy into their notebooks. Continue the question numbers to 8.

Question	Name:_____	Name:_____
1		
2		

- Students interview two other students and note their answers in the second and third columns. Make sure students do not show each other their charts. Encourage confident students to give more information.

8 WRITING

- Ask one or two students to tell the class about the answers they got for the first question. Use this information to show students how to form one sentence if the responses were the same *If …, both X and Y will …* and if the responses were different *If …, X will … and/ but Y will …*
- Students write a paragraph comparing the two students they interviewed. Set a 10-minute time limit.
- Students exchange writing and check each other's work for spelling, grammar and punctuation.

Extension Students can write their own answers to the questions in the questionnaire.

LANGUAGE WORKOUT

- Ask students to complete the Language box. Confident students can complete first and then check, while others can look back at the text in exercise 2 and then complete.
- Students turn to page 116 of the Language File to check their answers.

Answers

If write, won't won't, don't will, don't

- Highlight that:
  - even when we are talking about the future, a present verb form is used after *if*.
  - the order of the clauses can be reversed, e.g. *You'll talk to Matt if you press that button.*
  - there is a comma between the clauses when the sentence begins with the *if* clause, but there is no comma when the sentence begins with the main clause.
- Drill the examples for pronunciation.

PRACTICE

- Ask students to look at Practice exercise 13 of the Language File on page 116 and complete the sentences.

Answers

1 You'll feel better if you take more exercise.
2 He'll have an accident if he drives so fast.
3 They'll pass the exam if they work hard.
4 I won't spend any money if I stay at home.
5 You'll get a prize if you win the competition.
6 We won't go to the gig if we don't get free tickets.
7 She'll find her keys if she tidies her room.
8 I won't get lost if I take a map.

Follow-up activities

- ♦ In groups, students write (and illustrate) eight points similar to those in exercise 5 but based on home. Do one as an example, e.g. *If you don't tidy your room, your Mum will get angry.*
- ♦ Give students a selection of pictures from recent magazines, etc. In groups, students choose two or three and write captions using the first conditional.

HOMEWORK

Students write a story that begins with the words *Jack said, "If we don't hurry ..."*

WEBLINK

Students may like to visit http://www.helpguide.org/life/improving_memory.htm where they can read more about improving their memory.

Revision and Extension p57

Language File p116

Workbook Unit 4 Lesson 3 pp42–43

Photocopiable worksheet p173, notes p157

4 Integrated Skills Telling a story

Skills

Reading *Rebecca* story
Speaking Continuing the story based on pictures and prediction outcomes
Listening Listening to check predictions
Writing Retelling the end of a story

Learner Independence

Guessing the meaning
Word creation: noun → adjective, verb → noun

Vocabulary

Useful expressions

Optional Aids

Follow-up activity: small cards for Vocabulary box

WARMER 1

Write jumbled first conditional sentences on the board. Set a time limit for students to re-order them in pairs.

WARMER 2

Game *Shark* For instructions see Unit 1, Lesson 3, p33. Play with the word *Rebecca* and tell students that it's a girl's name. Afterwards, students say if they know anyone called Rebecca or the equivalent, if there is one, in their native language.

Useful information

Rebecca was first published in 1938 and is Daphne du Maurier's (1907–1989) most famous novel. It is a haunting thriller in which the name of the main character, the second Mrs de Winter, is never known. In 1940 the film, directed by Alfred Hitchcock, won the Oscar for Best Picture.

1 OPENER

- Ask students to look at the book cover. Ask *What type of story do you think it is going to be? Would you like to read this book?*
- Ask students to read the short introduction. Check comprehension by asking *Who is Rebecca? Does Maxim talk about her? What about other people?* Students discuss the problems the new wife might have.

2 READING

- Play the recording. Students listen and read. With a confident class, play the recording first with books closed for students to get a general idea of the story without worrying about individual words.
- Students read the questions and look in the text to find the answers. They write short answers. Encourage students to guess the meaning of new words from context. Students compare their answers in pairs. Check the answers with the whole class.

2.10 Recording
See text on page 54 of the Student's Book.

Answers
1 *In Monte Carlo*
2 *Maxim de Winter's first wife*
3 *She drowned in a boating accident.*
4 *On the south-west coast of England*
5 *She was shy and young, she was in charge of a huge house with lots of servants and Rebecca seemed to haunt the house.*
6 *Unfriendly*
7 *Because it held bad memories.*
8 *Rebecca*

Optional activity

Fast finishers prepare further comprehension questions to test their partner, e.g. *How old was the second Mrs de Winter when she first met Maxim?*

3 SPEAKING

- Students look at the pictures and read the captions. Check students understand *fancy dress ball* (a formal party where you wear costumes) and *wig*.
- Ask *Who are they? Where are they? What are they talking about?* in relation to the first picture. In pairs, students say what is happening in the other three pictures.
- Play the recording. Students listen and check whether their ideas were correct.

2.11 Recording
The second Mrs de Winter wanted to be the perfect wife at Manderley's annual fancy dress ball.
'What are you going to wear for the ball?' asked Mrs Danvers in a friendly voice.
'I don't know,' replied Mrs de Winter.
'Why don't you copy one of the paintings in Manderley?' suggested Mrs Danvers. 'I like the picture of the girl in white with a hat.'
Mrs de Winter went to look at the picture of the girl in white, who was very beautiful with curly hair. 'I'll have to wear a wig,' she thought.
She began to feel very excited about the ball. She made a drawing of the girl in the painting, and sent it to a shop in London, with instructions to make the dress, the hat and the wig. When Maxim asked her about her costume, she said it was a secret.

'You won't know it's me – you'll have the surprise of your life.' Mrs de Winter felt pleased and happy. She hoped to show everyone that she was the right woman for Maxim de Winter and for Manderley.
But when she appeared in her costume on the evening of the ball, Maxim became white with anger. 'Go and change immediately!' he said. 'It doesn't matter what you put on.' She was extremely upset, and ran up to her room.

4

- Students read the questions. Check students understand *a diver, to confess*. In pairs, students discuss possible answers. Ask some students to report back to the class with their ideas but do not confirm or correct them at this stage.

Optional activity

Students make a note of their ideas at this stage. These notes can be used to write an alternative ending.

5 LISTENING

- Tell students they are going to hear the answers to these questions. Play the recording. Students listen and check/correct their answers.

2.12 Recording

Then Mrs de Winter found out that Rebecca wore exactly the same costume at the last fancy dress ball. She changed her dress and went downstairs again. But Maxim didn't say another word to her that evening.
The next day, she spoke to Mrs Danvers.
'You wanted this to happen, didn't you? Are you happy now?'
'Why did you ever come to Manderley?' said Mrs Danvers. 'No one wanted you here.'
'You seem to forget I love Mr de Winter,' the young girl replied. 'Why do you hate me?'
'You tried to take Rebecca's place. She's the real Mrs de Winter, not you.'
That night, it was very foggy, and a ship hit the rocks off the coast. When a diver went down to look at the ship, he found Rebecca's boat – and Rebecca's body.
Mrs de Winter went to talk to Maxim. He put his arm round her.
'I was angry with you last night, wasn't I?' he said.
'Maxim, can't we start again?'
'It's too late, darling. Rebecca has won,' he replied.
'What are you trying to tell me?' she asked.
'Rebecca didn't drown. I killed her – I shot her in the cottage and I carried her body to the boat. Then I took the boat out and sank it.'
'What are we going to do? Does anyone know?' asked his wife.
'No', said Maxim. 'There was no one else there. It was dark.'
'Why didn't you tell me?' she asked. 'I thought you loved Rebecca.'
'You thought I loved Rebecca? I hated her, I tell you! We never loved each other. Rebecca was a terrible woman and she did terrible things. One night I couldn't stand it any longer, I took a gun to the cottage and found Rebecca there, alone. She looked ill, strange. But she smiled at me. She said, "If I have a child, Max, everyone will think it's yours. But you will never know." And she smiled at me again. When I killed her she was still smiling. And now they've found the boat and they've found Rebecca.'
'But no one saw you that night,' said his wife. 'No one else knows what really happened. They'll think Rebecca's death was an accident.'
'I don't know,' Maxim replied. 'I don't know.'

Answers

1 Rebecca wore the same costume at the last fancy dress ball.
2 Because she wanted to cause a problem between Mrs de Winter and her husband.
3 She asked Mrs Danvers why she suggested wearing the dress.
4 She said she didn't want the new Mrs de Winter at Manderley.
5 Rebecca's boat and her body
6 He killed Rebecca.
7 No
8 No

- Ask students to predict what happens next.

6

- Students look at the phrases. Be prepared to explain *inquest, verdict, suicide*. Ask students to use the phrases to complete the story orally. Do the first sentence or two together as an example. Students continue in pairs.
- Before playing the recording, ask students what they think happened at the end.
- Play the recording to listen and check.

2.13 Recording

There was an inquest into Rebecca's death, and the verdict was suicide. But Rebecca's diary showed that she visited a doctor in London on the day she died. The next day, Maxim and his wife went to London and asked the doctor about Rebecca.
'She was very ill,' said the doctor. 'She had only six months to live. And she could never have a child.'
Later, while they were having dinner in a restaurant. Maxim said, 'I think Rebecca wanted me to kill her. That's why she was laughing when she died.'
His wife didn't reply. It was all over now. But Maxim looked very worried and suddenly said, 'We must drive back to Manderley tonight. Something's wrong, I know it is.'
In the early hours of the morning, they reached the top of the hill near Manderley. The sky above their heads was black. But the sky above Manderley wasn't dark at all. It was red, like blood. And Maxim de Winter and his wife watched Manderley burning down.

- Ask students if they liked the story and why/why not.

7 GUIDED WRITING

- Students use the phrases in exercise 6 to write the last part of the story. Monitor and help as necessary.

Optional activity

With a confident group, write the key words of the final part of the story on the board, e.g. *inquest, suicide, diary, doctor*. Books closed, students use just these words to reconstruct the ending.

8 LEARNER INDEPENDENCE

- The aim is to encourage students to use the clues in the context and within the form of an unfamiliar word to guess the meaning. This is a skill which we use when listening or reading in our native language but don't always transfer to other languages.
- Ask students to read the questions. Do a demonstration with the students using a word from exercise 2, e.g. *drowned*: from the context we know that it is a verb in the past related to death and boating accident. Accept any possible ideas: a general understanding of the meaning of the word is enough.
- Ask students to note other new words in the reading. In pairs, students choose some and answer as many of the questions as possible for each one.

9 WORD CREATION

- The aim is to make students aware of some typical noun, adjective and verb forms and expand their vocabulary.

Answers

Noun	*Adjective*	*Verb*	*Noun*
cheer	*cheerful*	*calculate*	*calculator*
fright	*frightening*	*conclude*	*conclusion*
importance	*important*	*differ*	*difference*
luck	*(un)lucky*	*investigate*	*investigator*
memory	*memorable*	*paint*	*painter/ painting*
superstition	*superstitious*	*predict*	*prediction*

10 PHRASEBOOK

- Play the recording, pausing after each expression for students to repeat.
- Ask students to look through the unit to find the expressions, and look at how they are used.

2.14 Recording and answers

Take no notice. (L2, Ex2)
It makes no difference. (L2, Ex2)
Touch wood. (L2, Ex2)
I'll keep my fingers crossed! (L2, Ex2)
Have a safe journey. (L2, Ex5 – not previously recorded)
Don't get lost! (L2, Ex5 – not previously recorded)
Keep in touch. (L2, Ex5 – not previously recorded)
Come back soon. (L2, Ex5 – not previously recorded)
You're not the only one. (L3, Ex2)
It's a secret! (L4, Ex2 – not previously recorded)

- Students match one expression to each of the four definitions and add expressions they like to their Personal Phrasebooks.

Answers

1 Keep in touch. 2 You're not the only one.
3 It makes no difference. 4 Take no notice.

Optional activity

Students work in pairs and write a short dialogue using at least three of the expressions in the box. Invite confident pairs to act out their dialogues.

Follow-up activities

- ♦ In groups, students choose a scene from the story to act out. Ideally each group has a different scene. Give students ten minutes to prepare their dialogue together. Tell students to write notes rather than the entire script. Give students another five minutes to prepare a 'stage' and practise their scene. Students act it out for the other groups.
- ♦ In groups, students think about converting the book into a film. *Where will be a good place in their country to film it? Which actors will they choose for each role and why?* etc. Each student in the group makes notes on their ideas. Students then regroup and explain their ideas to a new group.
- ♦ Students write new words from the lesson on vocabulary cards. These can be added to the Vocabulary box if you have one and/or used to play *Password* (see Unit 2, Lesson 1, p43).

HOMEWORK

Students write a letter as the second Mrs de Winter, after she arrives in Manderley, to a friend to say how she feels, or as Maxim writing to the second Mrs de Winter explaining what happened with Rebecca.

WEBLINK

Students may like to visit www.imdb.com/title/tt0032976/ and also hitchcock.tv/mov/rebecca/rebecca.html where they can read about the film *Rebecca*.

Revision and Extension p57

Workbook Unit 4 Lesson 4 pp44–45

Inspiration EXTRA!

Optional Aids

Project: information from the Internet on some mysteries/unusual events

PROJECT MYSTERY REPORT

1
- Ask students to look at the pictures. Ask *What is the man doing? What do you know about bird migration? What is the connection between the pictures?* (They both show unexplained mysteries.)
- Ask students to look in the text and find how far some birds fly when they migrate and how far they fly in a single day (70,000km and between 330 and 520km a day).
- Students read the text again and find five possible explanations for how birds migrate (the position of the stars, the sun, temperature, smells, memory).
- Explain to students that the aim of the project is to write about a mystery or unusual event.
- Divide the students into groups and give them three minutes to make a list of mysteries. Each group then chooses one/two to write about.

2
- Students look at the prompts and make notes about their mysteries. Encourage students to bring pictures to class to illustrate their file.

3
- Working together in a group, students compare the information they have found. They decide in which order to put the information and form and link the sentences. Students read the text(s) through carefully to correct any mistakes. They copy their texts out neatly and illustrate their file(s) with photos or drawings.
- Students show their Mystery File(s) to other groups. Display the files in the classroom if possible.

GAME WHERE AM I?

- Students imagine they are somewhere outside the classroom. Suggest some places, e.g. *in the library*. Give students five minutes to read and note their answers.
- Read the example and ask students to guess where you are (a horse race). Students work in pairs and do the same. Allow students to use their notes at the beginning. After describing their experience once or twice, encourage them to talk about it without their notes.

Language File p116

Workbook Unit 4 Inspiration EXTRA! pp46–47

REVISION

Lessons 1–2
Students' own answers

Lesson 3

Answers

1 look, will go 2 will be, eat 3 leave, will lose 4 will be, point 5 is, will bring

EXTENSION

Lessons 1–3
Students' own answers

YOUR CHOICE!

- Organise students into groups depending on their learning style. Set a 10-minute time limit for all groups.

CONSTRUCTION

Answers

1 remember 2 repeat 3 respond 4 reporter 5 realise

REFLECTION

Answers

going to, 'm going to; will, shall, 'll, Shall; will, 'll; will, 'll; going to, 's going

ACTION

- Organise students into groups of three and make sure there is enough space for B to run between A and C.

INTERACTION

- Divide students into groups. Give them three minutes to think about their answers first.
  You may now like students to do the song *Celebrate The Future*. See p161 for the notes and p187 for the worksheet.

Song – photocopiable worksheet p187, notes p161

Units 3–4

1 Check general comprehension: ask students to look at the picture and the headline and predict the story. Give students one minute to read the story and check their predictions. Students read the story again and choose the appropriate word for each space. Do the first one together as an example. This can be done in pairs or individually as a short test.

Answers
1 B 2 A 3 C 4 B 5 B 6 C 7 A 8 C 9 B 10 A 11 B 12 A

Optional activity

Confident students can attempt the task before looking at the word options.

2 Students use the prompts to write responses. Point out that students must also choose the correct pronoun: *it, he, she* or *they*. Do the first one together as an example.

Answers
1 He can't be Italian – he must be Brazilian.
2 It can't be a parrot – it must be a penguin.
3 They can't be curtains – they must be windows.
4 She can't be a pilot – she must be a doctor.
5 It can't be rain – it must be snow.
6 They can't be cucumbers – they must be bananas.
7 They can't be reporters – they must be actors.
8 It can't be a helicopter – it must be a plane.

3 Students read and complete the school rules choosing the appropriate word. Do the first one together as an example.

Answers
1 mustn't 2 mustn't 3 must 4 must 5 mustn't 6 mustn't

Optional activity

Fast finishers write more rules.

4 Students replace the words in italics. Point out that some sentences are in the present and some are in the past.

Answers
1 Do we have to 2 You don't have to 3 You have to 4 He has to 5 We had to 6 They didn't have to

5 **Answers**
1 myself 2 yourself 3 her 4 ourselves 5 them 6 yourselves 7 myself 8 him

6 Point out that students write *'d better (not)* where possible; *should(n't)* is possible in all the spaces.

Answers
1 should 2 'd better 3 'd better not 4 should 5 'd better 6 should

7 **Answers**
1 It's hard to remember dates.
2 It's good to see you again.
3 It's rude to stare at people.
4 It's important to tell the truth.
5 It's wrong to cheat.
6 It's nice to meet you.

Optional activity

Students invent other endings for the adjectives, e.g. *It's hard to wake up in the morning, It's rude to interrupt.*

8 Students complete the sentences. Confident students can attempt the task without looking at the words in the box and then look to check.

Answers
1 playing 2 burning 3 waiting 4 running 5 eating 6 singing

9 Give students one minute to read the conversation and find out who is talking, what the relationships are between them and what they are talking about. Check answers (Jack and Tim are friends and Tim is also speaking to his father – they are talking about what Tim is doing this afternoon). Students then choose a verb form for each space.

Answers
1 'm going to 2 's going to 3 'll 4 'll 5 won't 6 'll 7 'm going to 8 aren't going to 9 'll 10 won't 11 'll 12 're going to

10 Students complete the sentences with the correct form of the verb in brackets. Remind students that the correct form may be negative. Do one together as an example.

Answers
1 I'll cook dinner tonight if you like.
2 If we don't hurry, we'll miss the plane.
3 My sister will be a doctor if she passes her exams.
4 If the team score(s) another goal, they'll win the game.
5 We won't get lost if we look at the map.
6 If it rains tomorrow, we won't have a barbecue.
7 You'll sleep better if you open the window.
8 If I don't finish my project, I'll be in trouble!

Optional activity

Students write other ways of finishing the sentences, e.g. *I'll cook dinner tonight if you wash up.*

VOCABULARY

11 Students complete the sentences with the words in the box. Confident students cover the words in the box and guess which words are missing before checking against the list.

Answers
1 election 2 concentrate 3 haunted 4 honeymoon 5 electricity 6 army 7 communicate 8 ladder 9 horoscope 10 bruise

Optional activity

Fast finishers mark the stress on words of more than one syllable.

12 Students match the words with their definitions. Confident students can attempt the task without looking at the words in the box and then look to check.

Answers
1 forbidden 2 nasty 3 improve 4 increase 5 recall 6 mood 7 purpose 8 lie 9 ignore 10 adore

Optional activity

Students write definitions of other words from Units 3 and 4. They exchange definitions and try to guess each other's words.

13 Remind students that it can be very useful to learn words that go together like this.

Answers
1 boil water 2 break the law 3 fall asleep 4 switch off the lights 5 pay attention 6 tell lies

Optional activity

In pairs, one student says a word or phrase from list B and their partner recalls the verb.

LEARNER INDEPENDENCE SELF ASSESSMENT

- Explain to students that the aim of the self assessment is to help them check their own progress and take any action necessary to improve. Point out that the list 1–7 covers language from Units 3 and 4.
- Have students look at the table and tick the Fine box for language they feel confident using or put a question mark in the Not sure box if they feel they still have some difficulties.
- Encourage students to look at the Language File and re-do exercises from the lessons, the Revision and Extension section and the Workbook in areas where they have problems.
- Students write an example sentence for each language area in the list. You may like to elicit the language students need for each example before students write sentences, e.g. *Making logical deductions and discussing possiblity.* Students can refer back to the lessons and the Language Workout box and Language File.

Follow-up activities

♦ **Game** *Word game* This can be played in teams. Say a topic, e.g. *things you hear in the street, superstition* and give students one minute to write as many words as they can related to that topic. The group with the most correct words wins a point.

♦ Write the sentences on the board which use grammar presented in Units 3 and 4, e.g. *She must be famous. You don't have to go. You should talk to them.* In pairs, students invent a short dialogue which includes at least four of them. Set a 10-minute time limit. Students practise and act out their dialogue. The rest of the class listen and identify the relationship between the two speakers and what they are talking about.

HOMEWORK

Students try to find English song lyrics which include some grammar from previous units. They can look through their current albums or search on the Internet. Some examples: Madness *It must be love*, The Clash *Should I stay or should I go now?*

WEBLINK

Students may like to visit www.bbc.co.uk/science/space/life/aliens/ufos/index.shtml where they can read more about UFOs and the arguments for and against their existence.

Language File pp114–116

Workbook Review Units 3–4 pp48–49

Units 5–6

Activities		Game	Vocabulary	Optional Aids
Identifying communicative aims Categorising vocabulary	Contextualising listening extracts	What kind of person?	Sport Materials Household items	Follow-up activities: slips of paper

WARMER 1

Students look back at Units 3–4 in their books and talk in pairs about the activities or reading texts that they enjoyed or didn't like. Encourage them to give reasons for their feelings.

WARMER 2

Put anagrams for words related to superstition on the board, e.g. *DELDAR* (ladder), *IMRRRO* (mirror), *SCPROHOOE* (horoscope), *TIRTHENE* (thirteen). Students rearrange the letters to make the correct spellings. This could also be done as a race with the first pair to finish with all the correct spellings being the winner.

WARMER 3

Write five *if* clauses on the board, e.g. *If it rains at the weekend …*, *If I have time this evening …* Students work in pairs and finish the sentences. Ask different students to read out their complete sentences to the whole class.

1

- The aim is to introduce the students to the main areas of communicative language they will cover in Units 5–6, and to encourage them to think about the function of the language.
- Explain the task to the class. Students should look at the photos and match them with the communicative aims, using the captions to help them. Point out that there are four pictures and six communicative aims so two of them are not used.
- Ask students to do the task individually and then compare their answers in pairs. Check the answers with the whole class.

Answers

A 5 B 1 C 6 D 4

Optional activity

Ask students to work in pairs and make a list of the most important inventions of the 20th and 21st centuries. Ask them to report their ideas to the whole class and list them on the board, e.g. *mobile phone, television, word processor, aeroplane, helicopter*. Ask students to vote for the three most important inventions in the list.

2

- Explain that the words in the box are related to three different categories and that each word has one letter missing. There are two words that both consist of two words and there is a letter missing in each part of the word. Point out that if students do not know the meaning of one or more words in the box, they should guess the possible spelling and what category they go into. Tell students you will explain the meaning of any words they are not sure about when you check the answers.
- This exercise could be done in pairs. Check the answers with the whole class. Write the three categories on the board and invite students to come to the board without their books and write any words they can remember in the correct category. Highlight that *glass* could go into two different categories: glass is a material and a glass is a household item.

Answers

sport – cycling, ice hockey, running, sailing, skiing, surfing
materials – cotton, glass, metal, plastic, paper, wool
household items – carpet, cupboard, curtains, mirror, saucepan, vacuum cleaner

Optional activity

Ask students if they can add one or more words to each of the groups. Possible words include *tennis, basketball, football; steel, nylon, stone; dish, plate, chair.*

3

- The aim of the activity is for students to contextualise a short listening extract by working out what kind of passage it is extracted from.
- Explain to students that they should listen for the main gist of each passage and that it does not matter if they do not understand every word.
- Play the recording. Students match each extract 1–3 with the summaries A–C.

2.15 Recording

1

Kite surfing started in France in the 1980s and has recently become very popular worldwide. You use a small surfboard and a large kite on 30-metre lines. The kite pulls you through the water and you can steer with the lines. You can just speed through the water, or you can do jumps as high as a house. 'I've never had so much fun,' says a kite-surfer. 'It's much more exciting than water-skiing behind a boat.'

2

'My best friend in the world is still NJ, or Nugent Walker Junior. We've been friends ever since we met on the first day of primary school and I can't remember ever falling out with him. We hit it off straight away and now he's my personal assistant, someone I can turn to at any time of day or night, who is always, always there for me.'

3

Californian Krysta Morlan was 16 when she invented a special waterbike. She thought of the idea when she was doing exercises in the swimming pool. She had spent a lot of time in hospital and needed to do exercises to recover her strength. 'I loved cycling, but I hadn't ridden a bicycle for a long time,' she explained. 'The idea of the waterbike was to have fun and still get the advantage of a workout in the pool.'

Answers

1 C 2 A 3 B

Optional activity

2.15 Write *Where did kite surfing start? When did it start? How long are the lines? When did the writer meet NJ? How old was Krysta when she invented the waterbike?* on the board. Play the recording again and ask students to write down the answers. Check the answers with the whole class. (France, in the 1980s, 30m, on the first day of primary school, 16)

4
- The aim of this activity is for students to write descriptions of other people using words from general categories that could be associated with those people. You could introduce this activity by asking students *If you were a colour, what colour would you be? If you were an animal, what animal would you be?*
- Ask students to look at the photo and the description of the girl. Point out that the description includes a word or phrase for each of the items in the *What kind of person?* list.
- Students work in pairs. Ask them to write similar descriptions of four members of their class. Make sure both students in each pair write out the descriptions.
- Put students into large groups of five or six. Make sure that they are not in the same group as the student they worked with when writing the descriptions. Students read out their descriptions to the group and the other group members guess which student they are describing.

What kind of person? Project

- Students use the descriptions in the *What kind of person?* activity as the basis of a short paragraph. Ask them to choose two of the descriptions they wrote and expand them into paragraphs by including reasons for their choice of words or phrases. For example, *I wrote blue for this person because she has blue eyes and she often wears a blue T-shirt. I associate her with Friday because she is always happy and smiling on Fridays. I chose May as the month because I think her birthday is in May* and so on.
- Ask students to stand up and find the classmates they wrote about. They explain their choice of descriptions and check that they are accurate. For example, *I wrote May as the month because I think your birthday is in May. Is that correct? I wrote chocolate as the food because I'm sure you like chocolate!*

- Books closed. Write the phrase *The world's greatest inventor* on the board. Tell the students this person holds the record for the greatest number of inventions. Elicit suggestions from the class for the number of things this person has invented.
- Ask students to open their books and check their predictions in the Believe it or not! box.

Optional activity

Ask students what they would invent if they could invent the perfect invention.

Follow-up activities

- Students think of three more headings to add to the *What kind of person?* list, e.g. *car, sport, country, profession, drink, type of music.*
- Do the activity in Preview 1–2 follow-up activities on page 26 of this book but using the three categories in the vocabulary exercise on page 60 of the Student's Book: sport, materials and household items.

HOMEWORK

Ask students to use the *What kind of person?* activity to write a description of a famous person in the same way.

1 Has she learnt first aid yet?

Communicative Aims	Language	Pronunciation	Vocabulary	Optional Aids
Talking about what has and hasn't happened	Present perfect with *just, already, yet*	/eə/ where /eɪ/ way	Countries Phrases with *go, learn* and *ride*	Exercise 5 optional activity: world map

WARMER 1

Give students the beginning to the story: *If I have enough money, I'll buy a motorbike. If I buy a motorbike, …* In pairs/small groups, students complete the story. Tell students they must continue the pattern of first conditionals that follow on from each other and they must finish the story in no more than five lines. Set a five-minute time limit. Pairs/groups read their stories to each other.

WARMER 2

Game *Alphabet game* Ask students to write the letters A–Z down the margin of a piece of paper. In pairs or small groups, give students two minutes to think of a country for as many of the 26 letters as possible. Do an example, e.g. *A, Australia*. Use the example to show that students do not write continents, e.g. *Africa*, or cities, e.g. *Amsterdam*. After two minutes, ask the group with the most countries to read out their list. Check spelling and pronunciation. Ask students to tell their partner which countries on the list they would most like to visit and why.

1 OPENER

- The aim is to generate interest and set the scene for the listening.
- Ask students to look at the photos and say which of the activities in the 10 things to do before you're 20 list they represent (ride a horse, go skiing, hold a baby, go camping with friends).
- Students look again at the list of 10 things to do before you're 20 and tick the ones they have already done. Ask them to compare their lists in pairs. Find out which students have done the most things.

2 LISTENING

- The aim here is for students to listen to the interview and mark the things the girl and the boy have already done. Explain that the interviewer asks them about the 10 items in the list in exercise 1 and that all the activities are mentioned but the girl and the boy say they haven't done some of them.
- Play the recording once. Check that students have got all the answers. If not, play the recording again.

2.16 Recording

INTERVIEWER *OK, Lisa, let's look at this list of ten things to do before you're twenty. Have you been to a gig yet?*
LISA *Yes, I have. I've already been to lots of gigs.*
INTERVIEWER *Have you learnt first aid?*
LISA *No, I haven't yet. I should, though, shouldn't I?*
INTERVIEWER *Have you performed in a play?*
LISA *Yes – I've been in two school plays.*
INTERVIEWER *The next one is: ride a horse.*
LISA *Yes, I've already ridden a horse. I didn't like it much – I fell off.*
INTERVIEWER *Bad luck! Have you written a poem yet?*
LISA *Yeah, I've written a couple of poems for the school magazine.*
INTERVIEWER *OK – have you been camping with friends?*
LISA *Not yet, but I'm going camping with friends this summer.*
INTERVIEWER *Nice! Have you organised a birthday party?*
LISA *Yes, I've just had my 16th birthday party and I organised it all myself.*
INTERVIEWER *Cool. Next – have you been skiing?*
LISA *No, not yet. I'd like to, but it's expensive …*
INTERVIEWER *True. Have you learnt to drive?*
LISA *Er, no, I haven't done that yet either. But I want to learn as soon as possible.*
INTERVIEWER *And the last one. Have you held a baby yet?*
LISA *Yes, I've held my little brother lots of times!*
INTERVIEWER *Great – you've already done six of the ten things.*
LISA *And what about you?*
INTERVIEWER *I'm not telling you. Perhaps I'm over 20! And now it's Steve's turn. Are you ready?*
STEVE *Sure! Ready when you are.*
INTERVIEWER *They're the same questions that Lisa has answered. So, have you been to a gig yet?*
STEVE *Yes, of course I have!*
INTERVIEWER *Have you learnt first aid?*
STEVE *Yes, I have actually. It was very interesting. Everyone should learn. But I haven't had a chance to use it yet.*
INTERVIEWER *Now, have you performed in a play?*
STEVE *No, but it's something I've always wanted to do – perhaps next year.*
INTERVIEWER *And what about horses? Have you ridden a horse yet?*
STEVE *No, I'm afraid I haven't. To tell the truth I'm a bit frightened of horses.*

INTERVIEWER	*What about poetry?*
STEVE	*Am I frightened of poetry? What kind of question is that?*
INTERVIEWER	*No, Steve, I meant have you written any poems?*
STEVE	*No again – I like reading poetry but I've never written any. Perhaps I should try!*
INTERVIEWER	*Good idea! Right, have you been camping with friends yet?*
STEVE	*Yes, loads of times. There's a whole group of us who go camping together.*
INTERVIEWER	*Sounds great! Now have you organised a birthday party?*
STEVE	*Yes, my brother was 15 in the summer and I helped organise a barbecue for him.*
INTERVIEWER	*And what about skiing? Have you been skiing yet?*
STEVE	*Yes, I went to Switzerland with my parents last winter. It was brilliant – even though I fell over a lot.*
INTERVIEWER	*Sure, that always happens the first time. And have you learnt to drive?*
STEVE	*Not yet – but I'm having my first driving lesson next week.*
INTERVIEWER	*Great! And last question: have you held a baby yet?*
STEVE	*Not yet, but my sister has just got married, so I'm sure I will quite soon.*
INTERVIEWER	*Five 'yes's and five 'no's, Steve – you've already done half of the things!*

Answers

	Lisa	*Steve*
Go to a gig	✓	✓
Learn first aid	✗	✓
Perform in a play	✓	✗
Ride a horse	✓	✗
Write a poem	✓	✗
Go camping with friends	✗	✓
Organise a birthday party	✓	✓
Go skiing	✗	✓
Learn to drive	✗	✗
Hold a baby	✓	✗

Optional activity

2.16 Write *How many plays has Lisa performed in? What happened when she rode a horse? How old is she? Why hasn't Steve ridden a horse yet? How old is his brother? Where did Steve go skiing?* on the board. Play the recording again and ask students to note down the answers. Check the answers by asking individual students to read out their answers. (Two, She fell off, 16, He's a bit scared of horses, 15, Switzerland)

LANGUAGE WORKOUT OPTION

If you want to pre-teach the language students will be using in the following activities, you may like to go to the Language Workout box now.

3 SPEAKING

- Ask two students to read the examples aloud: one student is A, one student is B.
- Students continue in pairs. Monitor, making sure students are using *yet* and *already*. Students may also remember that she has just had her 16th birthday.

Answers

Has she performed in a play yet? Yes, she's already done that.
Has she ridden a horse yet? Yes, she's already done that.
Has she written a poem yet? Yes, she's already done that.
Has she been camping with friends yet? No, she hasn't done that yet.
Has she organised a birthday party yet? Yes, she's just had her 16th birthday.
Has she been skiing yet? No, she hasn't done that yet.
Has she learnt to drive yet? No, she hasn't done that yet.
Has she held a baby yet? Yes, she's already done that.
Has Steve been to a gig yet? Yes, he's already done that.
Has he performed in a play yet? No, he hasn't done that yet.
Has he ridden a horse yet? No, he hasn't done that yet.
Has he written a poem yet? No, he hasn't done that yet.
Has he been camping with friends yet? Yes, he's already done that.
Has he organised a birthday party yet? Yes, he's already done that.
Has he been skiing yet? Yes, he's already done that.
Has he learnt to drive yet? No, he hasn't done that yet.
Has he held a baby yet? No, he hasn't done that yet.

- Tell students to write the numbers 1–10 down the side of a page. In pairs, students ask each other about the 10 things and note the answers next to the number. Encourage confident students to provide more information, e.g. *When did they do these things? Are they going to do these things in the future?*

Optional activity

Fast finishers add three things to the list of things to do before you are twenty.

4 WRITING

- Ask some students to tell you about the student they interviewed. Use this information to demonstrate forming a longer sentence which uses *just, already* or *yet* and links the ideas with *and* or *but* as in the example.
- Have students write sentences about the person they interviewed. Set a time limit of 10 minutes. Monitor and note examples of good language and errors for feedback later.

Optional activity

Students hand in the writing. Read some of them to the class without saying who it is describing. Students listen and guess who it is about.

Extension Students write a list of things to do before you are sixteen. To help less confident students, write a list of general categories on the board, e.g. *travel, transport, sport, books, food*. In pairs students ask and answer questions about their lists, using *Have you ...?*

5 READING

- Students read and listen to find out how many countries they have visited.
- Ask students to look at the box with the route of the journey. Ask *Where are they now?* (Kazakhstan) and *When did they arrive in Kazakhstan?* (1 May).

2.17 Recording

See text on page 63 of the Student's Book.

Answers

They've been to six countries so far: Belgium, Germany, Czech Republic, Slovakia, Ukraine, Russia

Optional activity

Students look at a world map and find the countries McGregor and Boorman travelled through.

6 AFTER READING

- Students look at the example. Highlight the use of *been* instead of *gone*. Elicit/explain that they are both the past participle of *go* but *been* is used when the visit is finished and *gone* is used when the person is still there, e.g. *My sister has just gone to the shops* means she is there now.
- Students use the prompts to write complete questions. They use the route of the journey to answer the questions. Check students know that it is now 1 May. Ask students when McGregor and Boorman visited Germany (15 April). Elicit the first answer, given as an example.

Answers

1 *Have they been to Germany yet? Yes, they've already been to Germany.*
2 *Have they reached Alaska yet? No, they haven't reached Alaska yet.*
3 *Have they been to Russia yet? Yes, they've just been to Russia.*
4 *Have they crossed Mongolia yet? No, they haven't crossed Mongolia yet.*
5 *Have they travelled through Ukraine yet? Yes, they've already travelled through Ukraine.*
6 *Have they arrived in Canada yet? No, they haven't arrived in Canada yet.*

- Ask students to look at the example sentences and ask them to use the information in the route of the journey to make three more sentences about the journey.

Suggested answers

They've already been to/travelled through Belgium, the Czech Republic, Slovakia, Ukraine.
They haven't been to/reached/crossed Mongolia, the USA/ Alaska, Canada yet.

Your response

Students work individually and note their answers in their notebooks. Ask them to give reasons for their choice of transport. Ask them other questions, e.g. *How long would you go for? How would you pay for it?* e.g. working in different places, fundraising. *Which charity would you raise money for?* Ask them to compare their answers in pairs. Ask each pair to report back to the whole class.

7 VOCABULARY

- Write *bicycle* on the board and elicit the verb which goes with it. Students complete the word maps with the appropriate words and phrases.
- Students compare answers before answers are checked as a whole class.

Answers

go: camping; on holiday; skiing; to a gig
learn: an instrument; a language; first aid; to drive
ride: a bicycle; a horse; a motorbike

Optional activity

Fast finishers think of other things you can *learn, go* or *ride* and add them to the word map.

8 PRONUNCIATION

- Write /eə/ on the board. Ask students if they remember this sound (Unit 4, Lesson 1). Elicit some words which have this sound, e.g. from Unit 4, Lesson 1: *hair, air, chair, fair, dare, wear*. Write *way* on the board. Elicit the pronunciation of the word and then the sound /eɪ/. Compare how the two sounds are formed: with /eə/ the mouth remains open while with /eɪ/ it begins open and then closes slightly.
- Ask students to look at the words in the chart. Play the first part of the recording, pausing after each word for students to repeat.

2.18 Recording

/eə/ *where bear dare hair pair stare their*
/eɪ/ *way bay day hey pay stay they*

- Play the second part of the recording. Students listen and write the words they hear. Ask students to compare answers. If necessary, play the recording again. Have different students say and spell the answers.

2.18 Recording and answers

bear dare hey pair stay their way

9 WRITING

- Each student writes a list of ten things they would like to do in the future. Ask for some suggestions, e.g. *learn to surf, go skiing, stay in a five-star hotel*. Encourage students to write realistic achievements rather than improbable ones.
- Students give their list to their partner who writes sentences saying which ones they have already done and which they have not done yet. Monitor and help as necessary.

Extension Students work with a different partner and write five sentences about themselves, three true and two false, e.g. *I haven't been to France. I've run a marathon.* Students exchange papers and guess which of the sentences are true and which are false.

LANGUAGE WORKOUT

- Ask students to complete the Language box. Confident students can complete first and then check, while others can look back at exercise 5 and then complete.
- Students turn to page 117 of the Language File to check their answers.

Answers

just already yet yet
just already yet

- Highlight that:
  - the present perfect simple is formed with *have/has(n't)* + past participle.
  - *have* and *has* are shortened to *'ve* and *'s*
  - *just* and *already* are used in positive sentences and are placed between the auxiliary verb (*have*) and the main verb (past participle).
  - *yet* is used in negative sentences and questions and is placed at the end of the sentence.
- Highlight the effect of using *already* and *yet*. Write the following sentences on the board: *I have done that. I have already done that.* Ask *Which has a stronger meaning?* (the second) *I haven't done that. I haven't done that yet.* Ask *Which one suggests that you will do it in the future?* (the second)
- Drill examples from exercise 5 in chorus for pronunciation, paying particular attention to the contracted form and weak pronunciation of *have*, e.g. *They've* /ðeɪv/ *already travelled across Europe.*

Optional activities

- With a less confident class, review irregular past participles: Students look at the Irregular Verb List on p127 of the Student's Book and test each other.
- Ask what has *just/already/not yet* happened in this lesson, e.g. *The teacher has just explained the grammar, but we haven't done the exercise in the Language File yet.*

PRACTICE

- Ask students to look at Practice exercise 14 of the Language File on page 117 and complete the sentences with the present perfect of the verbs. Do the first one together as an example.
- Check the answers by asking different students to say the completed sentences.

Answers

1 's just started 2 've already seen 3 Have; read; yet
4 've just watched 5 hasn't replied; yet
6 's already scored 7 have already been 8 has just sent

Follow-up activities

- Organise students into teams. Say an action, e.g. *have lunch*. Each team must write a sentence using *just, yet, already* which is true, e.g. *We have just had lunch*. The first team to run to the front and show you a correct sentence wins a point. Continue with other actions, e.g. *do the homework, finish the class*.
- **Game** *Are we ready?* Ask students what you need to do before you go on a trip/holiday. Write a list of six things on the board, e.g. *pack the suitcases, find the passports*. Students copy the list into their notebooks. They then each choose three things they have done and tick them, and three things they have not done and put a cross next to these. Students then stand up and move round the class asking different students *Have you … yet?* The aim of the game is to find a student who has done the three things that you have not and therefore you are ready to go away together.

HOMEWORK

Students write a short newspaper article on McGregor and Boorman when they arrive in the USA. They can use the reading in exercise 5 as a model but change some of the information.

WEBLINK

Students may like to visit www.longwayround.com/journeys.htm where they can read more about Ewan McGregor and Charley Boorman and their trip.

Revision and Extension p71

Language File p117

Workbook Unit 5 Lesson 1 pp50–51

Photocopiable worksheet p174, notes p157

5.2 CHALLENGES

Have you ever wondered ...?

Communicative Aims	**Language**	**Pronunciation**	**Vocabulary**
Talking about experiences	Present perfect with *ever* and *never* Present perfect and past simple	Word stress: compound nouns	Sport

WARMER 1

Game *Play or pass* Organise students into teams. Ask team A to spell a word. Choose words that your students have had difficulty with. Possible words include: *mystery, bruise, whistle, embarrassed, disappear, beautiful*. They can choose to spell it or pass it to another team. If they spell it correctly themselves, they win a point. If they get it incorrect, they get no points. If they pass it to team B and they get it correct, then team B get the point. If they pass it and team B get it incorrect, then team A get the point. Continue until all the words have been spelled and there is a winner.

WARMER 2

Game *Mime the sport* Organise students into teams. One student from each team comes to the front. Show them a card with a sport written on it. Students mime this sport for their team. The first team to shout the correct word wins.

1 OPENER

- The aim is to set the context and generate interest in the reading.
- Ask students to cover the magazine extracts and look at the photos. Ask *What are they doing?* Students do not need to name the sport at this stage. They only need to say what is happening. Ask *Are these normal sports?* Elicit/teach *extreme sports* (sports which are dangerous and exciting).

Optional activity

Write some of the words from the reading on the board, e.g. *to steer, bouncy, a surfboard, a washing machine, to float, speed, a parachute*. Students check the meaning in an English-English dictionary, and predict which sport each word will be used to describe.

2 READING

- The aim is for students to read for general comprehension. Set a short time limit for students to quickly read and match the definitions to the pictures. Students then listen and check their answers.

2.19 Recording

See text on page 64 of the Student's Book.

Answers

A Para-skiing B Zorbing C Free running D Kite surfing

3 AFTER READING

- Students read the questions. They answer as many questions as possible from memory before reading the text again to check and complete their answers. Encourage students to work out the meaning of new words from context and ignore words which are not necessary to complete the exercise.
- Check the answers by choosing different pairs to ask and answer the questions.

Answers

1 Free running 2 Zorbing 3 Kite surfing
4 Free running 5 Kite surfing 6 Zorbing
7 Free running 8 Free running and kite surfing
9 Para-skiing and kite surfing 10 Zorbing
11 Para-skiing 12 Kite surfing

Your response

Ask students *Which sport do you think is the most dangerous? Which one do you think is the most exciting? Why? Which sports would you most and least like to try?* and have them give reasons for their choices.

4 PRONUNCIATION

- Students look at the words in the box. Check students understand the words using pictures or by giving descriptions, e.g. *It's an attraction at a theme park – you sit in a small car and it goes up and down and round in circles.*
- Ask students why these words are called compound nouns (because they are formed using two nouns together). Ask which one of the two nouns, the first or the second, is used as an adjective (the first one – it describes the type, e.g. what type of hockey, what type of surfing).
- Students copy the words into their notebooks. Play the recording one word at a time. Students listen and repeat the word and mark the stress over one of the syllables.
- Check answers by asking students to read the words and exaggerate the part of the word which is stressed. Ask *What do you notice about the pronunciation of compound nouns?* (The first noun is always stressed.)
- In pairs, students read the words aloud to each other to practise pronunciation.

2.20 Recording and answers

bungee jumping *ice hockey* *kite surfing* *paragliding*

roller coaster *water-skiing*

Optional activity

Define other examples of compound nouns, e.g. *music teacher, surfboard, homework*. Students listen and call out the correct compound noun. You could run this as a team competition. Make sure they pronounce the correct syllable in each compound noun, e.g. *music teacher*.

LANGUAGE WORKOUT OPTION

If you want to pre-teach the language students will be using in the following activities, you may like to go to the Language Workout box now.

5 SPEAKING

- Students copy the chart into their notebooks. Nominate two students to read the example conversation aloud. With a less confident class, check students understand *What was it like?* means *Describe it* and not *Did you like it?*
- Tell students that the aim is to find one person who answers *Yes* for each question. They only need one name for each activity. They must note the name and extra information when a student answers *yes*. Encourage confident students to ask more follow-up questions, e.g. *Where was it? Who were you with? How did you feel?* and provide more information in their answers.
- Ask students to stand up and move around, asking different students the questions. Monitor and help as necessary. Make a note of examples of good language and errors.
- When one student has completed the chart, stop the activity. In groups, students compare their charts. Ask a few students to tell you something interesting they learnt.
- Write on the board some examples of good language and some errors. Praise the former and ask students to correct the latter.

Extension Students add five more activities to the chart. In groups of four they ask and answer questions to complete the chart.

6 WRITING

- Students write about the activities they have tried. Set a 10-minute time limit to write a paragraph. Monitor and help as necessary.
- Students exchange their paragraphs in pairs and read and correct each other's work.

7 VOCABULARY

- Students copy the word map into their notebooks. They look back through the lesson and add all the sports they find to the map. Students then compare their answers and work in pairs or small groups to add their own ideas to the map. You could set a target for the total number of words to add to the map, e.g. 15.

Answers

Air: para-skiing, bungee jumping, paragliding, skydiving
Water: water-skiing, kite surfing, scuba diving, sailing
Land: football, ice-hockey, zorbing, free running

Suggested answers

Air: parachute jumping, hang gliding, parascending
Water: surfing, windsurfing, swimming, diving, canoeing
Land: mountain biking, rock climbing, horse riding, cycling, jogging, tennis, aerobics

Optional activities

- ♦ With a less confident class, dictate all the sports in a random order. Students listen and write the name in the correct place on the map.
- ♦ Organise the students into three groups (A, B, C). Each group works on one category within the word map, e.g. A works on Air. Students then regroup into groups of three (one A, one B, one C).
- ♦ Students write [✓✓] next to sports they have tried and like, [✓✗] next to ones they have tried and didn't like, [✓] next to ones they would like to try and [✗] next to ones they would not like to try.

8 SPEAKING

- Students look at the example. Nominate two students to read the example aloud. Tell students they are going prepare some more questions starting *Have you ever wanted to …?* and using the different verbs in the box. Give students two minutes to think of ways to finish the last three questions.
- In pairs, students ask and answer the questions. Remind students to ask *Why/Why not?* Monitor and help as necessary.

Optional activity

Fast finishers invent more questions to ask each other.

9 WRITING

- Ask students to think about things they have always wanted to do but have never done. Brainstorm possible topics, e.g. *sports, skills, travel, leisure activities*.
- Set a 10-minute time limit for students to write about five things they haven't done and why they have never done them.

Optional activity

Students read each other's paragraphs and offer advice on how to achieve these goals using *should/shouldn't*, e.g. *You should go the gym on Saturday morning – they have judo lessons there then.*

LANGUAGE WORKOUT

- Ask students to complete the Language box. Confident students can complete first and then check, while others can look back at exercise 2 and then complete.
- Students turn to page 117 of the Language File to check their answers.

Answers

ever ever never never
ever; never
present perfect past simple

- Highlight that:
  - *ever* means 'any time in the past until now'
  - *never* with the present perfect means 'not once in the past until now'
  - 'an indefinite time in the past' means you do not know exactly when it happened
- With a confident class, point out that the choice between the past simple or present perfect often depends on how we see the action. If we think it is related to now we use the present perfect. If we think it is something finished and in the past we use the past simple, even if the time is not mentioned. Compare *I've had skiing lessons but I've never been on a skiing holiday* (I might have more skiing lessons in the future), *My mother had skiing lessons but she didn't enjoy them.* (She probably won't have any more lessons).
- Drill the examples in chorus and individually for pronunciation.

PRACTICE

- Ask students to look at Practice exercise 15 of the Language File on page 117 and complete the sentences with the present perfect of the verbs and *ever* or *never*. Do the first one together as an example.
- Check the answers by asking different students to say the completed sentences.

Answers

1 *She's never seen anything like it.*
2 *Have you ever thought about going on holiday on your own?*
3 *I've always wanted to, but I've never had enough money.*
4 *Why haven't you ever learnt to swim?*
5 *Because I've never lived near the sea, and I hate swimming pools.*
6 *Have your parents ever left you at home when they've been on holiday?*

- Ask students to look at Practice exercise 18 of the Language File on page 118 and complete the sentences with the correct form of the verb – present perfect or past simple. Do the first one together as an example.
- Ask students to compare their answers in pairs. Check the answers by asking different students to say the completed sentences.

Answers

1 Have; tried 2 had; was 3 Have; let
4 had; did; let 5 Have; done 6 felt; stole; was; have; forgotten

Follow-up activities

♦ **Game** *Is it true?* Write the following activities on the board: *sleep under the stars, fly in a small plane, eat something unusual, see a very frightening film, lie to your parents*. Students ask each other *Have you ever …?* and must answer *Yes, I have* to every question. Their partner then asks follow-up questions to guess to whether they are telling the truth or lying.

♦ **Game** *Guess who* Organise students into groups of four. Write the following on the board:
All of us have …
Three of us have (never) …
Two of us have (never) …
One of us has (never) …
Students copy the sentence heads and finish the sentences so they are true for their group. To do this they will need to think of activities they have done and find out how many other students in their group have done it. Groups read their completed sentences to the class who can guess the student(s) in each case.

HOMEWORK

Students write an article to promote an experience doing a sport, visiting a place or learning a skill. The article should start *Have you ever wondered what … is like? Have you ever wanted to …?*, e.g. *Have you ever wanted to dance like a professional dancer?* Tell them to use the texts in exercise 2 as models.

WEBLINK

Students may like to visit www.exelement.co.uk or www.bbc.co.uk/worldservice/learningenglish/newsenglish/britain/extreme_sports.shtml to read more about extreme sports.

Revision and Extension p71

Language File pp117–118

Workbook Unit 5 Lesson 2 pp52–53

Photocopiable worksheet p175, notes p157

3 We've been friends ever since we met

Communicative Aims	**Language**	**Pronunciation**	**Vocabulary**	**Optional Aids**
Talking about achievements and important events	Present perfect with *for* and *since*	Syllable stress	Sport Prepositions Personal information	Follow-up activity: small cards for Vocabulary box

WARMER 1

Write the following time expressions on the board: *This week ... Last week ... Yesterday ... Today ...* Dictate true endings for the four sentences, e.g. *I've drunk four cups of coffee, I ate too much.* Students match endings and beginnings, then they make their own sentences and work with a partner.

WARMER 2

Tell the students that you have a puzzle for them. Say: *It's an event. People from all over the world take part in it. It happens every four years. You can win a gold, silver or bronze medal.* Elicit the answer *Olympic ® Games.*

1 OPENER

- The aim is to set the context and generate interest.
- Students look at the photo. Ask *Where is he from? Do you know his name? How is he feeling? What has he done?*

2 READING

- Play the introduction. Pause and check *How many medals did Usain win in Beijing?* (three). *Which two world records did he set in 2009?* (100 metres and 200 metres). Ask students to read the six headings. Tell them they will hear six quotations from Usain Bolt's autobiography (a book about his own life). They should match the headings to the quotations. Students read and listen.

2.21 Recording

See text on page 66 of the Student's Book.

Answers

1 Winning 2 Someone I rely on 3 What I do at a race 4 Something I'd like to change 5 Charity work 6 Drugs

3 AFTER READING

- Students read the questions and answer as many as they can before reading the text again to check and choose their answers from the list a–h. Point out that two of the answers are not used. Be prepared to explain *hit it off* (like each other from the start), *achievement* (something that you succeed in doing), *novelty* (the excitement something new creates), and *wear off* (gradually disappear).
- Check the answers and ask students where they found the answer in the text.

Answers

1 h 2 d 3 e 4 b 5 f 6 c
The two answers not used are a and g.

Optional activity

Students note all words in the text connected with sports events, e.g. *to win, gold medal, race, world record.*

Your response

Students work individually and answer the three questions, making notes. Ask them to work in pairs and compare their answers and then share their ideas with the class.

4 VOCABULARY

- Students complete the expressions from memory and then look back though the lesson to check their answers. Check students understand *fall out with someone* (have an argument with someone and stop being friends), *cut out something* (stop a bad habit).

Answers

1 at/in 2 to 3 about 4 with 5 in 6 in 7 at 8 in

Optional activity

Noughts and crosses (See Unit 2, Lesson 1 page 45) Play this to review these and other verbs and adjectives with dependent prepositions, e.g. *fed up with, dream of.*

5 PRONUNCIATION

- Write *achievement* on the board and elicit the number of syllables and where the main stress falls. Students look at the words in the box. In pairs, students decide where the main stress is.
- Play the recording for students to listen and check and then pause after each word for students to repeat.

2.22 Recording and answers

achievement attitude authorities
community development entertain
fortunate novelty opportunity primary

LANGUAGE WORKOUT OPTION

If you want to pre-teach the language students will be using in the following activities, you may like to go to the Language Workout box now.

6 SPEAKING

- Students read the two examples. Ask which tense is used and why. (The present perfect simple is used in the first example because the question is *How long …?* and the past simple is used in the second example because the question is *When …?*) Ask students to demonstrate the activity by asking and answering the example questions.
- Tell students to note their partner's answers. Be ready to help with the first part of question 3 as the choice of tense is less obvious: it is present perfect because the action is unfinished. Suggest students say the more natural *All my life* in answer to questions 7 or 8, rather than *Since I was born*.

Answers

1 *How long have we had this coursebook?*
2 *When did you start learning English?*
3 *Who have you known the longest in the class? When did you first meet them?*
4 *Which friend have you had the longest? How long have you been friends?*
5 *What's your favourite band? When did you first hear them?*
6 *What's your favourite sport? How long have you played it?*
7 *How long have you lived in this town?*
8 *How long have you lived in the same house or flat?*
9 *What colour are your favourite shoes? When did you get them?*
10 *Has your family got any pets? How long have you had them?*

- Students tell another partner about the most interesting answers. Ask some students to report back to the class.

Extension Students work in different pairs and interview their partner. They should give some false answers and have their partners work out which answers are false.

7 WRITING

- Students look back at exercise 6 and write their own answers to questions 3–10 as full sentences. Set a 10-minute time limit. Monitor and help as necessary.

LANGUAGE WORKOUT

- Ask students to complete the Language box. Confident students can complete first and then check, while others can look back at exercise 2 and then complete.
- Students turn to pages 117 of the Language File to check their answers.

Answers

since *for*
present perfect *past simple*

- Drill the example sentences in chorus and individually.

PRACTICE

- Ask students to look at exercise 16 of the Language File on p117 and complete the sentences.

Answers

1 for 2 since 3 since 4 for 5 for 6 since
7 since 8 for 9 for 10 since 11 for 12 since
13 since 14 since 15 for

- Tell students to look at exercise 17 of the Language File on p117. They put the verb in the present perfect and complete the sentences with *for* or *since*.

Answers

1 have asked; since 2 's been; since 3 's lived; since
4 's been; for 5 's won; since 6 's known; for

Optional activity

Game *Left or right?* For instructions see Unit 1, Lesson 2, p32. Play with the phrases *for* and *since*.

Follow-up activities

- Write *Olympic Games*® vertically down the board. In pairs students race to think of one word connected with the games for each letter.
- Students write new vocabulary from the lesson on cards to add to the Vocabulary box or to play *Password* (see Unit 2, Lesson1 p43).

HOMEWORK

Students write about a famous sportsperson of their choice. Have them use the reading on page 66 as a model.

WEBLINK

Students may like to visit www.usainbolt.com where they can read more about Usain Bolt.

Revision and Extension p71

Language File p117

Workbook Unit 5 Lesson 3 pp54–55

Photocopiable worksheet p176, notes p158

Integrated Skills
Describing personal experiences

Skills		Learner Independence	Vocabulary	Optional Aids
Reading Connecting ideas: blog about a journey *Listening* Checking details: conversation about an itinerary	*Speaking* Planning a backpacking trip *Writing* Blog describing a trip	Self assessment Word creation: noun suffix *-ity*	Countries Geographical features Useful expressions	Exercise 7: maps of different areas of the world

WARMER 1

Write the following sentences on the board.
I've been awake today for/since …
I've been at school today for/since …
I've been in this classroom for/since …
Students copy, choose *for* or *since* and complete the sentences so two are true and one is false. They read their sentences to their partner who guesses which one is false.

WARMER 2

Give students one minute to write down as many countries in South America as possible, with their capital cities. Tell students you will only accept the English name for the country. The pair with the most countries at the end of the minute writes them on the board. Other pairs call out countries which can be added to the list. Students say what they know about each country, e.g. what it is famous for, the food, the drink, tourist attractions.

1 OPENER

- The aim is to set the scene and generate interest in the reading.
- Students look at the photos. Ask where students think they were taken but do not provide the answers at this stage. Students use the words in the box to describe what they can see. Use the pictures to explain *llama, ruins, lake*.
- Students answer the quiz questions in pairs. Check the answers with the whole class. Note that Peru also has borders with Ecuador, Colombia, Brazil and Chile.

Answers
1 B 2 A 3 A 4 B 5 B

2 READING

- The aim is to complete the text by selecting appropriate connecting phrases.
- First, check general comprehension: Give students one minute to read the travelogue and say which country Julie is mainly writing about and the name of the two places in the photos. Check the answers (Peru, Machu Picchu, Lake Titicaca) and then give students a further five minutes to read the text more carefully and choose the appropriate phrase for the spaces.
- Students compare answers. Play the recording for students to listen and check.

2.23 Recording

We've been busy since we arrived in Peru from Ecuador a week ago! It's our fourth country so far. First we took a bus from Lima, the capital, to Cuzco (24 hours!). Somewhere on the journey I lost my watch, but it wasn't valuable, so it didn't really matter. Cuzco is a beautiful old town surrounded by the Andes mountains – it was the capital of the Inca empire. We spent a night in a hostel, and the next morning we started to walk the Inca trail to the city of Machu Picchu. The trail is often very steep and rises to over 4,000 metres in some places, so lots of people suffer from altitude sickness. I've been lucky because I haven't felt ill, but Simon has had a bad headache for a couple of days.
The trek along the Inca trail took four days and it was exhausting. But it was well worth it. On the last day, we got up at 4am to reach Machu Picchu in time for sunrise. When we got there, the city was invisible because it was covered in cloud. But suddenly the cloud lifted, and there was Machu Picchu on the edge of the mountain. It was magic!
We spent several hours wandering round the site – what an incredible place! Then back to Cuzco by bus and train for a hot shower and a rest before dinner. We've had some interesting food in Peru. I've already tried llama, which tastes a bit like beef. A local speciality in Cuzco is roast guinea pig, but I couldn't face it!
Tomorrow we're going to Lake Titicaca, on the border between Peru and Bolivia. It's the largest freshwater lake in South America and one of the highest in the world – it's 3,809 metres above sea level. The weather has been great – let's hope it stays that way.

Answers
1 c 2 a 3 f 4 e 5 b 6 d

Optional activity

In pairs/groups, students write five comprehension questions. They exchange their questions with another group and try to answer from memory.

3

- The aim is to encourage students to deduce meaning from context.
  Students look at the highlighted words in the text and match them to the correct meaning.

Answers

1 hostel 2 altitude 3 wandering 4 trail 5 steep 6 exhausting 7 valuable 8 invisible

4

- Students find and note examples of sentences in the text with *so* and *because*. They use the examples to complete the rules. Check answers.
- Use the examples to further check comprehension: Ask which part of the sentence happened first, e.g. *It wasn't valuable* (1), *so it didn't really matter* (2). *The city was invisible* (2) *because it was covered in cloud* (1).

Answers

Examples in text: It wasn't valuable, so it didn't really matter. The trail is often very steep, so lots of people suffer from altitude sickness. I've been lucky because I haven't felt ill. The city was invisible because it was covered in cloud.
We use because to talk about reason or cause.
We use so to talk about consequence or result.

- Students complete the sentences with *so* or *because*.

Answers

1 because 2 so 3 because 4 because 5 so

5 LISTENING

- Students look at the map of South America and read out the different countries they can see. Drill the names of the countries chorally.
- Play the recording. Students listen and put the countries in order.

2.24 Recording

ROD *So how long have you guys been on the road?*
JULIE *About two months – we left Britain eight weeks ago.*
ROD *And have you enjoyed it so far?*
SIMON *Oh yes, it's been absolutely great!*
ROD *Where did you start?*
SIMON *Well, we flew from London to Venezuela – and we spent a couple of weeks there.*
JULIE *Then we took a bus to Colombia – we've had an awful lot of long bus rides!*
SIMON *Some more comfortable than others!*
JULIE *That's right, but it's a great way to see the countryside.*
ROD *And it's cheap.*
SIMON *Yeah, really cheap. So we were in Colombia for three weeks, and then we went down to Ecuador.*
ROD *I loved Ecuador.*
JULIE *Yes, we did too. We stayed there for two weeks, and then we came to Peru.*
ROD *Did you spend any time in Lima?*
SIMON *No – we came straight to Cuzco. But we'll be back to Lima on our way to Chile.*
ROD *And after Chile?*
SIMON *From Chile we go to Argentina, and then from Buenos Aires across the River Plate to Uruguay.*
ROD *And then I guess you're going to Brazil.*
JULIE *Oh yes! We go over the border to Brazil – up the coast to Rio and Salvador, and then up the mouth of the Amazon.*
SIMON *And then we fly home.*
ROD *Sounds great.*

Answers

1 Venezuela 2 Colombia 3 Ecuador 4 Peru 5 Chile 6 Argentina 7 Uruguay 8 Brazil

Optional activity

In groups of three, students act out the dialogue.

6 SPEAKING

- Read the example. In pairs, students talk about the journey using *already* and *yet*.

Answers

They've already visited Venezuela, Colombia, Ecuador and Peru.
They haven't been to Chile, Argentina, Uruguay and Brazil yet.

Optional activity

Students work in pairs or small groups and tell each other which countries in general they have visited and which they haven't visited yet.

7

- Tell students they are going to plan a backpacking trip with their partner. They are going to go during their long holiday from school so they need to plan for that length of time and consider the weather around the world at that time of year.
- In their pairs, students decide which country or countries they are going to visit. If possible, provide a map of this area for them. Students decide which places they are going to visit.

Optional activities

- ♦ Give students time to research the country/countries they have chosen at the library or on the Internet.
- ♦ Students present their plans to the class. Students vote on which trip sounds most enjoyable, dangerous, cultural, or relaxing.

8 GUIDED WRITING

- Tell students they are now on the road (on their backpacking trip somewhere). Give students five minutes to discuss the answers to the questions with their partner and take notes.
- Tell students they are going to write a blog including this information. Ask *How do you usually start a travel blog?* (I/We're in …). Ask them to refer to the text in exercise 2.
- Give students 10 minutes to write their blog. This could be done in pairs with both students writing the same blog or individually. Encourage students to use a range of adjectives to describe the journey and the places, and to link sentences with *so* and *because*.

9 LEARNER INDEPENDENCE

- The aim is to encourage students to review the language in this unit, to build confidence by showing them what they have learnt, and to allow students to focus on individual areas of weakness.
- Students make a list of what they have learnt. Check that students have a complete list of the language and information covered in the unit.
- Students choose one or more areas which they would like to review. Students wishing to review the same area, could work together. For grammar, students can look at the examples and re-read the Language File at the end of the Student's Book. For vocabulary, students can make a new list or mind map, or think of ways to remember particularly difficult words.

10 WORD CREATION

- The aim is for students to learn one way in which nouns can be formed from adjectives and extend their vocabulary.
- Students complete the sentences individually and then compare in pairs. Check answers as a whole class.
- Tell students to think about the pronunciation of the nouns. Ask *What is the rule?* (The main stress is always on the syllable before the *-ity* ending).

Answers

1 speciality *2 activity* *3 possibility* *4 popularity*
5 nationality *6 responsibility* *7 electricity* *8 reality*

11 PHRASEBOOK

- Ask students to look through the unit to find the expressions, and look at how they are used. Be ready to help as necessary.
- Play the recording, pausing after each expression for students to repeat.
- Students can add expressions they like to their Personal Phrasebooks.
- Ask students to work in pairs to make up the five-line dialogue. Invite some pairs to act out their dialogues in front of the class.

2.25 Recording

I didn't have a clue. (L2, Ex2)
Have you ever wondered what it's like? (L2, Ex2)
I've never had so much fun. (L2, Ex2)
I've never done anything like it before. (L2, Ex2)
It didn't really matter. (L4, Ex2)
It was well worth it. (L4, Ex2)
It was magic! (L4, Ex2)
What an incredible place! (L4, Ex2)
I couldn't face it. (L4, Ex2)
Let's hope it stays that way. (L4, Ex2)

Follow-up activities

- ♦ In groups, students choose one area of grammar, vocabulary or information from the list made in exercise 9 and prepare a short test on the area for the rest of the class.
- ♦ **Game** *Shark* For instructions see Unit 1, Lesson 3, p33. Play with new words from the unit.

HOMEWORK

Students design a word map with the word *TRAVEL* in the centre. They each decide on their own sub-categories, e.g. *transport, accommodation* and add as many words as they can including words from this unit.

WEBLINK

Students may like to visit www.lonelyplanet.com/peru for travel information about Peru and photos.

Revision and Extension p71

Workbook Unit 5 Lesson 4 pp56–57

Inspiration EXTRA!

Optional Aids

Game: slips of paper

LANGUAGE LINKS

- Write the word *colours* on the board. Tell students there are eleven words to describe basic colours in English. Students work in pairs and write down as many words for colours as they can.
- Students read the text and check their answers.
- Ask students to read the list of colours and find out if they know any of them. Students use their dictionaries or the Internet to find the meaning of each word and identify which of them are colours of the rainbow (violet and indigo).

Optional activities

- Write these languages on the board: *Japanese, Hanunóo, Navaho* and *Dani*. Ask students to read the text again and say what is strange about the words for colours in each of these languages, e.g. *Japanese has one word which means 'blue', 'green' or 'pale'.*
- Students rank the six extra colours in order of preference and give reasons for their choice.

GAME HELP!

- Organise students into groups. Ask students to read the instructions carefully. Check comprehension by asking: *Who has a problem?* (the tourist). *Where is he/she?* (in a foreign country). *Can he/she speak the language?* (No). First, give students five minutes in their groups to write possible problems on slips of paper. Encourage them to be creative, as in the examples.
- Collect the problems from each group and pass them, face down, to the next group. One student in each group takes one of these problems and mimes it to their group. The other students in their group guess the problem. The student who guesses correctly takes the next problem and so on.

Optional activities

- You could make this more competitive by saying that the winning group is the group that guesses the most in five minutes.
- Once the groups have worked out the problems they could try and think of some solutions.

SKETCH THE INTERVIEW

- The aim is for students to enjoy using their English while also reviewing language presented in this unit and getting valuable stress and intonation practice.
- Ask the students to look at the title and the cartoon and establish that the sketch is about a job interview. Students guess which one is the interviewer, the man or the woman, and what the job is.
- With a more confident class, play the recording with books closed. With a less confident class, play the recording while the students follow in their books. Check the answer (the man is interviewing the woman for a deep-sea diving job and the woman is interviewing the man for an interviewer job!).

2.26 Recording

See text on page 70 of the Student's Book.

- Divide the class into two equal groups and play the recording again, with one group repeating the man's role in chorus and the other group repeating the woman's role. Encourage students to exaggerate stress and intonation.
- Ask the students to close their books and play the recording again. Then ask the students to work in pairs and practise the sketch. Choose several pairs to act out the sketch in front of the class.

Optional activity

Make an audio or video recording of students performing the sketch.

REVISION

Lesson 1

Answers
She's already been to lots of gigs.
She hasn't learnt first aid yet.
She has already performed in two school plays.
She's already ridden a horse.
She's already written a couple of poems.
She hasn't been camping with friends yet.
She's already organised a birthday party.
She hasn't been skiing yet.
She's already held a baby.
He's already been to a gig.
He hasn't performed in a play yet.
He hasn't ridden a horse yet.
He hasn't written a poem yet.
He's already been camping with friends.
He's already organised a birthday party.
He's already been skiing.
He hasn't learnt to drive yet.
He hasn't held a baby yet.

Lesson 2
Students' own answers

Lesson 3
- You could insist on students writing sentences that are true.

Students' own answers

EXTENSION

Lesson 1

Suggested answers
Have they been to/travelled across/crossed … yet? Yes, they've already been to/travelled across/crossed …
Have they travelled 20,000 miles yet? Yes, they've already travelled 20,000 miles.
Have they been on the road for three months yet? Yes, they've already been on the road for three months.
Have they had any accidents yet? No, they haven't had any accidents yet.
Have they arrived in the USA yet? Yes, they've just arrived in the USA.
Have they completed their journey yet? Yes, they've just completed their journey.

Language File pp117–118

Lesson 2
Students' own answers

Lesson 3
Students' own answers

YOUR CHOICE!

- Organise students into groups depending on their learning style. Each group does the activity for their own learning style. Set a 10-minute time limit for all groups.
- Monitor and help groups. Check if necessary. You could provide written answers for groups to check their own work.
- Encourage students to experiment with other learning styles and try one of the other activities of their choice.

CONSTRUCTION

Answers
1 haven't tried 2 invented 3 wanted
4 didn't work 5 tried 6 have opened
7 has tried 8 have had

REFLECTION

Answers
A B B A A A B

ACTION

- Students follow the instructions in the box, taking it in turns to remember and add to the sentence.
- When one round has finished, remind students to try with another verb and change their order in the group.
- Students could report back on who has the best memory.

INTERACTION

- Divide students into small groups. Suggest students take two minutes to think about what they have always wanted. They then take turns to tell their group.
- Students could report back to the rest of the class on any interesting points.

Workbook Unit 5 Inspiration EXTRA! pp58–59

5 CULTURE

Tourism

Optional Aids

Exercise 2 Optional activity: small cards
Exercise 3 Optional activity: photos of Machu Picchu, Angkor Wat, Pompeii and the Taj Mahal

1 READING

- Ask students to look at the two photos. Ask *Where do you think this is? What can you see in the photos?*
- Students read and/or listen to the texts A–E and answer questions 1–3. With a less confident class, students work in pairs and help each other. With a more confident class, students work individually and then compare answers. Check answers with the whole class.
- Students answer questions 4–6 individually then compare their answers in pairs or as a class.

2.27 Recording

See text on page 72 of the Student's Book.

Answers

1 C; E; B/D; A
2 less than a third
3 be careful; be tidy; respect what the local people have planted; not take the locals for granted
4–6 Students' own answers

Optional activity

2.27 Play the poem (text E) again and ask students to read it aloud in time with the recording to give practice in rhythm and intonation. Point out that *give someone an earful* means to criticise someone angrily, and *practise what you preach* is behave in the same way you expect other people to behave.

2 VOCABULARY

- Students find the words in the different texts and use the context to match to the definitions.

Answers

1 c 2 h 3 g 4 b 5 f 6 d 7 e 8 a

Optional activity

Fast finishers check any new vocabulary from the texts in a dictionary and put these words, together with an example or definition, on cards for the Vocabulary box.

3 LISTENING

- Tell students they are going to hear more about the effect of tourists on some well-known tourist destinations. Ask students to look at the names of the four destinations. Ask *Do you know them? Where are they? What are they? Have you been there?*
- Students read the text and guess the answers. With a less confident class, check how each of the options is said.
- Play the recording. Students listen and choose the correct option. If necessary, play the whole or part of the recording again. Ask four different students to read the four texts aloud to check answers.

2.28 Recording

See text on page 73 of the Student's Book.

Answers

1,000,000; in a group; reducing; $20; 863,000; two; 3,000,000

Optional activities

- ♦ Bring in photos of the four tourist destinations for students to look at.
- ♦ Ask students to comment on the ideas suggested in the listening, e.g. *you are only allowed to visit in a group, foreigners pay more.* Ask *Do you think these are good ideas?*

4 MINI-PROJECT RESPONSIBLE TOURISM

- Students read the instructions. Point out that the second paragraph is about possible problems with responsible tourism, not normal tourism. With a less confident class, students discuss their ideas and make notes together first.
- Set a 15-minute time limit. Monitor and prompt students to connect their ideas into longer sentences using *which* and *who*, *however*, *so* and *because*. Note examples of good language use. Put these on the board.

Optional activity

In groups, students use their ideas from the mini-project to make an oral presentation on either point.

WEBLINK

Students may like to visit www.responsibletravel.com where they can read about holidays offered by one responsible tourism company.

Workbook Culture pp60–61

1 He had won awards

Communicative Aims	Language	Pronunciation	Vocabulary	Optional Aids
Describing a sequence of past events	Past perfect	Syllable stress	Disability	Follow up activity 1: magazine photos of non-famous people

WARMER 1

Elicit the words *blind* and *deaf* from the students and find out if they know anyone who suffers from these conditions. In pairs, ask students to try to imagine what it is like to be blind or deaf and write a list of things which must be more difficult or impossible to do, e.g. *blind – It must be difficult to use public transport.* You could take a class vote on which condition they think would be most difficult to cope with.

WARMER 2

Game *Guess what?* Tell students that you are going to slowly draw something on the board and that they should try to guess what it might be, as you are drawing. Start with a circle and then slowly add extra lines and circles to draw a bicycle. The first student to guess correctly is the winner. In pairs, students then discuss if they like/dislike cycling, giving their reasons and describing their own bike if they have one.

1 OPENER

- The aim is to set the context for the reading in exercise 2, which introduces some inventions connected to hands/bodies.
- Ask the students to look at their hands and in pairs make a list of things they can do with them. Give *wave* as an example. The pair with the longest list should read it to the rest of the class.

Suggested answers

wave, shake hands, point, eat, write, type, cook, wash, build, paint, read Braille

2 READING

- Ask students to look at the photos and predict which of the four inventions the pictures might represent. Use the photos to elicit vocabulary such as *glove, disabled, Braille, dots* and *blind*. Play the recording. Students read and listen and check their predictions. Encourage them to guess unfamiliar words from context. Be prepared to check/explain *workout, recycled, inspiration, limited mobility* and *recover strength*.

2.29 Recording

See text on page 74 of the Student's Book.

Answers

From school project to successful business – B
The glove that translates – D
The waterbike – A
Braille – C

3 AFTER READING

- Students read and listen to the dialogue again and answer questions 1–9. Remind students that there may be more than one correct answer for each. Explain that the expression *to do with* in questions 2, 4 and 9 means connected/related to.
- Check the answers by asking different students to ask and answer the questions.

Answers

1 Louis Braille's invention.
2 Louis Braille's and Ryan Patterson's inventions.
3 Ruth Amos's and Krysta Morlan's inventions.
4 Krysta Morlan's invention.
5 Ryan Patterson's invention.
6 Louis Braille's invention.
7 Ryan Patterson's invention.
8 Krysta Morlan's invention.
9 Ryan Patterson's, Ruth Amos's and Louis Braille's inventions.

Optional activity

Fast finishers could write other *Whose invention …?* questions to ask their partner or the whole class.

Your response

Have students discuss the questions in pairs and then as a class.

4 PRONUNCIATION

- Ask students to copy the words in the box into their notebooks and work in pairs to decide which are stressed on the first syllable.
- Play the recording, pausing after each word for students to repeat and asking which syllable is stressed. Make sure students mark the stressed syllable on the words in their notebooks.

2.30 Recording and answers

advantage balance bicycle communicate disabled

electronics enemy inspiration invention

mobility realise recover simplify translator

university

Optional activities

- With their books closed, students remember which of these words related to which of the four inventions from exercise 2. Confident students could try to remember exact sentences from the text. They check in the text afterwards.
- Students look back through earlier units of the book and find five words of more than two syllables for which they know the stress pattern. They write the words in a list and give them to another student to mark the stressed syllables.

LANGUAGE WORKOUT OPTION

If you want to pre-teach the language students will be using in the following activities, you may like to go to the Language Workout box now.

5 SPEAKING

- Ask students to look at the photo. Ask *Why were they celebrating/happy/delighted?* Ask students to find a reason from those in the box (win the match) and elicit a sentence with the past perfect: *The players were delighted because they had won the match.*
- Ask the students to read sentences 1–8 and match each with a reason from the box. In pairs, students must complete the sentences using the reason and the past perfect. Encourage students to speak and to use contractions.
- Ask different pairs to tell their answers to the rest of the class.

Answers

1 *I didn't do my homework because I had left my books at school.*
2 *She was exhausted because she hadn't slept all night.*
3 *He didn't call her back because he had forgotten her number.*
4 *She couldn't get into the house because she had lost the key.*
5 *They were really happy because they had passed the exam.*
6 *I was hungry because I hadn't eaten anything all day.*
7 *We couldn't go to the gig because the tickets had sold out.*
8 *The players were delighted because they had won the match.*

Optional activities

- Fast finishers make up similar sentence stems and ask their partner to complete them with a reason, using the past perfect.
- In pairs, only one student has their book open. This student reads the *because* clause from the sentences in exercise 5. Their partner tries to remember or invent a suitable beginning to the sentence.

6

- Ask students to read the questions first and think about any of the experiences they had last year. Be prepared to give any vocabulary they might need to discuss these experiences or ask them to check it in their dictionaries.
- In pairs, students then interview each other using the questions. Remind students to note down their partner's answers.
- Ask one or two confident students to tell the class something they found out about their partner.

Extension Students write sentences about their partner using their notes to help.

7 WRITING

- The aim is to enable students to write about things they did yesterday using the past perfect and past simple.
- Ask students to make a list of things they did yesterday after coming home from school, if possible in chronological order. Encourage students to use the prompts to give them ideas and to give further details, e.g. *eat some chips* rather than *have something to eat.*
- Ask a confident student to read the example sentence. Check with the students which tense the verbs are in and why.
- Students write similar sentences about their own day, using *after*, the past perfect and past simple.

Optional activity

Students read some of their sentences to a partner and try to find two things which they both did after coming home from school. Confident students could report back to the rest of the class, using *After we'd come home from school, we …*

Extension Students work in pairs and interview their partner about what they did yesterday after school.

LANGUAGE WORKOUT

- Ask students to complete the Language box. Confident students can complete first and then check, while others can look back at exercise 2 and then complete.
- Students turn to page 118 of the Language File to check their answers.

Answers

had won had been had I'd
past perfect

- Highlight that:
  - we use the past perfect when we want to make it clear that one past event happened before another. We do not use it if the order of events is chronological and clear, e.g. *She put her helmet on and got on her bike.*
  - *had* is used as the auxiliary verb for all persons.
  - *hadn't* is used in the negative form.
  - the *'d* contraction is generally used and represents *had*, not *would*.
  - past perfect is often used with time expressions *by* and *after*.
- Drill the examples in chorus for pronunciation and stress. Encourage students to use contractions.

Optional activity

Ask students to look back at the text in exercise 2 and find more examples of the past perfect.

PRACTICE

- Ask students to look at Practice exercise 19 of the Language File on page 118 and complete the sentences with the past simple or past perfect of the verbs. Do the first one together as an example.
- Check the answers by asking different students to say the completed sentences.

Answers

1 didn't; had invented 2 hadn't left; created
3 was; had designed 4 loved; hadn't ridden
5 visited; had been 6 developed; had told

Follow-up activities

♦ **Game** *Good/bad day* Show students a magazine photo of a person (not a famous person). Ask the students to give the person a name, age and occupation. Write *(Person's name) arrived home at 11pm feeling terrible. It had been an awful day …* on the board. Invite a student to give an example of what the person had done that day which had made them feel bad, e.g. *She'd argued with her boyfriend.* Another student repeats the story so far and adds another bad thing that had happened that day. Students continue repeating the story so far and adding one extra thing. Students who cannot remember are out of the game. This can be played in small groups once students have understood what to do, and can be repeated with *a wonderful day, a frightening day, a surprising day*, etc.

♦ **Game** *Truth or lie* Students write five sentences about what they had done by different ages in their lives, e.g. *By the age of 5, I'd learnt to ride a bike.* Some sentences should be true and some false. They read them to their partner who asks them further questions, e.g. *Was it difficult? Who taught you?* and guesses if their sentences are true or false.

HOMEWORK

Students find a photograph, either of their own or from a magazine and write five sentences about what they know or think had happened before the moment of the photograph being taken, e.g. *a photo of a barbecue – we'd lit the barbecue, we'd invited friends round, we'd bought sausages at the supermarket.*

WEBLINK

Students may like to visit www.inventionreaction.com/weird-inventions for details of weird and wonderful suggestions for new inventions.

Revision and Extension p83

Language File p118

Workbook Unit 6 Lesson 1 pp62–63

Photocopiable worksheet p177, notes p158

2 People didn't use to throw things away

Communicative Aims	Language	Pronunciation	Vocabulary	Optional Aids
Talking about past habits and states	*used to* + infinitive	/eɪ/ *waste* /e/ *west*	Recycling Household items Materials	Warmer 2: some small reusable objects Exercise 5 Optional activity: materials on sticky notes Follow-up activity: large pieces of paper and scissors

WARMER 1

If you set the homework from lesson 1, ask students to work in groups to show each other their photos. Other students guess what was happening and what had happened before.

WARMER 2

Game *Recycle it!* Divide students into small groups of about four students and give each group an object such as a stone, a plastic cup, a plastic bottle, a juice carton. Tell students they have five minutes to think of new uses for their object, e.g. a stone could become a paperweight, a plastic bottle could become a pen pot by cutting off the top. Groups report back to the rest of the class to see which group had the best/most ideas.

Useful information

In the last 20 years, the amount of rubbish produced by each citizen in the industrialised world has tripled. In a recent survey of recycling rates in 25 countries, Switzerland and Austria came out on top, whilst the UK, Ireland and Mexico were among the lowest recyclers.

1 OPENER

- The aim is to set the context and predict the content of the reading in exercise 2.
- Explain that the items in photos 1–5 are all recycled. Check that students understand *recycled* by eliciting some materials which are commonly recycled, e.g. *glass and paper.* Ask students to discuss in pairs what the items in the photos are, and what they might be made from. The emphasis is on generating ideas and students might not have the exact answers.
- Listen to their ideas as a class. On the board make a list of the items and possible materials they suggest.

2 READING

- Play the recording. Students read and listen to the text and check their predictions.
- Encourage students to guess unfamiliar words from context. Be prepared to explain *mend, wear out* (past simple: wore), *consume, campaign* and *waste.*

2.31 Recording

See text on page 76 of the Student's Book.

3 AFTER READING

- Students read the text again and answer questions 1–6.
- Check the answers by asking different students to ask and answer the questions.
- Ask them to tell you what items 1–5 in the pictures used to be.

Answers

1 Because we used to mend our clothes and we didn't throw things away.
2 Because we used to wear shoes until they wore out.
3 Because we consume more.
4 Metal cans, glass bottles and paper
5 Cans and plastic bags
6 Yoghurt pots and glass bottles
The chair used to be books.
The house used to be a jet plane.
The vase used to be a shoe.
The T-shirt used to be plastic bottles.
The pencil case used to be a rubber car tyre.

Optional activities

Fast finishers could find examples of materials vocabulary in the text, in preparation for exercise 5.

Your response

Students work individually to answer the questions and make some notes. Then they compare their answers in pairs or small groups. Each pair or group reports back to the whole class.

LANGUAGE WORKOUT OPTION

If you want to pre-teach the language students will be using in the following activities, you may like to go to the Language Workout box now.

4 SPEAKING

- Ask students to look at the picture of a sitting room 200 years ago. Ask students if they can see anything in the picture which seems wrong. Go through one example as a class, eliciting a sentence with *didn't use to* to explain the mistakes in the picture and *used to* to give the correction.
- Ask the students to make similar sentences in pairs, using the phrases.
- Ask one or two pairs to tell the rest of the class one of their sentences.

Answers

1 *They didn't use to have electric light.*
2 *They didn't use to have vacuum cleaners.*
3 *They used to light candles.*
4 *They didn't use to make phone calls.*
5 *They used to paint pictures.*
6 *They used to play cards.*
7 *They didn't use to take photos.*
8 *They didn't use to watch TV.*
9 *They used to write letters.*

Extension Read the example aloud to the class. Students work individually and think of ten other differences between life now and life 200 years ago. Then they compare their lists in pairs. You may need to help less confident students by suggesting items that didn't exist 200 years ago, e.g. *cars, washing-machines, fridges*. Listen to their ideas as a class and make a list of items on the board.

Optional activity

In pairs, ask students to discuss how school life might have been different 50 years ago, e.g. *There didn't use to be a computer room.*

5 VOCABULARY

- Before students look at the exercise, ask them how many different materials they can think of. They then check if they can see these materials in the box in exercise 5, and can ask *What does … mean?* or check in their dictionaries if there are materials they don't know.
- Ask two confident students to read the example A/B dialogue out loud and elicit the end of the sentence: *It's made of … (plastic/metal).*
- In pairs, students have similar conversations discussing what the other objects are made of. Note that there are often several possibilities so be prepared for some argument!
- Check the answers by asking pairs to repeat their conversations to the whole class.

Optional activities

- Fast finishers could think of all the other possible materials for the objects in the box.
- **Game** *Run and grab!* Write the materials from exercise 5 on sticky notes and stick them to the board. Divide the class into two teams and choose a student from each team to stand at an equal distance from the board. Say the name of an object made from one of the materials, e.g. *a pullover*. The two students must run to the board and try to grab the note with the correct material. The one who reaches it first wins the material for their team. Repeat with two new students, until all the materials have gone from the board.

6 PRONUNCIATION

- Model the two sounds by saying the example words *waste* and *west*. Highlight the more relaxed mouth position for /e/ and the two-sound nature of /eɪ/ beginning with /e/ and ending in /ɪ/.
- Play the recording, pausing after each word for students to repeat.
- Students listen to the rest of the recording, writing down the words they hear in their notebooks. They then compare what they have written with a partner.
- Check the answers as a class, writing each word on the board to show spelling. Check for each example if the sound is /eɪ/ like *waste* or /e/ like *west*.

2.32 Recording

/eɪ/ *waste later pain paper saint tale wait*
/e/ *west letter pen pepper sent tell wet*

2.32 Recording and answers

west letter pain paper sent tale wait

Optional activity

Students try to add two more words containing the correct sound to each column.

7 SPEAKING

- Tell students they are going to talk about how they have changed since becoming a teenager.
- Ask confident students to read the example sentences out loud. Find out if any of the sentences are also true for your students.
- Ask students to make notes about changes in their lives for the topics in the instruction.
- In pairs, students use their notes to tell each other about how they are now different to what they used to be. Remind them to note down their partner's answers.
- Ask one or two students to tell the class something they found out about their partner.

Optional activity

Students change partner and tell their new partner about their previous one, using their notes to help.

8 WRITING

- The aim is for students to write about how they and other students have changed, using *used to* where appropriate.
- Remind students to use their notes from exercise 7 and to write about themselves and other students. Encourage students to organise their writing into separate paragraphs for each topic.
- Students give their writing to another student to read and check for accuracy.

Extension Ask students to write about how their town or city has changed. Elicit one or two examples to help less confident students before they start writing, e.g. *There used to be a hotel opposite the school but now there's a supermarket. We didn't use to have a metro.*

LANGUAGE WORKOUT

- Ask students to complete the Language box. Confident students can complete first and then check, while others can look back at exercises 2 and 3 and then complete.
- Students turn to page 118 of the Language File to check their answers.

Answers

used to *used to* *did(n't) use* *did ... use*

- Highlight that:
  - *used to* can express past habits and states. Check that students can give an example of a state and non-state verb.
  - The negative form is *didn't use to* and the question form *did ... use to?*
  - the past simple can be used in place of *used to* in all cases.
- Drill the examples in chorus for pronunciation and stress. Highlight the /s/ sound in *used to,* in contrast with /z/ when used as a main verb. Remind students that *used* has only one syllable. Encourage students to produce the weak form of *to*, putting greater stress on *used* so the whole phrase sounds like one word /'juːstə/

PRACTICE

- Ask students to look at Practice exercise 20 of the Language File on page 118 and complete the sentences with the correct form of *used to.*
- Students complete the sentences with *used to* [✓], *didn't use to* [✗] or the question form of *used to* [?].
- Check the answers by asking different students to say the completed sentences.

Answers

1 didn't use to *2 used to* *3 didn't use to*
4 Did ... use to *5 didn't use to* *6 Did ... use to*

Optional activity

Fast finishers look back at the text in exercise 2 to find more examples of *used to.*

Follow-up activities

- Students work in small groups to make an advertising poster for the *Recycle Now* campaign to be started in their school. Give suggestions for things to include on their poster: the aim of the campaign, reasons why we need to recycle more nowadays, examples of materials that can be recycled, illustrations, descriptions or photos of items made from recycled materials, suggestions for how the campaign can be introduced in the school.
- On the board, write the names of ten famous people, e.g. *Tom Cruise, David Beckham.* Read out sentences with *used to* about these people, e.g. *He used to be married to Nicole Kidman, He used to play for Manchester United.* In small groups, students write down which person each sentence refers to. The group with the most correct answers wins.

HOMEWORK

Students interview an older person, e.g. a parent, guardian, teacher or grandparent about how life was different when they were a teenager. Give topic areas that could be covered in the interview, e.g. school, entertainment, family, fashion, communications, money. Students can conduct the interview in their own language, but should write up five of the questions and answers in English, using *used to* where appropriate.

WEBLINK

Students may like to visit www.allfreecrafts.com/recycling-crafts/index.shtml to find out more about recycling everyday items.

Revision and Extension p83

Language File p118

Workbook Unit 6 Lesson 2 pp64–65

Photocopiable notes p158, worksheet p178

3 The first car was invented by him

Communicative Aims	Language	Pronunciation	Vocabulary	Optional Aids
Talking about inventions	Past simple passive	Syllable stress	Inventions Phrases with *do* and *make*	Warmer 2: a list of objects and inventions that students can draw

WARMER 1

Write the word *Inventions* on the board and tell the students that this is the theme of the lesson. Ask students to work in pairs to make as many other words as possible using only letters from this word, e.g. *ten, note, vote, in, sent, son, on, stone, tin, nest*. The first pair to find seven words are the winners and must read their list to the class.

WARMER 2

Game *Pictionary* Write a list of the names of objects and inventions, e.g. *robot, bicycle, plane, mobile phone, computer, MP3 player*. Divide the class into three teams. Ask a student from each group to come to the front of the class and show them the first word on the list. They must run back to their team and draw the object. The 'artist' cannot speak. The first team to guess correctly wins a point.

1 OPENER

- The aim is to set the context for the reading.
- Students decide which of the question words are used in each question. Ask them to work individually and then compare their answers in pairs. Check that they have chosen the correct question words.
- Students match the questions with the answers. Do not check their answers at this point. They can do this when they listen to the recording and/or read the text in exercise 2.

Useful information

Leonardo da Vinci's best known works of art include *Mona Lisa* (painted 1503-1515) and *The Last Supper* (1498). In recent years there has been a surge of interest not only in his art, but also in the man himself. Much of this is due to the success of Dan Brown's fictional novel *The Da Vinci Code*.

2 READING

- Play the recording. Students read and listen to the text. Ask them to check their answers from exercise 1.
- Encourage students to guess unfamiliar words from context. Be prepared to explain *attempt*, *replica*, *clockwork* and *sketch*.

2.33 Recording

See text on page 78 of the Student's Book.

Answers

1 Who 2 What 3 When 4 When 5 What
1d 2a 3e 4b 5c

Your response

Students work individually and decide which fact about Leonardo's inventions is the most surprising. Encourage them to think of reasons for their choice. Students compare their ideas in pairs and then report back to the whole class.

LANGUAGE WORKOUT OPTION

If you want to pre-teach the language students will be using in the following activities, you may like to go to the Language Workout box now.

3 SPEAKING

- Read the example question aloud to the class. Point out that all the questions are in the past using the past simple passive. Students work in pairs to fill the gaps to complete the questions using the verbs in brackets at the end of each question.
- If students find it difficult to formulate the questions, check the answers before students ask and answer them with their partner.
- Students ask and answer the questions in pairs.
- Check the answers by playing the recording. Be prepared to pause the recording after each question to give students a chance to correct their work.

2.34 Recording

1 *The first telephone call was made in 1876.*
2 *The zip was invented in 1893.*
3 The Last Supper *and* Mona Lisa *were painted by Leonardo da Vinci.*
4 Hamlet *was written by William Shakespeare.*
5 *The Pyramids of Giza were built over 4,000 years ago.*
6 *X-rays were discovered in 1895.*
7 The Marriage of Figaro *was composed by Mozart.*
8 The Simpsons *were created by Matt Groening.*

Answers

1 *When was the first telephone call made?* – A
2 *When was the zip invented?* – A
3 *Who were* The Last Supper *and* Mona Lisa *painted by?* – B
4 *Who was* Hamlet *written by?* – B
5 *When were the Pyramids of Giza built?* – A
6 *When were X-rays discovered?* – A
7 *Who was* The Marriage of Figaro *composed by?* – B
8 *Who were* The Simpsons *created by?* – A

Extension Students work in small groups and write five more questions about inventions using *who, what, when* and the past simple passive. They exchange questions with another group and try and answer their questions.

Optional activities

- Fast finishers write questions about the text in exercise 2 using the question words from exercise 1.
- Ask students to find examples of past participles in the text.

4 READING

- Set the context for the text before students do the exercise by checking that students understand *survey* and asking them to guess what were the most and least popular inventions of the last 150 years.
- Ask students to read the text and fill the gaps in the text with suitable nouns.
- Play the recording so that they can check their answers.

2.35 Recording and answers

Best and worst inventions
In a recent radio survey, the [1] ***bicycle*** *was chosen by UK listeners as their favourite invention of the last 150 years. It was invented in Paris by Pierre Lallement in 1866. Atomic and nuclear* [2] ***bombs*** *were voted the least favourite inventions.*
Listeners were invited to nominate their favourite and least favourite inventions. Then a shortlist of ten 'best' and ten 'worst' inventions was drawn up for the poll. The computer, the [3] ***light bulb*** *and the World Wide Web were included in the list of ten 'best' inventions. Plastic* [4] ***bags****, mobile* [5] ***phones*** *and car alarms were listed among the 'worst' inventions.*
Interestingly, three inventions were selected for both lists: [6] ***television****, the telephone and the internal combustion engine.*

Optional activity

Ask students to write true and false sentences about the poll, e.g. *the lightbulb* was included in the list of ten 'worst' inventions (false). They read these to their partner who identifies if they are true or false and corrects the false sentences.

5 VOCABULARY

- Before students look at the exercise, write *do* and *make* on the board, and ask students if they know any expressions with these verbs. If they don't have any ideas, give a suggestion, e.g. *a noise*, and ask students which of the two verbs it goes with.
- In pairs, students look at the list and choose the correct verb, *do* or *make*.

Answers

1 make 2 do 3 make 4 do 5 make 6 make
7 make 8 do 9 make 10 make 11 do 12 do

Optional activity

Game *Left or right?* For instructions see Unit 1, Lesson 2, p32. Read out expressions from the exercise without *make* or *do*.

6 PRONUNCIATION

- Write *artist* and *attempt* on the board and ask students which syllable is stressed.
- Ask students to copy the table into their notebooks and work in pairs to decide which words go in each column.
- Play the recording, pausing after each word for students to repeat and to check they have the word in the correct column.

2.36 Recording and answers

■▪ *artist clockwork damage engine practice robot surface*
▪■ *attempt believe compose create display invent machine*

7 SPEAKING

- Elicit from the class any inventions from this lesson and make a list on the board.
- Ask students to decide which they think are the best and worst. Give students a minute to decide and make a few notes giving their reasons for their choices.
- In pairs, students compare and justify their choices. Encourage them to try to change their partner's mind if they disagree.
- Ask confident students to report their choices to the rest of the class. Have a class vote on the best and worst invention.

Optional activity

Students work in small groups to think of three new inventions they hope to see in the future, e.g. *a computer that can do your homework for you.*

8 WRITING

- The aim is for students to write about what they think are the best and worst inventions of all time, using the past simple passive where appropriate.

- Brainstorm possible inventions as a whole class first, if you think some students may need ideas.
- Ask students to write a paragraph each about the best and the worst invention. Remind students to include answers to the three questions.
- Students give their writing to another student to read, check that they have included all the necessary points and that the writing is accurate.

Optional activity

Ask students not to write the name of their invention in their writing. Students read each other's paragraphs and try to guess which inventions are being described.

LANGUAGE WORKOUT

- Ask students to complete the Language box. Confident students can complete first and then check, while others can look back at exercises 2 and 3 and then complete.
- Ask students to look at the sentences and p119 of the Language File to check their answers.

Answers

was *were* *was*
be

- Highlight that:
  - the past simple passive is formed in a similar way to the present simple passive. We still use the past participle, but with auxiliary verb *was* (singular) or *were* (plural) instead of *is/are*.
  - as with the present simple passive, the subject is not the 'doer' of the verb. If we mention the 'doer' we use *by*. Refer students back to Unit 2, Lesson 3 if necessary.
- Drill the examples in chorus for pronunciation and stress. Encourage students to produce the weak forms of *was* /wəz/ and *were* /wə/.

Optional activities

♦ Fast finishers look back at the text in exercise 2 to find more examples of the past simple passive.
♦ Read out sentences from the article in either the active or passive forms. Ask students to transform from active to passive or vice versa where possible.

PRACTICE

- Ask students to look at Practice exercise 21 of the Language File on page 119 and complete the sentences using the past simple passive.
- Check the answers by asking different students to say the completed sentences.

Answers

1 *The first petrol-driven car was built in 1885.*
2 *The first newspapers were published in 1609.*
3 *The Eiffel Tower was completed in 1889.*
4 *Modern safety matches were invented in 1855.*
5 *The tomb of Tutankhamun was discovered in 1923.*
6 *The Channel Tunnel was opened in 1994.*
7 *The first postage stamps were used in 1840.*
8 *Barack Obama was elected US President in 2008.*

Follow-up activities

♦ Divide students into groups of four. They work together to write five survey questions about 'bests' and 'worsts' to ask the rest of the class, e.g. *What's the best/worst food in the school canteen?* They then interview different students in the class, noting down answers. Students get back into their group, share their findings and work together to write a survey report, similar to the one in exercise 4. Groups read their report to the class and the class discuss any surprising findings.
♦ Ask students to work in pairs to make a word map for either *make* or *do*. They write this word in the centre of the page. At the end of each line, they write an expression that goes with their verb, as well as an example of it in a sentence. Encourage students to use those from exercise 5 and to find more examples in a dictionary.

HOMEWORK

Ask students to research and write a paragraph about a famous building, painting or invention. They should try to include five verbs in the past simple passive in their writing.

WEBLINK

Students may be interested to visit inventors.about.com/od/astartinventions/a/FamousInvention.htm to find out more about when things were invented.

Revision and Extension p83

Language File p119

Workbook Unit 6 Lesson 3 pp66–67

Photocopiable worksheet p179, notes p158

4 Integrated Skills Describing a process

Skills

Reading Connecting ideas: *Ancient Inventions* article
Listening Ordering the stages in a process
Speaking Describing a process
Writing Process description

Learner Independence

Self assessment
Word creation: noun suffixes *-or, -er* and *-ist*

Vocabulary

Inventions
Useful expressions

Optional Aids

Follow-up activities: names of famous people on sticky notes

WARMER 1

Elicit the word *chocolate* from the students by giving clues like *It's sweet, It can be white, milk or plain*, etc. Tell students they are going to ask each other questions in pairs about chocolate. Elicit possible questions, e.g. *What's your favourite kind of chocolate? How often do you eat chocolate? Do you think chocolate is good or bad for you?* and give them two minutes to ask each other.

Useful information

The world's best-selling chocolate bar is Kit-Kat, whilst Britain's best-seller is Cadbury's Dairy Milk (a simple bar of milk chocolate). The Swiss are the world's biggest consumers of chocolate.

WARMER 2

Give students a short test on vocabulary from previous lessons. Choose words from the Vocabulary box, read out the definition and ask students to write down the word. Check their answers and spelling.

1 OPENER

- The aim is to set the context for the reading in exercise 2.
- Ask students to work in pairs to guess where and by whom the things in the box were invented. Check students know *plastic surgery* by asking *What do you call operations in hospital to make a part of your body (e.g. nose) look more beautiful?*

2 READING

- Ask students to read the text and check their predictions from exercise 1.
- Check the answers as a whole class.

Answers

1 C 2 B 3 A 4 C 5 A 6 B

3

- Ask students to read the text again and match the topics with the paragraphs.
- Play the recording for students to check their answers.
- Discuss which words in the phrases helped them choose the right answers.

2.37 Recording

See text on page 80 of the Student's Book.

Answers

1 Medicine 2 Clothing 3 Mathematics
4 Food and drink 5 Written communication

Optional activities

- ♦ Fast finishers could find examples of the past simple passive in the text.
- ♦ On the board, write information from the text which could be answers to questions, e.g. *AD 499* (When was zero invented?), *50* (How many cups of chocolate did Montezuma drink a day?). Ask students to write possible questions for these answers.
- ♦ Write the six inventions from exercise 1 on the board and ask students to close their books and remember as much as they can about each. They then discuss which they think was the most important discovery.

4 LINKING WORD: *although*

- Ask the students to find examples of *although* in the Ancient Inventions text.

Answers

Although we call them Arabic numbers, the numbers that we use today came from India …
Although the Mayans and Aztecs loved chocolate, Europeans didn't discover it for another two thousand years.
Although paper was introduced into Japan in AD 610, it didn't reach the West until much later.

- Highlight that:
  – *although* expresses contrast. The idea of the second clause is surprising or unexpected because of the contrast with the first.

– *although* often introduces the first clause, but the clauses can be reversed, e.g. *The numbers we use today come from India, although we call them Arabic numbers.* In this case, *but* can be used in place of *although*.

- Elicit a transformation of an *although* sentence from the text into a *but* sentence.
- Ask the students to rewrite sentences 1–6 using *although* instead of *but*.

Answers

1 *Although paper was made Japan in AD 610, it wasn't made in Europe until 1151.*
2 *Although printing was invented in the 3rd century, it didn't reach Europe until 1455.*
3 *Although the Mayans and Aztecs loved xocolatl, the Spanish thought it tasted awful until they added sugar.*
4 *Although Leonardo da Vinci lived 500 years ago, he designed the first car.*
5 *Although Krysta Morlan was only 16, she invented a waterbike.*
6 *Although Louis Braille couldn't see, he developed a reading system for the blind.*

Optional activity

Dictate sentence stems including *although* for students to write down and complete in their own words, e.g. *Although it was raining …, She decided to buy it, although …*

5 LISTENING

- Ask students to look at the six pictures showing the process of making paper. In pairs, they predict the correct order. Check the meaning of *bark* (the hard substance that covers a tree) and *pulp* (a thick soft substance made by boiling something).
- Play the recording and ask students to check their predictions.
- Establish the correct order with the whole class.

2.38 Recording

The process of making paper was invented by Cai Lun in China in AD 105. Before that the Chinese used to write on silk or bamboo. To make paper, bark and leaves from the mulberry tree were collected and put in water. Then the bark and leaves were boiled to make a pulp. When the pulp was soft, it was spread on a bamboo tray with small holes in it. After water from the pulp had run away through the holes, a thin sheet of pulp was left on the tray. Then this sheet was dried to remove any water that was left. Finally the paper was ready!

Answers

The correct order is: E, A, D, F, C, B

6 SPEAKING

- Remind students to use the past simple passive as they describe the process.
- In pairs, students use the sentences in exercise 5 to tell each other how paper was made. Confident students can cover the sentences as they speak, while less confident students can refer to them during the activity.

Optional activity

Read the audio script to the students again, but include some mistakes, e.g. *The bark and leaves were cooled to make a pulp.* Students must shout *Stop!* when they hear a mistake, and correct you, e.g. *They weren't cooled; they were boiled.*

7 GUIDED WRITING

- Books closed. Tell students they are going to write a description of the process of how paper was made. Ask if they can remember any expressions from the recording which introduced new stages of the process, e.g. *then …, after …*
- Ask the students to complete the process description using the list of prompts. Remind them to look back at the sentences in exercise 5 to help.
- Students exchange their writing with another student and check it for accuracy.

Optional activity

Ask students to leave out or to put correction fluid over all the examples of the past simple passive in their paragraph. They then exchange texts with a partner and try to complete the gaps from memory with the correct passive forms.

8 LEARNER INDEPENDENCE

- Ask students to look back over the unit, think about what they have learnt and complete the sentences.
- With a less confident class, look at the sentences as a whole class first and elicit possible ways to finish the sentences, e.g. *I have difficulty in* + verb + *-ing* (describing processes in the past).
- Ask students to compare their sentences in pairs and find similarities and differences.

9 WORD CREATION

- Write the name of an actor, designer and artist on the board, e.g. *Julia Roberts, Jean-Paul Gaultier, Leonardo da Vinci* and elicit the three words, highlighting the three different suffixes.
- Students copy the table into their notebooks and write the 'people' nouns in the correct columns, choosing the suffix, *-or, -er, -ist.* Remind students that there may be spelling changes.
- Students can check back in the book or in dictionaries, before checking as a class. Drill in chorus and individually for pronunciation and stress.

Answers

-or: actor, director, inventor, professor, translator
-er: designer, engineer, painter, reporter, runner
-ist: artist, journalist, novelist, scientist, tourist

Optional activity

Game *Password* Use the 'people' nouns to play the game, e.g. actor, designer. For instructions see Unit 2, lesson 1, p43.

10 PHRASEBOOK

- Play the recording for the students to listen and repeat the expressions.
- Students look through Unit 6 to find the expressions, noting how they are used.
- Highlight the exclamation marks in two of the expressions and ask students to think of other situations where each exclamation could be used.

2.39 Recording and answers

It's doing really well. (L1, Ex2)
The idea was to … (L1, Ex2)
in the first place (L2, Ex2)
The possibilities are endless! (L2, Ex2)
Believe it or not … (L3, Ex2)
It's no secret. (L3, Ex2)
It works! (L3, Ex2)

Optional activity

Students can add expressions which they like to their Personal Phrasebook. Be ready to help as necessary.

Follow-up activities

- Ask students to think of a process that they know and could mime/act out for other students, e.g. *a cup of tea being made, money being taken out of a cash machine, a bicycle being repaired.* In small groups, each student then performs their process for the other students, who should guess what is happening and take notes. When the mime is finished, the other students work together to describe what they think was done during the process and the actor confirms if they are right or not.
- **Game** *Guess who?* Write the names of famous artists, inventors, scientists, etc. on sticky notes and stick one on each student's back or forehead, so they cannot see what it says, but other students can. Students must circulate, asking each other *yes/no* questions, e.g. *Am I a designer? Am I an artist? Am I male? Am I from this country?* to try to guess their identity.

HOMEWORK

Ask students to think of and/or research a process and write one paragraph describing it. If possible, they should provide illustrations to accompany each stage of the description.

WEBLINK

Students may like to visit science.discovery.com/tv/how-its-made to find out how things are made.

Revision and Extension p83

Workbook Unit 4 Lesson 4 pp68–69

Inspiration EXTRA!

Optional Aids

Poem, optional activity: card or paper, pictures/photos to be cut out and used as illustrations

PROJECT AN EXTRAORDINARY PERSON

1 • Explain to students that the aim of the project is to write a profile of an extraordinary person. Divide the students into groups. Give students five minutes to choose a person to write about and make some preliminary notes. Ask them to read the paragraph about Tanni Grey-Thompson as an example of a profile of an extraordinary person. Point out that her profile contains a lot of facts and figures.

2 • Students find out more about their extraordinary person by using the Internet or a library or by interviewing a local person or e-mailing him/her. Encourage students to divide subjects for research among the group members.

3 • Students work together in their groups to share their research findings. They should decide how to group together and order their information and how to illustrate it with pictures or photos. Remind students to include *used to* (Unit 6, Lesson 2) and the past simple passive (Unit 6, Lesson 3) as appropriate. Students show their file to other groups. Display the files in the classroom if possible.

Optional activity

Students could act out interviews with their extraordinary person and perform these for the rest of the class.

POEMS CHANGES: THE THINGS WE USED TO DO

- The aim is for students to be creative with their English while also focusing on the *used to* form.
- Divide the students into groups of three or four and ask them to think about how their lives/their friends' lives have changed in the last year. Point out the example topics to give them ideas.
- Students then use these ideas to help them think of ways to complete sets of the three *used to* sentences.
- They then decide the best sets of three sentences and put them together to make a poem.
- Students give you their poems to be read out to the whole class. Other students guess which group wrote each.

Optional activities

- Fast finishers can add two more lines to their poems.
- Students copy their poems out on card and illustrate with images. These can then be displayed on classroom walls.
- Ask students to think of a place they used to go to when they were younger, e.g. *a holiday destination, a playground, their primary school, a friend's house.* They tell a partner their memories of this place and what they used to do there.

REVISION

Lesson 1
Students' own answers

Lesson 2
Students' own answers

Lesson 3

Answers
1 was invented 2 was heated 3 was filled
4 were put 5 was seen 6 were followed

EXTENSION

Lesson 1
Students' own answers

Lesson 2
Students' own answers

Lesson 3

Answers
1 Who was (title of book) written by?
2 When was (name of building) built?
3 Who was (title of song) sung by?
4 When was (name of continent) discovered?

YOUR CHOICE!

- Ask students to look back at the questionnaire on page 7 and remember which learning style they were. Divide the class into groups according to their learning style to do the relevant activity.
- Monitor and help groups. Check answers if necessary, or provide written answers for groups to check their own work against.
- Encourage students to experiment with other learning styles and try one of the other activities of their choice.

CONSTRUCTION

- Students complete the gaps with past simple active or passive.

Answers

1 knew 2 was understood 3 was used 4 changed
5 were replaced 6 appeared 7 were invented
8 was made 9 exploded 10 killed

REFLECTION

- Students match the examples a–f with the language functions 1–3.

Answers

1 c, e
2 b, d
3 a, f

Language File pp118–119

Workbook Unit 6 Inspiration EXTRA! pp70–71

ACTION

- Divide students into small groups.
- Students then follow the instructions in the box, taking it in turns to think of a famous person who is no longer alive, and telling the group one fact about this person.
- The other students in their group ask *used to* questions to try to guess the person.
- Students could decide in their group who chose the most interesting famous person, to repeat their clue and question procedure with the whole class.

INTERACTION

- Divide students into small groups.
- Ask students to remember a dramatic event in their life, making notes about what happened, when it happened and why they felt the way they did.
- Students take it in turns to tell each other about the event, using their notes to help and ending *I'd never been so … before!*
- Students could report back to the rest of the class on who experienced the most dramatic event.

You may now like students to do the song *Brown-eyed Girl*. See p161 for the notes and p188 for the worksheet.

Song – photocopiable worksheet p188, notes p161

UNITS 5–6

1 Check general comprehension: Ask students to look at the picture and the headline and predict the story. Give students one minute to read the story and check their predictions. Students read the story again and choose the appropriate word for each space. Do the first one together as an example. This can be done in pairs or individually as a short test.

Answers

1 C 2 B 3 B 4 C 5 A 6 B 7 A 8 C 9 A 10 C 11 C 12 B

Optional activities

- Confident students can attempt the task before looking at the word options.
- Fast finishers can find expressions connected with sleep in the text, e.g. *sleepwalk, sleepwalker, fall asleep, be fast asleep, wake up.*

2 Students rewrite the sentences using the present perfect with *just*. Remind the students that *just* will replace the time expression in the sentence. Do the first one together as an example.

Answers

1 The plane has just landed.
2 We've just seen the film.
3 It has just started raining.
4 The students have just left school.
5 I've just bought some new trainers.
6 We've just heard the news.

Optional activity

Fast finishers write three sentences about what has just happened or what they have just done.

3 Before students look at the exercise, set the context and ask them to predict what the two students will have to do before going backpacking. They then read the list and check their predictions. Students then write sentences using the present perfect with *yet* and *already*.

Answers

1 They haven't booked anywhere/somewhere to stay the first night yet.
2 They've already applied for visas.
3 They've already planned their route.
4 They haven't bought a phrasebook yet.
5 They've already had the necessary vaccinations.
6 They've already saved up enough money.
7 They haven't packed their rucksacks yet.
8 They haven't organised travel insurance yet.

4 Students ask and answer questions using the present perfect with *ever*.

Answers

1 Has Sophie ever been on a roller coaster? Yes, she has.
2 Has Steve ever eaten sushi? No, he hasn't.
3 Has Lisa ever tried bungee jumping? Yes, she has.
4 Have Julie and Simon ever visited Mexico? No, they haven't.
5 Has Lisa ever won a race? Yes, she has.
6 Have Julie and Simon ever been on TV? No, they haven't.

Students then write sentences using this information.

Answers

1 Sophie has been on a roller-coaster.
2 Steve has never eaten sushi.
3 Lisa has tried bungee jumping.
4 Julie and Simon have never visited Mexico.
5 Lisa has won a race.
6 Julie and Simon have never been on TV.

5 Students complete the gaps with the present perfect or past simple.

Answers

1 Have 2 made 3 have 4 wanted 5 did 6 Did 7 enjoy 8 was 9 jumped 10 opened 11 felt 12 've been

6 Students write sentences using the present perfect with *for* and *since*. Encourage them to use contracted forms.

Answers

1 He's had guitar lessons for six months.
2 She hasn't contacted us since last Friday.
3 I've been awake since 6 a.m.
4 You've known each other for two weeks.
5 My parents have been married for 25 years.
6 We've lived here since I was born.
7 You haven't been on holiday for ages.
8 I've had a headache since yesterday.

7 Students complete with the past perfect where possible, otherwise using the past simple.

Answers

1 invented 2 was 3 had been 4 had been 5 retired 6 knew 7 had taught 8 painted 9 had thought 10 sold 11 hadn't expected 12 earned

Optional activity

Students try to remember as much as possible about the four teenage inventors from Unit 6, Lesson 1.

8 Ask students to think about how life was different 300 years ago. They then use the prompts 1–8 to make sentences about what people used to do and didn't use to do.

Answers

1 They didn't use to drive cars.
2 They used to travel by boat.
3 They used to cook food over a fire.
4 They didn't use to buy frozen food.
5 They didn't use to send emails.
6 They didn't use to listen to the radio.
7 They used to read by candlelight.
8 They used to wash clothes by hand.

9 Students write sentences using the prompts and the past simple passive. Remind students that they may need to add words such as articles and prepositions.

Answers

1 Radium was discovered by Marie and Pierre Curie in 1898.
2 The first printed books were produced in China.
3 The electric light bulb was invented by Swan and Edison in 1879.
4 Mount Everest was first climbed by Tenzing and Hillary in 1953.
5 Mobile phones were first used in 1978.
6 The London underground was opened in 1863.
7 The first colour photos were taken by James Maxwell in 1861.
8 Potatoes were brought to Europe in the 16th century.

VOCABULARY

10 Students complete the sentences with the words in the box. Confident students can cover the words in the box and guess which words are missing before checking against the list.

Answers

1 kite 2 mend 3 carpet 4 cans 5 habit 6 float 7 accident 8 medal 9 inspiration 10 award

11 Students match the words with their definitions. Confident students can attempt the task without looking at the words in the box and then look to check.

Answers

1 entertain 2 combine 3 sphere 4 blind 5 deaf 6 recycle 7 vehicle 8 reduce 9 foreigner 10 simplify

12 Remind students that it is often more useful to learn words that go together like this than single words.

Answers

1 become well-known 2 do damage 3 earn money 4 light a candle 5 perform in a play 6 reduce by 50% 7 think of an idea 8 translate a language 9 swim underwater

LEARNER INDEPENDENCE SELF ASSESSMENT

- Explain to students that the aim of the self assessment is to help them check their own progress and take any action necessary to improve. Point out that the list 1–6 covers language from Units 5 and 6.
- Have students look at the table and tick the Fine box for language they feel confident using or put a question mark in the Not sure box if they feel they still have some difficulties.
- Encourage students to look at the Language File and re-do exercises from the lessons, the Revision and Extension section and the Workbook in areas where they have problems.
- Students write an example sentence for each language area in the list. You may like to elicit the language students need for each example before students write sentences, e.g. *Talk about experiences: present perfect.* Students can refer back to the lessons and the Language Workout box and Language File.

Follow-up activities

♦ **Game** *Outburst* Divide students into groups of three and give each group a vocabulary area, e.g. *materials, geographical features, machines.* Groups write a list of six examples in their category, e.g. *materials: cotton, denim.* Groups then take it in turns to tell the other students their category name and the other groups write a list of items they guess have been included in the list. After one minute, the original list is read out and other groups score points for how many they correctly guessed.

♦ **Game** *Noughts and crosses* For instructions see Unit 2, Lesson 1, p45. Put the following words in the grid: *yet*, past perfect, *already, used to*, past simple passive, *although, however, since, ever.*

HOMEWORK

Ask students to find an interesting story in a newspaper or magazine with an accompanying photo. It can be in their own language or in English. They should write an English headline to accompany the photo and write three or four sentences to summarise the key points of the story.

WEBLINK

After exercise 1, students may like to visit www.helpguide.org/life/sleep_tips.htm for tips on how to sleep well.

Language File pp117–119

Workbook Review Units 5–6 pp72–73

Units 7–8

Activities		Project	Vocabulary	Optional Aids
Identifying communicative aims Categorising vocabulary	Contextualising listening extracts	News survey	Animals Geographical features Weather and climate	Project: sheets of A3 paper Follow-up activities: slips of paper

WARMER 1

Students look back at Units 5–6 in their books and talk in pairs about the activities or reading texts that they enjoyed or didn't like. Encourage them to give reasons for their feelings.

WARMER 2

Put anagrams for words related to sports and extreme sports on the board, e.g. *INRZOGB* (zorbing), *IGSLIAN* (sailing), *HKOCEICYE* (ice-hockey). Students rearrange the letters to make the correct spellings. This could also be done as a race with the first pair to finish with all the correct spellings being the winner.

WARMER 3

Write five famous places, inventions or people in one circle on the board and five dates in another in random order, e.g. *Barack Obama, the Channel Tunnel, 1994, 2008.* Students work in pairs and make five complete sentences using the past simple passive, e.g. *The Channel Tunnel was opened in 1994.*

1
- The aim is to introduce the students to the main areas of communicative language they will cover in Units 7–8, and to encourage them to think about the function of the language.
- Explain the task to the class. Students should look at the six photos and match them with the communicative aims, using the captions to help them. Point out that there are six pictures and seven communicative aims so one of them is not used.
- Ask students to do the task individually and then compare their answers in pairs. Check the answers with the whole class.

Answers

1 D 2 C 3 E 4 A 5 F 7 B

2
- Explain that the words in the box are related to three different categories and that each has one letter missing. Point out that if students do not know the meaning of one or more words in the box, they should guess the possible spelling and what category they go into. Tell students you will explain the meaning of any words they are not sure about when you check the answers.
- This exercise could be done in pairs. Check the answers with the whole class. Write the three categories on the board and invite students to come to the board without their books and write any words they can remember in the correct category.

Answers

Animals: bear; crocodile; elephant; gorilla; kangaroo; pig
Geographical features: desert; forest; lake; mountain; river; waterfall
Weather and climate: monsoon; rain; sunshine; temperature; thunderstorm; wind

Optional activity

Ask students if they can add one or more words to each of the groups. Possible words include *lion, cow, giraffe, sea, hill, valley, snow, fog, cloud.*

3
- The aim of the activity is for students to contextualise a short listening extract by working out what kind of passage it is extracted from.
- Play the recording. Students match each extract 1–3 with the summaries A–C.

3.01 Recording

1
(Unit 7 Lesson 2, Exercise 2)
A: How do you feel about spam and viruses?
B: I get annoyed when I get spam. It's a tough problem but we're going to solve it. So far the solutions aren't working – they either filter too much or not enough. We must find a better way to stop spam. Viruses are another problem and you usually get them from an email attachment. An ISP could throw away all emails with attachments, but then email wouldn't be any use. We'll have to find a solution.
2
(Unit 7 Lesson 4, Exercise 4)
Two teenagers capsized in the sea off the south coast of Britain and called Japan on a mobile phone to ask for help. Brother and sister Ken and Emily Booth were on a sailing holiday near Southampton. But because of strong winds, their dinghy capsized and they were thrown into the sea.

3
(Unit 8 Lesson 3, Exercise 2)
It's the tallest skyscraper in the world. It's in Dubai and it's 828 metres high. And it's got 160 floors.

Answers
1 C 2 B 3 A

Optional activity

3.01 Write *Where do you usually get viruses from? What were the teenagers doing? Where did their dinghy capsize? Where is the tallest skyscraper in the world? How many floors has it got?* on the board. Play the recording again and ask students to write down the answers. Check the answers with the whole class. (email attachments, sailing, off the south coast of Britain, Dubai, 160)

4
- Explain to students that the aim of the exercise is to write a survey about different ways of getting the news.
- Ask students to look at the photos and identify the different ways of getting the news they show.
- Divide the students into groups and appoint a 'secretary' for each group. The 'secretary' is responsible for taking notes for the group.
- Give students three minutes to make a list of ways of getting the news including the examples given.
- Students look at the list on page 87. Elicit an example for each type of news, e.g. *school news – someone is coming to visit the school*. Tell students they are going to interview each other about how they usually find out about each type of news. Point out that they need to record details such as which TV or radio programme.
- Ask students to copy the list. Make sure they leave plenty of space on the right for a variety of answers. Give students five minutes to think about and note their own answers to the question.
- Students interview other students in the group about where they usually hear the news. Remind them to be specific in their answers and to note each other's answers. Encourage more confident students to ask and provide more information, e.g. why they like this programme, how often they watch the programme.
- Working together in their group, students decide in which order to put the information. Then they form and link the sentences. Students read the texts through carefully to correct any mistakes. Monitor and help as necessary. They copy their texts out neatly and illustrate the file with photos or drawings.
- Students show their News Survey to other groups. Display the surveys in the classroom if possible.

Optional activity

Each group focuses on one type of news. They research how students in their group usually get this type of news and present their findings to the class.

News Survey Project

- Students build on the information from the previous activity to formulate a statistical overview of the news habits of the whole class. Ask them to transfer the six categories in the list in exercise 4 to a large sheet of paper.
  Students stand up, walk around the class and note down answers to each question from all the other class members.
  Then they work in their groups from exercise 4 and create a poster to display this information. The poster could contain simple statistics such as *50% of the students in our class get news about world events from the Internet*, or this information could be conveyed via a simple bar chart or pie chart.
- Encourage students to use colour and illustrations to make their posters more visually attractive. Display the posters on the classroom wall. Students vote for which poster is the most impressive.

- Books closed. Write the phrase *oceans and seas* on the board. Elicit an example of an ocean, e.g. *the Pacific* and a sea, e.g. *the Mediterranean*. Ask the students to work in pairs and discuss what percentage of the world's surface is covered by oceans and seas, what the average depth of the world's oceans is and what percentage of life on Earth lives in the sea.
- Ask students to open their books and check their predictions in the Believe it or not! box.

Follow-up activity

Remind students of the three categories in exercise 2: animals, geographical features and weather and climate. Do the same activity as in Preview 1–2. Follow the instructions on page 26.

HOMEWORK

Ask students to use the News Survey to ask a friend or a family member how they get news about local, national and world events.

7.1 COMMUNICATION

He asked her not to go

Communicative Aims
Reporting requests and commands

Language
ask/tell + object + infinitive

Pronunciation
Linking

Vocabulary
Animals
Phrasal verbs: opposites

Optional Aids
Follow-up activity: sentences on slips of paper

WARMER 1

Game *Which word next?* Organise the students into one large or two smaller circles. Everyone stands up. Choose a student in the circle and give them a starting word, e.g. *invention*. The student to the left has to say a word beginning with the last letter of the previous word, e.g. *night*. The next student then has to say a word beginning with '*t*', and so on around the circle. If a student cannot think of a word in 15 seconds, they sit down and are out of this round of the game.

WARMER 2

Game *Alphabet game* Ask students to write the letters A–Z down the margin of a piece of paper. In pairs or small groups, give students two minutes to think of an animal for as many of the 26 letters as possible. Tell students it can be any type of animal including insects, reptiles and birds. Do an example, e.g. *A, ant, ape*. After two minutes, ask the group with the most animals to read out their list. Check spelling and pronunciation.

1 OPENER

- The aim is to set the scene and generate interest in the reading text.
- Students read the four statements and decide if they are true or false. Ask them to compare their answers in pairs. Check the answers with the whole class. In fact, all the statements are true.
- Students look at the photos. Ask students to name the bird and animal (parrot and chimpanzee) and ask what they can do that is unusual. Do not tell them the answer at this stage.

2 READING

- Tell students they are going to read and hear about these two animals and one other. Ask them to note down the names of the three animals and one thing they can do. With a confident class, do this as a listening exercise first. With a less confident class, students read and listen. Check the names (the parrot is Alex, there is a gorilla called Koko, the chimpanzee is Kanzi) and elicit one thing they can each do.

3.02 Recording

See text on page 88 of the Student's Book.

3 AFTER READING

- Students read the statements and complete as many as possible from memory. They then read the text again to check and complete their answers. Encourage students to guess the meaning of unknown vocabulary from context.
- Ask different students to read the sentences aloud to check the answers. Ask questions to check students have understood the meaning of: *sign language* (When is it normally used?), *a keyboard* (Which part of a computer is it?), *to count* (What do you do when you count?).
- Ask students if they had heard about these animals before. Are they surprised by what they have read? Have they ever heard about any other animals who could communicate?

Answers

1 Koko 2 Alex 3 Kanzi 4 Alex 5 Koko
6 Kanzi 7 Alex 8 Koko 9 Kanzi

Optional activity

Fast finishers note new words in the text and check the meaning in a dictionary.

LANGUAGE WORKOUT OPTION

If you want to pre-teach the language students will be using in the following activities, you may like to go to the Language Workout box now.

4

- Students read sentences 1–5 and note first which are requests and which are commands. Check the answers.
- Students then find the matching reported requests and commands in exercise 2. Ask different students to read the answers aloud.

Answers

1 Command. She told him to put a tomato in the fridge.
2 Command. She told him to take a red ball into the office.
3 Request. She asked him to get a ball.
4 Command. She told him to turn off the water.
5 Request. The trainer asked Kanzi to get them back for her.

Your response

Students work individually to think about their answers to the questions and to make notes. Then ask them to work in pairs and compare their ideas. Ask each pair to report back their views to the whole class.

5 PRONUNCIATION

- The aim is to make students aware of how words link together in spoken English. At this stage, this is more important than students actually being able to produce the linking themselves.
- Students look at the sentences in the box and the linking. Play the recording, pausing after each sentence for students to repeat.

3.03 Recording

See the text in the Student's book on page 89.

Optional activity

Choose other sentences in which words link together from this or previous lessons. (Many sentences have an example where a word beginning with a vowel sound links with the previous consonant sound.) Dictate them to the students. Students then compare and practise saying them naturally with their partner.

6 LISTENING

- Students read the instructions. Ask *Who is talking? Who is she talking to?* Students read the sentences. Tell students that the trainer says something different. They need to listen and note the mistake. Do the first one together as an example.
- With a confident class, do not check the answers at this stage. They can use the next part of the exercise to compare and check their answers. With a less confident class, check the mistakes first.

3.04 Recording and answers

1 'Charlie, can you pick up the blue box?'
2 'No, don't eat the apple.'
3 'Take off my hat, Charlie.'
4 'Charlie, put the ball on the desk.'
5 'Could you open the door, please, Charlie?'
6 'No, please don't sit on the table.'

- Ask students to look at the example. Complete the example with the students: *No, she asked him to pick up the blue box*. Students continue in pairs. Monitor and help.
- If necessary, ask different pairs to ask and answer the questions in open class to confirm answers.

Answers

1 Did she ask Charlie to pick up the red box? No, she asked him to pick up the blue box.
2 Did she tell him not to eat the banana? No, she told him not to eat the apple.
3 Did she tell him to take off her shoe? No, she told him to take off her hat.
4 Did she ask him to put the ball on the desk? No, she told him to put the ball on the desk.
5 Did she ask him to open the window? No, she asked him to open the door.
6 Did she tell him not to stand on the table? No, she told him not to sit on the table.

Optional activity

In pairs, one student asks the questions and their partner responds from memory. To make it more challenging, the first student can change the question, e.g. *Did she ask Charlie to pick up the green book? Did she ask him not to eat the pizza?* After two minutes, students reverse roles.

7 VOCABULARY

- Students match the opposites. Students then race to find as many as they can in the lesson (There are five, see below).

Answers

1 e 2 c 3 b 4 f 5 a 6 d
In this lesson: turn off (the water), bring back (the stolen keys), sit down, pick up (the red box), take off (my shoe)

Extension Students look at the example. Students think of at least two things that *it* could be in the phrases.

Suggested answers

Put it on/Take it off: It could be a jacket/a cap (any kind of clothing).
Pick it up/Put it down: It could be a pen/a glass (any kind of moveable object).
Take it away/Bring it back: It could be a chair/a plate (any kind of moveable object).
Turn it on/Turn it off: It could be a tap/a television/a radio/a light/a mobile phone (any kind of electrical equipment with an on/off switch).

8 SPEAKING

- Ask *Do your parents ask or tell you to do things or not to do things?* Ask students for examples and how often this happens.
- In pairs, students tell each other how often their parents ask/tell them (not) to do the things in the pictures. Do one as an example: ask different students to say how often their parents ask/tell them to turn down their music. If necessary, point out that the present simple tense is used to talk about how often things happen, e.g. *They ask/tell me to turn my music down every evening.*
- With a less confident group, review the language of frequency: *never, every day/week/month, once/twice/three times a day/week/month.* Encourage more confident students to ask for and provide more information, e.g. *Is it the same for your brother or sister? Do you usually do it when they tell you to? When was the last time they told you to do this?*
- Monitor and help as necessary. At the end, ask some students to report back on some things they learnt.

9 WRITING

- Ask students to think about yesterday. What did their parents ask/tell them (not) to do yesterday? Set a 10-minute time limit for students to write their sentences. Monitor and help as necessary. Make a note of good language examples and errors. Put these on the board and ask students to identify and correct the errors. Then give students a further minute to improve/ correct their writing.

Optional activity

Students exchange sentences. Before they read each other's, they make one prediction about what it will say, e.g. *I think your parents told you to tidy your room yesterday.* Students then read and see if they were right.

LANGUAGE WORKOUT

- Ask students to complete the Language box.
- Students turn to page 119 of the Language File to check their answers.

Answers

asked him to *not to*
told her to *not to*

- Highlight that:
  - *asked* in these examples does not mean 'asked a question' but is used to report a request.
  - not all requests end in a question mark, e.g. *Please don't go!* Elicit ways in which you make a request, e.g. *Can you …? Could you …? Would you …? Please …*
  - *tell* is always followed by an object: you always *tell someone something.*
  - the negative form of reported requests and commands is *ask/tell* + object + *not* + infinitive.
- Drill the examples in chorus and individually for pronunciation, paying particular attention to the pronunciation of *asked* /ɑːskt/ and the weak pronunciation of *to* /tə/.

PRACTICE

- Ask students to look at exercise 22 on page 119 of the Language File. Ask which word in the first sentence shows that it is a command (*should*). Point out that this word is not necessary when you report the command because the form (*tell* + object + infinitive) shows that it was a command. With a less confident class, point out that they may also need to change pronouns in the sentence, e.g. sentence 3 *give me* becomes *give him*.

Answers

1 *The teacher asked Anya to clean the board.*
2 *The mother told the children to go to bed.*
3 *Rob asked his mother to give him some money.*
4 *The coach told the team they had to win the match.*
5 *The fire-fighter asked everyone to keep calm and leave the building.*
6 *Julie asked Simon if he would carry her rucksack.*
7 *The pilot told the passengers to fasten their seatbelts.*
8 *The teacher told everyone to sit down.*

Optional activity

Fast finishers cover the exercise and transform the sentences back from reported to direct speech.

Follow-up activities

- ♦ **Game** *Mime the sentence* Use sentences from this lesson or invent others which include a reported request or command, e.g. *The coach told him to run faster*. Organise students into teams. One student from each team comes to the front and reads the sentence. They mime it to their team. When the team thinks they have the sentence they write it down. The first team to show you the correct sentence wins a point. A different student from each team does the next mime and so on.
- ♦ **Game** *Act it out* Brainstorm famous people and write them on the board. Brainstorm people who they talk to during a typical day, e.g. *partner, child, coach*, and write these on the board. In pairs, students invent a short conversation between the famous person and one of the people they talk to. It must include at least one request or command. Give a 10-minute time limit. Students then act out their mini-dialogues for the class. The class listens/ watches and decides who the famous person is and who they are talking to. They then report the request and/or command, e.g. *Beckham told his son not to wear black football boots.*

HOMEWORK

Students use the following line as either the beginning or end of a short story of their own invention: *He told them to forget everything they had seen.*

WEBLINK

Students may like to visit www.sciencemuseum.org.uk/onlinestuff/snot/can_animals_talk_and_what_do_they_say.aspx where they can read more about how animals communicate.

Revision and Extension p97

Language File p119

Workbook Unit 7 Lesson 1 pp74–75

Photocopiable worksheet p180, notes p159

7.2 COMMUNICATION

He said he couldn't remember

Communicative Aims	Language	Pronunciation	Vocabulary	Optional Aids
Reporting what someone said	Reported statements: *say* and *tell*	/g/ dog /k/ dock	Communication technology	Follow-up activity: cards for Vocabulary box

WARMER 1

Students tell their partner one request and one command they have made since the last lesson, e.g. *Yesterday I asked my brother to lend me his leather jacket.* Their sentences may be true or invented. Their partner listens and decides if they are true or not.

WARMER 2

Dictate three or four website or email addresses that you know, e.g. *www.bbc.co.uk/learningenglish* and *jsmith@hotmail.com*. Do one or two with the students so they learn *at, dot, slash, backslash*. Students guess what the websites are or who the email addresses are for. Students then write three or four that they know and dictate them to their partner who guesses the relevance.

1 OPENER

- The aim is to set the scene and personalise the topic of the lesson.
- Students ask and answer the questions in pairs/small groups. Ask some students to report back on the least and most popular forms of communication in their pair/group. With a confident group extend the discussion: Ask *When do you phone/write a letter/send an email? What are possible problems with phoning/writing a letter/sending an email? Do you think people will stop writing letters in the future?* You could include text messaging in the discussion.

2 READING

- Write @ on the board. Ask students how you say this in English (at). Ask what it is in their language and how it translates into English. Find out if they know any other names for it. Tell students they will hear and/or read what it is called in ten other countries. Play the introduction once for them to note the countries and repeat it for students to note what it is called in each country. Check answers and ask which one the students like best.
- Ask students to listen to the recording and/or read the text and note down the advantages and disadvantages of email the speaker mentions. Check the answers with the whole class.

3.05 Recording

See text on page 90 of the Student's Book.

Answers

Advantages: more communication, easier to communicate, can send attachments
Disadvantages: spam, viruses

3 AFTER READING

- Students read the text again and decide if the sentences are true or false (or no information). Encourage students to work out the meaning of unknown vocabulary from context, e.g. spam, attachment, and ignore words which are not necessary to complete the exercise.
- Check the answers before asking them to correct the false sentences. Point out that students only need to change one or two words in the false sentences and not the whole sentence.

Answers

1 False. He invented email.
2 True
3 False. Stopping spam is a tough problem.
4 True
5 False. He said that so far the solutions weren't working.
6 True
7 No information
8 False. He said it was easier to communicate with more people than before.

Optional activity

Students find and note all the words in the text relating to computers and email, e.g. *spam, filter, virus, email attachment, ISP*. Note that ISP will be explained in exercise 5.

LANGUAGE WORKOUT OPTION

If you want to pre-teach the language students will be using in the following activities, you may like to go to the Language Workout box now.

4

- Students read the reported statements and match them to Ray's words in exercise 2. Ask students to note which words have changed. This will draw attention to the pronoun changes as well as the verb changes.

Answers

1 *'It was a fun thing to try out.'*
2 *'I can't remember exactly how long it took.'*
3 *'I get annoyed when I get spam.'*
4 *'We're going to solve it.'*
5 *'We must find a better way to stop spam.'*
6 *'I don't think people are really different now.'*

Optional activity

Confident students transform the sentences into direct speech first and then check their answers in the reading text.

Your response

Ask students to work in pairs or small groups and make a list of the advantages and disadvantages of email, text messages, instant messaging and social networking sites. Listen to their ideas as a class. Examples could include that email doesn't require paper or postage, texting reduces face-to-face or voice communication, people may actually be more lonely because of virtual contact through social networking sites.

5 VOCABULARY

- Students find the five words in exercise 2 and use the context to help match the words and definitions.

Answers

1 Internet 2 virus 3 ISP 4 attachment 5 spam

Optional activity

In pairs/groups, students think of other words related to computers, e.g. *screen, mouse, keyboard, file, document, website, search engine, download, save, open.* Write them on the board. Check comprehension by giving a definition and asking students for the word. Students define one for their group. The group listens and says the word.

6 PRONUNCIATION

- Write *dog* and *dock* on the board. Elicit the pronunciation. Model and drill the pronunciation of the two sounds, /dɒg/ and /dɒk/.
- Ask students to look at the words in the chart. Play the first part of the recording, pausing after each word for students to repeat.

3.06 Recording

/g/ *dog pig dug bag game good*
/k/ *dock pick duck back came could*

- Play the second part of the recording. Students listen and write the words they hear. Ask students to compare answers. If necessary, play the recording again. Ask different students to say and spell the answers.

3.06 Recording and answers

dock pick dug bag came good

Optional activities

♦ If these are difficult sounds for your students, ask them to write five of the words from the chart in their notebook. They then dictate them to their partner and compare to see if the communication was successful. Monitor and help as necessary.
♦ Students race to think of three more words for each sound.

7 LISTENING

- Students look at the photos of Peter and Natasha. Ask *How old do you think they are?* Tell students that they are boyfriend and girlfriend but Peter is having problems with Natasha. Students read what Natasha said. They could then use the sentence heads to predict what actually happened before listening to check.
- Play the recording. Students note the answers. With a less confident class, check what happened before asking students to make complete sentences. With a confident class, students go straight into telling each other what Natasha said and what actually happened. Check answers as a whole class.
- Ask students what they think Peter should do.

3.07 Recording and answers

She said she would meet him at 8, but she didn't turn up until 8.30.
She said the film began at 8.30, but it started at 7.30.
She said he could borrow her MP3 player, but she lent it to her best friend.
She said she had left his birthday present at home, but she hadn't bought him one.
She said she had to get home early, but she went out again later.
She said he hadn't phoned her, but her phone was switched off.

8 WRITING

- Students work in pairs and interview each other. Elicit that the first question they need to ask is *When did you last hear some good news about sport/family/etc.?* Ask two students to demonstrate a question and answer. Direct students' attention to the other questions below the box. Remind students to note down their partner's answers. They do not have to write complete sentences.
- Monitor and help as necessary. Make a note of good examples of language use and errors to focus on at the end of the activity. Ask students to tell you about any interesting answers they heard.
- Students use their notes to write two sentences about each topic. Set a 10-minute time limit. Monitor and help as necessary.

Optional activity

Fast finishers/confident students can add more good news for one of the topics or for another topic of their choice, e.g. *films, football teams, holidays, school.*

Extension Students work in pairs and tell each other about the most important news they have had or heard in the past few days or weeks. Then students work with a different partner and report what their first partner told them.

LANGUAGE WORKOUT

- Ask students to complete the Language Workout box.
- Students turn to page 119 of the Language File to check their answers.

Answers

Past simple *Past continuous* *Past perfect*
Past perfect *was/were going to* *had to*
could *would*

- Highlight that:
  - when we report someone's words, the verb usually moves one tense back into the past. Both the past simple and the present perfect become the past perfect in reported speech.
  - the verbs *say* and *tell* are usually used to report someone's words but they are used differently. With a confident class, ask students to look at the examples and elicit the different use. With a less confident class, explain that you use *tell someone* (that) + subject + verb and *say* (that) + subject + verb.
  - *say* and *tell* can be followed by *that* but it is not necessary

Optional activity

In pairs, one student, with the Student's Book open, reads the direct speech and their partner, with their book closed, tries to make the reported speech. After two minutes, students reverse roles.

PRACTICE

- Students look at exercise 23 on p120 of the Language File. Ask them to read through Ray's ideas quickly to find out if he agrees or disagrees (he agrees that the way we communicate is changing but he doesn't think people are changing because of this – friendly people are still friendly people).
- Students then transform his direct speech into reported speech. Monitor and help as necessary. Check answers as a whole class.

Answers

1 *He said he wasn't a household name for inventing email.*
2 *He said it didn't bother him – it wasn't the centre of his life.*
3 *He said computer experts knew what he'd done.*
4 *He said we had to look at how people communicate.*
5 *He said people could communicate more easily by email.*
6 *He said in the past people had gone to libraries.*
7 *He said in the future they would use the Internet.*
8 *He said Internet use was going to increase enormously.*
9 *He said it was exciting because so much was happening.*

Optional activity

In small groups, students discuss their own answers to the question *A lot of people say email has changed society – do you agree?* Students then use reported speech to tell the whole class what their group said.

Follow-up activities

- ♦ Organise students into two teams. Write the beginning of a sentence on the board, e.g. *Today/ Last night/Yesterday the headmaster/(name of student)/ (famous person) said that …* Each team races to complete the sentence so that it is grammatically correct but also true. Continue with other sentences. You could also revise *asked* and *told* in this activity.
- ♦ Students record new vocabulary from the lesson in their vocabulary notebook and/or on cards for the class Vocabulary box.

HOMEWORK

Students think of a scene from a well-known film and write (approximately) what the characters said to each other in the scene using reported speech.

WEBLINK

Students may like to visit www.teenforumz.com where they can read messages posted by teenagers. The language is quite informal and so may be difficult but the topics and sense of humour should appeal.

Revision and Extension p97

Language File pp119–120

Workbook Unit 7 Lesson 2 pp76–77

Photocopiable worksheet p181, notes p159

3 They asked how he had got the idea

Communicative Aims	Language	Pronunciation	Vocabulary	Optional Aids
Reporting what someone asked	Reported questions	Syllable stress	Education Phrasal verbs with *go*	Follow-up activity: questions on slips of paper

WARMER 1

If you set the homework from the previous lesson, students read their description of the scene to their partner who tries to identify the film.

WARMER 2

Write the word *energy* on the board. Students work in pairs or small groups and brainstorm as many possible sources of energy as they can. Set a time limit of three minutes for this. Listen to their ideas as a class and write their suggestions on the board, e.g. *water* (hydro-electric), *nuclear energy, wind power, coal, gas, the sun* (solar energy).

1 OPENER

- The aim is to set the scene and personalise the topic.
- Ask students to look at the photo and tell you what the object is and what it is used for.

Answer

It's a windmill. It's used to generate (make) electricity.

2 READING

- Ask students to read the question first. Then they read and/or listen to the text and find the answer. More confident students can do this with their books closed and just listen to the story.
- Students compare their answers in pairs. Check the answer with the whole class.

3.08 Recording

See text on page 92 of the Student's Book.

Answer

To generate electricity so that his family had electric light and could pump water, because his village had no electricity.

3 AFTER READING

- Tell students that these five questions are reported in the text. Students read the text again and find the reported questions. Point out to less confident students that they are all in the final paragraph.
- When students have found the reported questions, they match them with the answers a–e. Check the answers.

Answers

1 *They also wanted to know if he had gone back to school – b*
2 *Reporters asked the teenage inventor how he had got the idea. – c*
3 *They asked what he called his windmill. – a*
4 *They asked what else the windmill was used for. – e*
5 *They asked if other villages were building windmills. – d*

Optional activity

Fast finishers note any more new words in the reading and look them up in a dictionary.

Your response

Have students work in pairs to discuss the questions. Then conduct a feedback session with the whole class.

4 ROLE PLAY

- Give students one minute to read the reported interview and then ask comprehension questions, e.g. *How long did he work on the windmill? What did the villagers think of his 'electric wind'? Has he visited other countries?*
- With a less confident class, give students five minutes to re-write the interview in direct speech. Students then roleplay it in pairs. With a more confident class, students go directly into roleplay. Ask some pairs to act out the role play for the class.
- Students listen and compare their version with the original.

3.09 Recording and answers

REPORTER *How long did you work on the windmill?*
WILLIAM *I built it in three months.*
REPORTER *What did the villagers think of your 'electric wind'?*
WILLIAM *At first they said it was magic.*
REPORTER *Have they changed their minds?*
WILLIAM *Yes, they have. Because now they can charge their mobile phones.*
REPORTER *What's the best thing about your windmill?*
WILLIAM *It's free! The parts are free and the wind is free.*
REPORTER *How did you get a place at ALA?*
WILLIAM *I won a scholarship.*
REPORTER *Do you like being at ALA?*
WILLIAM *It's great. There are students there from 53 countries.*

REPORTER *Have you visited other countries?*
WILLIAM *I've been to the USA, and to a conference in Tanzania.*
REPORTER *Did you enjoy the conference?*
WILLIAM *Yes. I was very scared but it went all right.*
REPORTER *What do you want to do next?*
WILLIAM *I want to go on with my studies and get a place at a college in the USA.*

5 VOCABULARY

- Students match the phrasal verbs with their meaning. Students then race to find as many as they can in the lesson.

Answers
1 go up 2 go ahead with 3 go down 4 go away
5 go on 6 go back
In this lesson: go down, go ahead with, go back

Extension Students put each phrasal verb into a sentence. Encourage students to use the examples in the lesson and/or in the dictionary. This will help avoid unnatural sentences.

6 PRONUNCIATION

- Ask students to copy the chart into their notebook. Students look at the words in the box and predict the word stress. Play the recording. Students write the words in a column and then compare answers in pairs.

3.10 Recording and answers
■▪▪ *educate leadership library secondary*
▪■▪ *electric inventor reporter starvation*

- Play the recording for students to check their answers. Pause after each word for students to repeat.

7 WRITING

- With a less confident class, give students time to prepare some questions to ask their partner. Remind students to use *if* in reported questions that do not contain a question word (when, who, what). Give students five minutes to interview each other. Remind students to note their partner's answers.
- Set a 10-minute time limit for students to write sentences reporting the questions and answers.

Extension Students write sentences reporting the questions they were asked and the answers they gave. Make sure they report all five questions.

LANGUAGE WORKOUT

- Ask students to complete the Language box.
- Students turn to page 119 of the Language File to check their answers.

Answers
if he had gone what; was used
how he had got if

- Highlight that:
  – the verb and pronoun changes in reported questions are the same as in reported speech.
  – the word order in reported questions is the same as in normal statements. This means that the auxiliary verb *do/does/did* is not used.

PRACTICE

- Students do exercise 24 on p120 of the Language File.

Answers
1 Anna asked Will what his mobile phone number was.
2 Anna asked Will if he used his phone mainly to send texts or to make calls.
3 Anna asked Will if he was thinking of changing his mobile phone.
4 Anna asked Will when he first got a mobile phone.
5 Anna asked Will if he had ever forgotten to charge his mobile phone.

Follow-up activities

- **Game** *What did they say?* Give each student a different question, e.g. *Can you play an instrument?* Students move around, asking and answering the questions. In pairs, students recall who asked them what and how they replied, e.g. *Simon asked me if I could play an instrument and I told him that I played the guitar.* They win one point for remembering who asked the question and one point for a correct reported question and answer.
- Write jumbled reported questions, commands or requests on the board. Students race to re-order them and transform them into direct speech.

HOMEWORK

Students interview a friend or relative about their mobile phone use, e.g. *How often …? Who do you phone most?* The interview need not be in English. Students then write up the interview in English in reported speech.

WEBLINK

Students can visit www.ted.com/speakers/william_kamkwamba.html for more news on William Kamkwamba.

Revision and Extension p97

Language File pp119–120

Workbook Unit 7 Lesson 3 pp78–79

Photocopiable worksheet p182, notes p159

4 *Integrated Skills* Telling a Story

Skills
Reading Details: *Amazing Rescue* newspaper story
Listening Details: radio news
Speaking Comparing newspaper and radio news report of same story
Writing News story about a rescue

Learner Independence
Using the Internet to practise language skills
Word creation: noun suffix *-tion*

Vocabulary
Sailing and the sea
Useful expressions

Optional Aids
Exercise 8: pictures of people, places and ways of rescuing people
Follow-up activity: large piece of paper

WARMER 1

Game *Noughts and crosses* For instructions see Unit 2, Lesson 1, p45. Use the following verbs: *go ahead with, pick up, turn off, bring back, go into, go on, take away, go through, put down.*

WARMER 2

Draw a circle and write the letters for *AMAZING RESCUE* on the board. In pairs, students write as many words as they can in two minutes using the letters in the circle. When they have finished, ask the pair with the most words to write them on the board.

1 OPENER

- The aim is to set the scene and pre-teach some of the vocabulary for the reading.
- Ask students to look at the headline and the photos and predict what the story is about.
- Ask students to read the words in the box. Give definitions of some of the more difficult words and ask students to say which word you are defining, e.g. *Someone who watches the sea near a coast for boats that are having problems is a … coastguard.* In pairs, students say which words they think they will find in the story. More confident students can discuss how these words will fit into the story.

2 READING

- The aim is for students to read to find specific details.
- Check general comprehension first: Give students one minute to read through the text quickly and find out if their predictions for the story were right.
- Students then read the comprehension questions and read the story again to find the answers.

Answers
1 Off the south coast of England.
2 Because of huge waves.
3 30 minutes
4 After they'd been in the water for about 40 minutes.
5 They felt very cold.
6 It's 6,000 miles away.
7 By helicopter
8 They should contact the coastguard direct on 999.

3

- Students read the definitions and find the corresponding words in the text. Encourage students to use the context to work out the form and meaning of the word.

Answers
1 dinghy 2 capsized 3 watertight 4 success 5 container 6 coastguard 7 safety 8 contact 9 right

4 LINKING WORDS

- Students find and note examples of sentences in the text with these linking words. Ask students to say how these words help the reader. (They make it clear to the reader the order in which the actions happened.)
- Highlight that:
  – *after* introduces the first of two actions: *After they did/had done …, they did …*
  – *afterwards* introduces the second action and means that the first activity is finished: *They did … Afterwards, they were/did …*

Answers
1 After they'd been in the water for about 40 minutes, the situation was getting serious. / After they had held on to the dinghy for nearly an hour, they heard a helicopter.
2 Then Emily remembered her mobile phone …
3 Ten minutes later … they heard a helicopter.
4 Next, everything happened very quickly …
5 Afterwards, the coast guard said that the teenagers were lucky to be alive …

5 LISTENING

- Tell students they are going to hear the same story as a radio news report but some of the information is different or said in a different way. Students look back at the questions in exercise 2.
- Play the recording. Students listen and note the answers. Students compare their answers in pairs. If necessary play the recording again, pausing after each answer is heard to check. Check comprehension of *lifeboat* and *emergency services.*
- Ask students to identify the different words used to express the key information, e.g. *thirty minutes/half an hour.*

3.11 Recording and answers

Two teenagers capsized in the sea off the south coast of ***Britain*** *and called Japan on a mobile phone to ask for help.*
Brother and sister Ken and Emily Booth were on a sailing holiday near Southampton. But because of ***strong winds****, their dinghy capsized and they were thrown into the sea. Ken, 17, and Emily, 16, spent* ***half an hour*** *trying to right the capsized dinghy, but without success. They couldn't get back into the dinghy, and they couldn't attract the attention of passing ships. After they'd been in the water for about* ***three quarters of an hour****, the situation was getting serious, and they felt very* ***tired****. Then Emily remembered her mobile phone in its watertight container in her pocket and reached for it.*
But she didn't think of dialling 999, the emergency number. Instead she phoned their father, who was ***10,000 kilometres*** *away in Tokyo on a business trip. Emily explained: 'I thought it would be quicker to phone someone I knew and tell them our position. I dialled Dad's number and he contacted the coastguard.'*
About ten minutes later, after they had held on to the dinghy for nearly an hour, they heard a ***lifeboat****. Next, everything happened very quickly, and Ken and Emily were picked up and carried to safety.*
Afterwards, the coastguard said that the teenagers were lucky to be alive and very, very lucky that the mobile had worked. 'Anyone in trouble should contact the ***emergency services*** *direct on 999,' he added.*

6 SPEAKING

- Ask two students to read the example aloud. In pairs, students continue comparing the newspaper and the radio report.

Answers

2 *In the newspaper it said that their dinghy had capsized because of huge waves. On the radio it said that it had capsized because of strong winds.*
3 *In the newspaper it said that they had spent 30 minutes trying to right the dinghy. On the radio it said that they had spent half an hour trying to right it.*
4 *In the newspaper it said that Emily had remembered her mobile after about 40 minutes. On the radio it said that she had remembered it after about three-quarters of an hour.*
5 *In the newspaper it said that they had felt cold. On the radio it said that they had felt tired.*
6 *In the newspaper it said that Tokyo was 6,000 miles from Southampton. On the radio it said that it was 10,000 kilometres from Southampton.*
7 *In the newspaper it said that they had been rescued by helicopter. On the radio it said that they had been rescued by lifeboat.*
8 *In the newspaper it said that the coastguard had said that anyone in trouble should contact the coastguard direct on 999. On the radio it said that the coastguard had said that anyone in trouble should contact the emergency services direct on 999.*

7

- Tell students they are going to roleplay an interview between a journalist and Emily.
- With a less confident group, organise students into two groups: one group are interviewers and one group are Emily. Give the groups five minutes to prepare their roles.
- Students do the role play in pairs. Confident students can add more questions or more information.

Suggested answers

Where were you when you capsized? Off the south coast of England/Britain.
Why did the dinghy capsize? Because of huge waves/strong winds.
What did you do when you fell into the sea? We spent 30 minutes/half an hour trying to right the dinghy.
Why didn't you dial 999? Because I thought it would be quicker to dial someone I knew and tell them our position.
How were you rescued? By helicopter/lifeboat.
How did you feel after the rescue? Relieved/Great.

8 GUIDED WRITING

- Students write their own news story about two people in an amazing rescue using the questions as prompts. You could brainstorm dangerous locations/situations to help start students off, e.g. *walking or cycling in mountains, on safari in the jungle*. Alternatively, you could provide pictures of people, possible locations and ways of rescuing them to help prompt students. Students could work individually or in pairs. Give students five minutes to get their ideas together.
- Set a 10-minute time limit to write the story. Encourage students to use the linking words from exercise 4 and to think of an exciting headline. Monitor and help as necessary.
- Students read or listen to each other's stories. Hold a class vote on which one is the most amazing rescue.

Optional activities

♦ Students copy their story out neatly and make it look like a real newspaper article adding maps or pictures if possible. These can then be displayed around classroom.
♦ Students write five comprehension questions for readers of their news story to answer.

9 LEARNER INDEPENDENCE

- The aim is to encourage and motivate students in their English studies by showing them stimulating material which they can use to practise their reading and listening.
- Ask *Do you use the Internet? Do you have the Internet at home? Do you ever look at English websites? Which ones?*
- Tell students about this excellent website and encourage them to look at it before next lesson and report back on what they read/listened to and how they found it.

10 WORD CREATION

- The aim is for students to learn one way in which nouns can be formed from verbs and extend their vocabulary.
- Warn students that the spelling of the word changes sometimes when the ending is added. Students complete the sentences individually and then compare in pairs. Check the answers and how to spell them as a whole class.
- Tell students to think about the pronunciation of the nouns. Ask *What is the rule?* The main stress is always on the syllable before the *-tion* ending.

Answers
1 invention 2 operation 3 communication 4 attention 5 invitation 6 information 7 situation 8 description

Optional activity

Give students two minutes in pairs to invent a story using as many of the nouns as possible. Ask the pair that has managed to include the most nouns to tell their story to the class.

11 PHRASEBOOK

- Play the recording, pausing after each expression for students to repeat.

3.12 Recording and answers
Calm down! (L1, Ex2)
I can't remember exactly. (Ray L2, Ex2)
I get annoyed when … (Ray L2, Ex2)
It's a tough problem. (Ray L2, Ex2)
There isn't an easy answer. (Ray L2, Ex2)
How did you get the idea? (L3, Ex3)
… but without success (L4, Ex2)
It said on the radio that … (L4, Ex5)

- Ask students to look through the unit to find the expressions, and look at how they are used.
- Students can add expressions they like to their Personal Phrasebooks.
- Ask students to work in pairs to make up the five-line dialogue. Invite some pairs to act out their dialogues in front of the class.

Follow-up activities

- Students choose ten words from this lesson and previous lessons in the unit and make anagrams. In pairs, they exchange lists and see who can rewrite all the words correctly first.
- Write *Communication* on the board. Elicit different categories from the class and write them on the board to create a word map e.g. *Internet, phone, letter* or *speaking, writing, signs*. Divide students into small groups to draw their own word map on a large piece of paper.

HOMEWORK

If students have access to the Internet, ask them to read and/or listen to one news item on the CBBC news website and be prepared to talk about it in the next lesson (www.bbc.co.uk/newsround/). If students do not have access to the Internet, ask them to choose a current news story which interests them.

WEBLINK

Students may like to visit news.bbc.co.uk/cbbcnews/hi/world/default.stm. Here they can read the latest stories from around the world.

Revision and Extension p97

Workbook Unit 7 Lesson 4 pp80–81

Inspiration EXTRA!

Optional Aids

Your choice! Action: blindfolds

LANGUAGE LINKS

- Books closed. Write the word *recycling* on the board. Elicit from the class examples of things that can be recycled, e.g. *paper, cardboard, glass, plastic, metal, clothing*. Find out what students do with old computer equipment or household appliances like washing machines. Point out that electronic equipment like this can also be recycled.
- Ask students to open their books. Tell them that this text is part of a leaflet with the same message about recycling in six different languages. Ask them to underline any words they recognise in any of the languages. If their mother tongue is one of the languages in the list, they do not need to underline the words in that particular section.
- Students compare their answers in pairs and answer the other questions. They then share their ideas with the whole class.
- At home students look at other leaflets or instruction booklets for different electronic appliances and look for recognisable words.

Answers

The languages are French, English, German, Italian, Spanish and Turkish.
German has the longest words and uses the most capital letters (all nouns in German begin with a capital letter).

Optional activity

Ask students which of the languages in the leaflet contains the most recognisable words and which contains the least. Ask which language uses the most words to convey the message and which language is the most concise.

GAME GUESS WHAT THEY SAID

- Organise students into groups of four. Ask students to read the instructions carefully. Check comprehension by asking: *What do you have to do first?* (Choose a topic) *What does A do?* (Write a question on the topic) *What does B do?* (write a reply) *What do C and D have to try to do?* (Guess the question and answer) *How many questions can they ask?* (Five) Point out that C and D need to use reported speech to guess the question and answer.
- Ask one group to demonstrate the game. Point out that A and B, C and D then change roles.
- Students play in their groups. Monitor and help as necessary. Play for 10 minutes or until topics have been used twice. At the end ask how many they guessed correctly.

Optional activities

- ♦ Add more specific topics relevant to your students' lives and interests.
- ♦ Make the game competitive by awarding two points to the player who correctly guesses the question and one point to the player who correctly guesses the answer. Players take it in turns to guess.

SKETCH HOTEL RECEPTION

- The aim is for students to enjoy using their English while also reviewing language presented in this unit and getting valuable stress and intonation practice.
- Ask the students to look at the title and the cartoon and establish that the sketch is set at the hotel reception and is a conversation between the manager and a guest.
- With a more confident class, play the recording with books closed. With a less confident class, play the recording while the students follow in their books. Play the first time just for enjoyment.
- Check students comprehend the sketch fully: Students read the sketch and identify the five communication problems the manager and the guest have (1 – his surname is Watt, she thinks he says 'What?'; 2 – she says 'Right', he thinks she understands his surname is 'Wright'; 3 – she asks him for his first name, he thinks she asks again for his surname; 4 – She says 'Address?', he thinks she is offering him a dress; 5 – she says 'Room 420', he thinks he is in a room for twenty people).

3.13 Recording

See text on page 96 of the Student's Book.

- Divide the class into two equal groups and play the recording again, with one group repeating the man's role in chorus and the other group repeating the woman's role. Encourage students to exaggerate stress and intonation.
- Ask the students to close their books and play the recording again. Then ask the students to work in pairs and practise the sketch. Choose several pairs to act out the sketch in front of the class.

Optional activity

Make an audio or video recording of students performing the sketch.

REVISION

Lesson 1
Students' own answers

Lesson 2

Answers
She said she would meet him at 8, but she didn't turn up until 8.30.
She said the film began at 8.30 but it started at 7.30.
She said he could borrow her MP3 player but she lent it to her best friend.
She said she had left his birthday present at home but she hadn't bought him one.
She said she had to get home early but she went out again later.
She said he hadn't phoned her but her phone was switched off.

Lesson 3

Answers
He asked why she hadn't phoned him.
He asked what she was doing that evening.
He asked if she would have dinner with him.
He asked if she liked Japanese food.
He asked if she had ever tried sushi.
He asked how often she ate fish.

EXTENSION

Lesson 1
Students' own answers

Lesson 2
- Students complete the questions first, then interview each other and finally write up the answers in reported speech.

Students' own answers

Lesson 3
Students' own answers

Language File pp119–120

YOUR CHOICE!

- Organise students into groups depending on their learning style. Each group does the activity which relates to their own learning style. Set a 10-minute time limit for all groups.
- Monitor and help groups. Check if necessary. You could provide written answers for groups to check their own work.
- Encourage students to experiment with other learning styles and try one of the other activities of their choice.

CONSTRUCTION

Answers
1 He asked her to close the window.
2 I asked him not to shout.
3 The teacher told them to be quiet.
4 She said that she didn't mind the rain.
5 I told them that the taxi was waiting.
6 You told us that we had to hurry.
7 She asked him what the time was.
8 He wanted to know if the answer was right.

REFLECTION

Answers
1 e, g   2 a, f   3 b, d, h, i   4 c, j

ACTION

- Students follow the instructions in the box. Encourage students to check what their partner said before they move to avoid bumping into things.
- Students change roles when A reaches their destination.
- Students could report back on who successfully directed their partner round the class.

INTERACTION

- Divide students into small groups. Suggest students take two minutes to think about how their parents would describe them. They then take turns to tell their group. Finally they report to the group what they learnt/found surprising.
- Students could report back to the rest of the class on any interesting points.

Workbook Unit 7 Inspiration EXTRA! pp82–83

7 CULTURE

Global English

Optional Aids

Exercise 3 Optional activity: small cards for Vocabulary box

1 READING

- Students look at the photos. Ask them to describe what they can see and guess what country it might be.
- Tell students they are going to read about people learning and using English around the world. Ask them to look at the paragraph headings. Explain that there are seven headings but they only need to use four of them. Set a time limit of four minutes for students to match the headings to the paragraphs. Point out that they do not need to understand the whole paragraph to match it to a heading.
- Students compare answers and then listen to check.

3.14 Recording

See text on page 98 of the Student's Book.

Answer

1 Young readers of English
2 New kinds of English
3 Working in English
4 Reasons for teaching English

Optional activity

With a confident class, ask students to predict the paragraph headings before looking at the options.

2

- Ask students to look at the information in the box. Then ask them to look at the questions. Explain that they should use the words and numbers in the box to answer the questions. They can check their answers by looking in the text.
- Students do the task individually and then compare their answers in pairs. Check the answers with the whole class. Note that 76.8% is pronounced 'seventy-six point eight per cent' and 1.2 million 'one point two million'.

Answers

1 76.8%   2 Singapore and Switzerland   3 Belgium
4 6,661   5 1.2 million   6 India and Japan

Optional activities

- ♦ Close the book. Ask students to ask you questions about the text. Students then continue in pairs.
- ♦ Write the following sentence heads on the board: *I didn't know that …, I am surprised that …, I think … is a good/bad idea.* In pairs, students complete the sentences orally with reference to the text, e.g. *I am surprised that people in Switzerland speak to each other in English at work.*

3 VOCABULARY

- Ask students to find words 1–8 in the text. Students use the context to help match the words to the definitions.

Answers

1 b   2 f   3 a   4 e   5 h   6 g   7 c   8 d

Optional activities

- ♦ With a confident class, students cover the words 1–8 and try to find/recall the word in the text for each definition.
- ♦ Students write these words, together with an example or definition, on cards for the Vocabulary box.

4 MINI-PROJECT LEARNING LANGUAGES

- Students read the questions. Check students understand the meaning of *particular* in this context (a specific one).
- Give students a few minutes to think about their answers to the questions. Then ask them to work in pairs and compare their answers. They can use the library or the Internet to check that their answers are correct.
- Ask each pair to write a report giving information about language learning in their country. Monitor while they are writing and give help if required.
- Pairs exchange their reports with other pairs and compare the facts.

WEBLINK

For more information, students may like to visit wikipedia.org/wiki/English_language

Workbook Culture pp84–85

1 They should have thought …

Communicative Aims	Language	Pronunciation	Vocabulary	Optional Aids
Criticising past actions	*should(n't) have/ought to have*	/dʒ/ jump /ʃ/ shark /tʃ/ punch	Water	Follow-up activity: cards with example situations written on them

WARMER 1

Game *Cross the river* On the board, draw a picture of three stepping stones across a river. Divide the class into two teams and tell them that for their team to score a point, they must 'cross' the river by successfully answering one vocabulary question, one grammar question and one pronunciation question. Give students a definition and have them say the word for the first. For the second give a 'grammar' word (*since, although, ever,* etc.) for students to put into an example sentence, and for the last, write a word and ask students to identify the stressed syllable. Teams take it in turns to attempt to 'cross the river' as many times as possible.

WARMER 2

Game *Water word race* In pairs, ask students to write a list of ten words connected with water, e.g. *drink, tap, fish,* as quickly as possible. Remind them of the shark attack article in Unit 1, Lesson 3 for ideas. The fastest pair should shout *Stop!* and read out their list to the rest of the class.

1 OPENER

- The aim is to set the context for the reading.
- Ask the students to discuss in pairs how much water they think they have used that day and for what. Ask a few pairs to tell the rest of the class what they have used water for and create a list of uses on the board.
- Students do the quiz. Ask them to answer the questions individually and then compare their answers in pairs.
- Play the recording so that students can check their predictions.

3.15 Recording and answers

1 The answer is A. 97.5% of the water on Earth is salt water, which humans can't drink.
2 The answer is C. Most fresh water can't be used because it's frozen in the polar ice caps. Only 1% of the world's fresh water is available for use. That's 0.01% of Earth's total water.
3 The answer is A. Humans can only live for three days without water.
4 The answer is C. It takes 42,500 litres of water to produce a kilo of beef.
5 The answer is B. The recommended minimum amount of water per person per day for cooking, drinking and personal hygiene is 50 litres.
6 The answer is B. The average citizen of the Gambia in West Africa uses 4.5 litres of water a day.

2 READING

- Ask students to look at the photos and say what they show. Use the photos to elicit vocabulary such as *dam* and *environmental campaigner*.
- Explain the task. Students read and/or listen to the text and identify two problems the environmental campaigner is concerned about.
- Play the recording for students to listen to as they read the whole text. Encourage them to guess unfamiliar words from context. Be prepared to explain *shortage, species, wipe out, flood, displace* and *underway*.

3.16 Recording

See text on page 100 of the Student's Book.

Answers

Two-thirds of the world's population will face a shortage of water by 2025 and the environmental damage caused by building dams.

Optional activity

More confident students can do exercise 2 as a listening activity.

3 AFTER READING

- Students read the text again and match questions 1–5 with answers a–h. Remind students that three of the answers will not be used.
- Check the answers by asking different students to ask and answer the questions.

Answers

1 h 2 c 3 e 4 f 5 b

Your response

Students work in pairs to discuss the questions. Then have class feedback to see what the general opinions are.

Optional activities

- Fast finishers write other questions that are answered in the text. They can later read one out to the class, who find the answer in the text.
- In pairs, students take the roles of Kate and the interviewer. Less confident students can read directly from the text, while more confident students try to do this without looking at the text.
- Students discuss in pairs which of the water facts from the article they found most surprising.

LANGUAGE WORKOUT OPTION

If you want to pre-teach the language students will be using in the following activities, you may like to go to the Language Workout box now.

4 SPEAKING

- Ask the students to look at the pictures and think about which of the phrases in the box they are connected to. Use the pictures to check any vocabulary that students are unsure of, e.g. *hosepipe, watering can*.
- In pairs, students make sentences to say what the people in the photos should/shouldn't have done to save water using the phrases.
- Check the answers by asking different students to say their sentences.

Answers

1 *He shouldn't have had a bath. He should have had a shower.*
2 *He shouldn't have used a hosepipe. He should have used a watering can.*
3 *She should have turned off the tap.*
4 *She shouldn't have washed the car every day.*
5 *He should have gone to a public swimming pool.*
6 *She should have saved the rainwater.*

5 PRONUNCIATION

- Ask students to look at the cartoon. Elicit the words *shark, chew* and *Jaws* (the name of the famous shark from the Spielberg film).
- Play the recording. Students listen and repeat.
- Highlight the three sounds, drilling in chorus the individual words which contain these sounds. Highlight the increasing tension and forward movement of the lips from /ʃ/ (ship) to /dʒ/ (Jaws) to /tʃ/ (punch). Also highlight the stressed content words of the sentence and the resulting rhythm.
- Students practise saying the sentence to their partner.

3.17 Recording

George shouldn't have watched the shark chew the ship – he should have jumped in shouting 'Jaws!' and punched it.

Optional activities

- Dictate some words containing the three sounds for the students to write down, e.g. *July, cheap, sheep, gel, shell, wash, message, watch*. In pairs, students compare what they have written and sort the words into three groups according to which sound they contain.
- In pairs, students invent another sentence including as many examples of the three sounds as possible. The pair that manages to include the greatest number reads their sentence out to the class and the other students practise repeating it.

6 SPEAKING

- Ask students to think about a situation in the past when they did or didn't do something they are not happy about now. Highlight the CD example given in the book. Students then make notes under the four headings about the experience and how they feel about it now.
- Students then use their notes to tell another student about it.

Extension Students work individually and think of situations where things went wrong and mistakes were made. Give them a few minutes to make notes about what the people involved should have done or shouldn't have done, e.g. *My sister failed her exam because she didn't study hard enough. She should have studied harder.*

Optional activity

Students tell a new partner about the same experience, but this time their partner finishes the story by saying what they think they should/shouldn't have done.

7 WRITING

- The aim is for students to write about the situations from exercise 6, using *should/shouldn't have*.
- Remind students to write two paragraphs, one about their own situation and the other about their partner.
- Ask students to show their paragraphs to their partner to check the accuracy of the situation and the language.

LANGUAGE WORKOUT

- Ask students to complete the Language box. Confident students can complete first and then check, while others can look back at exercises 2 and 3 and then complete.
- Students turn to page 120 of the Language File to check their answers.

Answers

have *shouldn't have* *ought to have*

- Ask students questions about the sentences in the Language Workout box, to check that they understand the meaning, e.g. *Did they go ahead with the project? Does the speaker (Kate) think that was a good idea?*
- Highlight that:
  - we can use *should have* or *ought to have* with the same meaning. Both are followed by the past participle.
  - *should* is not followed by *to*, unlike *ought*.
  - *shouldn't have* is more common than *ought not to have/oughtn't to have.*
  - *ought to haven't/should haven't* are not possible for the negative forms.
- Drill the examples in chorus for pronunciation and stress. Encourage students to use the weak form of *have* /həv/ and the contractions in the negative form. Remind students of the correct pronunciation of *ought* /ɔːt/ rhyming with *bought* and *sort*.

PRACTICE

- Turn to Practice exercise 25 in the Language File on page 120. Ask a confident student to read the example out loud to the rest of the class. Highlight the change from *you* to *I* and *your* to *my*. Do the first sentence as an example with the whole class. Students then write similar sentences for 2–8.
- Check the answers together as a whole class.

Answers

1 *I should have made my bed this morning.*
2 *I should have finished my homework before I went out.*
3 *I shouldn't have left my sports bag at school.*
4 *I shouldn't have been rude to the bus driver on the way home.*
5 *I should have remembered to bring my dictionary home.*
6 *I should have phoned my teacher back.*
7 *I should have helped to clear the table after dinner.*
8 *I shouldn't have come home after midnight/I should have come home before midnight.*

Optional activities

- ♦ Fast finishers replace *should/shouldn't have* with *ought to have/ought not to have.*
- ♦ Students cover the phrases and try to remember the *should/shouldn't have* sentences by looking at the pictures.

Follow-up activities

- ♦ **Game** *Right or wrong?* Before the game starts, prepare some short examples of 'debatable behaviour' on cards, e.g. *a homeless man stole fruit from a supermarket, a man phoned the police when his neighbours were playing loud music at midnight.* Divide students into groups of five and give each group a few cards. One student in each group chooses a card and reads it to the rest of the group. Each group member secretly writes a tick in their notebook if they think the behaviour was right in the situation and a cross if they think it was wrong. The 'reader' then guesses what other students have written, e.g. *You don't think he should have done that. You think he did the right thing.* The group then discuss the situation further and try to reach a decision on what should have been done in each situation.
- ♦ Divide students into two groups, parents and teenagers. Set the context: the parents have been away for the weekend, leaving the teenagers in charge of the house. The teenagers have had a party, damaged several things in the house, played loud music late at night and finished all the food and drink in the house. Teenagers work together first to prepare how they will explain their behaviour. Parents work together to plan how to explain to the teenagers that their behaviour was wrong, using *should(n't) have*. Students then work in parent/teenager pairs to roleplay the discussion.

HOMEWORK

Ask students to write a short message to an Internet problem page, explaining an imaginary difficult situation they are in because of their own behaviour, e.g. *They can't go to college because they failed their exams*. They should then write two different reader responses commenting on what they should/shouldn't have done and/or what they should do now.

WEBLINK

Students can find out more about water and its uses by visiting ga.water.usgs.gov/edu

Revision and Extension p109

Language File p120

Workbook Unit 8 Lesson 1 pp86–87

Photocopiable worksheet p183, notes p160

What would you do?

Communicative Aims	**Language**	**Pronunciation**	**Vocabulary**	**Optional Aids**
Talking about imaginary or unlikely situations Giving advice	Second conditional	Pronunciation of *gh*	Geographical features Weather Illnesses and ailments Survival kit	Follow-up activity: large pieces of paper and coloured pens

WARMER 1

Ask students to work in pairs to try to remember three of the facts they learnt about water from the last lesson. After a couple of minutes, they can check back in their books and see if they remembered correctly.

WARMER 2

Introduce the topic of survival by asking students if they have seen any reality TV shows such as *Survivor* or dramas/films such as *Lost* or *Castaway*. Tell students to imagine they have to live alone on an island for a week. They can take one song, one book/film and one luxury item. Students tell their partner what they would take and why.

1 OPENER

- The aim is to set the context and pre-teach vocabulary for the Questionnaire in exercise 2.
- Check first that students understand *survival* by asking *What things do we need for survival?* (water, food, heat, shelter, etc.) and *In what places/situations is survival difficult?* (the desert, space, jungle, etc.).
- Ask students to look only at the pictures in the questionnaire and guess which of the words from the box they expect to find in the questionnaire.

Answers

bear, desert, oasis, thunderstorm, lightning, forest, fire, wind, river, waterfall

2 READING

- Students read and answer the questionnaire. Be prepared to translate or explain *shelter, crouch* and *hold on tight.*
- Ask students to compare their answers in groups.

3 AFTER READING

- Students turn to page 121 to find out their scores.

Your response

Ask students which of the situations they would enjoy and which they would be frightened in.

4 LISTENING

- Play the recording for students to listen to and write down Simon's answers to the questionnaire.
- Check that students have correctly calculated his score.

3.18 Recording

JULIE *Simon, would you like to answer this questionnaire?*
SIMON *What kind of questionnaire is it?*
JULIE *It's a survival questionnaire – about what you'd do to survive in difficult situations.*
SIMON *OK, let's have a look.*
JULIE *Question 1: What would you do in the desert if you didn't have enough water?*
SIMON *I dunno, I think I'd eat a lot because there's water in food. So that's A.*
JULIE *Right. Here's question 2: what if you were in an area where there were lots of snakes?*
SIMON *Um, I think I'll go for A. I'd walk as quietly as possible.*
JULIE *Next question: What if you were outside in a thunderstorm and lightning was near?*
SIMON *You know I hate thunderstorms. Erm, I think I'd take off all metal objects and crouch on the ground.*
JULIE *So you're going for C.*
SIMON *Yes.*
JULIE *I see. And this is question 4: If you were lost in a forest without a phone, how would you let your friends know where you were?*
SIMON *Mm. That's an interesting one. I'm not much good at shouting or screaming so I'd probably whistle loudly.*
JULIE *That's C. All right – now question 5. What would you do if you were out walking and met a bear?*
SIMON *I haven't a clue! I think I'd climb up the nearest tree. That's C again.*
JULIE *Question 6: If you had to cross a fast river with waist-high water, which way would you face?*
SIMON *I think I know this one. I'd face upstream because that's where the water is coming from. Answer: A.*

JULIE	*And now question 7: What would you do if you were in a forest fire?*
SIMON	*Oh, that's a tricky one. Er, I think I'd work out which way the wind was blowing, and run in the same direction.*
JULIE	*Um, so your answer is B.*
SIMON	*That's right.*
JULIE	*Here's question 8: If you were on a steep hill covered in large slippery rocks, what would be the safest way to climb it?*
SIMON	*Um, that's hard. I think I'm going to go for B: I'd keep my socks and boots on.*
JULIE	*And here's question 9: If you were lost in a forest and very hungry, how would you decide which plants were safe to eat?*
SIMON	*Um, I don't know a lot about plants and I don't like the idea of putting something which could be poisonous in my mouth so I think I would choose B – I'd look and see what the birds were eating and do the same.*
JULIE	*And now for the last question: What would you do if you were in a boat on the edge of a waterfall?*
SIMON	*And you know I'm afraid of heights! Well, I wouldn't jump, I'd stay in the boat and hold on tight.*
JULIE	*You've chosen C again. OK – now let's find out your score!*

Answers

1 A 2 A 3 C 4 C 5 C 6 A 7 B 8 B 9 B 10 C

Simon's score: 1 point

LANGUAGE WORKOUT OPTION

If you want to pre-teach the language students will be using in the following activities, you may like to go to the Language Workout box now.

5 SPEAKING

- In pairs, students ask and answer questions about the imaginary situations 1–6, using the second conditional.
- Ask one or two pairs to ask and answer about one of the situations in front of the class. Other students can say if they had different or similar answers.

Extension Students add three more imaginary situations to the list. They then work in pairs and ask their partner what they would do/say/feel in each case.

6 LISTENING

- Ask the students to read problems 1–6 and predict which phrases from the box will be used. Check that students understand *cough* and *hiccoughs* by asking for a demonstration. Drill *hiccoughs* /ˈhɪkʌps/ and *cough* /kɒf/.
- Play the recording for students to check their predictions, matching advice with problems 1–6.

3.19 Recording

1 I've got hiccoughs.
If I were you, I'd take a deep breath, and count to 100. Or I'd drink a glass of water.
2 I've got toothache.
If I were you, I'd take an aspirin and see a dentist.
3 I think I'm getting a cold.
If I were you, I'd eat lots of oranges.
4 I can't get to sleep at night.
If I were you, I'd take more exercise and go to bed later. You could read a boring book in bed. And you could try counting sheep!
5 I've got a headache.
If I were you, I'd take an aspirin and lie down.
6 I've got a cough and a sore throat.
If I were you, I'd drink hot lemon and honey. And I'd stop talking!

Answers

1 take a deep breath and count to 100, drink a glass of water
2 take an aspirin, see a dentist
3 eat lots of oranges
4 take more exercise, go to bed later, read a boring book, count sheep
5 take an aspirin, lie down
6 drink hot lemon and honey, stop talking

Extension In pairs, students give their own advice to problems 1–6, using *If I were you, I'd/I wouldn't ...* Ask the students to tell the rest of the class if they had any better ideas.

7 PRONUNCIATION

- Ask students to look at the words in the box and, in pairs, decide which words contain the sound /f/.
- Play the recording. Pause after each word for students to repeat and check their answers.

3.20 Recording

cough enough ghost hiccough high laugh lightning night thought through tight weight

Answers

/f/ *cough, enough and laugh*

Optional activity

Students group together words from the box which have the same pronunciation of *gh*, e.g. *high, tight*.

8 SPEAKING

- Ask students to imagine they were going backpacking with another student and had to choose ten items from the box which they would include in their pack.
- Check first that students understand and can pronounce all the items, by asking questions, e.g. *Which do you need for sewing? Which makes something look bigger?* Drill any problem words.
- In pairs, students discuss what to choose. Remind students to give reasons why items would(n't) be useful,

using the second conditional, like the examples.

- Set a time limit for students to reach joint decisions.
- Students work with a different partner to compare what they have decided they would take and why.
- Students report back to the whole class using the example sentences as a model.

Optional activity

In small groups, students make second conditional sentences about the objects, without saying the name, e.g. *If you had this thing, you wouldn't get sunburnt.* Other students guess/remember the name of the object.

9 WRITING

- The aim is for students to write some useful advice, using the expression *If I were you …* and the second conditional where appropriate. Ask students to give reasons for their advice.
- Set the context by asking a confident student to read the instruction out loud. Remind students to look back at the vocabulary in exercise 8 for ideas and help.
- Ask students to show their paragraphs to their partner to see who wrote the best advice.

LANGUAGE WORKOUT

- Ask students to complete the Language box. Confident students can complete first and then check, while others can look back at exercises 2 and 3 and then complete.
- Students turn to page 120 of the Language File to check their answers.

Answers

would stand *were; wouldn't jump*
would you do; didn't have *if; were*

- Highlight that:
  - the second conditional is formed with *If* + past simple, *would(n't)* + infinitive.
  - *If I/he/she/it was* is often used instead of *were* in spoken English.
  - The condition and result clauses can be reversed.
  - We use the second conditional to talk about imaginary present or unlikely future situations. Its choice in preference to the first conditional suggests the speaker considers the situation hypothetical/less possible.
- Drill the examples in chorus for pronunciation and stress. Encourage students to use the *'d* contraction and to pronounce *would you* with natural linking and the weak form of *you* /'wʊdʒʊː/.

Optional activity

Read out one half of some of the conditional sentences, either the condition or the result clause, from the questionnaire. Students must shout out a possible second half of the sentence, e.g. *I'd run uphill as fast as I could …* (Student: if I were in a forest fire).

PRACTICE

- Students do exercise 26 in the Language File on page 120.

Answers

1 How would you survive if you got lost in the mountains?
2 If my mobile worked, I'd dial the emergency number.
3 What would you do if the battery was/were flat?
4 If I had a mirror, I'd try to send signals.
5 Would you feel scared if you were alone?
6 I'd sing rap songs if I felt scared.
7 What if you had to spend the night in the mountains?
8 If I was cold, I'd make a fire.

Follow-up activities

- ♦ Pairs of students make up a *What would you do if …?* question, e.g. *What would you do if you won the lottery/were President of this country/had only one day to live?* Students ask their question to as many different students as possible, noting down the answers of each student. They then display their answers on posters, with illustrations/photos and the question as the title.
- ♦ **Game** *Guess the question* Before the class, prepare a couple of *What would you do if …* questions and three possible answers to each. Read out only the answers to the students, e.g. *I'd be frightened, I'd dial 999, I'd run out of the house.* Students work in pairs to guess what the question was and write it down, e.g. *What would you do if there was a fire in your house?* Ask pairs of students to do the same.

HOMEWORK

Students interview someone outside school asking them five *What would you do if …?* questions. They can use the survival questions, those from exercise 6 or their own. They can do the interview in their own language, but then write it up in English.

WEBLINK

Students can find more advice and trivia on survival in a variety of situations by visiting www.wildsurvival.com

Revision and Extension p109

Language File p120

Workbook Unit 8 Lesson 2 pp88–89

Photocopiable worksheet p184, notes p160

8.3 NATURAL WORLD

You'd like to stay there, wouldn't you?

Communicative Aims	Language	Pronunciation	Vocabulary	Optional Aids
Asking for agreement and checking information	Question tags	Intonation in question tags	Buildings	Follow-up activity: question tags on sticky notes

WARMER 1

Game *Password* Play Password using vocabulary from the previous lesson, such as *survival kit words, illnesses and geographical features*. For instructions, see Unit 2, lesson1, p43.

WARMER 2

On the board, put anagrams of words for living spaces, e.g. *sohue* (house), *aflt* (flat), *vcae* (cave). Tell students they are all places where you can live and ask them to work in pairs to solve the anagrams as quickly as possible.

1 OPENER

- The aim is to set the context and pre-teach vocabulary for the reading in exercise 2.
- Ask the students to look at the photos and match each one with a word from the box.
- Check the answers together, drilling in chorus where necessary to practise pronunciation.

Answers

A skyscraper B igloo C exhibition pavilion D hotel E museum

2 LISTENING

- Students listen to the conversation between Sophie and Zak. Ask them to listen out for the order in which the five places from exercise 1 are mentioned.

3.21 Recording

ZAK *Hey, what's all this, Sophie?*

SOPHIE *It's a website about unusual buildings around the world. You can see that, can't you?*

ZAK *Sure, but why have they chosen these particular buildings? What's unusual about them?*

SOPHIE *This one's the world's biggest igloo. It's 40 metres round, 12 metres across and five metres high. It can hold 500 people! It's in a place called Puvirnituq in northern Canada.*

ZAK *I get it – they're all special in some way. Oh, and I know what that one is – it's the tallest skyscraper in the world. It's in Dubai and it's 828 metres high. And it's got 160 floors. You didn't expect me to know that, did you?*

SOPHIE *No, I didn't! And look! That building has been in the news recently, hasn't it?*

ZAK *Yes, it was an exhibition pavilion in the Shanghai World Expo 2010. It was made out of recycled CD cases and it changed colour when people moved around inside it! But the most amazing thing is that after the Expo was over they recycled the whole building!*

SOPHIE *Hey, look at this! It's a modern art museum in Vienna in Austria and it's got an upside down house on the roof.*

ZAK *That's cool. It says it's called 'House Attack'! But why's that huge hotel room on the website?*

SOPHIE *Let's see. Oh yes. It's in Athens in Greece and it's one of the world's most expensive hotel suites. It's called the Governor Villa and costs £4,500 a night! It even includes a gym and a swimming pool! You'd like to stay there, wouldn't you!*

ZAK *You must be joking – they wouldn't let someone like me in, would they?*

Answers

B, A, C, E and D

3

- Students listen to five extracts from the recording 3.22 and choose the best answer in each case.
- Ask students to compare their answers in pairs. Check the answers as a class.

Answers

1 Vienna 2 Dubai; 828 metres 3 colour 4 Greece; £4,500 5 40; northern

Your response

Ask students to work individually and think about their answers to the question. Have them compare their answers in pairs and then share their ideas with the whole class.

LANGUAGE WORKOUT OPTION

If you want to pre-teach the language students will be using in the following activities, you may like to go to the Language Workout box now.

4 PRONUNCIATION

- Students complete the sentences using the question tags in the box and compare answers in pairs.
- Play the recording for students to check their answers. Point out the two intonation patterns and play the

recording again for students to identify rising or falling intonation. Pause after each question for students to identify and practise the intonation pattern.

3.23 Recording and answers

1 *The hotel room is in Athens, isn't it? [rising]*
2 *You don't know what that is, do you? [falling]*
3 *The photos were of special places, weren't they? [rising]*
4 *Zak asked Sophie about the photos, didn't he? [falling]*
5 *Sophie didn't expect Zak to know about the tallest skyscraper, did she? [falling]*
6 *Zak wouldn't like to stay in the Governor Villa, would he? [falling]*
7 *Zak likes the modern art museum, doesn't he? [falling]*
8 *The igloo can't hold 500 people, can it? [rising]*

Optional activity

If students are having difficulty identifying intonation, model some example words, which, when said with a rising intonation, become a question, e.g. *Finished? Alright? Tired? Coffee?* Ask students to identify when you are saying them as questions and when not.

5 SPEAKING

- Ask students to look at the photographs and see if they can remember what any of them show.
- In pairs, students do the quiz. Remind students that they are not allowed to look back in the book yet. Highlight the A/B example at the end of the quiz and encourage students to use question tags in the same way, where appropriate. Set a time limit and do this as a competition to see which pair has the best memory.
- Check the answers as a class.

Answers

1 Tunnels Beach 2 59 3 Ron Hornbaker
4 Mercury 5 9 billion 6 Manderley
7 Ewan McGregor and Charlie Boorman 8 Three
9 The car, flying machine, parachute, robot and scuba diving
10 About 100 11 Ray Tomlinson 12 Electric wind

Extension Ask students to look back through the book and write five more questions. Students then work in pairs and see if their partner can remember the answers without looking in their book.

6 WRITING

- Ask students to write two paragraphs describing other people or places from earlier in the book. Do the example with the whole class, asking the students *Who/What is it?* (Machu Picchu). Remind students not to include the name, but encourage them to give as much descriptive detail as possible.
- In small groups, students exchange their writing and try to guess the subject of each paragraph. Encourage them to ask for confirmation with tag questions, e.g. *It's Machu Picchu, isn't it?*

LANGUAGE WORKOUT

- Ask students to complete the Language box.
- Students turn to page 120 of the Language File to check their answers.

Answers

can't you? wouldn't you? hasn't it? did you?

- Highlight that:
  - if the main clause is positive, the question tag is negative and vice versa.
  - question tags are formed with the appropriate auxiliary or modal verb according to the verb and tense in the main clause: *can→can, would→would, be→be*, present perfect→*has/have*, past simple→*did*, present simple→*do/does*. The subject pronoun is then repeated.
- Drill the examples in chorus for pronunciation and stress.

PRACTICE

- Ask students to do exercise 27 in the Language File on page 120. They complete the sentences using question tags.

Answers

1 wasn't it 2 did you 3 can he 4 don't you
5 doesn't she 6 hasn't she 7 are we 8 wouldn't they

Follow-up activity

Game *Run and grab* Write about 18 typical tag questions, e.g. *isn't it? doesn't he? wouldn't you? didn't she?* Stick these to the board and divide the students into three teams. A student from each team stands at equal distance away from the board. Read out a statement, e.g. *She won the medal …* The three students run to the board and grab the appropriate question tag.

HOMEWORK

Ask the students to imagine how their life would be different if they lived in one of the living spaces from exercise 1. They should write at least one sentence for each place, e.g. *If I lived in the igloo, I'd have very cold feet.*

WEBLINK

Students may like to visit www.nordicexperience.co.uk/icehotel-experience, the website of an ice hotel.

Revision and Extension p109

Language File p120

Workbook Unit 8 Lesson 3 pp90–91

Photocopiable worksheet p185, notes p160

Integrated Skills Describing a country

Skills

Reading Topics: Australia website description
Listening Specific information: description of Canada
Speaking Exchanging information
Writing Describing a country

Learner Independence

English resources outside school
Word creation: adjective suffix *-al*

Vocabulary

Geographical features
Animals
Climate
Useful expressions

Optional Aids

Warmer 1: 10 pictures of places from different countries
Exercise 6 Optional activity: paper/card, photos, coloured pens
Follow-up activity 1: maps of Canada and Australia

WARMER 1

Stick pictures of places from different countries on the classroom wall, e.g. *Ayers Rock, the Grand Canyon*, labelling pictures 1–10. Students walk around the room in pairs, looking at pictures and guessing which country each is from, keeping a list 1–10. Check the students' ideas as a class, before telling them the correct answers and eliciting anything they know about these places

WARMER 2

Game *Guess who?* Tell students you are thinking of a famous person, and they must ask you *yes/no* questions to try to guess who it is, e.g. *Is it an actor?* Continue until they have guessed correctly. Choose a famous person from Australia or Canada, e.g. *Kylie Minogue, Nicole Kidman, Celine Dion, Avril Lavigne*. Then ask students if they know any other famous people from these countries.

Useful information

Geographical terms:
Prairie – a treeless, but grass-covered plain, typical of central North America.
Tundra – an arctic plain with frozen sub-soil.
Outback – remote and sparsely populated areas of the interior of Australia.
Grassland – areas permanently covered in grass.
Monsoon – caused by the seasonal winds of the Indian Ocean, this is a period of heavy rain. The term is also used for similar weather outside India.
Coral reef – formed from the dead skeletons of invertebrate sea creatures. It builds up into multi-coloured banks at the bottom of the sea.

1 OPENER

- The aim is to set the context and pre-teach vocabulary for the reading in exercise 2.
- Ask students to work in pairs to look at the words in the box and decide which they associate with Australia, which with Canada and which refer to weather.
- Check their ideas as a whole class. Check that they understand the vocabulary by asking questions, e.g. *What's the weather like if there's a drought? And a monsoon?* Drill the words in chorus. Highlight that *drought* rhymes with *out*.

Answers

Australia: coral reef, desert, outback, rainforest, drought, cyclone, monsoon
Canada: forest, grasslands, prairie, tundra, ice
Weather: cyclone, drought, ice, monsoon

Optional activity

Ask students if they associate any of the words with their own country and to provide others.

2 READING

- Encourage students to share any knowledge they may have of Australia, asking them if they know the names of the capital, famous animals, famous people etc.
- Ask students to read the text and match the headings to paragraphs 1–5. Point out that there are six headings but only five paragraphs so one heading isn't used. Encourage them to read for gist by setting a time limit of no more than five minutes. Remind students it is not necessary to understand every word, and encourage them to deduce the meaning of unknown words from context.
- Play the recording for students to check their answers.
- Ask students which of the words from exercise 1 they noticed in the text.

3.24 **Recording**
See text on page 106 of the Student's Book.

Answers

1 Key facts 2 The people 3 Geography 4 Wildlife 5 Weather

3

- Ask the students to work in pairs to ask each other questions about the text. Student A starts by asking questions 1–7 and B continues with 8–14. Encourage students to scan the text to try to find the answers as quickly as possible. Ask pairs of students to read out a question and the answer. Encourage them to identify in which paragraph they found the answer.

Answers

1 7,686,900 square km 2 Canberra 3 250,000
4 4.5 million 5 Mount Kosciuszko, 2,228m
6 It's the largest living structure in the world.
7 Warm with lots of sunshine and little rain
8 22 million 9 50,000 years 10 Over 70%
11 The Murray-Darling
12 Off the south-east coast of Australia
13 Animals: kangaroo, koala and platypus; Birds: emu and kookaburra
14 In the tropical north

Optional activity

Students make vocabulary lists under the five paragraph headings, finding useful words from the text and adding their own ideas, e.g. *geography – interior, desert, plain, grassland, mountain range.*

4 LISTENING

- Encourage students to share any knowledge they may have of Canada, e.g. the currency, the capital, major cities.
- Ask students to look at the factfile in pairs and tell each other if they can guess any of the missing words.
- In each pair, one student is A and the other is B. Play the recording and ask As to complete the notes in the yellow sections and Bs those in blue.

3.25 Recording and answers

CANADA
Key Facts
Canada is the second largest country in the world, smaller only than Russia and its area is nearly ***10*** *million square kilometres. Canada occupies 41% of North America, with the USA to the south. The population of Canada is* ***34 million*** *and the capital city is Ottawa. The official languages are English and* ***French****, and the currency is the Canadian dollar.*
The people
Native Canadians have lived in Canada for at least 10,000 years. There are now only about ***800,000*** *Native Canadians, approximately 2.5% of the total population. About* ***75%*** *of Canadians live in cities or towns, and about* ***80%*** *live within 200 kilometres of the US border. The largest city is Toronto, with a population of* ***5.5*** *million.*
Geography
The ***north*** *of Canada is mainly forest, tundra, ice and snow. The Rocky Mountains cover a large part of* ***western*** *Canada and the highest mountain is Mount Logan (****5,951 metres****). West-central Canada is mostly prairie grassland – the main farming area. On the plains of the* ***east-*** *central part of Canada are the major industrial areas. The St Lawrence is Canada's most* ***important*** *river, but its* ***longest*** *river is the Mackenzie (4,241 kilometres), in the north-west.*
Niagara Falls, near the US border, are the ***largest*** *falls in the world. Canada also has around* ***two million*** *lakes, over 60% of all the lakes in the world, and shares four of the five Great Lakes with the USA.*
Wildlife
Well-known Canadian animals include the polar ***bear****, moose and caribou. The Rocky Mountains are home to a huge variety of wildlife, including the elk, brown bear, grizzly bear, and wild cats.* ***Whales*** *can be seen off the east and west coasts. Canada also has over* ***500*** *different kinds of birds.*
Weather
The typical climate of ***central*** *Canada is short hot summers and long cold winters. On the east and* ***west*** *coasts the winters are warmer, but the summers are cooler. Average temperatures in Ottawa are minus 6 to minus 15 degrees Celsius in January and 15 to* ***26*** *degrees Celsius in July. The* ***north*** *of Canada is extremely cold all year. Western and south-eastern Canada get a lot of* ***rain****, but other areas are much drier.*

Optional activity

Students use the factfile information as a basis for either a presentation or for writing a paragraph on Canada. Encourage students to work in pairs to transform the notes into full sentences.

5 SPEAKING

- In A/B pairs, students use their notes to tell each other what they learnt about Canada.
- In pairs, students discuss whether they would visit Australia or Canada, if they had the chance. Remind them to use a second conditional form in their answer and to give reasons for their choice.

Optional activities

- Students write three sentences comparing Canada and Australia. Two should be true and one false. They read the sentences to their partner, who identifies if they are true or false.
- Read out ten pieces of information from the Australia text or Canada recording, without saying which it comes from, e.g. *The capital is Canberra.* In pairs, students decide which country it is about and write down their answers, before checking them as a class to find the winning pair.

6 GUIDED WRITING

- Ask students to write a description of their country or another country, based on the Australia text model.
- Put the headings from the Australia text on the board and brainstorm possible information/vocabulary to include in each section. If your students have access to the Internet, encourage them to do some research on the country before they start writing.
- Students exchange writing with a partner to read and check each other's work. If they have written about different countries, encourage students to discuss which of the countries they would prefer to visit or live in.

Optional activity

Students make their paragraph into a guidebook entry by adding titles, illustrations, photos, facts and quotations from visitors/residents. Display these on the classroom wall if possible.

7 LEARNER INDEPENDENCE

- Before students look at the table, ask them if they can think of anywhere they can read or hear English outside school. They then look at the chart and compare it with their ideas.
- Ask students to tick the read/listen columns as appropriate and to add other headings if they had other ideas.
- Students compare their charts in pairs. Encourage them to give examples of the things they can see and hear in English.
- Ask those students who had ideas for other headings to report back on their ideas to the rest of the class.

8 WORD CREATION

- Write *music* on the board and ask *What's the adjective made from it?* (musical). Highlight the *-al* suffix and ask if students know any other adjectives with the same suffix.
- Ask students to complete the chart with the adjectives ending *-al*. Remind students that there may be spelling changes.
- Check the answers as a class, drilling the adjectives and highlighting the stressed syllables, especially if the adjective is stressed differently to the noun.

Answers

central coastal continental electrical environmental global musical natural official tropical

9 PHRASEBOOK

- Play the recording for the students to listen and repeat the expressions.
- Students look through Unit 8 to find the expressions, noting how they are used.
- Ask students to think of three ways to complete each of the incomplete expressions.

3.26 Recording and answers

What would you do? (Julie L2, Ex 4)
What if ...? (Julie L2, Ex 4)
If I were you, I'd ... (V2/4/6/8 L2, Ex6)
I've got hiccoughs. (V1 L2, Ex 6)
I've got toothache. (V3 L2, Ex 6)
I've got a headache. (V11 L2, Ex 6)
I get it. (Zak L3, Ex 2)
You must be joking. (Zak L3, Ex 2)

Optional activity

Students can add expressions which they like to their Personal Phrasebook.

Follow-up activities

♦ Divide students into two groups, one to be visitors to the country (your own country or Canada or Australia) and the others to be tourist officers. The visitors should imagine they have just arrived in the country and prepare five questions they want to ask, e.g. *Where should I visit?* Tourist officers should draw a map of the country, marking key features and think of any important facts which they may want to tell tourists. Provide students with maps they can use as a model. After preparation time, students work in tourist/tourist officer pairs to roleplay a dialogue at the tourist office.

♦ **Game** *Outburst* Play the game with categories from this lesson, e.g. *weather, animals*. See Review 5–6, p122 for instructions.

HOMEWORK

Ask students to research another country and write a factfile similar to the Canada factfile. Encourage students to follow the same topics/headings and remind students to write in their own words rather than copying long sections from web pages.

WEBLINK

Students may like to visit www.earthfromtheair.com to view aerial pictures of places all over the world.

Revision and Extension p109

Workbook Unit 4 Lesson 4 pp92–93

Inspiration EXTRA!

Optional Aids

Project: paper/card, pictures/photos and scissors

PROJECT EXTREME PLACES

1
- Explain to students that the aim of the project is to write about an extreme place – a place where it is very difficult to live because of geographical or climatic conditions.
- Ask students to look at the pictures of examples of extreme places and elicit why they are extreme. (Picture 1 – Bakers Lake, Canada, extremely cold, Picture 2 – Lake Titicaca, Peru, a very high altitude, Picture 3 – a desert, very dry, Picture 4 – a remote island). Ask students to read the short text about Tristan da Cunha and encourage them to write their report in a similar format.
- Divide the students into groups of four and appoint an 'editor' for each group. Ask them to make a list of extreme places, using the examples in the pictures to help them.
- Each group then chooses two of the places on their list to write about in their report.

2
- Students read the questions in the box and make notes to answer them. Encourage them to use the Internet or the school library to check facts.

3
- Students work together in their groups to share their notes from the questions in exercise 2 and write their report. Different students or pairs of students in the group can take responsibility for different sections, e.g. languages, geography. They should decide how to order and present their information and how to illustrate it with pictures or photos they can find online or in magazines.
- Students can show their report to other groups. Display the reports in the classroom if possible.

Optional activity

In pairs, one student is a city-dweller, while the other lives in the Australian outback. They imagine they are going to swap lives for one month and must give advice to each other about how to cope. Confident students could perform their dialogue for the rest of the class.

GAME WORD RACE

- In small groups, students choose a topic from the list and write as many words as possible about that topic in one minute. Encourage them to work as quickly as possible, but remind them to be careful with spelling. Groups exchange lists after one minute and check that all the words in the list are correct for the topic. Any words they are unsure about should be checked in their dictionaries. Students then count how many correct words were included in the list they marked and report back to the rest of the class, mentioning any new or interesting words that were included. The team with the longest list is the winner. Repeat for the other topics.

Optional activities

- ♦ Students suggest further topics to use in the same game.
- ♦ Instead of showing their lists to other groups, each group has two minutes to give definitions/explanations of words on their list to see how many can be guessed by the rest of the class.

LIMERICK

- Play the recording and ask students to read and listen to the limerick.
- Drill the limerick line by line in chorus, paying attention to stress and rhythm.
- Students practise saying the limerick to their partner, either reading the whole verse each or alternating lines.

3.27 Recording

See the text on p108 of the Student's book.

Optional activities

- ♦ Ask students to find rhyming groups from the limerick and add another rhyming word to each group, e.g. *should, would, could, good.*
- ♦ Before students read and listen to the limerick, write only the final word(s) of each line on the board and ask students to sort them into rhyming groups. Students then listen to the limerick and order the words according to when they appear, writing 1 next to the first and 5 next to the last.

REVISION

Lesson 1

Suggested answers

1 You shouldn't have missed the bus.
2 You should have got up earlier.
3 You should have woken up on time.
4 You shouldn't have forgotten to set your alarm clock.
5 You shouldn't have gone to bed late.

Lesson 2
- Remind students to use the second conditional.

Students' own answers

Lesson 3
Students' own answers

EXTENSION

Lesson 1
Students' own answers

Lesson 2
Students' own answers

Lesson 3
- Ask students to make two lists: one of the lessons they enjoyed most and the other of the lessons they found difficult. They should then do the same to guess their partner's preferences, before checking with their partner. Highlight the example and remind students to use questions tags.

Students' own answers

YOUR CHOICE!

- Divide the class into groups according to their learning style to do the relevant activity.
- Monitor and help groups. Check answers if necessary, or provide written answers for groups to check their own work against.
- Encourage students to experiment with other learning styles and try one of the other activities of their choice.

CONSTRUCTION

- Students complete the gaps with the correct question tag.

Answers
1 weren't they 2 hadn't she 3 wouldn't you 4 hasn't he 5 isn't it 6 doesn't she 7 didn't she 8 wouldn't he

REFLECTION

- Students match the beginnings of the rules 1–4 with the endings a–d.

Answers
1 b 2 d 3 a 4 c

ACTION

- Students work in small groups.
- Ask students to look back through the unit for vocabulary items to use in the game.
- Students then follow the instructions in the box to play the guessing game.
- Students change roles and repeat with other words.

INTERACTION

- In pairs or small groups, students ask each other *If you were a …, what … would you be?* questions using the words in the box. Encourage students to give reasons for their choices and discuss if they agree with each other's choices.

You may now like students to do the song *I Will Survive*. See p161 for the notes and p189 for the worksheet.

Language File p120

Workbook Unit 8 Inspiration EXTRA! pp94–95

Song – photocopiable worksheet p189, notes p161

UNITS 7–8

1 Check general comprehension: Ask students to look at the picture and the headline and guess how the teenager saved the tourist. Give students one minute to read the story and check their predictions. Students read the story again and choose the appropriate word for each space. Do the first one together as an example. This can be done in pairs or individually as a short test.

Answers

1B 2C 3A 4B 5A 6C 7B 8A 9C 10A 11B 12C

2 Students write sentences reporting the requests with *asked* and the commands with *told*. Remind students to use *ask/tell* + someone + infinitive, and that they may need to change parts of the sentences, e.g. possessive adjectives. Do the first one together as an example.

Answers

1 *Mrs Flynn asked Rob to tidy his room.*
2 *The teacher told the students not to make so much noise.*
3 *Julie told Simon that he had to take it easy.*
4 *The researcher asked Kanzi if he would get her keys back.*
5 *Bethany's father told her to try it one more time.*
6 *Peter told Natasha not to be late.*
7 *The police officer told the thief to stop.*
8 *Adam told the contestants to try out new dance routines.*

Optional activity

Fast finishers can write a similar sentence with direct speech and give it to another student or read it to the class to be transformed in the same way with *ask/tell*.

3 Students transform the direct speech into reported speech. Remind students they may have to change parts of the sentence, e.g. pronouns and time expressions.

Answers

1 *Rob said he wasn't looking for a girlfriend.*
2 *Sophie said she wanted to be a doctor.*
3 *Joni said she had danced for five hours.*
4 *Lara said she couldn't concentrate for long.*
5 *Sherlock Holmes said they'd try to solve the mystery.*
6 *Steve said he'd never ridden a horse.*
7 *Ray said they had to find a way to stop spam.*
8 *Bill Hobbs said he wouldn't go back.*

4 Students write sentences reporting Sophie's questions using *asked*.

Answers

1 *She asked him what the matter was.*
2 *She asked him where he had lost it.*
3 *She asked how much money was in it.*
4 *She asked if he knew the number of the bus.*
5 *She asked if he had told the police.*
6 *She asked if he was going to phone them.*
7 *She asked why he wasn't more careful.*

5 Students re-write the sentences using *should/shouldn't have*.

Answers

1 *You should have asked me to help you.*
2 *I shouldn't have stayed out so late last night.*
3 *The students should have worked harder.*
4 *We shouldn't have sailed the dinghy in the storm.*
5 *You shouldn't have read my diary.*
6 *You should have phoned the police.*
7 *The team should have won the match.*
8 *I shouldn't have listened to you.*

Optional activity

In pairs, ask students to imagine situations in which sentences 1–8 might have been said, e.g. 1 *a mother speaking to her teenage daughter after discovering she was being bullied at school.*

6 Students write sentences using the correct form of the verbs: past simple or *would*.

Answers

1 *If I had toothache, I'd go to the dentist.*
2 *You wouldn't get hiccoughs if you didn't eat so quickly.*
3 *Where would you live if you could live anywhere?*
4 *If you were on a roller coaster, how would you feel?*
5 *If I knew the answer, I'd tell you.*
6 *The singer wouldn't perform well if she had a sore throat.*
7 *If we didn't have water, we'd die.*
8 *What would you say if your country won the World Cup?*

Optional activity

Fast finishers write answers to the questions in 3, 4 and 8.

7 Before students look at the sentences, ask them if they can think of any advice for someone who can't sleep at night. Students then give advice using *If I were you, I'd/I wouldn't* … and the phrases.

Answers

1 If I were you, I wouldn't drink coffee in the evening.
2 If I were you, I'd buy a new bed.
3 If I were you, I'd try to relax.
4 If I were you, I wouldn't eat cheese for dinner.
5 If I were you, I wouldn't read ghost stories in bed.
6 If I were you, I'd stop worrying about it.

8 Students complete the questions with the appropriate question tags.

Answers

1 didn't he 2 did it 3 wouldn't you 4 do you 5 has it 6 don't we 7 can they 8 haven't they

Optional activity

Fast finishers can write alternative question stems for the same question tags.

VOCABULARY

9 Students complete the sentences with the words in the box. Point out that there are twelve gaps but sixteen words in the box, so four are not used. Confident students can cover the words in the box and guess which words are missing before checking against the list.

Answers

1 guilty 2 shortage 3 annoyed 4 solution 5 attachment 6 snail 7 honey 8 electricity 9 shelter 10 currency 11 emergency 12 beef

Optional activity

Fast finishers choose three of the words and write another example sentence for each.

10 Students match the words with their definitions. Confident students can attempt the task without looking at the words in the box and then look to check.

Answers

1 safety 2 plain 3 igloo 4 bracelet 5 peak 6 trunk 7 cool 8 firm 9 a dozen 10 consequence

Optional activity

In pairs, students try to remember where in the unit they met these vocabulary items.

11 Remind students that it is often more useful to learn words that go together like this than single words. Note that *change your shoes* is also possible.

Answers

1 attract attention 2 take off your shoes 3 hold on tight 4 keep calm 5 solve a problem 6 take a deep breath 7 change your mind 8 turn off the tap

LEARNER INDEPENDENCE SELF ASSESSMENT

- Explain to students that the aim of the self assessment is to help them check their own progress and take any action necessary to improve. Point out that the list 1–7 covers language from Units 7 and 8.
- Have students look at the table and tick the Fine box for language they feel confident using or put a question mark in the Not sure box if they feel they still have some difficulties.
- Encourage students to look at the Language File and re-do exercises from the lessons, the Revision and Extension section and the Workbook in areas where they have problems.
- Students write an example sentence for each language area in the list. You may like to elicit the language students need for each example before students write sentences, e.g. *Criticising past actions: should/shouldn't have*. Students can refer back to the lessons and the Language Workout box and Language File.

Follow-up activity

Game *Categories* Students work in small groups of three. On the board, write some vocabulary categories, e.g. *animals, materials, geographical features*. Ask students to think of one item in each category beginning with a letter of your choice. The first team to find one for each shouts *Stop!* and wins 10 bonus points (but loses 10 points if any of their words are wrong). Teams then read out the word they had in each category. They score 10 points if they had a unique suggestion, 5 if another team has the same word. Check how many points each team has before moving on to a new letter.

HOMEWORK

Ask students to write a paragraph about the things they enjoyed most or remember most in the book. They should mention the stories that interested them and the characters/ people they remember and give reasons for their preferences.

WEBLINK

If students enjoyed listening to the songs throughout the book, they may like to visit www.elyrics.net for more song lyrics or www.songfacts.com for facts and trivia about many well-known songs.

Language File pp119–120

Workbook Review Units 7–8 pp96–97

1.1 What are we like?

Activity Survey

Language focus Present tenses review; adverbs of frequency

Preparation Photocopy the worksheet for every 12 students and cut it up into strips. Photocopy the blank question and answers sheet for each student.

Procedure

1. Give each student in a group of 12 a sentence card and a question and answers sheet. Tell them to make a question from the statement on the card and write it on the top of the question and answer sheet.
2. The students should walk about the classroom and ask at least 12 people their question. They should write down the person's name and make notes under the name, e.g. *Carla: (is worried about) her exams.*
3. When time is up, the students can give feedback in open class, or in groups. The students should make general comments about their findings rather than going through details about every person. Revise language such as *a lot of people, not many people, a few people, nobody.*
4. Based on the information they have found, the students write a profile of their class and put the sheets on the walls for everyone to read.

1.2 Story secrets

Activity Story completion

Language focus Past simple (regular and irregular)

Preparation Photocopy a worksheet for each group of three and cut the first part into three. Give one copy of the key (Your secrets revealed!) to each group.

Procedure

1. Divide the class into three groups and give each group either part A, B or C of the story.
2. The students in each group work together to complete the verbs in the past tense, tell them they can refer to the irregular verb list on p127 of the Student's Book if necessary. Tell them to ignore the words in italic for now.
3. Each student then circles the words in italic that they prefer.
4. Re-order the groups, so that there is a student with an A, B and C part of the story in each group.
5. Each person reads out their part of the story.
6. Then have students look at the key 'Your secrets revealed!' to see what it says about them.

1.3 What were you doing?

Activity Pelmanism

Language focus Past simple and past continuous (with *when/while*)

Preparation Photocopy the worksheet for each pair of students and cut them up into cards (10 of each type).

Procedure

1. Divide the students into pairs and give each pair a set of 10 picture cards and 10 sentence cards. Tell each pair to mix them up well and spread the cards out in front of them face down.
2. Explain or demonstrate the activity. Each student should pick up two cards – one sentence card and one picture card – and try to make a full sentence with them, e.g. *I was having a shower when the phone rang./While I was having a shower, the phone rang.* If the sentence is correct, the student keeps the two cards. He/she could also try to say what happened next. The next student then has a turn. If they cannot make a sentence with the cards, they turn the cards over again, and miss a turn.
3. When all the cards are finished, or neither student can make another sentence, the game is over. The winner is the person with the most cards.

2.1 Gwyneth Paltrow

Activity Jigsaw reading

Language focus Verb + gerund; opinion adjectives

Preparation Photocopy one worksheet for each pair and cut out the two cards along the dotted lines.

Procedure

1. Show the students the activity and explain that they will be working in pairs to discover missing information from a text. They will all get the same text, but Student A has the information Student B is missing and vice versa.
2. Divide the students into two groups, A and B. Give Students A, Card A and Students B, Card B.
3. Tell the students to work together with a person from the same group to write all eight of their questions. There are cues in brackets to help them. Monitor to offer help and to check the correct formation of questions.
4. Tell the students they should now divide up so that a student from group A works with a student from group B. They can now begin asking their questions. They write the answers on their cards. Monitor to correct any mistakes.
5. When the students have finished asking and answering questions, ask them to compare their pieces of writing to make sure they are the same.

2.2 How well do you know your classmates?

Activity Questionnaire

Language focus Verb + infinitive; verb + object + infinitive; present simple questions

Preparation Photocopy the worksheet for each student.

Procedure

1. Show the students a copy of the worksheet and explain that they need to make guesses about 12 of their classmates. Tell them to make guesses about as many different classmates as possible. Give each student a worksheet and tell them to write down their guesses. Monitor and offer help where needed.
2. Explain that the students now need to ask each other questions to find out if their guesses were correct or not. Let them walk around the classroom to ask each other their questions. They have to mark on their worksheets whether their guesses were correct or not.
3. When the students have finished, ask them to sit down and do some open class feedback by asking some students to share their correct guesses with the rest of the class.

2.3 Making a film

Activity Gap-fill and ordering

Language focus Present simple passive (*be* + past participle)

Preparation Photocopy one worksheet for each group and cut it into 12 strips.

Procedure

1. Split the students into groups of 12. Give each student a strip of paper and tell them that they need to complete the sentence by putting the verb in brackets into the correct form (present simple passive). Remind them that there is a list of irregular verbs in the Student's Book on page 127.
2. Each student then dictates their sentence to the other members of the group.
3. When they have finished, ask the students to work together to put the 12 sentences in the correct order to make the film making process. (The order is correct on the activity sheet.)
4. When all the groups have finished, do some open class feedback by eliciting the correct order. There may be some variations so encourage the students to explain and discuss their reasons for the order they chose.

3.1 Who could it be?

Activity Guessing game

Language focus *must; can't; could be; may be; might be*

Preparation Photocopy the worksheet for each group of students and cut it into four sets of five sentences.

Procedure

1. Divide the students into groups of four. Explain that they must work as a group to guess who the celebrities are. They will receive five clues and the earlier they guess correctly, the more points they will get. If they guess correctly after one clue, they receive five points, after two clues they receive four points, and so on.
2. Give out the first card to one member of each group. Ask the group member to read the first clue and give the other members some time to discuss who they think it could be. When they have reached a decision, they should write down the answer. The student with the card can then read out the second clue. Repeat the procedure until all the clues have been read out.
3. Elicit the answer from the class. Collect the number of points received on the board for each group.
4. Give out the next card to a different member of the group and repeat Steps 2 and 3.

Key 1 Nelson Mandela 2 Will Smith 3 Britney Spears 4 Princess Diana

3.2 Unusual laws from around the world

Activity Information gap

Language focus *must/mustn't; can't; have to/don't have to; may; might*

Preparation Photocopy the worksheet for each pair of students and cut it along the dotted lines.

Procedure

1 Divide the class into two groups, A and B. Put the students into pairs with a Student A and a Student B and ask them to sit face to face. Explain that they will each get the same sheet with fifteen unusual laws from around the world but that different information is missing from each sheet.

2 Give Student A and Student B the appropriate parts of the worksheet. Tell them to ask each other questions to fill in the spaces on their worksheets.

3 When the students have completed their worksheets, tell them to compare their worksheets to check spelling mistakes.

4 Then ask them to discuss together which laws they believe are true.

Key 1T 2F 3T 4F 5T 6F 7T 8T 9F 10F 11T 12F 13–15T

3.3 Problems at school, problems at home!

Activity Role play

Language focus *should; have to; ought to; had better*

Preparation Photocopy the worksheet for each pair of students and cut it along the dotted lines.

Procedure

1 Tell the students that they are going to imagine that they are experiencing a teenage problem and that they are going to talk to their best friend about it.

2 Divide the class into pairs of students and ask them to sit face to face.

3 Give out the cards for Situation 1 and give the students two minutes to think about what they want to say.

4 Ask the students to act out the role play. Monitor and give feedback. Find out what advice was given and if Student A felt the advice was useful.

5 Give out the cards for Situation 2 and explain that Student B is now the student experiencing a problem. Give the students two minutes to think of what they want to say.

6 Ask the students to act out the role play. Monitor and give feedback. Again find out what advice was given and if Student B felt the advice was useful.

4.1 What did we see going on?

Activity Memory game

Language focus *(can) see/hear/notice someone doing something*

Preparation Photocopy the worksheet for each student and cut it into two along the dotted lines.

Procedure

1 Hand out the picture and have the students memorise as much as they can in the picture. Set a time limit.

2 When the time is up, take the pictures away and give each person a copy of the sentences. Tell them they should complete them on their own first according to how much they remembered.

3 Tell the students to work in pairs to compare their results.

4 Get the students to feed back to the rest of the class and find out which pair had the best memory.

4.2 What are you going to say?

Activity Card game

Language focus *will/shall* and *going to*

Preparation Photocopy the worksheet for each group and cut it up into thirty cards.

Procedure

1 Divide the students into groups of three. Shuffle the response cards. Each person should have five response cards. Put the statement cards in the middle of the table, face down and well shuffled.

2 Allow time for the students to look at their cards and ask about any vocabulary.

3 Explain that, depending on the situation, they will use *will/shall* or *going to* in their response.

4 Going anti-clockwise, one student should turn over a statement card. The person with the correct response card – this includes the person who turned over the statement card – should make a sentence with *will* or *going to*, as appropriate. If it is correct, they keep the statement card. If not, it is put back.

5 The game ends when all the cards have been used up. The winner is the person with most cards.

4.3 I hope I'm a winner!

Activity Board game

Language focus first conditional; *will/won't; be going to; hope to*

Preparation Photocopy the worksheet for each group, enlarged to A3 size. Have a dice for each group and counters for each student.

Procedure

1 Give each group one copy of the board game and a dice and counters.

2 Explain the rules of the game to the class:
– All students put their counters on the Start square.
– The youngest player throws the dice first and moves the counter around the board to the correct square.
– Once on the square the player must talk for thirty seconds about the topic on the square.
– The other students must listen and ask at least two follow-up questions.
– If the student cannot think of anything to say then they stay on that square on their next turn and try again.
– Play continues with the player on the left of the youngest player.
– The winner is the first player to reach the Finish square.

3 The students play the game. Monitor and support as necessary, taking note of any errors for feedback.

5.1 Getting ready to go

Activity Information gap

Language focus Present perfect with *already*, *just* and *yet*

Preparation Photocopy one worksheet for each pair and cut it into two.

Procedure

1 Show the students a role card and explain that the card shows all their jobs and their friend's jobs. Explain that they need to find out which jobs their friend has already done and which they haven't done yet and tick the appropriate box.

2 Show the students how they should find out and give their information. Elicit a question, e.g. *Have you bought a first aid kit yet?* Tell the students they bought one last week and elicit the answer *I've already bought one*. Then tell the students they bought one this morning and elicit the answer *I've just bought one*. Now tell the students they are going to buy one next week and elicit the answer *I haven't bought one yet*.

3 Divide the class into two groups, A and B. Give the students in groups A and B the appropriate role cards and ask them to think about their questions and answers (with extra details) for a few minutes.

4 Now split the students into pairs with one A and one B student and ask student A to begin by asking a question.

5.2 South American adventure

Activity Information gap

Language focus Present perfect with *ever*, *never*; revision of present and past simple

Preparation Photocopy one worksheet for each group of six and cut out the cards.

Procedure

1 Brainstorm South American countries and what things you can see and do there and write ideas on the board. Pre-teach *sand dune*, *lost city* and *falls*. You could show them pictures of the places on the cards if you have time.

2 Show the students a card and explain that the three points on the left are three things they have done. Tell them that they need to find out who has done the three points on the right by speaking to other members of their group. When they find out, they write the student's name next to the activity.

3 Tell students that you want them to describe what they have done in a story-like manner rather than just reading the points on their card. Give an example, e.g. *I went to the beach in Brazil. It was great. I have never been to such a nice beach. I stayed in Rio and saw all the sights.*

4 Give out the cards and give students five minutes to think about how they will describe their experiences.

5 Have the students stand up and mingle describing their experiences and find out about the experiences of others in their group.

6 When they have finished, split them into pairs to discuss their findings.

5.3 Interviewing a star

Activity Interview

Language focus Present perfect; past simple; *for/since*

Preparation Photocopy one worksheet for each pair of students.

Procedure

1 Tell the students that they are going to work in pairs to act out an interview. Explain that one of them will be a world famous athlete and one a TV presenter.

2 Tell the students that first they need to spend 10 minutes writing notes to prepare for the interview. Presenters write questions and athletes write about their lives.

3 Put the students into pairs of two athletes or two presenters and give out the role cards. Monitor to offer help where necessary.

4 When the students are ready, separate them into pairs of one presenter and one athlete and ask them to begin the interview.

5 When the interviews have finished, ask the presenters to report back to the class one interesting fact they discovered about the athlete, and give any feedback needed on the uses of present perfect and past simple.

6.1 Crime never pays

Activity Puzzle stories

Language focus Past perfect; past simple

Preparation Photocopy the worksheet and cut it into six cards for each group of six.

Procedure

1 Divide the class into six groups (A, B, C, D, E and F) and explain that each group is going to read a different story about a robbery. Give out the cards so that Group A has Story A, Group B has Story B, etc. Give the students two minutes to read the cards and check with each other that they understand.

2 Regroup the students so that there are six people in each group, each with a different story. Tell them that they need to read their stories aloud for the other members of the group and that the other students need to discuss together why the story happened, using the past perfect. Point out the Help part of the card and tell the students to read that part aloud if the rest of the group cannot solve the mystery.

3 Student A reads his/her story aloud and the others guess using the past perfect in their guesses. If they can't guess, Student A can read the Help sentence. If the others still do not know, Student A can tell them. It is then Student B's turn.

4 When all the stories have been discussed, the students can vote for their favourite story.

6.2 Mayans and Incas

Activity Comparing texts

Language focus *used to/didn't use to*

Preparation Photocopy one worksheet for each pair and cut it up along the dotted lines.

Procedure

1 Divide the class into two groups, A and B, and ask each student to work with a partner from the same group. Hand out the text about the Incas to the students of group A and the text about the Mayans to the students of group B. Ask them to read the texts and to note down information using the questions on the board to help them. They have to use *used to/didn't used to* in their answers.

2 Tell the students that they should now divide up so that a student from group A works with a student from group B. Using their notes, they have to tell their partner all about the people that they read about in order to find as many differences as they can between the groups of people.

6.3 Who invented it?

Activity Memory game

Language focus Past simple passive

Preparation Photocopy the worksheet for every eight students and cut it up as indicated. Copy the questions for each pair.

Procedure

1 Tell the students that they will be given a card with some information about an invention on it and that they are going to describe the invention.

2 Give each student a card and tell them to read it and to think about the sentences that they are going to make.

3 Ask the students to work in groups of eight and to tell each student in their group their information.

4 After five minutes ask the students to sit down in pairs. Give each pair a copy of the eight questions and ask them to try to answer as many questions as they can.

7.1 She told him *what*?

Activity Information gap

Language focus Reported commands and requests; contrastive stress

Preparation Photocopy the worksheet for each pair and cut it in half along the dotted lines.

Procedure

1 Tell the students that they are going to look at some pictures of a man travelling by plane and that there are going to be a number of differences.

2 Demonstrate the activity using picture 1 with a student:

Teacher: The man asked her to give him an aisle seat in my picture.

Student: The man asked her to give him a *window* seat in my picture.

Draw the students' attention to the contrastive stress that should feature on the differing word.

3 Divide the class into two pairs of students, A and B. Give out the worksheet. Tell the students to report what is being said in each picture of the journey.

4 Monitor and give assistance as required.

7.2 What a holiday!

Activity Role play

Language focus Reported speech

Preparation Photocopy one worksheet for each group and cut it into four role cards.

Procedure

1 Separate the students into pairs of A and B and C and D and give out the role cards. Explain that Students A and B need to work together to plan their stories and C and D to plan their questions. Ask the students to be as detailed as possible. Give them 10 minutes to plan and monitor to help where needed.

2 When the students are ready, separate them into pairs of A and C and B and D to perform the interview. Ask the managers to make notes so that they can compare the customers' answers later.

3 When the interviews have finished, ask the students to return to their original partners to discuss what was said in the interview. The friends should discuss what they were asked and what answers they gave to see if they told the same story. The managers should discuss the answers the friends gave to see if they told the same story and decide if they will give them a refund or not. They must give the friends a refund if their stories were the same. Remind all students to use reported speech constructions during their discussions, using the example on the board to help them.

4 When the managers have decided, all four students should come together so that the managers can give their decision and the reasons for their decision.

7.3 Grammar gamble

Language focus Reported speech; reported questions

Preparation Photocopy one worksheet for each group of three.

Procedure

1 Divide the class into groups of three and ask each group for a team name that can be written on the board. Give one worksheet to each team.

2 Explain that each team starts with 100 gold coins. Each team should look at the first sentence on their worksheet and decide if it is grammatically correct or incorrect. Each team bets a number of gold coins that their answer is right. The minimum bet is 10 gold coins. If they are confident that their answer is right they should bet a large number and if they are not confident they should bet a small number.

3 When they are ready, the teacher asks each group for their answer and their bet. The teacher then reveals the right answer and the groups that were right add their bet to their 100 gold coins whilst the groups that were wrong subtract their bet from their 100 gold coins. The teacher writes the totals on the board. Continue in this way for sentences 2 to 12.

4 When all 12 sentences have been looked at, the team with the most gold coins is the winner. Ask the students for the correct sentences and write them up on the board.

8.1 Why did you do that?

Activity Simulation, responding to situations

Language focus *should(n't) have/ought to have*

Preparation Photocopy the worksheet and cut it up into 12 strips. Copy enough sheets so that each student has one strip.

Procedure

1 Tell the students that you are going to give each of them a situation in which something happened in the past. They should read the situation, memorise it if possible, and then go around the class and tell people, as if it had happened to them. The students they tell their story to should respond with criticism or advice using *should(n't) have/ought to have*.

2 Give the students a time limit to mill around the class, telling people what happened, and waiting for a response. Tell them to make a note of the best responses.

3 Students give feedback to the class, saying what the situation was and what other students said.

8.2 If I were you ...

Activity Questionnaire

Language focus Second conditional

Preparation Photocopy the worksheet for every student.

Procedure

1 Distribute the worksheets to every student and ask them to spend a few minutes reading it, and to ask you if there are any words they don't understand.

2 Put the students into pairs. Tell the students to complete the first sentence, imagining they are their partner: *I would be really scared if I ...* . Then tell them to ask their partner if their guess was correct.

3 Give them a time limit to complete the remaining sentences. They should then take turns to ask and answer their questions. If they guessed correctly, they should put a tick in the ✔ column. If they were wrong, they should write the correct response under ✘.

4 In groups, the students should tell each other anything interesting they learned about their partners.

8.3 It's fun, isn't it?

Activity Dominoes

Language focus Question tags, intonation

Preparation Photocopy the worksheet for each group and cut it up into 20 dominoes along the dotted lines.

Procedure

1 Ask the students to work in groups of three and give each group a set of dominoes. Ask them to deal out five dominoes each and put the rest in a pile in the middle, face down.

2 Give them the instructions, or demonstrate with one of the groups:

– The youngest player puts down a domino, face up.

– The next player puts down one of his/her dominoes, making sure one of the sides matches one of the sides of the first player's domino, e.g. *won't she? | Humans can't drink salt water, can they? | The Incas lived there,*

– The first player must say if he/she thinks it's incorrect. If they haven't got the correct one, they can pick up one from the pile, but they miss a turn.

– The winner is the first person to get rid of all their dominoes.

3 Give them a time limit and tell the students to start the game. Monitor and give help where needed.

You've Got A Friend

Activity Song

Language focus Revision of language and vocabulary from Units 1–2

Preparation Photocopy one sheet for each student. Get the recording ready. 3.31

Procedure
1 Ask students to work in pairs and try to guess which words go in each space.
2 Play the recording so students can check their answers.
3 Students listen to the whole song again and choose the best answer to 2. They compare their answers in pairs.
4 Students work individually to answer 3 and 4. They then check their answers in pairs.

Key
1 a) eyes b) night c) name d) spring e) sky f) wind g) door h) people
2 b 3 a) right b) call c) loud d) desert
4 a) down b) troubled c) brighten up d) fall e) desert

Celebrate The Future

Activity Song

Language focus Revision of language and vocabulary from Units 3–4

Preparation Photocopy one sheet for each student. Get the recording ready. 3.32

Procedure
1 Students look at the words in the box. They read the song and guess which word goes in each space. Ask them to compare their answers in pairs.
2 Play the recording so students can check their answers.
3 Students listen to the whole song again and choose the best answer to 2. They compare their answers in pairs.
4 Students work individually to answer 3 and 4. They then check their answers in pairs.

Key
1 a) hand b) make c) world d) tomorrow e) celebration f) true g) history h) share i) world
2 c) 3 a) unfold b) fade away c) fairy tale d) harmony
4 a) hold b) put c) catch d) join e) make

Brown-eyed Girl

Activity Song

Language focus Revision of language and vocabulary from Units 5–6

Preparation Photocopy one sheet for each student. Get the recording ready. 3.33

Procedure
1 Students look at the words in the box. They read the song and guess which word goes in each space. Ask them to compare their answers in pairs.
2 Play the recording so students can check their answers.
3 Students listen to the whole song again and choose the best answers to 2. They compare their answers in pairs.
4 Students work individually to answer 3 and 4. They then check their answers in pairs.

Key
1 a) rain b) game c) hearts d) radio e) used f) own g) grown h) used
2 a) fog b) mine c) waterfall d) stadium
3 a)
4 a) hollow b) thumping c) rainbow d) overcome

I Will Survive

Activity Song

Language focus Revision of language and vocabulary from Units 7–8

Preparation Photocopy one sheet for each student. Get the recording ready. 3.34

Procedure
1 Students look at the words in the box. They read the song and guess which word goes in each space. Ask them to compare their answers in pairs.
2 Play the recording so students can check their answers.
3 Students listen to the whole song again and choose the best answer to 2. They compare their answers in pairs.
4 Students work individually to answer 3 and 4. They then check their answers in pairs.
5 Students tell each other about any other songs they know which tell a story or convey a message or strong feelings and emotions.

Key
1 a) afraid b) strong c) sad d) stupid e) welcome f) alive g) broken h) sorry i) high j) new k) free
2 b)
3 a) along b) face c) anymore d) die e) heart
4 a) do b) mend c) hold d) learn e) change

What are we like?

Sentence cards

I worry about …	I'm scared of …
I really care about …	At the moment I'm reading …
At weekends I usually …	I play/watch (the following sports):
My favourite school subjects are …	I'm really looking forward to …
In the future I'd like to …	My friends and I usually talk about …
I'd love to travel to …	I like wearing …

Question and answers

Name	Answer

Story secrets

A

I ________________ (wake) up and slowly ________________ (get) out of bed. I ________________ (look) out of the window. It was a *snowy* / *sunny* / *frosty* day. I ________________ (put) on my clothes and some shoes. Then I ________________ (run) downstairs, and ________________ (open) the *heavy* / *wooden* / *creaky* back door into the garden. I ________________ (walk) along the grassy path towards the woods at the bottom of the garden.

B

I ________________ (cross) the *stile* / *river* / *bridge* and went into the woods. Suddenly I ________________ (see) an *old* / *rusty* / *shiny* key on the ground. When I ________________ (pick) it up, I ________________ (hear) a bird tweeting loudly. I ________________ (follow) the noise, holding the key tightly in my hands. Suddenly in front of me there ________________ (be) a tree. Walking closer, a bright light ________________ (begin) to shine.

C

The tree was *leafy* / *tall* / *scary* with a hollow inside. I ________________ (feel) with my hand inside the hollow and my fingers ________________ (touch) something hard. It was a box. I ________________ (look) at the *colours* / *shape* / *weight* of it. Then I ________________ (remember) the key, and ________________ (put) it in the lock. The lid ________________ (open) and inside I ________________ (find) the most amazing thing.

YOUR SECRETS REVEALED!

The day represents your personality
Snowy: you keep your friends close to your heart, and always need them around you.
Sunny: the brighter the day you imagine, the smilier a person you are.
Frosty: you are sensitive, but you seem tough on the outside!

• • • • • •

The type of door reveals your nature
Heavy: you're caring and never tell lies.
Wooden: you are honest, and secrets are safe with you.
Creaky: you always say the right thing, friends rely on you.

Your route represents a decision
Stile: you never run away from a challenge.
River: don't be shy to ask your friends for help if you are in trouble.
Bridge: you have a problem to solve but it will be fine afterwards.

• • • • • •

The key – a secret in your life
Old: a visitor from your past will bring some adventure to your life.
Rusty: a difficult time for you is now finished.
Shiny: you always have lots of good ideas. Try to use them.

The tree describes your future
Leafy: the more leaves on the trees, the more friends you will have.
Tall: you dream a lot and some of them will come true.
Scary: you will have a very up-and-down year.

• • • • • •

The type of box represents a mystery
Colours: you will have good luck.
Shape: you will have a very nice surprise.
Weight: you will help to solve a problem and make a new friend.

1 3 What were you doing?

Picture cards

listen/radio

cook/dinner

live/Paris

swim/sea

dream/about you

ride/my bike

visit/fortune teller

make/the bed

run/for a bus

work/in the garden

Sentence cards

… when I (*hear*) my favourite song.	… when I (*fall*) off.
… when I (*burn*) my hand.	… when she (*tell*) me some good news about my future.
… when I (*meet*) my boyfriend.	… when I (*find*) my ring.
… when I (*see*) the shark.	… when I (*drop*) my phone.
… when the alarm clock (*wake*) me up.	… when I (*hurt*) my back.

2.1 Gwyneth Paltrow

A

GWYNETH PALTROW is a (**1**) ______________ (*what?*) and is most famous for acting in the romantic film *Shakespeare in Love*. She has also acted in comedies, science fiction, and action films.

Gwyneth was born in Los Angeles on (**3**) ______________ (*when?*). She attended the University of California for one year but gave up studying in 1991 because she wasn't interested in learning about (**5**) ______________ (*what?*). Gwyneth was interested in acting and dreamt of winning an Oscar. She started acting (**7**) ______________ (*when?*) in a film called *Shout*. After playing a small part in the thrilling film *Seven*, Gwyneth began dating the famous actor Brad Pitt. This relationship later ended and she married Coldplay singer Chris Martin in 2003.

Gwyneth has spent some time in Spain and is good at (**9**) ______________ (*what/good at/do?*). She likes eating healthy food and is keen on (**11**) ______________ (*what/keen on/do?*). Gwyneth enjoys watching funny films but is not keen on (**13**) ______________ (*what/not keen on/do?*).

Gwyneth loves acting but says she has acted in some terrible films. She thinks that being an actress is disappointing at times but that winning an Oscar® is thrilling and shows that she has succeeded in being a good actress.

B

GWYNETH PALTROW is a brilliant actress and is most famous for acting in (**2**) ______________ (*what film?*). She has also acted in comedies, science fiction, and action films.

Gwyneth was born in Los Angeles on the 28th of September 1972. She attended the University of California for one year but gave up (**4**) ______________ (*what/do?*) in 1991 because she wasn't interested in learning about the history of art. Gwyneth was interested in acting and dreamt of (**6**) ______________ (*what/do?*). Gwyneth started acting in 1991 in a film called *Shout*. After playing a small part in the thrilling film *Seven*, Gwyneth began dating (**8**) ______________ (*who?*). This relationship later ended and she married Coldplay singer Chris Martin in 2003.

Gwyneth has spent some time in Spain and is good at speaking Spanish. She likes eating (**10**) ______________ (*what?*) and is keen on singing. Gwyneth enjoys watching (**12**) ______________ (*what?*) but is not keen on watching scary films.

Gwyneth loves (**14**) ______________ (*what/love/do?*) but says she has acted in some terrible films. She thinks that being an actress is disappointing at times but that winning an Oscar® is thrilling and shows that she has succeeded in being a good actress.

How well do you know your classmates?

Guesses	I was right ☺	I was wrong ☹
______ hopes ______ in the future.		
______ refuses to eat ______		
______ never manages ______		
______ would like to learn ______		
______ wants to speak ______ very well.		
______ expects his/her parents ______		
______ always helps friends ______		
______ wants ______ one day.		
______ would like ______ better.		
______'s parents ask him/her to ______		
______ sometimes pretends ______		
______ refuses ______		

2 3 Making a film

A story line ______________________________ (*create*).

Details ______________________________ (*add*) to the story line.

The script ______________________________ (*write*).

The budget ______________________________ (*produce*).

The actors and actresses ______________________________ (*choose*).

The sets ______________________________ (*build*) and costumes ______________________________ (*make*).

The film ______________________________ (*rehearse*).

The sound and lighting ______________________________ (*set up*).

The film ______________________________ (*shot*).

The film ______________________________ (*edit*).

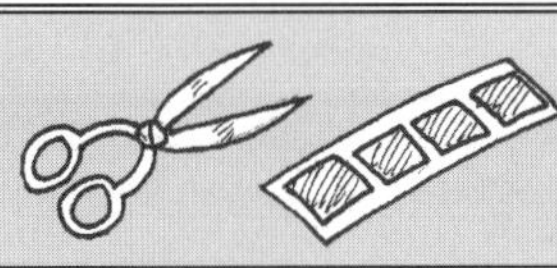

The film ______________________________ (*promote*).

The film ______________________________ (*release*) and ______________________________ (*watch*) at the cinema.

Who could it be?

Mystery celebrity number 1

1 This man was born in 1918.

2 He was in prison from 1964 to 1990.

3 He is not a sportsman.

4 He is from South Africa.

5 He was the president of South Africa from 1994 to 1999.

Mystery celebrity number 2

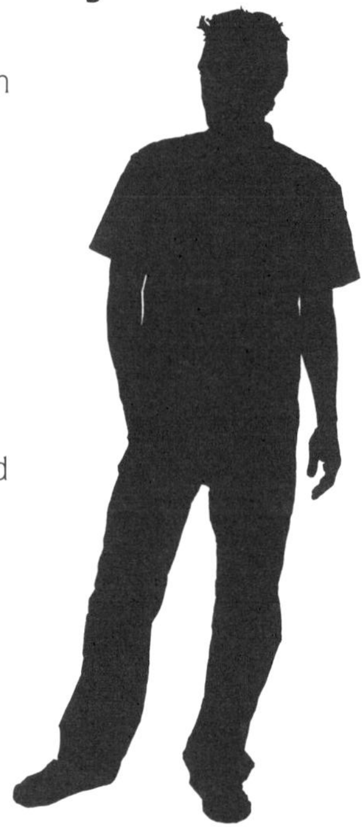

1 This man was born in America in 1968.

2 He is an actor on TV and in films.

3 He is also a singer.

4 He has black hair and brown eyes.

5 He acted in the films *Men in Black*, *Hitch*, and *Wild, Wild West*.

Mystery celebrity number 3

1 This American woman was born in 1981.

2 She has sold more than fifty-five million records around the world.

3 She made a film in 2002.

4 She had her first child in 2005 and called him Sean Preston.

5 Her most famous song is 'Hit Me Baby One More Time'.

Mystery celebrity number 4

1 This English woman was born in 1961.

2 She is now dead.

3 Many people watched her wedding on television.

4 Her two sons are also famous all over the world.

5 She died in a car crash in Paris in 1997.

3.2 Unusual laws from around the world

STUDENT A

1. In Thailand you can't leave your house when ______________________________ .
2. You can't have a microwave if you don't have a licence in the UK.
3. ________________________ can't be used in New Year's celebrations in Cambodia.
4. In Iceland you must not say the word *shark* on Wednesdays.
5. In Canada you are not allowed to take ____________________________ off in public.
6. You don't have to pay for a train ticket in France if you are older than eighty.
7. You cannot enter the Houses of Parliament in London if you are wearing ______________ .
8. It is illegal to run out of petrol in Germany when you are driving on the motorway.
9. You have to have a special licence to change a light bulb in ____________________ (*which country?*).
10. In Japan all men must take their glasses off when they go into a temple.
11. You are not allowed to ______________________________________ in Singapore.
12. All married Turkish women must ask their husband's permission if they want to have a job.
13. You must let somebody into your house in Scotland if they knock on the door and ask to ____ .
14. You don't have to pay for a meal in restaurants in Denmark if you do not feel full after eating it.
15. In Mexico you mustn't ________________________ when you are riding a bicycle.

STUDENT B

1. In Thailand you can't leave your house when you are not wearing any underwear.
2. You can't have a __________________________ if you don't have a licence in the UK.
3. Water guns can't be used in New Year's celebrations in Cambodia.
4. In Iceland you must not ____________________________________ on Wednesdays.
5. In Canada you are not allowed to take bandages off in public.
6. You don't have to pay for ________________________ in France if you are older than eighty.
7. You cannot enter the Houses of Parliament in London if you are wearing a suit of armour.
8. It is illegal to run out of ________________ in Germany when you are driving on the motorway.
9. You have to have a special licence to change a light bulb in China.
10. In Japan all men must take their ______________________ off when they go into a temple.
11. You are not allowed to go bungee jumping in Singapore.
12. All married Turkish women must ____________________________ if they want to have a job.
13. You must let somebody into your house in Scotland if they knock on the door and ask to use your toilet.
14. You don't have to pay for a meal in restaurants in ____________________ (*which country?*) if you do not feel full after eating it.
15. In Mexico you must not take your feet off the pedals when you are riding a bicycle.

Problems at school, problems at home!

STUDENT A

Situation 1

You are a fifteen-year-old student and you have always worked hard. You have a new Maths teacher who does not like you. He/She gives you bad marks even though your work is excellent and better than most of the other students in your class. Last week you told the head teacher but he/she does not believe you. This morning a letter arrived from the school telling your parents about your bad marks in Maths and they are furious. You really do not know what to do and you are going to talk to your best friend to ask for some advice.

You need to:

- explain the problem;
- ask your best friend for advice;
- decide what you are going to do.

STUDENT A

Situation 2

Your friend is going to talk to you about a very serious problem that he/she has.

You need to:

- listen to your friend as he/she explains the problem;
- offer some advice on what you think he/she should/ought to/shouldn't/had better do.

STUDENT B

Situation 1

Your best friend is going to talk to you about a very serious problem that he/she has.

You need to:

- listen to your friend as he/she explains the problem;
- offer some advice on what you think he/she should/ought to/shouldn't/had better do.

STUDENT B

Situation 2

You are a fifteen-year-old student and last week you 'borrowed' your friend's digital camera without his permission. Unfortunately, you broke it. Your friend has told you that he is going to tell your parents. He told you that he won't tell them if you give him £300 but you don't have the money. You really don't know what to do and you are going to talk to your best friend.

You need to:

- explain the problem;
- ask your best friend for advice;
- decide what you are going to do.

What did we see going on?

What do you remember hearing and seeing? Complete these sentences.

I could see a policeman ____.

There was an old man ____________________ and ____________________ on a bench.

____________________ wearing a long dress and ____________________.

I heard a man in a car ____.

I saw a young man and woman ____.

I saw a ____ playing with a ball.

I could hear the birds ____.

I noticed a teenager ____.

A mother was watching her child ____ a bike.

4.2 What are you going to say?

Statement cards	Response cards
Look at those black clouds!	Yes, I think it rain.
I've got a maths exam tomorrow.	I keep my fingers crossed for you.
We're staying in tonight.	You watch TV?
The phone's ringing!	I answer it.
That person's going too fast.	Yes, he fall off.
I'm thirsty.	I get you a drink?
Here are the tickets.	Thanks. I pay you later.
It's my 18th birthday soon.	Congratulations. You have a party?
I need some chocolate!	I go to the shops for you?
It's a secret!	OK. I promise I (not) tell anyone.
My team's playing well at the moment.	You think they win the cup?
We want to go to London at the weekend.	You drive?
I've lost my glasses.	I find them for you.
Do you want to come round later?	I can't. I visit my grandmother.
I'm scared of sharks.	You (not) see any in Britain!

I hope I'm a winner!

5.1 Getting ready to go

Student A

Your jobs	Last week (already)	This morning (just)	Next week (not yet)
book / the car			✔
buy / a guidebook	✔		
buy / sun cream and sun hats 			✔
get / a passport		✔	
buy / a first aid kit 	✔		
order / a visa		✔	
buy / a new camera	✔		

Your friend's jobs	Last week (already)	This morning (just)	Next week (not yet)
change / money			
buy / travel insurance 			
book / the flights			
make / list of things to see			
book / the hotels			
buy / insect spray 			
order / a visa			

Student B

Your jobs	Last week (already)	This morning (just)	Next week (not yet)
book / the hotels			✔
make / list of things to see		✔	
buy / insect spray 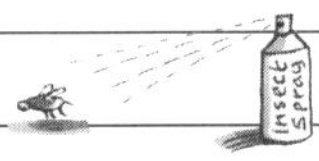			✔
book / the flights	✔		
buy / travel insurance 	✔		
order / a visa		✔	
change / money		✔	

Your friend's jobs	Last week (already)	This morning (just)	Next week (not yet)
buy / a first aid kit 			
buy / a new camera			
get / a passport			
buy / sun cream and sun hats 			
order / a visa			
buy / a guidebook			
book / the car			

South American adventure

STUDENT A

You ...	Find out who ...
• visit / Iguazu Falls in Argentina • watch / football in Brazil • go / to Easter Island near Chile	• visit / Machu Picchu in Peru Name ____________ • see / Angel Falls in Venezuela Name ____________ • go / on a cruise boat in Colombia Name ____________

STUDENT B

You ...	Find out who ...
• visit / Machu Picchu in Peru • go / shopping in Santiago in Chile • visit / the Tiahuanaco ruins in Bolivia	• visit / a culture museum in Uruguay Name ____________ • go / salsa dancing in Colombia Name ____________ • go / to the beach in Brazil Name ____________

STUDENT C

You ...	Find out who ...
• visit / a lake in Peru • climb / a volcano in Chile • visit / a culture museum in Uruguay	• go / to Easter Island near Chile Name ____________ • climb / sand dunes in Venezuela Name ____________ • visit / the lost city in Colombia Name ____________

STUDENT D

You ...	Find out who ...
• visit / the lost city in Colombia • see / Angel Falls in Venezuela • go / to the beach in Brazil	• go / skiing in Chile Name ____________ • visit / a lake in Peru Name ____________ • walk / in the rainforest in Ecuador Name ____________

STUDENT E

You ...	Find out who ...
• walk / in the rainforest in Ecuador • climb / sand dunes in Venezuela • go / salsa dancing in Colombia	• go / shopping in Santiago in Chile Name ____________ • watch / football in Brazil Name ____________ • go on / a nature trek in Uruguay Name ____________

STUDENT F

You ...	Find out who ...
• go / on a nature trek in Uruguay • go / skiing in Chile • go / on a cruise boat in Colombia	• climb / a volcano in Chile Name ____________ • visit / the Tiahuanaco ruins in Bolivia Name ____________ • visit / Iguazu Falls in Argentina Name ____________

5.3 Interviewing a star

Famous athlete

You are a world famous athlete. Today you are being interviewed on a TV chat show called *The Fame Game*. Write some notes about your life before you begin the interview. Use the notes below to help you.

Your sport:
Which one(s)?
How long for?
Why start?
Training?

Competitions you've won:
How many?
Which ones?
When?
How you feel?

Travel:
Which countries?
Favourite? Why?
Most recent?

Home:
Where?
Since when?

Married:
Who to?
When meet?
Love at first sight?
Children yet?

Hobbies:
Which ones?
Why?
How long for?

Presenter

You are a presenter on a TV chat show called *The Fame Game*. Today you are going to interview a world famous athlete. Write some questions before you begin the interview. Use the notes below to help you.

His/her sport:
Which one(s)?
How long for?
Why start?
Training?

Competitions he/she has won:
How many?
Which ones?
When?
How he/she feel?

Travel:
Which countries?
Favourite? Why?
Most recent?

Home:
Where?
Since when?

Married:
Who to?
When meet?
Love at first sight?
Children yet?

Hobbies:
Which ones?
Why?
How long for?

6.1

Crime never pays

Story A

A robber went into a bank with a gun and a note written on the back of an envelope. He gave the note to the cashier. It said 'I have a gun, so give me one million dollars.' The cashier gave the robber the money and he went away. One hour later the police went to his home and arrested him. How did the police know where to find him?

Help: What else was written on the envelope?

Answer: The robber hadn't noticed that his name and address were on the back of the envelope. The cashier had seen them and told the police.

Story B

One day in January last year two robbers broke into a bank at night and stole more than one million dollars. There were no cameras in the bank and nobody saw the robbers commit the crime. They were caught as they were eating breakfast the next morning. How did the police know who had robbed the bank?

Help: What had the weather been like on the night of the robbery?

Answer: The robbers had left footprints in the snow and the police had followed them from the bank directly to their house.

Story C

A robber went into a bank and gave the cashier a note that said 'I have a gun. Put 16 million dollars in the bag. If you ever tell anybody I will come and find you and kill you.' The cashier put the money in the bag. She never told the police but the robber was never able to spend any of the money. Why?

Help: What money had the cashier given him?

Answer: The cashier had given the robber Australian dollars and he had robbed a bank in the USA.

Story D

Two robbers broke into a bank late one night and stole the safe. There were no cameras and nobody saw the robbery. They were never caught by the police and never went to prison but the robbers never became rich. Why?

Help: What had been in the safe?

Answer:

Story E

Two robbers went into a bank and gave the cashier a note. The cashier gave the robbers 20 million dollars and the robbers left with the money. They got into a car and the police followed them. They were arrested on a quiet country road two hours later. How?

Help: Why had the robbers stopped driving?

Answer: The robbers had forgotten to fill the car with petrol before the robbery.

Story F

A group of robbers robbed a bank last year and escaped with 25 million dollars. They were driving along the motorway when the police stopped them. The police didn't arrest them and after a short conversation the robbers left. Why?

Help: Why had the police stopped the robbers?

Answer: The police had seen the robbers driving too fast and had stopped them to give them a speeding ticket.

6

2

Mayans and Incas

The Incas

The Incas used to live in small towns and villages in the mountains of Ecuador, Peru and Chile, from the 12th to the 16th century.

They used to be very good builders and engineers and built many fantastic tunnels and bridges. They were also rich and used to have lots of silver and gold.

They used to believe in a Sun god and they built many temples to please him. Many of these can still be seen today. They used to travel from their towns and villages into their cities for special festivals when they would pray to the Sun god. They used to believe that when a person died they went to heaven or hell.

They used to speak a language called Quechua and some people in the Andes, a group of mountains in South America, still speak it. Even though their language has survived, the Incas have disappeared because they were conquered by the Spanish in the 1560s.

The Mayans

The Mayans were a group of people who used to live in Honduras, El Salvador, Guatemala and southern Mexico, mostly in the years between 300 and 900AD.

They used to have many different gods; most of them looked like lizards. The Mayans used to give human blood to their gods to keep them happy. They believed that only very special people went to heaven when they died and most people went to hell.

Priests used to be very important to Mayans and only they were allowed to live in the wonderful big cities that the Mayans built. Most Mayans, however, used to live in small villages in the rainforest.

They used to speak a language called Mayan and this is still spoken by a small number of people today. A few Mayans still live in some parts of Central America.

6.3 Who invented it?

– invent / 1860 / Antonio Meucci / in Italy
– Used for?

– make / 1889 / for King Umberto I of Italy
– first pizzeria / open / 1830 / in Naples
– Made of?

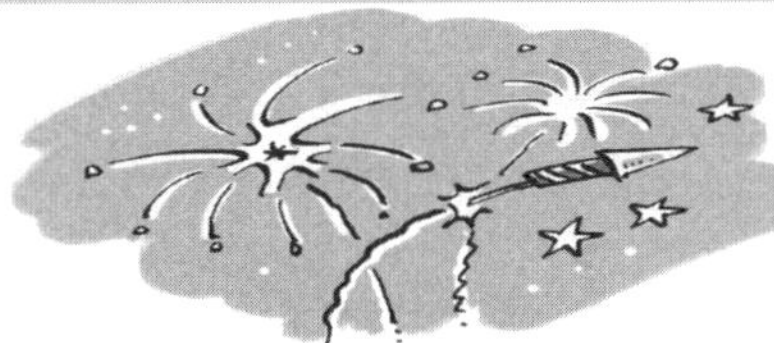

– invent / AD 1000 / China
– first use / for weapons in war
– Used for now?

– make / 5,000 years ago / Ancient Egypt
– Used for?

– invent / 1879 / USA / Thomas Edison
– Used for?

– invent / 1790s / France
– Used for?

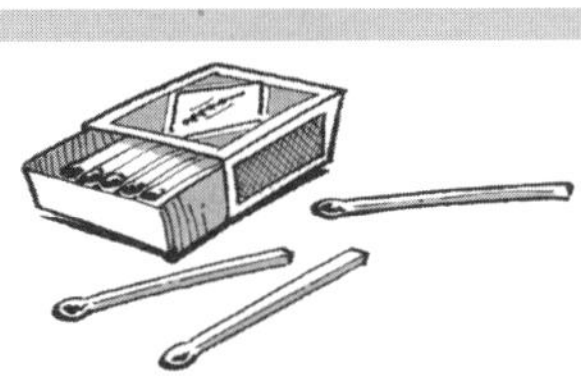

– invent / 1827 / John Walker / England
– make / of wood
– Used for?

– invented / 1284 / Salvino D'Armate / Italy
– make / of glass
– Used for?

1 Which three things were first invented in Italy? ______
2 When was the first pizzeria opened? ______
3 Which thing was first invented in France? ______
4 What was invented by a man called John Walker? ______
5 Which invention was first used in battles? ______
6 Which invention came from Egypt? ______
7 Which four things were invented in the nineteenth century? ______
______
8 Which invention came from the USA? ______

7 1

She told him *what*?

What a holiday!

STUDENT A

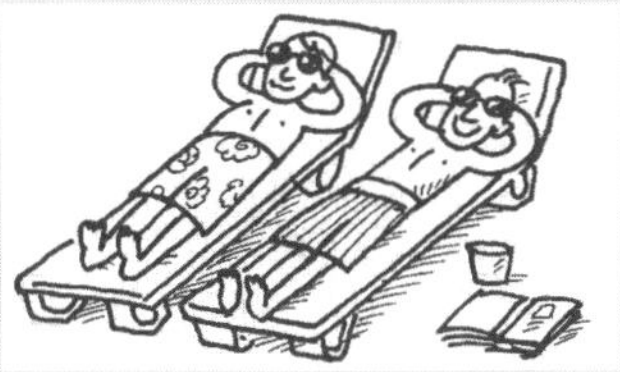

You and your best friend have recently come back from a holiday that was arranged for you by a travel company. You had a lovely time but it was very expensive and now you haven't got any money. You and your friend have decided that you will tell the holiday company that the holiday was terrible and ask them to refund your money.

Today you are both being interviewed by managers of the holiday company. The only problem is that you are being interviewed separately and they will only refund your money if you tell them the same story about the holiday. Before your interview, discuss the details of the holiday with your friend. Use these notes to help you:

Where / go?	How long?
How / travel?	Where / stay?
What activities / do?	What problems / have?

STUDENT C

You are a manager of a travel company. Today you and your colleague are interviewing two friends who recently bought a holiday through your company. They want you to refund their money because they say the holiday was terrible. You and your colleague are going to interview the friends separately because you think they are lying and will tell different stories about the holiday. You will only refund their money if they both tell the same story. Before the interview, discuss with your colleague the questions you will ask them. Use these notes to help you:

Where / go?	How long?
How / travel?	Where / stay?
What activities / do?	What problems / have?

STUDENT B

You and your best friend have recently come back from a holiday that was arranged for you by a travel company. You had a lovely time but it was very expensive and now you haven't got any money. You and your friend have decided that you will tell the holiday company that the holiday was terrible and ask them to refund your money.

Today you are both being interviewed by managers of the holiday company. The only problem is that you are being interviewed separately and they will only refund your money if you tell them the same story about the holiday. Before your interview, discuss the details of the holiday with your friend. Use these notes to help you:

Where / go?	How long?
How / travel?	Where / stay?
What activities / do?	What problems / have?

STUDENT D

You are a manager of a travel company. Today you and your colleague are interviewing two friends who recently bought a holiday through your company. They want you to refund their money because they say the holiday was terrible. You and your colleague are going to interview the friends separately because you think they are lying and will tell different stories about the holiday. You will only refund their money if they both tell the same story. Before the interview, discuss with your colleague the questions you will ask them. Use these notes to help you:

Where / go?	How long?
How / travel?	Where / stay?
What activities / do?	What problems / have?

Grammar gamble

Sentence	Correct	Incorrect	Gold coins bet	Total
1 They had wanted to buy a new mobile phone, but decided against it. 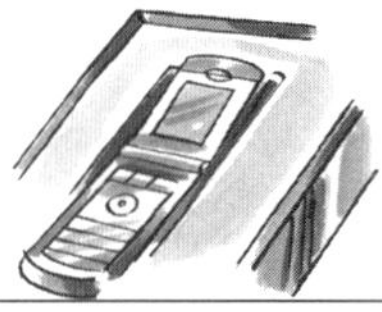				
2 I asked her does she like animals.				
3 My friend told me that she was going to go shopping in Warsaw.				
4 He asked me how long I worked on the air ambulance before becoming a teacher. 				
5 Her father told her to do the washing up.				
6 She said she must do her homework.				
7 I told him if he had sent an email today.				
8 He told me that he could play the piano. 				
9 My brother said that his mobile phone wasn't work.				
10 My mum asked me help with the cooking.				
11 She said it was still early days.				
12 They wanted to know has anyone seen a parrot. 				

Why did you do that?

You had already bought a ticket to a football match before your sister invited you to her 21st birthday party. The ticket was expensive, so you decided to go to the match and now your sister won't speak to you.

You went walking in the mountains on a school trip and you and your friend decided to go off for a while on your own. You got lost and it was more than 24 hours before someone found you.

At Christmas you couldn't buy anybody any presents because you had spent all your pocket money on a new games console. You felt really guilty.

You told a friend that you were good at skiing and his/her family invited you to go with them on a skiing holiday. In fact you had never done it before! You went, and it was really embarrassing.

You borrowed your sister's best dress for a party without telling her and then spilt something on it. So you hid it, and she was really upset that she had lost it.

While you were babysitting for your aunt, you invited a couple of people to come round. They brought some friends, woke up the children, drank your aunt's wine and made a mess. Your aunt was very angry with you.

You told your friend that her boyfriend was dating someone else at the same time as her. It was true, but she hasn't spoken to you since then.

Your mother told you to wear a coat when you went out; you didn't and got very wet when it started to rain. You now have a bad cold and can't go out.

You didn't leave the party until 2am yesterday. You have an important exam today and feel very tired.

You stayed off school because you didn't feel too well. Then at about 10am you felt fine and went shopping in town. One of the teachers saw you and now you are in trouble.

You went to a friend's house after school yesterday and forgot to tell your mother. When you got home much later, your mother was very upset and had called the police.

You saw someone stealing a CD from a shop near your house. You didn't say anything to the shop assistant because you knew the person and you were scared.

8.2 If I were you ...

Imagine you are your partner, and complete the following statements.	✔	✘
I would be really scared if ______ ______	☐	______
If I could change one thing about my country, ______ ______	☐	______
If I were an animal, I'd be ______ ______	☐	______
If I could have the ideal job, ______ ______	☐	______
I would be thrilled if ______ ______	☐	______
If I could choose one thing to take with me to a desert island, ______	☐	______
If someone was really angry with me, ______ ______	☐	______
If I could live anywhere in the world, ______ ______	☐	______
The world would be a better place if ______ ______	☐	______
If I could meet anyone in the world, ______ ______	☐	______
If I could be somewhere else now, ______ ______	☐	______
If I had 24 hours to live, ______ ______	☐	______

It's fun, isn't it?

can they?	The Incas lived there,	didn't they?	You'd like to go,
wouldn't you?	John didn't go,	did he?	
	You've got a car,	haven't you?	You forgot your bag,
didn't you?		can't they?	
would you?		have you?	The hotel isn't expensive,
is it?	Lucy doesn't know where we are,	does she?	Jake hasn't seen the exhibition,
has he?	People use too much water,	don't they?	It's been on TV,
hasn't it?	His dog doesn't bite,	does it?	Mario's got a sister,
hasn't he?	You know each other,	don't you?	You won't tell him what I said,
will you?	I'm sure she'll come,	won't she?	Humans can't drink salt water,

1–2 Song: You've Got A Friend

1 Read the song and complete it with words you think are appropriate. Listen and check.

When you're down and troubled
And you need some loving care
And nothing, nothing is going right
Close your (a) ___________ and think of me
And soon I will be there
To brighten up even your darkest (b) ___________

Chorus:
You just call out my (c) ___________
And you know wherever I am
I'll come running to see you again
Winter, (d) ___________, summer or fall
All you have to do is call
And I'll be there
You've got a friend

If the (e) ___________ above you
Grows dark and full of clouds
And that old north (f) ___________ begins to blow
Keep your head together
And call my name out loud
Soon you'll hear me knocking at your (g) ___________

Chorus

Ain't it good to know that you've got a friend
When (h) ___________ can be so cold?
They'll hurt you, and desert you
And take your soul if you let them
Oh, but don't you let them

Chorus

2 What is the main message of the song? Tick the correct box.

a) There are a lot of bad people in the world. ☐
b) I'm your friend and you can rely on me. ☐
c) Never forget to call your friends. ☐

3 Find words in the song that rhyme with these words:

a) night ___________
b) fall ___________
c) cloud ___________
d) hurt ___________

4 Find words in the song that have a similar meaning to these words:

a) depressed ___________
b) having problems ___________
c) make bright ___________
d) autumn ___________
e) leave someone ___________

3–4

Song: Celebrate The Future

1 Read the song and complete it using the words in the box. One word is used twice. Listen and check.

celebration hand history make share
tomorrow true world

The future's coming
You got to catch it if you can
The magic's unfolding
When you can hold it in your (a) __________
We can touch tomorrow today
To (b) __________ some memories that never fade away
Put your hands on the future
There are dreams together around the (c) __________
With the voice from every country
Face from every land
We'll celebrate the future hand in hand
We'll celebrate the future hand in hand

The magic of (d) __________
Lives inside of you
Join the (e) __________
It's a fairy tale come (f) __________
Harmony
It's harmony
All of us together making (g) __________
Put your hands on the future
(h) __________ our dreams together around the (i) __________
With the voice from every country
Face from every land
We'll celebrate the future hand in hand
We'll celebrate the future hand in hand
We'll celebrate the future hand in hand

2 Tick the sentence that best describes the way the songwriter is feeling.

a) He/she is pessimistic about the future. ☐
b) He/she believes that it is important to make history. ☐
c) He/she believes it's important to make the future together. ☐

3 Find words in the song that have a similar meaning to these words:

a) develop __________
b) disappear gradually __________
c) a story for children __________
d) a situation in which people live and work well with other people __________

4 Complete these phrases from the song using the verbs in the box.

put make join hold catch

a) __________ something in your hands
b) __________ your hands on something
c) __________ it if you can
d) __________ the celebration
e) __________ history

5–6 Song: Brown-eyed Girl

1 Read the song and complete it using the words in the box. One word is used twice. Listen and check.

game grown hearts own radio rain used

Hey, where did we go
Days when the (a) __________ came?
Down in the hollow
Playing a new (b) __________
Laughing and a-running, hey, hey
Skipping and a-jumping
In the misty morning fog
With our (c) __________ a-thumping
And you, my brown-eyed girl,
You, my brown-eyed girl

Whatever happened to Tuesday and so slow
Going down the old mine
With a transistor (d) __________
Standing in the sunlight, laughing
Hiding behind the rainbow's wall
Slipping and a-sliding
All along the waterfall
With you, my brown-eyed girl
You, my brown-eyed girl

Do you remember when we (e) __________ to sing?
Sha la la la la la la la la la dee da, just like that
Sha la la la la la la la la la dee da, la dee da

So hard to find my way
Now that I'm all on my (f) __________
I saw you just the other day
My, how you have (g) __________
Cast my memory back there, Lord
Sometimes I'm overcome thinking about
Laughing and a-running, hey, hey
Behind the stadium
With you, my brown-eyed girl,
You, my brown-eyed girl

Do you remember when we (h) __________ to sing?
Sha la la la la la la la la la dee da, just like that

2 Listen to the song again and choose the correct words.

a) They used to laugh and run in the misty morning **fog** / **rain**.
b) On Tuesdays they used to take a radio to the old **park** / **mine**.
c) They used to slip and slide along the **river** / **waterfall**.
d) They used to laugh and run behind the **stadium** / **station**.

3 Tick the correct box.

a) The song is about the past. ☐
b) The song is about the present. ☐
c) The song is about the future. ☐

4 Find words in the song that have the following meanings:

a) a small area in the ground that is lower than the ground around it __________
b) when your heart is beating very fast __________
c) a curved line of colours in the sky __________
d) emotional __________

7–8 Song: I Will Survive

1 Read the song and complete it using the words in the box. Listen and check.

sad	afraid	free	new	high	broken
stupid	strong	sorry	welcome	alive	

First I was (a) ____________
I was petrified
Kept thinking I could never live
Without you by my side
But I spent so many nights
Thinking how you did me wrong
And I grew (b) ____________
And I learned how to get along
And so you're back
From outer space!
I just walked in to find you here
With that (c) ____________ look upon your face
I should have changed that (d) ____________ lock
I should have made you leave your key
If I'd known for just one second
You'd be back to bother me

Chorus:
Go on now, go!
Walk out the door!
Just turn around now
'Cause you're not (e) ____________ anymore
Weren't you the one
Who tried to hurt me with goodbye?
Did you think I'd crumble?
Did you think I'd lay down and die?
Oh no, not I!
I will survive
Oh, as long as I know how to love
I know I'll stay (f) ____________
I've got all my life to live
I've got all my love to give
And I'll survive
I will survive
Hey, hey

It took all the strength I had
Not to fall apart
Kept trying hard to mend
The pieces of my (g) ____________ heart
And I spent oh so many nights
Just feeling (h) ____________ for myself
I used to cry
But now I hold my head up (i) ____________
And you see me
Somebody (j) ____________
I'm not that chained up little person
Still in love with you
And so you felt like dropping in
And you expect me to be (k) ____________
Now I'm saving all my loving
For someone who's loving me

Chorus (twice)

2 How would you describe the feelings of the singer? Tick the correct box.

a) Sad and depressed ☐
b) Angry and determined ☐
c) Sorry and apologetic ☐

3 Find words in the song that rhyme with these words:

a) wrong ____________
b) space ____________
c) door ____________
d) goodbye ____________
e) apart ____________

4 Complete the phrases from the text using the verbs in the box.

hold	mend	change	do	learn

a) ____________ someone wrong
b) ____________ a broken heart
c) ____________ your head up high
d) ____________ how to get along
e) ____________ a lock

5 Write down the titles of three other songs you know that tell a story or have strong emotions or feelings.

____
____
____
____

WORKBOOK
Answers

UNIT 1 LESSON 1

1
1 lives, doesn't 2 speaks, doesn't
3 works 4 go, play 6 wants

2
1 *Is Rob reading anything at the moment? No, he isn't.*
2 *Is he feeling excited? Yes, he is.*
3 *Is he wearing jeans? Yes, he is.*
4 *Are Rob's friends waiting for him? No, they aren't.*
5 *Is Rob looking forward to the holidays? Yes, he is.*
6 *Is he looking for a girlfriend? No, he isn't.*

3
1 are/'re 2 is/'s 3 are staying/'re staying
4 are going/'re going 5 is/'s 6 has
7 wants 8 is working/'s working
9 am writing/'m writing
10 am eating/'m eating 11 love

4
1 *do (you usually) do*
2 *do (you) watch*
3 *are (you) sitting*
4 *do (you usually) talk*
5 *are (you) looking*

5
1 *is coming/'s coming*
2 *am helping/'m helping*
3 *am meeting/'m meeting*
4 *are playing/'re playing*
5 *am having/'m having*
6 *are watching/'re watching*

6
1 every 24 hours 2 eight times a month
3 twice a month 4 three times a year
5 52 times a year 6 12 times a year

7

T	R	A	I	N	E	R	S	M
Z	B	F	G	I	D	S	C	H
B	R	L	C	H	N	K	M	O
O	F	E	Y	S	D	I	O	O
O	I	E	S	H	I	R	T	D
T	T	C	U	W	E	T	O	I
S	J	E	A	N	S	L	P	E

8
1 street crime 2 sixth form college
3 science fiction 4 girlfriend 5 half term
6 part-time 7 shoe shop 8 school trip

9
1 ✓ *2* ✓ *3* ✓ *4* ✓ *5* ✓ *6* ✗
7 ✓ *8* ✓

UNIT 1 LESSON 2

1
1 F Sara and Joni are on holiday in Newquay.
2 T 3 F Joni didn't go to the cinema.
4 F Sara didn't see Joni's mother. 5 T

2
1 weren't, were 2 Was, was 3 weren't
4 were 5 was, wasn't 6 weren't, were
7 Was, wasn't

3
1 *Did Joni go on holiday in June?*
No, she didn't. She went on holiday in July.
2 *Did Joni's mum apologise for writing?*
No, she didn't. She apologised for phoning.
3 *Did Joni want to stay in Newquay?*
No, she didn't. She wanted to go home.
4 *Did Joni meet her friends in a disco?*
No, she didn't. She met them in a club.
5 *Did Joni nearly cry when she heard her father's voice?*
No, she didn't. She nearly cried when she heard her mother's voice.
6 *Did Joni fall asleep at the party?*
No, she didn't. She fell asleep on the beach.
7 *Did Joni have a picnic with Sara?*
No, she didn't. She had a picnic with some friends.
8 *Did Joni go for a swim in the pool?*
No, she didn't. She went for a swim in the sea.

4
1 *Did you make a new friend?*
2 *Did you phone someone?*
3 *Did you spend time with your friends?*
4 *Did you go for a swim?*
5 *Did you have a picnic?*
6 *Did you help your parents?*

5
1 scared 2 bored 3 excited 4 cheerful
5 pleased 6 embarrassed 7 lonely
8 miserable

6
1 fall asleep 2 feel angry 3 go for a swim
4 have a picnic 5 last all night
6 miss someone 7 say hello

7
1 spend time 2 have a good time
3 make new friends
4 mean something to someone
5 sound depressed 6 turn round

8
1 *place, fantastic, excited*
2 *lonely, someone, friendship*
3 *everything, together, phone*
4 *harbour, pleased, miserable*
5 *embarrassed, missed, depressed*
6 *right, enough, night*

9
*a**sleep** **cheer**ful de**pressed***
*em**bar**rassed ex**ci**ted fan**tas**tic*
***friend**ship **mi**serable **surf**ing to**ge**ther*
***yes**terday*

UNIT 1 LESSON 3

1
1 were surfing 2 were hoping
3 weren't thinking 4 was waiting 5 was losing
6 was saying 7 wasn't trying
8 was answering

2
What was Anna doing when the balloon landed? She was reading a newspaper.
What were Paul and Sue doing when the balloon landed? They were playing football.
What was Sam doing when the balloon landed? He was skateboarding.
What was Bill doing when the balloon landed? He was sunbathing.
What was Jane doing when the balloon landed? She was eating an ice cream.
When the balloon landed, Anna took a photo.
When the balloon landed, Paul waved.
When the balloon landed, Sam fell off (the skateboard).
When the balloon landed, Bill didn't notice.
When the balloon landed, Jane phoned a friend.

3
1 *Tiffany was dancing when Jake took a photo.*
2 *Jake was watching football on TV when Tiffany phoned him.*
3 *They were sitting in the park when it started to rain.*
4 *Tiffany was reading when Jake brought her some flowers.*
5 *Jake was painting a picture when Tiffany came to see him.*
6 *Tiffany was talking to her friends when Jake fell asleep.*

4
1 on 2 away 3 back 4 over 5 out

5

					↓				
					1 S	W	I	M	
				2 S	U	R	F		
					3 R	I	V	E	R
					4 F	I	S	H	
					5 B	O	A	T	
			6 P	O	O	L			
		7 S	P	L	A	S	H		
	8 C	L	E	A	R				
9 C	R	O	C	O	D	I	L	E	

6
1 bright, white
2 here, clear
3 four, jaw
4 thought, caught
5 water, daughter
6 morning, warning
7 seem, scream
8 splash, trash

UNIT 1 LESSON 4

1
1 separate 2 black 3 took 4 waited 5 walked 6 arrived 7 carried 8 started 9 light 10 hungry 11 voted 12 won 13 became 14 holiday

2
1 T
2 F, Nearly 16 million black people voted in the 1994 election.
3 F, 4 million white people voted in the 1994 election.
4 F, The election lasted 3 days.
5 F, Old and disabled people could go as well.
6 T

3

1 M	I	2 N	I	S	T	E	R			3 O
I		E						4 H	E	R
S		5 V	6 O	7 I	C	8 E				G
9 E	V	E	N	T		X				A
R		R				A		10 J		N
A			11 S	12 E	E	M		E		I
13 B	I	T		V			14 J	A	W	S
L				E				N		E
15 E	M	B	A	R	R	A	S	S	E	D

UNIT 1

Inspiration EXTRA!

Revision

Lesson 1
1 ~~are meeting~~ – meet
2 ~~is talking~~ – talks
3 ~~wears~~ – is wearing
4 correct
5 ~~goes~~ – go
6 ~~reads~~ – is reading
7 ~~think~~ – thinks

Lesson 2
1 Did Joni go for a swim in the morning? No, she didn't. She went for a swim in the afternoon.
2 Was Newquay a boring place? No, it wasn't. It was a great place.
3 Did Joni walk around the park? No, she didn't. She walked around the harbour.
4 Did Sara write to her mother? No, she didn't. She wrote to her best friend.
5 Did Joni's mother come to see her? No, she didn't. She phoned her.
6 Were Sara's friends friendly? No, they weren't. They were posh.

Lesson 3
1 Bethany was surfing with her friend Alana when the shark attacked.
2 Shane was helping his father when he decided to go for a swim.
3 Shane was swimming in the river when he heard a splash behind him.
4 Shane was answering his father when the crocodile took his arm.
5 Shane's father was waiting for him when he ran back to the garden.

Lesson 4
Suggested answers
1 Where did Rosa work?
2 Where did Rosa sit in the bus?
3 What did the bus driver tell Rosa?
4 What did the others do?
5 Why didn't Rosa give up her seat?
6 What happened as a result of Rosa's arrest?

Spelling
1 attack 2 boots 3 cheerful 4 college 5 depressed 6 embarrassed 7 feeling 8 freedom 9 happy

Extension

Lesson 1
1 Are you wearing jeans today? Yes, I am./No, I'm not.
2 Do you usually wear jeans to school? Yes, I do./No, I don't.
3 Do you go to the cinema every week?
4 Do you worry about exams?
5 Are you looking forward to the weekend?
6 What kind of music do you listen to?
7 What do you want to do today after school?

Lesson 2
1 What time did you get up? I got up at seven o'clock.
2 What did you have for breakfast?
3 What did you do after breakfast?
4 Who did you talk to in the morning?
5 When did you have lunch?
6 What did you do in the evening?

Lessons 3 and 4
Students' own answers

Spelling
1 money 2 activity 3 lonely 4 journey 5 movie 6 biology 7 monkey 8 suddenly 9 university 10 hockey

CULTURE
Women in the world

1
1 Miriam González Durántez
2 Michelle Obama 3 Carla Bruni
4 Samantha Cameron
5 Carla Bruni 6 Sarah Brown
7 Julia Gillard 8 journalists
9 Cherie Blair
10 (the French President) Nicolas Sarkozy

2
1c 2f 3a 4g 5d 6b 7e

3
1 journalist 2 criticise 3 soap opera 4 entertainment 5 Appearance 6 sleeveless 7 constant 8 put up with 9 press 10 inspire

UNIT 2 LESSON 1

1
1A 2C 3B

2
1T
2F, Hiccup didn't want to kill the dragon he caught.
3F They succeed in stopping the fighting.
4T 5T
6F The director is good at keeping viewers' attention.

3
1 thinking 2 playing 3 becoming 4 watching 5 crying 6 talking

4
1 so does 2 nor am 3 so can 4 so am 5 so are 6 nor does

5
1 love going to 2 So do I.
3 don't mind swimming
4 can't stand swimming 5 love watching
6 So do I. 7 don't mind playing 8 Nor do I.
9 can't stand ironing 10 Nor can I.
11 don't mind buying 12 love buying clothes.

6
1 about 2 of 3 in 4 on 5 of 6 for 7 in, with 8 at

7

A	W	F	U	L	T	B	A	D	B	C	U	T
E	L	U	P	T	A	S	C	A	R	Y	D	H
X	I	N	T	E	R	E	S	T	I	N	G	R
C	H	N	M	R	D	O	V	C	L	P	O	I
I	A	Y	Q	R	P	S	I	L	L	Y	O	L
T	E	M	R	I	D	I	C	N	I	G	D	L
I	K	N	T	B	I	B	S	R	N	N	H	I
N	F	G	I	L	B	O	R	I	N	G	C	N
G	E	X	C	E	L	L	E	N	T	Y	W	G

8

▪■	■▪
attack	horror
avoid	kidnap
enjoy	pirate
protect	planet
remove	rescue
succeed	drama

9
1✓ 2✓ 3✗ 4✗ 5✗ 6✓ 7✗ 8✓

UNIT 2 LESSON 2

1
1 Lorna 2 Nick 3 Nick 4 Nick 5 Lorna 6 Lorna

2
1 He refuses to do ballet.
2 She wants to learn ballet.
3 She promises to help everyone to sing better.
4 He offers to teach the contestants breakdancing.
5 He asks everyone to obey the rules.
6 Nick agrees (to try) to dance.

3

1 to become 2 you to listen 3 you to sing 4 to work 5 it to be 6 to know 7 to do 8 to try 9 you to develop 10 to work 11 to win 12 me to explain

4

1 writing 2 to give up 3 to tell 4 listening 5 dancing 6 to be 7 forgetting 8 to try

5

1 at 2 on 3 in 4 like 5 for 6 by 7 with 8 of

6

		1 V	O	I	C	E		
				2 C	O	A	C	H
	3 T	A	L	E	N	T		
4 R	E	A	L	I	T	Y		
	5 S	U	C	C	E	S	S	
		6 S	A	L	S	A		
7 B	A	L	L	E	T			
				8 J	A	Z	Z	
	9 P	A	R	T	N	E	R	
		10 P	O	E	T			

7

1G 2S 3O 4O 5G 6S 7O 8G 9G 10S

8

1 ballroom 2 breakdancing 3 songwriting 4 dance routine 5 thank-you letter 6 talent show

9

*con**test**ant, 3*	*re**al**ity, 4*
*de**vel**op, 3*	***song**writing, 3*
*ex**per**iment, 4*	***hope**ful, 2*
*im**por**tant, 3*	*question**naire**, 3*

UNIT 2 LESSON 3

1

1 The editor (does). 2 The designer gets it.
3 The designer lays out the text on the pages.
4 They choose photographs.
5 They are put together to make a book.

2

Past participle

bought	*I*	*produced*	*R*
drunk	*I*	*published*	*R*
found	*I*	*sold*	*I*
grown	*I*	*taken*	*I*
invited	*R*	*taught*	*I*
left	*I*	*visited*	*R*
made	*I*		

3

1 *Where is coffee grown? It's grown in Kenya.*
2 *Where are French, German and Italian spoken?*
They're spoken in Switzerland.
3 *Where is pasta eaten?*
It's eaten in Italy.
4 *Where are kimonos worn?*
They're worn in Japan.
5 *Where is champagne made?*
It's made in France.
6 *Where are penguins found?*
They're found in Antarctica.

4

1 *Newspaper stories are written by reporters.*
2 *Singing is taught by a voice coach.*
3 *This music is performed by a school band.*
4 *Pictures are drawn by artists.*
5 *Movies are made by film directors.*
6 *Books are produced by publishers.*

5

1 *His concerts are arranged for him.*
2 *His clothes are chosen for him.*
3 *His bags are carried for him.*
4 *His flights are booked for him.*
5 *His food is bought for him.*
6 *His flat is cleaned for him.*
7 *His hotel bills are paid for him.*
8 *His life is planned for him.*

6

1 grows 2 stood 3 turn 4 give 5 set 6 look

7

1 globe 2 borrow 3 public 4 character 5 unique 6 increasing

8

***char**acter, 3*	***li**brary, 3*
***com**ment, 2*	***pa**perback, 3*
*enthusi**as**tic, 5*	***re**gister, 3*
*in**creas**ing, 3*	*u**nique**, 2*
*invi**ta**tion, 4*	***vir**tual, 2*

9

1 ✗ *2* ✓ *3* ✓ *4* ✓ *5* ✓ *6* ✗

UNIT 2 LESSON 4

1

1c 2f 3a 4g 5d 6b 7e

3

1 E	X	2 C	E	3 L	L	4 E	N	5 T	
N		O		O		X		6 A	T
7 O		8 M	U	S	I	C	A	L	
R		E		T		I		E	
9 M	A	D	E		10 S	T	A	N	11 D
O		Y		12 B	E	E		13 T	O
14 U	15 S		16 F		17 A	D	18 D		W
19 S	E	C	R	E	T		20 O	W	N
	E		E			21 I	N		
22 I	N	T	E	R	E	S	T	E	D

Pronunciation

1 background 2 definitely 3 expression 4 realistic 5 war 6 painful 7 image 8 favourite

UNIT 2

Inspiration EXTRA!

Revision

Lesson 1

1 learning 2 swimming 3 flying 4 standing 5 going 6 forgetting 7 making 8 getting

Lesson 2

He promises to tell the truth. He wants to learn to windsurf and he would like to teach his friends to laugh at his jokes. He pretends to like olives, but he doesn't really like them. He refuses to eat cucumber. His parents ask him to wash the car and he doesn't really enjoy it. He can just manage to play the guitar but he would like to do better. He hopes to travel when he leaves school.

Lesson 3

1 is grown 2 are picked 3 are taken 4 are laid 5 are passed 6 is laid 7 are dried 8 is put 9 is sold

Lesson 4

1 *A documentary is a film which describes real people and events.*
2 *Foreground is the part of a picture which is at the front.*
3 *A coach is a person who teaches you a skill.*
4 *A contestant is someone who takes part in a competition.*
5 *A library is a place which has books you can read or borrow.*
6 *A paperback is a book which doesn't have a hard cover.*
7 *A pirate is a person who steals things from ships at sea.*
8 *Rice is a grain which is usually grown in water.*

Spelling

*1 balle**t** 2 bou**gh**t 3 fi**gh**t 4 fr**i**end 5 g**u**ard 6 han**d**kerchief 7 i**s**land 8 throu**gh***

Extension

Lessons 1 and 2

Students' own answers.

Lesson 3

1 see 2 are filmed 3 are turned 4 are sent 5 sends 6 are put 7 (are) carried 8 turn 9 become

Lesson 4

Students' own answers.

Spelling

1 bored 2 by/buy 3 right 4 our 5 know 6 peace 7 sea 8 sun

REVIEW UNITS 1–2

1

1D 2C 3B 4A 5C 6B 7B 8A 9D 10C 11A 12B 13B 14C 15C

2

1 discussion 2 worried 3 happiness 4 politician 5 realistic 6 successfully

3

1 *I'm really looking forward to seeing my parents again.*
2 *She apologised for being angry.*
3 *It all went wrong from the beginning.*
4 *She was waiting for the bus when she saw Tina.*
5 *Most people are good at surfing.*
6 *More and more books are being sold by online booksellers.*

4

1 beach 2 excited 3 cheerful 4 shout 5 paperback 6 coach 7 stage 8 boring

Learner Independence

1

Students' own answers

2

1 *I can't wait.*
2 *I couldn't believe it.*
3 *Everything went wrong.*
4 *I'll never forget the first time I …*
5 *Why not try it?*
6 *Do you promise to tell the truth?*
7 *You can't help laughing.*
8 *It reminds me of …*

UNIT 3 LESSON 1

1

1 can't 2 must 3 can't 4 can't 5 must 6 must 7 can't 8 can't 9 must 10 must

2

1 must 2 must 3 can't, must 4 can't, must 5 must

3

1 can't 2 must 3 could/might/may 4 can't 5 could/might/may 6 could/might 7 could/might/may 8 can't 9 could/might/may

4

1 star 2 solar system 3 surface 4 Gravity 5 orbit 6 atmosphere 7 Astronomers 8 light year

5

1 NEPTUNE
2 LIFE
3 GALAXY
4 UNIVERSE
5 TELESCOPE
6 ROBOT
(2 down: PLANET)

6

1 *rocky, rocket, Mercury*
2 *galaxy, gravity, regions*
3 *liquid, quarter, question*
4 *surface, universe, orbit*
5 *telescope, solar system, star*
6 *scientists, according, clouds*

7

1 ✗ 2 ✗ 3 ✓ 4 ✓ 5 ✓ 6 ✗

UNIT 3 LESSON 2

1

1T 2T 3F 4F 5T 6F 7F 8F

2

1 mustn't 2 don't have to 3 mustn't 4 don't have to 5 mustn't 6 don't have to 7 mustn't 8 don't have to

3

1 *In Denver, Colorado, your neighbour mustn't borrow your vacuum cleaner.*
2 *You can't go fishing in your pyjamas in Chicago.*
3 *In Ohio pets have to have lights on their tails at night.*
4 *You can't carry an ice cream in your pocket in Lexington, Kentucky.*
5 *You mustn't wash two babies in the same bath at the same time in California.*
6 *You can't walk backwards after dark in Devon, Connecticut.*
7 *In Utah you mustn't go fishing on a horse.*
8 *Men have to wear a matching jacket and trousers in Carmel, New York State.*

4

1 ourselves 2 herself 3 himself 4 themselves 5 myself 6 yourself 7 myself 8 itself

5

1 *stay awake*
2 *illegal*
3 *forbidden*
4 *carefully*
5 *buy*
6 *part-time*

6

1 *break a law*
2 *come up with an idea*
3 *keep a secret*
4 *leave school*
5 *get married*
6 *cross the road*
7 *vote in an election*
8 *spend time*

7

1 *lottery ticket*
2 *part-time job*
3 *school-leaving age*
4 *summer holiday*
5 *town square*
6 *TV licence*

8

■▪▪	▪■▪
carefully	*arrested*
continent	*election*
holiday	*forbidden*
lottery	*illegal*
motorbike	*permission*
possible	*reflexive*

UNIT 3 LESSON 3

1

1B 2G 3B 4B 5B 6G 7G 8B

2

1 *You ought to choose what to leave behind. You shouldn't take so many clothes with you.*
2 *You ought to queue up like everyone else. You shouldn't push in front of people.*
3 *You ought to calm down and take it easy. You shouldn't lose your temper.*
4 *You ought to concentrate on what you're doing. You shouldn't try to do two things at the same time.*
5 *You ought to talk to new students at your school. You shouldn't ignore students who don't know anyone.*
6 *You ought to stay awake at school. You shouldn't fall asleep in class.*

3

1 *You ought to tell the teacher if other students bully you.*
2 *We had better hurry or we'll be late.*
3 *You should keep a friend's secret.*
4 *You shouldn't cheat in exams.*
5 *You had better not forget your dictionary today.*

4

1 *difficult to hear*
2 *rude to point*
3 *good to learn*
4 *wrong to bully*
5 *normal to feel*
6 *possible to forget*

5

1 *keep a secret*
2 *break a promise*
3 *take it easy*
4 *feel nervous*
5 *have fun*
6 *laugh at someone*
7 *say no*
8 *tell lies*

6

1 CHEAT
2 COPY
3 NORMAL
4 SECRET
5 LIE
6 PANIC
7 TAKE
8 FAIR
9 BALANCED
10 CHAT
11 UPSET
(1 down: CONCENTRATE)

7

1 lie 2 calm 3 write 4 sit 5 Slow 6 turn

8

con**cen**trate em**bar**rassed ig**nore** **pan**ic
promise re**vi**sion up**set**

UNIT 3 LESSON 4

1

1 cost 2 die 3 richer 4 poorest 5 borrowed 6 pay 7 weapon 8 school 9 finish 10 much 11 themselves 12 fair 13 sell 14 dirty

2

Students' own answers

3

1 E	L	E	2 C	T	R	3 I	C	4 I	5 T	Y
D			H			D		6 N	O	
7 U	P	S	E	T		E		8 T	O	9 P
C			A		10 H	A	V	E		U
11 A	12 S		T					13 N	O	R
14 T	O		15 S	16 T	U	17 P	I	D		P
18 I	N			R		A			19 S	O
O		20 W		Y		R			21 A	S
22 N	E	E	D			23 T	R	A	D	E

UNIT 3

Inspiration EXTRA!

Revision

Lesson 1

1 It can't be a car. It must be a bus.
2 It can't be tea. It must be milk.
3 It can't be a cap. It must be a helmet.
4 It can't be Earth. It must be Venus.
5 It can't be a mirror. It must be a telescope.
6 It can't be a paperback. It must be an advertisement.
7 It can't be a metre. It must be a mile.
8 It can't be a wolf. It must be a dog.

Lesson 2

1 You must be 17 to drive a car.
2 You can't get married until you're 16.
3 You must have your parents' permission to join the army./You must be 17 to join the army.
4 You can't vote in an election if you're under 18.
5 You must be 16 to live by yourself.
6 You can't buy a pet if you're under 12.
7 You must be 16 to leave school.

Lesson 3

1 You should ignore them. You shouldn't show them that you are upset.
2 He shouldn't stay in bed so long. He should get up earlier.
3 They should be more polite. They shouldn't be rude to each other.
4 She should calm down. She shouldn't panic.

Lesson 4

1 What percentage of the people in the world live on less than $10 a day?
2 How many people live without electricity?
3 How many people don't have proper toilets?
4 How many children die each day because of poverty?

Spelling

1 arrest 2 bully 3 difference 4 forbidden 5 mood 6 illegal 7 lottery 8 married 9 mirror 10 allowed

Extension

Lessons 1–4

Students' own answers

Spelling

1 distance 2 secret 3 concentrate 4 difference 5 electricity 6 sensible 7 nicely 8 surface 9 stupid 10 responsible 11 independence 12 purpose

CULTURE

Good reads

Reading

1B 2A 3C
1b 2c 3a

UNIT 4 LESSON 1

1

1T 2F 3F 4T 5F 6F

2

1 reading a newspaper 2 playing football 3 sunbathing 4 skateboarding 5 eating an ice cream 6 waving 7 saying hello 8 taking a photo 9 phoning a friend 10 sitting on the ground

3

1 ringing 2 playing 3 describing 4 touching 5 sneezing 6 smiling 7 holding 8 cooking 9 getting 10 telling

4

1 coming 2 blowing 3 burning 4 cheering 5 melting 6 getting 7 crying 8 taking off

5

1 bruise, psychic, investigator
2 terror, record, scared
3 walking, knock, quickly
4 haunted, brought, furniture
5 float, daughter, hairbrush
6 different, strange, frightened

6

				1 L	A	U	G	H	
			2 R	I	N	G			
	3 W	H	I	S	P	E	R		
4 S	H	O	U	T					
		5 C	H	E	E	R			
		6 B	A	N	G				
				7 S	C	R	E	A	M

7

1 float, boat
2 fright, light
3 cheer, hear
4 bruise, shoes
5 speak, week
6 dare, wear
7 hold, cold
8 sneeze, knees

UNIT 4 LESSON 2

1

1 will fail 2 will pass 3 lazy 4 worried 5 yet

2

1 Ted's mother is afraid that he'll leave home.
2 Ted's father is worried that he won't pass his exams.
3 Ted's brother and sister think he'll be a famous rock star.
4 Ted's best friend is sure he'll be all right.
5 Ted's teachers expect he'll go to university.
6 Ted knows he'll pass his exams easily.

3

1 I'll do all I can to help.
2 I won't argue with you all the time.
3 I'll lend you my iPod®.
4 I'll cook you your favourite meal.
5 I won't ring you every five minutes.
6 I'll test you on your work.
7 I'll give you some practice tests.
8 I won't play loud music.

4

1 She's going to play tennis.
2 They're going to break the law.
3 They're going to dance all night.
4 He's going to take a break.
5 They're not going to answer the phone.

5

1 are/'re going to 2 won't 3 are/'re going to 4 won't 5 are/'re going to 6 will 7 am/'m going to 8 am/'m going to 9 will/'ll

6

1 cross your fingers 2 go to sleep 3 look like 4 keep in touch 5 read a horoscope 6 touch wood

7

1 find 2 Try 3 go 4 takes/took 5 Look 6 read

8

1 superstitious 2 horoscope 3 ladder 4 take no notice 5 haunted 6 accidentally

9

acci**den**tally **haun**ted **ho**roscope
ladder **no**tice **pain**ter super**nat**ural
super**sti**tious

UNIT 4 LESSON 3

1

1 *I'll tell the teacher.*
2 *I won't pay for your driving lessons.*
3 *we won't have enough money for the bus home.*
4 *I'll win a lot of money.*
5 *will/'ll be an accident.*
6 *you'll get a big surprise.*
7 *I'll give you some.*

2

1f 2h 3e 4g 5b 6a 7d 8c

3

1 *What will you do if it rains? We'll have the picnic indoors.*
2 *What will you say if she asks what happened? I'll tell the truth.*
3 *How will you get home if school finishes early? Anna'll give me a lift.*
4 *Who will you tell if you pass your driving test? I'll tell everyone.*
5 *What will you buy if your parents give you some money? I'll get a new pair of shoes.*
6 *Who will you ask if you need help? I'll ask my brother.*

4

C	O	N	N	E	C	T	I	O	N	S
E	A	W	Y	V	A	P	B	E	E	M
R	C	L	W	E	F	O	R	G	E	T
E	K	I	I	S	S	E	E	F	S	I
C	N	N	C	T	T	A	M	O	W	N
A	O	K	A	R	E	P	E	A	T	E
L	P	L	E	A	N	L	M	R	I	R
L	M	E	M	O	R	A	B	L	E	S
X	B	A	U	L	Y	P	E	R	L	S
C	O	N	C	E	N	T	R	A	T	E

1 remember 2 Repeat 3 forget 4 recall, connections 5 link 6 memorable 7 concentrate

5

■ ▪ ▪	▪ ■ ▪
calendar	*attention*
concentrate	*connection*
easier	*direction*
memorable	*remember*
memory	*together*
organise	
similar	

UNIT 4 LESSON 4

1

1d 2e 3a 4h 5c 6b 7f 8g

2

A1 B7 C3 D6 E4 F2 G5

3

1 *was very surprised and tried to pull away from him*
2 *the two men dancing together*
3 *in their faces*
4 *three cooks coming towards him with big kitchen knives in their hands*
5 *at the cooks*
6 *one of the cooks*
7 *Jo tried to move away and slipped on the wet floor.*
8 *a man hit him on the head and he fell to the ground, unconscious.*

4

(1) M	E	M	(2) O	R	I	(3) E	S			(4) U
E			N			Y		(5) L		N
(6) M	A	K	E		(7) R	E	C	A	L	L
O				(8) M		S		D		U
(9) R	E	(10) P	E	A	T			D		C
A		O		R			(11) W	E	E	K
(12) B	R	U	I	S	(13) E		(14) O	R		Y
L		R			A		R			
(15) E	A	S	I	E	R		(16) D	E	A	D

Learner Independence

1e 2c 3d 4b 5a

UNIT 4

Inspiration EXTRA!

Revision

Lesson 1

Suggested answers

1 *I could see a train leaving.*
2 *I could hear the fans cheering/shouting/ whistling.*
3 *I could see the birds flying.*
4 *I could feel the wind blowing.*
5 *I could smell the soup boiling/the cake burning.*
6 *I could hear people talking.*

Lesson 2

1 won't rain 2 'll have a party 3 'll like it 4 'll finish in time 5 'll see her again 6 won't happen again today 7 won't forget 8 won't be angry

Lesson 3

1e 2c 3b 4d 5a 6f

Lesson 4

1e 2b 3h 4g 5f 6c 7a 8d

Spelling

1 accidentally 2 confess 3 conclusion 4 forecast 5 honeymoon 6 horoscope 7 impatiently 8 ladder 9 notice 10 personalise 11 recall 12 supernatural 13 superstitious 14 terror 15 verdict 16 worried

Extension

Lesson 1–4

Students' own answers

Spelling

1 change 2 joke 3 cottage 4 original 5 June 6 jacket 7 January 8 jeans 9 job 10 charge 11 journey 12 gym 13 July 14 just

REVIEW UNITS 3–4

1

1A 2A 3C 4A 5B 6A 7C 8A

2

1 sensible 2 superstitious 3 dramatic 4 revision 5 cheerful 6 difference 7 electricity 8 memorable

3

1 *Your watch must be wrong.*
2 *This animal can't be a crocodile.*
3 *You don't have to book tickets for the film.*
4 *Children in the UK can't buy lottery tickets.*
5 *If you turn down the music, it will be easier to concentrate.*
6 *Shall I do the washing up?*
7 *You'd better phone to say you'll be late.*
8 *I'll email you every day.*

4

1 orbit 2 promise 3 bully 4 confident 5 energy 6 play 7 forget

Learner Independence

1

Students' own answers

2

1 *In other words …*
2 *What should I do?*
3 *I'm getting fed up with it.*
4 *I can't take it any more.*
5 *It makes no difference.*
6 *I'll keep my fingers crossed.*
7 *Have a safe journey.*
8 *You're not the only one!*

UNIT 5 LESSON 1

1

1 has become 2 have reached 3 have given up 4 has replaced 5 has climbed 6 has been 7 has, returned 8 has gone back 9 has, started

2

1 *They've just had an accident.*
2 *He's just scored a goal.*
3 *She's just missed the train.*
4 *He's just broken a window.*
5 *She's just won a prize.*
6 *They've just got married.*

3

1 *She's already invited all her friends.*
2 *She hasn't prepared the food yet.*
3 *She hasn't blown up the balloons yet.*
4 *She's already downloaded music onto her MP3 player.*
5 *She hasn't changed into new clothes yet.*
6 *She's moved the furniture already./She's already moved the furniture.*
7 *She hasn't put out plates and glasses yet.*
8 *She hasn't opened her presents yet.*

4

1 Have you chosen clothes to take? No, I haven't chosen them yet.
2 Have you bought some walking boots? Yes, I've already bought some.
3 Have you changed some money? No, I haven't changed any yet.
4 Have you booked a taxi to the airport? Yes, I've already booked one.
5 Have you looked at the map? Yes, I've already looked at it.
6 Have you found your passport? No, I haven't found it yet.

5

1S 2G 3S 4O 5G 6S 7O 8S

6

Go: camping, home, on holiday, red, skiing, to sleep, wrong
Have: an accident, fun, an idea, a look, a meal, a party, a picnic

7

/ɑː/ star	/ɔː/ wars
army	board
calm	law
charm	quarter
heart	toward
party	war
start	warm

UNIT 5 LESSON 2

1

1 They went camping yesterday.
2 They put it up in a field.
3 Holmes has woken Watson up because the tent has gone.
4 Watson can see millions and millions of stars.
5 Because someone has stolen their tent.

2

1 Have (you) ever wondered
2 has ever been 3 Have (you) ever imagined
4 've never wanted 5 Have (you) ever thought
6 've never heard 7 've never felt
8 've never enjoyed

3

1 Has Sophie ever been to Spain? Yes, she has. She went to Spain at half term.
2 Has Stella ever won a prize? Yes, she has. She won a prize last month.
3 Has Darren ever flown a plane? Yes, he has. He flew a plane two years ago.
4 Have Nick and Lorna ever performed their songs on TV? Yes, they have. They performed (their songs) on TV last night.
5 Has Anna ever played football? Yes, she has. She played (football) a week ago.
6 Have Emily and Alex ever tried salsa dancing? Yes, they have. They tried (salsa dancing) last weekend.

4

1 Have you ever flown a kite? No, I've never flown a kite/Yes, I have. I flew a kite last summer.
2 Have you ever rolled down a hill?
3 Have you ever climbed a mountain?
4 Have you ever done a parachute jump?
5 Have you ever driven a car?
6 Have you ever swum in a river or a lake?
7 Have you ever ridden a horse?

5

1 float 2 imagine 3 wonder 4 involves
5 roll 6 contain 7 steer 8 speed

6

1 beach ball 2 bungee jumping 3 ice hockey
4 kite surfing 5 motorbike 6 water-skiing

7

/k/	/tʃ/	/ʃ/
character	beach	champagne
psychic	challenge	machine
technique	change	parachute
Czech	cheer	

UNIT 5 LESSON 3

1

1 sent 2 since 3 crossed 4 for 5 broken
6 achieved 7 said 8 felt 9 Since 10 slept
11 for 12 been 13 told 14 landed
15 done 16 suffered 17 loved 18 since
19 saved 20 for

2

1F, Helen's trip was a non-stop round-the-world trip.
2T
3F, She felt thrilled; she was over the moon.
4F, She slept 30 minutes on average.
5F, It was difficult for her to describe how difficult it was.
6T

3

1 since 2 for 3 for 4 since 5 since 6 for
7 for 8 since 9 since 10 for 11 since
12 for 13 since 14 for 15 since 16 since

4

1 How long has Nicki known Tom? She's known him for two years.
2 How long have Lorna and Nick been at Star School? They've been at Star School since last month.
3 How long has Dan Deacon played in a rock band? He's played in a rock band since he left school.
4 How long have you had your new mobile? I've had it for ten days.
5 How long has Sophie lived in Liverpool? She's lived in Liverpool since she was 12.
6 How long has she wanted to be a doctor? She's wanted to be a doctor for a very long time.
7 How long have they been married? They've been married for six years.

5

1 The student apologized to the teacher **for** being late.
2 Why don't we go **for** a swim in the sea?
3 Did you get lots of presents **for** your birthday?
4 I went abroad **for** the first time when I was 13.
5 Usain Bolt is famous **for** winning Olympic® gold medals.
6 I'd like you to do this exercise **for** homework.
7 How much did you have to pay **for** your camera?
8 It's difficult **for** me to concentrate on my work.
9 Are you still waiting **for** the phone to ring?
10 I've looked everywhere **for** my glasses, but I can't find them.

6

1 world record 2 coursebook 3 drug test
4 gold medal 5 personal assistant
6 high school

7

1 done, won 2 sorry, lorry 3 gold, hold
4 head, said 5 case, race 6 start, heart
7 course, horse 8 year, steer 9 down, town

UNIT 5 LESSON 4

1

1 ever 2 so 3 since 4 ago 5 already
6 because 7 just 8 for 9 always
10 next 11 after 12 but 13 yet 14 never

2

We've just arrived in Alexandria. We got here by train. We've already been in Cairo and we've seen the Pyramids and the Sphinx. We've also sailed in a boat on the Nile. We've visited the Egyptian Museum and we've been shopping in the bazaars. We've ridden camels in the desert! We're going to return to Cairo and fly to Luxor. We're going to visit the temples of Luxor and Karnak. We haven't visited the Valley of the Kings and Queens yet and we haven't been scuba diving yet. But we're going to fly to the Red Sea and do that in four days. Then we're going to fly home.

3

1 W	O	N	D	2 E	R	E	3 D			4 C
O				V			5 R	I	C	H
6 R	A	7 P		E			E			A
L		L		R		8 M	A	9 P		M
10 D	E	E	P		11 C	A	M	E	U	P
		A		12 B	A	G				I
13 J	14 U	S	T		15 P	I	C	16 K		O
17 U	S	E		18 I		C		I		N
M			19 O	N			20 A	T		S
21 P	U	S	H		22 R	I	S	E	S	

UNIT 5

Inspiration EXTRA!

Revision

Lesson 1

1 *No – she's already seen it.*
2 *Yes – they haven't been there yet.*
3 *Yes – he hasn't sung his song on TV yet.*
4 *No – he has already read it.*
5 *No – they have already had lunch.*
6 *Yes – he hasn't downloaded it yet.*

Lesson 2

1 *Has Steve ever tried bungee jumping? No, he hasn't.*
2 *Has Lisa ever gone sailing? Yes, she has.*
3 *Have Joni and Sara ever played ice hockey? No, they haven't.*
4 *Has Lorna ever done aerobics? Yes, she has.*
5 *Has Rob ever won a race? No, he hasn't.*
6 *Has Ted ever ridden a motorbike? Yes, he has.*
7 *Has Julie ever skied down a mountain? No, she hasn't.*

Lesson 3

1 *How long have you been in the same class?*
2 *How long have you had English lessons?*
3 *How long have you had the same English teacher?*
4 *How long have you known your best friend?*
5 *How long have you slept in the same room at home?*

Lesson 4

1C 2G 3H 4D 5E

Spelling

1 accident 2 attitude 3 challenge 4 community 5 efficient 6 skiing 7 steer 8 strapped 9 suddenly 10 surround 11 travelling 12 uncontrollably

Extension

Lessons 1, 2 and 4

Students' own answers

Lesson 3

1 *He has won hundreds of medals* ***since*** *he was at school.*
2 *When* ***did*** *you* ***have*** *breakfast this morning?*
3 *I have wanted to be a doctor* ***for*** *over ten years.*
4 *How long* ***have*** *you* ***had*** *the jeans you're wearing?*
5 *We* ***have*** *lived in this house since 2001.*
6 *They* ***bought*** *a car yesterday.*
7 *My sister* ***has known*** *Lucy for five years.*
8 *How long* ***has*** *Mark had his car?*

Spelling

*1 enjoy**able** 2 horr**ible** 3 imposs**ible** 4 incred**ible** 5 invis**ible** 6 memor**able** 7 miser**able** 8 respons**ible** 9 sens**ible** 10 terr**ible** 11 uncomfort**able** 12 valu**able***

CULTURE

Tourism

1

1 problems 2 tourism 3 respect 4 fair 5 environment 6 groups 7 culture 8 wild 9 animals 10 share

2

1T 2F 3T 4F 5F 6F 7F

3

1c 2e 3d 4g 5b 6h 7i 8f 9a

4-6

Students' own answers.

UNIT 6 LESSON 1

1

1e 2c 3b 4a 5f 6d

2

1 *I'd never been there before.*
2 *He hadn't met her before.*
3 *She'd already seen it.*
4 *It'd already begun.*
5 *They'd eaten everything on the table*
6 *He'd forgotten his wallet.*
7 *She'd lost his address.*
8 *She'd left it on the bus.*

3

1 *Because she'd passed her driving test.*
2 *Because he hadn't heard the alarm clock.*
3 *Because he'd forgotten his keys.*
4 *Because she'd heard a good joke.*
5 *Because he'd failed his exam.*
6 *Because she'd already read it.*

4

1 workout 2 slide 3 blind 4 disabled 5 deaf 6 sign language

5

1 start a business 2 do exercises 3 recover your strength 4 make a sign 5 put on a glove 6 think of an idea

6

1 *successful, electronics, bicycle*
2 *inspiration, invention, simplify*
3 *advantage, realise, soldier*
4 *disabled, balance, language*
5 *exercise, fascinate, science*
6 *strength, translator, sign/sing*

7

1 swimming pool 2 computer screen 3 fast food 4 sign language 5 workout

8

▪■	■▪
appear	*business*
award	*metal*
design	*product*
explain	*soldier*
invent	*system*
translate	*workout*

UNIT 6 LESSON 2

1

1T 2T 3F 4F 5F

2

1 *She used to be a pilot.*
2 *He used to be a diver.*
3 *She used to be a soldier.*
4 *He used to be a painter.*
5 *She used to be an aerobics instructor.*
6 *He used to be a musician.*

3

1 *They didn't use to recycle plastic bottles, but they do now.*
2 *I used to walk to school, but I don't now.*
3 *People in the UK didn't use to recycle much rubbish, but they do now.*
4 *She used to drink coffee, but she doesn't now.*
5 *We used to play cards, but we don't now.*
6 *My shoes didn't use to wear out quickly, but they do now.*
7 *I didn't use to send emails, but I do now.*
8 *He didn't use to like salsa, but he does now.*
9 *She used to have long hair, but she doesn't now.*

4

1 *A bicycle tyre is made of rubber.*
2 *A book is made of paper.*
3 *A comb is made of plastic.*
4 *Gloves are made of wool.*
5 *Knives and forks are made of metal.*
6 *Shirts are made of cotton.*
7 *Tables are made of wood.*

5

1 bottle top 2 vacuum cleaner 3 car tyre 4 computer printer 5 hot water bottle 6 yoghurt pot

6

1 mend clothes 2 play cards 3 make phone calls 4 light candles 5 make a difference 6 write a letter

7

1 from 2 away 3 out 4 of 5 into

8

1✔ 2✘ 3✘ 4✔ 5✔ 6✘ 7✔ 8✘

UNIT 6 LESSON 3

1

1 was invented 2 was demonstrated 3 was bought 4 was designed 5 was called 6 was (first) seen 7 were sold 8 was invented 9 was developed 10 were sent

2

1f was invented, were discovered
2d were written
3h was developed, was called
4a was recorded
5e was built, weren't used
6b was called
7g was built, were made
8c was powered

3

1 The policeman was attacked by the lion.
2 The car was driven by the elephant.
3 The bicycle was ridden by the dog.
4 The horses were trained by the monkey.
5 The snake was bitten by the camel.
6 The ice cream was eaten by the polar bear.

4

1 compose music 2 do damage
3 run into something 4 put into practice
5 sketch a design 6 swim underwater

5

D	I	R	E	C	T	O	R	C
E	D	U	E	N	I	H	V	A
S	I	N	V	E	N	T	O	R
I	V	W	U	T	O	C	A	P
G	E	A	R	T	I	S	T	E
N	R	Y	P	U	T	N	I	N
E	N	G	I	N	E	E	R	T
R	S	O	L	D	I	E	R	E
A	R	F	K	N	O	O	R	R

6

1 light bulb 2 short list 3 flying machine
4 car alarm 5 parachute jump

7

bom~~b~~ b~~u~~ilt desi~~g~~n hi~~gh~~ly li~~gh~~t lis~~t~~ener
thou~~gh~~t w~~h~~ether

8

■▪▪	▪■▪
carpenter	atomic
institute	combustion
serious	connection
powerful	designer
replica	museum
vehicle	internal

UNIT 6 LESSON 4

1

1f 2c 3e 4i 5a 6g 7b 8d 9h

2

A6 B4 C8 D7 E5 F1 G3 H2

3

Students' own answers

4

1 I	M	A	2 G	I	N	3 A	4 T	5 I	V	6 E
N			E			7 D	O	T		N
8 T	U	R	N		9 T	V		10 E	G	G
R			11 I	D	E	A		M		I
12 O	13 W		U		14 A	N	15 Y		16 I	N
17 D	O		18 S	Y	S	T	E	M		E
19 U	N					20 A	S		21 M	E
C		22 U		23 T		G				R
24 E	X	P	L	O	D	E		25 G	A	S

Learner Independence

1f 2c 3b 4e 5a 6d

UNIT 6

Inspiration EXTRA!

Revision

Lesson 1

1 had got 2 had, seen 3 had won
4 had forgotten 5 had, invented
6 had, been, had changed

Lesson 2

1 didn't use to bother 2 used to be allowed to
3 didn't use to be possible 4 used to drive
5 didn't use to turn off 6 didn't use to recycle

Lesson 3

1 Colour television was invented in 1904 by a German.
2 The first BBC television show was broadcast in 1929.
3 The first TV interview was held in April 1930.
4 The first TV play was shown in July 1930.
5 The first horse race which was seen on TV was The Derby in 1931.

Lesson 4

1e 2c 3b 4a 5f 6d

Spelling

1 approximately 2 attempt 3 bottle
4 connect 5 endless 6 engineer 7 full-scale
8 possibility 9 process 10 self-propelled
11 supply 12 supporter

EXTENSION

Lesson 1

1 Because he'd left his books at school.
2 Because she'd fallen into the swimming pool.
3 Because he'd spent it all in the café.
4 Because he'd gone to the cinema with Tara.
5 Because she'd borrowed her mother's car without asking.
6 Because she'd promised not to be late.
7 Because she'd seen Carl fall off his chair.
8 Because he'd forgotten which day it was.

Lesson 2–4

Students' own answers

Spelling

connection inspiration instruction
invention suggestion combustion

REVIEW UNITS 5–6

1

1C 2A 3D 4B 5C 6A 7B 8B 9D
10B 11C 12D 13D 14C

2

1 challenging 2 popularity 3 speciality
4 inventor 5 connection 6 endless
7 possibility 8 powerful

3

1 The film has already started.
2 He has never tried ski-jumping before.
3 My parents have been married for 20 years.
4 He arrived at the party after she had left.
5 We used to have lunch together on Sunday.
6 Chocolate wasn't discovered by the Europeans until 1519.

4

1 runner 2 helicopter 3 vehicle 4 glass
5 race 6 brick

Learner Independence

1

Students' own answers

2

1 I didn't have a clue.
2 Have you ever wondered what it's like?
3 It didn't really matter.
4 Let's hope it stays that way.
5 It was well worth it.
6 The possibilities are endless!
7 Believe it or not …
8 It's doing really well.

UNIT 7 LESSON 1

1

1 remarkable 2 language 3 vocabulary
4 communicate 5 verbs 6 words 7 talk
8 teach 9 number 10 picture 11 asked
12 driver 13 parrot 14 memory 15 apes

2

1 He asked her to pass the salt.
2 She told them not to be afraid.
3 He told him to get out of the car.
4 He asked her to turn the music down.
5 He told them to work harder and run faster.
6 He told them not to touch anything.
7 She asked him to open his mouth wide.

3

1 pick 2 take 3 stand 4 put 5 make
6 go 7 take 8 Turn 9 come

4

M	W	O	L	F	C	N	U	T	L	K
I	B	R	L	H	P	A	L	I	O	N
X	W	F	A	D	G	Q	Y	G	I	Z
C	H	I	M	P	A	N	Z	E	E	E
P	A	F	A	A	S	L	T	R	M	B
O	L	Y	R	R	B	P	S	O	W	R
A	E	G	O	R	I	L	L	A	V	A
H	I	C	R	O	C	O	D	I	L	E
X	C	P	D	T	S	H	A	R	K	L

5

brou~~gh~~t b~~u~~ilding ca~~l~~m g~~u~~ilty of~~t~~en si~~g~~n
tau~~gh~~t

6

1 ✓ 2 ✓ 3 ✗ 4 ✓ 5 ✓ 6 ✗ 7 ✓
8 ✗

UNIT 7 LESSON 2

1

1 inventor 2 said 3 messages 4 remember
5 autumn 6 engineer 7 communication
8 had 9 programs 10 was 11 asked
12 thought

1 F It marked a communications breakthrough.
2 T
3 F He was developing a system which linked computers together.
4 F Ray didn't realize that his invention was important at first.
5 T
6 T

2

1 Sophie said that she wanted to go to university.
2 Jess said that not everyone could sing like a star.
3 Rob said that he was trying to do revision for his exams.
4 Anna said that she really didn't like pizza so she refused to eat it.
5 Lara said that she didn't want to panic, but she was really worried about her best friend.
6 Maxim said that they'd found Rebecca.
7 Janet said that she had heard someone walking around her room.
8 The free-runner said that he had never done anything like that before.
9 Julie said that they were going to Lake Titicaca the following day.
10 Rob said that he would walk home – he had just missed the last bus.

3

1 Mahatma Gandhi said that freedom was not worth having if it didn't include the freedom to make mistakes.
2 Napoleon Bonaparte said that history was the version of past events that people had decided to agree upon.
3 Woody Allen said that you could live to be a hundred if you gave up all the things that made you want to live to be a hundred.
4 Fred Allen said that he couldn't understand why a person would take a year to write a novel when he could easily buy one for a few dollars.
5 Oscar Wilde said that whenever people agreed with him, he always felt he must be wrong.
6 Clint Eastwood said that there was only one way to have a happy marriage and as soon as he learned what it was he would get married again.
7 Ann Landers said that television had proved that people would look at anything rather than each other.
8 Bernard Bailey said that when they discovered the centre of the universe, a lot of people would be disappointed to discover they were not it.
9 John F Kennedy said that the time to repair the roof was when the sun was shining.

4

1 says 2 tell 3 told 4 say 5 tell 6 said
7 say 8 told 9 tell 10 said

5

1 computer file 2 username
3 email attachment 4 social networking
5 breakthrough 6 worldwide

6

1 annoyed 2 solution 3 tough 4 filter
5 remember

7

at**ta**chment com**mu**nicate ef**fect** ex**change**
interviewer **pro**gram pro**vi**der **ser**vice
so**lu**tion **vi**rus

UNIT 7 LESSON 3

1

I asked the alien where he had come from. He said he was from a planet called Astra.
I asked the alien how long he had been here. He said he had arrived six months before/earlier.
I asked the alien why he had come here. He said he wanted to write a book about life on Earth.
I asked the alien where he was staying. He said he was staying at a hotel in New York.
I asked the alien if he liked New York. He said he thought it was an amazing city.
I asked the alien if he was happy about being the centre of media attention. He said he didn't like people taking photos of him.

2

1d How much are the jeans?
2 b Can we have two tickets, please?
3 f When did you last have your bag?
4 a Do you like my hair?
5 e Have you seen my trainers?
6 c Which street are you looking for?

3

1 Lorna asked Nick what time it was.
2 Rob asked his dad if he could lend him some money.
3 Lorna asked Nick why he had decided to come to Star School.
4 Dave asked Rob how long he had lived in north London.
5 Anna asked Will if he liked hip-hop.
6 The police officer asked Janet if she had ever seen a ghost.
7 Simon asked Julie if she knew where they were going.
8 The interviewer asked Ewan and Charley what they were going to do next.

4

1 secondary school 2 windmill 3 school fees
4 car parts 5 media interest

5

1 on 2 back 3 ahead 4 down 5 up
6 away

6

/ɒ/ dog	/ʌ/ month
blogger	become
borrow	country
crops	done
drop	dozen
gone	money
scholarship	southern
stock	won

7

borrowed, 2 phe**no**menal, 4
central, 2 re**mar**kable, 4
dis**ease**, 2 **scho**larship, 3
elec**tri**city, 5 star**va**tion, 3
media, 3

UNIT 7 LESSON 4

1

A3 B1 C5 D2 E4
1d 2h 3b 4c 5e 6i 7g 8a 9f

2

Suggested answer

In the science fiction novel The War of the Worlds, Martians land on Earth and attack Britain. Orson Welles' 1938 play was set in the USA and sounded like a realistic news broadcast. First, listeners heard on the radio that a huge burning object had fallen on a farm in New Jersey. Then they heard a description of the aliens coming out of their spaceship. There was enormous panic in New Jersey and New York. People called the police because didn't know how to protect themselves. Many people complained about the broadcast when they found out it was imaginary. Later, Orson Welles apologised for causing so much panic with his unlikely story.

3

1 C	H	2 I	M	3 P	A	4 N	Z	5 E	E
A		D		R		E		X	
6 P	H	E	N	O	M	E	N	A	7 L
S		N		G		D		8 M	E
9 I	N	T	E	R	N	E	10 T		N
Z		I		A		11 D	E	A	D
E		12 F	13 A	M	14 E		X		
15 D	16 A	Y	S		17 V	E	T		18 F
	P				E				A
19 R	E	S	E	A	R	C	H	E	R

UNIT 7

Inspiration EXTRA!

Revision

Lesson 1

1 She asked Robert to open the window.
2 She told Sara and Maria not to talk.
3 She told everyone to open their books.
4 She asked Pedro to clean the board.
5 She told Sara and Maria to stop laughing.
6 She asked Daniel to share his book with Anna.
7 She told Anna not to forget her book the next day.
8 She told everyone to listen to her carefully.

Lesson 2

1 'I can't remember the exact date.'
2 I'm looking forward to my birthday.
3 I go to parties every Saturday night.
4 I fell asleep on the beach.
5 I'll teach the contestants to sing.
6 I don't like pizza.
7 There are thousands of silly laws in the USA.
8 We have to drive back to Manderley.

Lesson 3

1 She asked what my phone number was.
2 They wanted to know when the film started.
3 I asked how much the bike cost.
4 The teacher asked where the students were going.
5 He wanted to know if his team had won.
6 We asked why the car had stopped.

Lesson 4

1 Where were they sailing?
2 Why were they thrown into the sea?
3 Where was Emily's mobile phone?
4 Who called the coastguard?
5 When did the coastguard arrive?
6 What did the coastguard say?

Spelling

1 attachment 2 attention 3 attract
4 borrow 5 business 6 blogger 7 command
8 communicate 9 correctly 10 windmill

Extension

Lesson 1

1 He told them to stop.
2 He asked her to marry him.
3 She told him not to smoke.
4 She asked them to wash the car.
5 He asked her to bring a(nother) bottle of water.
6 They asked him to turn down the music.

Lesson 2

1 Ray said it had probably **taken** four to six hours to invent email.
2 Sophie said she **had** never enjoyed herself so much.
3 The professor **said** the car was a very powerful machine.
4 Usain said NJ was still **his** best friend in the world.
5 Ken and Emily said they **couldn't** attract the attention of passing ships.
6 Ken told Emily they **would** have to call the coastguard.
7 Mrs Danvers said she **liked** the picture of the girl in white.
8 Rob **told** her that he was trying to do revision for his exams.

Lesson 3–4

Students' own answers

Spelling

1 believe 2 being 3 carried 4 either
5 field 6 friendly 7 height 8 interview
9 quiet 10 receive 11 replied 12 science
13 society 14 weight

CULTURE

Global English

1

1 How many speakers of English are there in the world?
2 When did people from Britain emigrate to North America?
3 How many languages were there in the world in 1966?
4 How many people spoke English in Shakespeare's time?
5 When did William Caxton print the first book in English?
6 How many people speak English as a foreign language?
7 How many European organisations use English as one of their working languages?
8 When did the Angles travel to England from southern Denmark and northern Germany?

2

1f 2j 3d 4i 5c 6g 7a 8b 9e 10h

3

1 French 2 Spanish 3 Spanish 4 Italian
5 German 6 Spanish 7 Greek 8 German
9 Greek 10 French 11 Polish 12 Greek
13 Spanish 14 Italian 15 French 16 Italian
17 Spanish 18 Greek 19 Spanish 20 Greek

4

1 answer 2 laugh 3 word 4 use 5 home
6 school 7 true 8 learn 9 first

UNIT 8 LESSON 1

1

1 He shouldn't have bought a large car. He should have bought a small one.
2 He shouldn't have washed it every day. He should have washed it once a month.
3 He should've used his bike more. He should've used his car less.
4 He shouldn't have driven to the shops.
5 For long journeys, he shouldn't have travelled by car. He should've taken the train.
6 He should've cared more about the environment. He should have cared less about his own fun.

2

1 She shouldn't have packed so many clothes.
2 He should've measured the table before he bought it.
3 He should've bought a ticket.
4 She shouldn't have forgotten her umbrella.
5 He shouldn't have believed everything the salesman said.
6 She should've thought of the consequences.
7 They shouldn't have been rude to the referee.
8 He should've turned the taps off.

3

1 She ought to have told him that she had a new pet.
2 She ought to have asked him what he wanted for his birthday.
3 He oughtn't to have arrived so early for the party.
4 She oughtn't to have been late for the cinema.
5 He ought to have remembered his passport.
6 She ought to have knocked on the door before she entered.

4

1 consequence 2 store 3 wipe out 4 essential
5 consider 6 available

5

1 build a dam 2 learn lessons
3 generate electricity 4 displace people
5 produce potatoes 6 turn off a tap

6

1 underway 2 hosepipe 3 ice cap
4 rainwater 5 watering can

7

▪■	■▪
amount concern displace effect mistake survive	hosepipe hygiene litre major polar shortage

UNIT 8 LESSON 2

1

1 he'd ask someone for help.
2 he'd try to find someone who could speak English.
3 he'd use a map.
4 he'd phone Sam on his mobile and ask for help.

2

1 What would you do if you were in the Arctic and didn't have enough water. I'd melt some snow.
2 What would you do if you were lost at sea and didn't have anything to eat? I'd catch some fish.
3 What would you do if you met a wild elephant in the jungle? I'd climb a tree.
4 What would you do if you woke up at night and heard a noise? I'd stay in bed.
5 What would you do if you saw an accident and had to get help? I'd call an ambulance.

3

1 If I were a millionaire, I'd give all my money away.
2 If she hurried, she'd catch the train.
3 If he asked me to go to the cinema, I'd be delighted.
4 If they worked harder, they'd finish the job today.
5 If you didn't worry so much, you'd be much happier.
6 If they asked me, I'd help them.

4

1 If I were you, I'd phone for a taxi.
2 If I were you, I wouldn't buy so many clothes.
3 If I were you, I'd send her some flowers.
4 If I were you, I'd join a gym.
5 If I were you, I'd do as much as possible.
6 If I were you, I'd ring and let her know.

5

1 magnifying glass 2 oasis 3 shelter
4 object 5 crouch 6 join 7 torch 8 dentist

6

H	I	C	C	O	U	G	H	S
E	H	U	L	A	E	J	T	O
A	S	P	I	R	I	N	O	R
D	E	N	T	I	S	T	O	E
A	T	W	R	L	H	A	T	T
C	O	U	G	H	G	N	H	H
H	M	V	I	D	L	U	A	R
E	D	O	C	T	O	R	C	O
E	T	C	O	L	D	P	H	A
S	N	B	R	I	G	K	E	T

1 sore throat 2 hiccoughs 3 cough 4 cold
5 aspirin 6 doctor 7 dentist, toothache

7

1 ✓ 2 ✓ 3 ✗ 4 ✓ 5 ✓ 6 ✓ 7 ✓
8 ✗ 9 ✓ 10 ✗

UNIT 8 LESSON 3

1

1 haven't you 2 isn't it 3 isn't he 4 doesn't it
5 weren't they 6 have you

2

1 weren't they 2 did he 3 hasn't it
4 couldn't you 5 didn't they 6 isn't it
7 did you 8 would they 9 haven't we
10 didn't I

3

1 isn't it 2 could he 3 didn't he 4 didn't they
5 don't they 6 isn't he 7 weren't they
8 aren't they

4

1 wasn't she 2 didn't she 3 was it
4 weren't they 5 could she 6 did she
7 didn't she 8 could she 9 hasn't she
10 didn't they

5

1 expect someone to know something
2 let someone in
3 be in the news
4 win a medal
5 ride a motorbike
6 make something out of something
7 change colour

6

				↓					
1 E	X	H	I	B	I	T	I	O	N
2 C	O	L	O	U	R				
	3 D	E	S	I	G	N	E	D	
			4 F	L	O	O	R	S	
				5 D	O	W	N		
			6 N	I	G	H	T		
7 E	X	P	E	N	S	I	V	E	
			8 I	G	L	O	O		

8

exhi**bi**tion ex**pen**sive **ig**loo pa**vi**lion
skyscraper un**u**sual

UNIT 8 LESSON 4

1

1g 2d 3a 4i 5b 6e 7h 8c 9f

2

1F 2F 3T 4T 5F 6T

3

Students' own answers

4

1 T	E	2 M	3 P	E	4 R	A	5 T	U	R	6 E
R		7 I	M		E		H			S
8 O	U	R		9 H	E	R	E			S
P		R			F		10 N	11 O	S	E
I		O		12 F				P		N
13 C	14 O	15 R	A	L			16 W	E	S	T
17 A	N		18 L	O	T			N		I
L			19 S	O		20 E				A
	21 A	B	O	R	I	G	I	N	A	L

UNIT 8

Inspiration EXTRA!

Revision

Lesson 1

1 should have remembered
2 should have been 3 shouldn't have forgotten
4 should have bought 5 shouldn't have fed
6 shouldn't have turned 7 should have replied
8 should have written

Lesson 2

1 If you listened carefully, you wouldn't get things wrong.
2 If she asked me, I would be delighted to help.
3 If the band practised more, they would play much better.
4 If you gave me your box of matches, I would light a fire.
5 If I had enough money, I would get some new trainers.
6 If it snowed, we would go skiing tomorrow.
7 If I won the lottery, I would travel to New Zealand.
8 What would you do if you saw a bear?

Lesson 3

1 isn't it 2 was it 3 wouldn't you 4 did they
5 didn't he 6 wasn't it 7 was she 8 didn't he

Lesson 4

1e 2b 3g 4c 5h 6f 7a 8d

Spelling

1 avail**a**ble 2 comm**o**n 3 consider**a**bly
4 essenti**a**l 5 extrem**e**ly 6 hicc**ough**s
7 interi**o**r 8 mount**ai**n 9 pres**e**rve
10 shelt**e**r 11 short**a**ge 12 typic**a**l

Extension

Lesson 1–4

Students' own answers

Spelling

1 Aborigin**al** 2 availab**le** 3 cand**le**
4 coast**al** 5 considerab**le** 6 continent**al**
7 environment**al** 8 essenti**al** 9 jung**le**
10 need**le** 11 nov**el** 12 offici**al** 13 trav**el**
14 tropic**al** 15 typic**al** 16 vehic**le**

REVIEW UNITS 7–8

1

1D 2B 3D 4C 5A 6C 7A 8C 9D
10D 11B 12C

2

1 shortage 2 attachment 3 tourism
4 attention 5 environmental 6 poisonous
7 coastal 8 Magnifying

3

1 to smile.
2 he couldn't remember.
3 how long she had been a surfer.
4 the weather was like in Australia.
5 have asked me for help.
6 have missed the last bus.
7 lost my bag, I would go to the police station.
8 were you, I would go to the dentist.

4

1 hospital 2 illness 3 cause 4 emergency
5 ask 6 average 7 lake 8 zebra 9 whistle
10 climate

Learner independence

1

Students' own answers

2

1 I can't remember exactly.
2 There isn't an easy answer.
3 How did you get the idea?
4 I've got a headache.
5 It's a tough problem.
6 You must be joking.
7 What would you do?
8 If I were you, I'd …

L.A. BLUES

L.A. Blues encourages students to read for pleasure, while consolidating language covered in *New Inspiration* 3. Chapters 1-8 of the story correspond to Units 1-8, and Chapter 9 revises language from the whole book. Each chapter begins with a question to focus students on the story and ends with a prediction question. The story is followed by a series of exercises testing comprehension. These stories can be read in class, or teachers can set the reading as homework. Teachers may also find that students read ahead because they are keen to know the end of the story!

It is a good idea to focus the students at the beginning of each chapter by asking them to retell the story so far or to describe the events of the previous chapter. This can be done in pairs or groups, with the students then sharing their ideas with the rest of the class, or as a whole-class activity. You can also use the illustrations to get the students to predict what will happen before they read the text. Ask questions about the pictures, such as *Who is this? Where are they? What is he/she doing?* to elicit ideas from the students. Sometimes get the students to read only part of a chapter and then stop and say what they think will happen next.

1 Someone was in my office

1

1 He's a private detective. 2 To pay for his new car.
3 He went to Al's Diner for a coffee. 4 He thought she had a gun.
5 Find Mark Jackson.

2

Clothes: suit, tie, shirt, jacket, trousers
Colours: midnight blue, dark blue, red, light blue, green
Parts of the body: feet, hand, hair, eyes

3

Students' own answers

2 Where was El Mayor?

1

1 Mark Jackson 2 Lenny Samuel 3 Julie
4 The man who was in Vargas's office 5 Mr Vargas
6 A piece of paper in one of the pockets
7 The gun in the man's hand
8 A pair of expensive cowboy boots

2

1 look in the mirror 2 ring the bell 3 search the room
4 turn on the stereo 5 wave goodbye 6 wear a jacket

3

1 with 2 at 3 to 4 on 5 behind 6 in

Optional activity

Books closed. Students answer questions about the story so far from memory.

3 You'd better get someone else

1

1 In Mr Samuel's office 2 Lenny arriving late 3 Ann
4 In Mexico 5 He wanted to see her again 6 Lenny and Julie
7 Mark working for Metro Rent-A-Car 8 Mr Vargas

2

She is Mark's sister. She's from Dallas, Texas. Mark called her on Monday and said he was somewhere in Mexico and he was there to collect a Metro car. He should be back in L.A. now but he isn't and he is possibly in real danger.

3

1 properly 2 slowly 3 nervously 4 quickly 5 quietly

Optional activities

- Books closed. Summarise the story so far but make some mistakes, eg ***Lenny works in London. He has lots of money. He met Ann at the coffee shop.*** Students listen. When they hear a mistake, they shout *Stop!* and correct the mistake.
- Students work in pairs. One is Lenny and one is Ann. They act out the conversation in Lenny's office. Less confident students can read the dialogue in the book. Confident students can use their own words. After everyone has practised, choose a confident pair to act out the scene to the class.

4 I heard someone coming

1

1 C 2 G 3 E 4 A 5 I 6 H 7 B 8 D 9 F

2

1 into 2 of 3 near 4 on 5 at 6 for 7 with 8 over

3

1 arrive in a town 2 cross the border 3 fall asleep
4 look through a book 5 order some food
6 park the car

Optional activity

Organise students into teams. Ask questions about details of the story, eg *What is the name of the town in Mexico where they are? What did they eat at the café?* Award points for correct answers.

5 Where have you been?

1

1 In the cabin 13 2 Ann 3 Swim out to the flag
4 A man's body 5 The dead man 6 In Casa Dorada
7 Ensenada 8 The ship

2

1 asked the way 2 breathed deeply 3 came up for air
4 dived down 5 looked excited 6 shook my head

3

1 into   2 in   3 by   4 for   5 on   6 of

4

Transport: boat, plane, ship
Seeing: saw, looked, stared, noticed

Optional activity

In pairs, students write comprehension questions about the chapter. Books closed, they then exchange their questions and try to answer each other's questions from memory.

6 It contained thousands of dollars!

1

1 Hank and a well dressed man of about 50
2 By motorboat   3 By the ladder
4 A metal box and a notebook   5 Thousands of dollars
6 To see if they were real

2

1 *become dark*
2 *count the money*
3 *make a trip*
4 *open a box*
5 *rent a motorboat*
6 *turn off the engine*

3

Students' own answers

Optional activity

Books closed. Students retell the story so far.

7 The driver had an accident

1

1 F   2 C   3 H   4 A   5 D   6 G   7 B   8 E

2

1 turned   2 go   3 woke   4 finds   5 looked   6 drove, got

3

Students' own answers

Optional activity

Books closed, students try to remember the dialogue between Julie and Lenny and Vargas at the Metro Rent-a-Car office. They write the dialogue, compare it with the original text and then act it out in groups of three, taking a role each. Less confident students can read it aloud from the text.

8 I should have guessed!

1

1 The man with long brown hair   2 Mark Jackson
3 Summers and Walter   4 Lenny and Ann
5 The diamonds   6 Walter   7 Ann   8 Mark Jackson

2

1 reply   2 told   3 asked   4 shouted   5 tell

3

Students' own answers

Optional activity

Books closed, students answer questions about the story so far from memory.

9 The L.A. blues had gone!

1

1 Summers   2 Jackson   3 Walter   4 Summers   5 Hank
6 Ann   7 Walter and Hank   8 Police officers   9 Ann
10 Ann

2

1 discovered   2 shore   3 nodded   4 marched
5 moustache   6 proof   7 smuggler   8 murderer

3

1 at, under   2 into, by, in   3 up   4 back   5 for   6 to
7 from, on   8 with   9 of

Optional activities

- **Game** *Who says this?* Read sentences from different chapters of the book. Students identify the speaker. Students could continue in pairs.
- Books closed. Summarise the story, but make some mistakes. Students listen. When they hear a mistake, they shout *Stop!* and correct the mistake
- Students retell the whole story.

After reading activities

Write the activities below on the board. Students choose the activities they are most interested in. The written work can be displayed in the classroom. The first activity could be videoed.

1 Choose one chapter of the story and act it out with another student/in a group.
2 Choose one chapter. Write as many questions as you can about this chapter of the story. Then give your questions to another student to answer.
3 Summarise each chapter in just one sentence.
4 Imagine you are Lenny or Ann. Write your diary for one of the days in the story.
5 Write a new ending for the story.
6 Write a study of one of the characters in the story. Include information about their personality, their importance in the story and why you chose this character.
7 Choose three pictures from the story. Ask a partner to describe what's happening in the picture, what had happened before and what's going to happen next.
8 You are a film director. You are going to make a film of the story. Choose your stars and make a film poster.

Unit 1–2 CLIL Teaching notes
Art

Pop Art

Aims To learn about the history and techniques of Pop Art.

Activities Guessing vocabulary from pictures; matching paragraphs and headings; reading for gist and specific information; matching vocabulary and definitions; doing a Pop Art quiz; researching and writing a critical analysis of an artist and a work of art.

Language Verb/preposition + gerund; *so/nor* + auxiliary verbs; verb and object and infinitive; present simple passive; linking words – *which* and *who*; likes and dislikes; agreeing and disagreeing; talking about skills, abilities and ambitions; adjectives for opinions; phrasal verbs with *up*; arts; styles; feelings.

To use After Unit 2, either in class, as self-study or as homework.

Procedure

- This CLIL spread can be given as homework or be done in pairs in class. For each activity, students can either check answers in pairs and then with the whole class, or use a monolingual dictionary to help with vocabulary if they are working at home.
- Ask students what they know about Pop Art. Then ask them to look at the pictures and solve the anagrams to find different artistic techniques.
- Ask students to read the text for overall understanding and match a heading with each paragraph.
- Next, ask students to scan the text and find the vocabulary listed and match it with the correct definition based on its use in the text.
- Ask students to do the Pop Art quiz. Tell them to read the text again and answer the questions individually.
- The project stage can be set as homework or done in class if you feel students have access to appropriate reference books, Internet, etc. Tell the students that they are art critics and ask them to prepare a short critical analysis of a Pop artist and a work of art. Remind them to include information about the artist and their style and techniques; a detailed analysis of the work using the technical language they have learnt from this worksheet; their own positive or negative opinion about the work of art, with reasons why they like or dislike it. Suggest they visit the listed websites as part of their research.
- As an extra activity in the following lesson, students can read or listen to each others' critical analysis and match it with the picture being described.

Key

Exercise 1
1 C 2 E 3 B 4 F 5 A 6 D

Exercise 2
1 A definition 2 The origins 3 Aims and criticisms
4 Pop Art in the USA 5 Pop Art in the UK

Exercise 3
1 critic 2 curator 3 stylised 4 depict 5 canvas 6 dot 7 realist
8 minimalist

Exercise 4
Part 1: 1D 2C 3A 4C 5B 6A 7D 8A
Part 2: 1c 2e 3b 4a 5d

Websites students could check:

www.artyfactory.com/art_appreciation/art_movements/pop_art.htm
www.tate.org.uk/collections/glossary/definition.jsp?entryId=226
www.visual-arts-cork.com

Unit 3–4 CLIL Teaching notes
Science

Science quiz

Aims	To learn about how the brain works and how to look after it.
Activities	Doing a pre-reading quiz about the brain, guessing vocabulary from context and completing sentences with vocabulary; reading for gist and specific information; labelling a diagram and completing a table about the different parts of the brain; researching and designing a brain health poster.
Language	Verbs of perception + present participle; *can/could* + verb of perception; future review; *will/won't*; *shall*; *going to*; first conditional; phrasal verbs with *out*; making predictions, promises and offers; talking about plans and intentions; talking about future possibility; memory; sensations and sounds; the brain.
To use	After Unit 4, in class, as self-study or as homework.
Procedure	• This CLIL spread can be given as homework or be done in pairs in class. For each activity, students can either check answers in pairs and then with the whole class, or use a monolingual dictionary to help with vocabulary if they are working at home. • Ask students to do the quiz about the brain individually. Then ask them to skim read the introductory text about the brain and check their answers. • Next, ask students to complete the sentences with the vocabulary from the text, referring back to the text to check meaning in context. • Ask students to read the second text about brain power and complete the missing information by labelling the diagrams and completing the table. • The project stage can be set as homework or done in class if you feel students have access to appropriate reference books, Internet, etc. Tell the students they are going to research and design a brain health poster for people of their own age. Remind them to make it eye-catching and age-appropriate and to include information about what is good and bad for the brain and why. Suggest they visit the listed websites as part of their research.

Key

Exercise 2

1T 2T 3T 4T 5F 6F 7F 8F 9F 10F

Exercise 3

1 organ 2 neurons 3 genes 4 hemispheres 5 stroke 6 regenerate

Exercise 4

1 cerebrum 2 meninges 3 limbic system 4 diencephalon
5 cerebellum 6 brain stem 7 parietal lobe 8 frontal lobe

Exercise 5 Suggested answers

The Cerebrum thinks and controls voluntary muscles.
The frontal lobe deals with speech, thought and emotion as well as coordinating movement.
The parietal lobe controls our sense of touch and tells us when to feel pain and temperature.
The cerebellum is responsible for accuracy, equilibrium and coordination.
The brain stem is responsible for all the body's vital, involuntary processes like breathing, digestion and circulation of the blood and is also responsible for monitoring sleep.
The limbic system manages emotions and instincts and so is vital to reading situations and in recognising when you're in danger.
The meninges protects the brain from injury.

Websites students could check:

www.ninds.nih.gov/disorders/brain_basics/know_your_brain.htm
faculty.washington.edu/chudler/introb.html
science.education.nih.gov/supplements/nih4/self/guide/info-brain.htm
www.bbc.co.uk/science/humanbody/body/interactives/organs/brainmap

Unit 5–6 CLIL Teaching notes
History

Inventions that shaped our world

Aims To learn about the history of inventions that have shaped our world.

Activities Matching vocabulary with pictures; a pre-reading quiz about inventions; reading for gist and specific information; completing a table; making sentences about what people used to do and what they do now; researching and writing about an invention that has shaped our lives.

Language Past perfect; *used to* + infinitive; past simple passive; linking words; *although*; describing past events; talking about past habits and states; writing about changes in life; talking about inventions; connecting ideas; recycling; household items; materials; inventions; phrases with *do* and *make*.

To use After Unit 6, in class, as self-study or as homework.

Procedure

- This CLIL spread can be given as homework or be done in pairs in class. For each activity, students can either check answers in pairs and then with the whole class, or use a monolingual dictionary to help with vocabulary if they are working at home.
- Ask students to look at the pictures and match them with the inventions.
- Ask students to do the quiz about inventions alone then skim the text to check their answers.
- Next, ask students to scan the text and complete the table.
- Then ask students to make sentences about what people used to do and what they do now, using the vocabulary provided. Suggest they refer back to the text if they need help.
- The project stage can be set as homework or done in class if you feel students have access to appropriate reference books, Internet, etc. Ask students to prepare a short description of an invention that has shaped their lives. Tell them not to say what the invention is so that their classmates can guess. Remind them to include information about: who invented it; when and where it was invented; past developments that led to the invention; recent developments; why they think it is so important to their life. Suggest they visit the listed websites as part of their research.
- As an extra activity in the following lesson, students can listen to each others' critical descriptions and guess what the invention is.

Key

Exercise 1
1B 2C 3A 4B 5A 6C 7C 8B 9B 10C

Exercise 3
These are suggested answers. Students' answers might vary in the last two columns.

Invention	*Inventors*	*Place and date of invention*	*Past developments*	*Recent developments*
Jeans	*Levi Strauss*	*USA, 1873*	*Clothes for men working in the mines during the Gold Rush*	*Fashion accessory*
Tooth brush	*Dupont de Nemours*	*USA, 1938*	*Wooden sticks* *Bamboo and pig's hair (China)* *Nylon*	*Electric toothbrush*
Plastic	*John Hyatt*	*USA, 1872*	*Celluloid* *Bakelite* *PVC* *PET*	*Many different goods like films, credit cards and bottles*
Text messaging	*Vodafone™*	*UK, late 1980s*	*Motorola's hand held mobile phone*	*One trillion texts sent annually.* *4 million mobile phone users* *Texting is more popular than telephoning*
World Wide Web	*Tim Berners-Lee*	*Switzerland, 1989*	*ARPANET*	*50% of the world's population now have internet access*

Exercise 4 Suggested answers
People used to send letters, but now they send text messages with their mobile phones.
People used to use analogue cameras to take pictures, but now they use digital cameras.
People used to do research at the library, but now they do research on the Internet.
People used to brush their teeth with wooden sticks, but now they have/use electric toothbrushes.
People used to catch up with friends in cafes, but now they use social networking sites.

Websites students could check:
www2.dupont.com/Heritage/en_US
www.levistrauss.com
smithsonian.yahoo.com
inventors.about.com/od/dstartinventions/
www.enchantedlearning.com/inventors
www.isoc.org/internet/history/brief.shtml
www.telegraph.co.uk/science/4981964/Top-10-inventions-that-changed-the-world.html

Unit 7–8 CLIL Teaching notes
Natural Science

Natural disasters

Aims	To learn about the causes and effects of natural disasters.
Activities	Matching texts with pictures; labelling diagrams of natural disasters; reading for gist and specific information; doing a quiz about natural disasters; researching and presenting and analysing a specific natural disaster.
Language	*Should have/ought to have*; second conditional; questions tags; criticising past actions; describing past situations; talking about imaginary or unlikely situations; giving advice; asking for agreement and checking information; writing descriptions; water; geographical features; weather; survival; buildings; geographical features; natural disasters.
To use	After Unit 8, in class, as self-study or as homework.
Procedure	• This CLIL spread can be given as homework or be done in pairs in class. For each activity, students can either check answers in pairs and then with the whole class, or use a monolingual dictionary to help with vocabulary if they are working at home. • Ask students to read the four texts quickly and match them with the pictures. • Ask student to read the texts again carefully and label the diagrams with the words listed. • Next, ask students to do the quiz about natural disasters alone, without referring back to the text. • The project stage can be set as homework or done in class if you feel students have access to appropriate reference books, Internet, etc. Ask students to research a short presentation about one of the natural disasters mentioned in the texts or another of their choice. Tell them they can use diagrams and pictures to illustrate their presentation. Remind them to include information about: when and where it happened; how it happened (explaining how cyclones, tsunamis, volcanic eruptions or earthquakes occur); what the effects were (on the people, the environment, the climate, the economy, etc.); what could have been done to prevent it being so bad.

Key

Exercise 1

1c 2d 3b 4a

Exercise 2

A 1 vent 2 crater 3 lava 4 magma
B 5 wave 6 shore 7 seabed
C 8 warm air 9 low pressure 10 high winds 11 heavy rain
D 12 fault 13 crust 14 tectonic plate

Exercise 3

1D 2A 3C 4B 5D 6B 7A 8A 9D 10B

Websites students could check:

earthquake.usgs.gov/learn/kids
environment.nationalgeographic.com/environment/natural-disasters
geology.com/volcanoes
home.vicnet.net.au/~hmwkhelp/hwh_natdis.htm
library.thinkquest.org/03oct/00758/en
news.bbc.co.uk/1/hi/sci/tech/7533950.stm
spaceplace.nasa.gov/en/kids/goes/hurricanes
www.fema.gov/kids/dizarea.htm
www.ready.gov/build-kit-kids

Audio Track List

CD 1

Track			
1.01	**Preview, Units 1 and 2**		Exercise 3
1.02	**Unit 1**	Lesson 1	Exercise 2
1.03			Exercise 4
1.04			Exercise 5
1.05		Lesson 2	Exercise 2
1.06			Exercise 4
1.07			Exercise 7
1.08		Lesson 3	Exercise 2
1.09			Exercise 3
1.10			Exercise 5
1.11			Exercise 7
1.12		Lesson 4	Exercise 2
1.13			Exercise 4
1.14			Exercise 9
1.15	**Inspiration EXTRA!** Sketch		
1.16	**Culture**	Exercise 1, Women in the World	
1.17	**Unit 2**	Lesson 1	Exercise 2
1.18			Exercise 5
1.19			Exercise 6
1.20		Lesson 2	Exercise 2
1.21			Exercise 4
1.22			Exercise 5
1.23		Lesson 3	Exercise 2
1.24			Exercise 4
1.25			Exercise 6
1.26			Exercise 9
1.27		Lesson 4	Exercise 2
1.28			Exercise 6
1.29			Exercise 11
1.30	**Inspiration EXTRA!** Project		
1.31	**Preview, Units 3 and 4**		Exercise 3
1.32	**Unit 3**	Lesson 1	Exercise 2
1.33			Exercise 7
1.34			Exercise 8
1.35		Lesson 2	Exercise 3
1.36			Exercise 5
1.37			Exercise 7
1.38		Lesson 3	Exercise 2
1.39			Exercise 4
1.40		Lesson 4	Exercise 1
1.41			Exercise 2
1.42			Exercise 6
1.43			Exercise 11
1.44	**Inspiration EXTRA!** Sketch		
1.45	**Culture**	Exercise 1, Good reads	
1.46	**Culture**	Exercise 2, Good reads cont.	

CD 2

Track			
2.01	**Unit 4**	Lesson 1	Exercise 2
2.02			Exercise 5
2.03			Exercise 6
2.04		Lesson 2	Exercise 2
2.05			Exercise 4
2.06			Exercise 6
2.07		Lesson 3	Exercise 2
2.08			Exercise 4
2.09			Exercise 6
2.10		Lesson 4	Exercise 2
2.11			Exercise 3
2.12			Exercise 5
2.13			Exercise 6
2.14			Exercise 10
2.15	**Preview, Units 5 and 6**		Exercise 3
2.16	**Unit 5**	Lesson 1	Exercise 2
2.17			Exercise 5
2.18			Exercise 8
2.19		Lesson 2	Exercise 2
2.20			Exercise 4
2.21		Lesson 3	Exercise 2
2.22			Exercise 5
2.23		Lesson 4	Exercise 2
2.24			Exercise 5
2.25			Exercise 11
2.26	**Inspiration EXTRA!** Sketch		
2.27	**Culture**	Exercise 1, Tourism	
2.28	**Culture**	Exercise 3, Tourism cont.	
2.29	**Unit 6**	Lesson 1	Exercise 2
2.30			Exercise 4
2.31		Lesson 2	Exercise 2
2.32			Exercise 6
2.33		Lesson 3	Exercise 2
2.34			Exercise 3
2.35			Exercise 4
2.36			Exercise 6
2.37		Lesson 4	Exercise 3
2.38			Exercise 5
2.39			Exercise 10

CD 3

Track			
3.01	**Preview, Units 7 and 8**		Exercise 3
3.02	**Unit 7**	Lesson 1	Exercise 2
3.03			Exercise 5
3.04			Exercise 6
3.05		Lesson 2	Exercise 2
3.06			Exercise 6
3.07			Exercise 7
3.08		Lesson 3	Exercise 2
3.09			Exercise 4
3.10			Exercise 6
3.11		Lesson 4	Exercise 5
3.12			Exercise 11
3.13	**Inspiration EXTRA!** Sketch		
3.14	**Culture**	Exercise 1, Global english	
3.15	**Unit 8**	Lesson 1	Exercise 1
3.16			Exercise 2
3.17			Exercise 5
3.18		Lesson 2	Exercise 4
3.19			Exercise 6
3.20			Exercise 7
3.21		Lesson 3	Exercise 2
3.22			Exercise 3
3.23			Exercise 4
3.24		Lesson 4	Exercise 2
3.25			Exercise 4
3.26			Exercise 9
3.27	**Inspiration EXTRA!** Limerick		
3.28	**Song** *You've Got A Friend*		
3.29	**Song** *Celebrate The Future*		
3.30	**Song** *Brown-eyed Girl*		
3.31	**Song** *I Will Survive*		